Becoming Dickens

Becoming Dickens

The Invention of a Novelist

ROBERT DOUGLAS-FAIRHURST

*The Belknap Press of
Harvard University Press*
CAMBRIDGE, MASSACHUSETTS
LONDON, ENGLAND

First Harvard University Press paperback edition, 2013

Book design by Dean Bornstein

Library of Congress Cataloging-in-Publication Data

Douglas-Fairhurst, Robert.
Becoming Dickens : the invention of a novelist / Robert Douglas-Fairhurst.
p.   cm.
Includes bibliographical references and index.
ISBN 978-0-674-05003-7 (cloth : alk. paper)
ISBN 978-0-674-07223-7 (pbk.)
1. Dickens, Charles, 1812–1870. 2. Novelists, English—19th century—Biography. I. Title.
PR4582.D68 2011
823'.8—dc22
[B]   2011004219

For Mac

Contents

Becoming Dickens

Prologue: Somebody and Nobody

One's real life is so often the life that one does not lead.
—Oscar Wilde

London, 1855. The old city is being swallowed up by change. Underfoot the ground trembles as excavation machines carve out new subway tunnels, adding a dull, thudding bass to the city's soundtrack and belching their fumes into the thick yellow air. Sleek steam-gurneys chug their way past a backdrop of nodding cranes and buildings furred with scaffolding. Shops hum with activity, as assistants key each customer's personal identification number into a credit machine, and then pull on the ebony handle to print out a receipt. Inventors gather to whip up public interest in the latest must-have gadgets: devices for crimping hair by electricity, or children's toys that play Beethoven, or schemes for electroplating the dead. And lurking behind everything else, out of sight but never quite out of mind, are the biggest and most sophisticated machines of all: the computers spawned by Charles Babbage's Difference Engine thirty years ago. It is Babbage whose vision saved Britain from anarchy in the 1830s, when the Reform Bill was defeated, Wellington was assassinated, and Lord Byron's Industrial Radical Party swept to power. Now it is his engines that dominate every aspect of life, from entertainment to national security, with their shiny cogs and pistons, their precisely engineered punchcards, their dedicated army of clackers.

❧❧ ❧❧

This isn't the Victorian age familiar from history books. That's because it didn't happen—at least not then, and not in this way. The Reform Bill was passed. Byron died fighting in Greece. Most important, the Difference Engine remained only a gleam of possibility until the end of the twentieth century, when technology finally became capable of realizing Babbage's plans. (A real version of the machine, massively yet delicately constructed from bronze and steel, now forms one of the key exhibits in London's Science Museum.)[1] The London of steam-gurneys and punchcards is a fiction—a revisionary alternative to the real city of 1855—created by William Gibson and Bruce Sterling in their 1990 novel *The Difference Engine*.[2] It is a story whose in-jokes and tricks of historical perspective start with its own title, which draws attention to the fact that a novel is another kind of difference engine: a verbal machine designed to help us look differently at the world. But although Gibson and Sterling set out to disorient us, their tactics are familiar enough.

Reimagining the past has long been a popular parlor game for historians, for whom what did happen cannot always be disentangled from what might have happened in its place. These counterfactual investigations are especially drawn to questions of "what if": "What if there had been no English Civil War? What if there had been no American War of Independence? What if Ireland had never been divided? What if Britain had stayed out of the First World War? What if Hitler had invaded Britain?"[3] Such speculations display a marked preference for the clash of armies and grand sweep of political movements over the smaller, more intimate occasions where history pauses on the brink. Whenever ordinary life makes an appearance, it is usually as the prelude to more satisfyingly earth-shaking events—as in Gibbon's suggestion that it was only an attack of gout that prevented Sultan Bajazet from sacking Rome in the fourteenth century, or Churchill's conclusion that a major war between Greece and Turkey was caused by the infected monkey bite which killed King Alexander of Greece in 1920.[4] Even Pascal, one of the earliest and best of counterfactual thinkers, is quick to move from the bedroom to the battlefield when he points out that, once Caesar fell in love with Cleopatra's nose, it became a tipping point in the history of civilization: "if it had been shorter the whole face of the earth would have been different."[5]

But global history is not the only thing that can be altered when one event happens rather than another, when one choice is made rather than another. Individual lives are similarly vulnerable to change, and here too the story of what did happen can never fully erase the ghostly outlines of history's rejected drafts. In *The Difference Engine* this produces a series of cameo appearances by literary figures, other than Byron, whose lives have taken a turn for the better, or at least a turn in a different direction. According to this version of history, Shelley has been exiled to St. Helena as a dangerous political subversive, Professor Coleridge and the Reverend Wordsworth are comfortably settled offstage in their Susquehanna pantisocracy, and a gray-haired Keats has abandoned medicine to become an expert operator of the kinetrope, an early form of cinema worked by thousands of mechanical pixels that click and whirr into place at the prompting of more punchcards. ("This London air will be the death of me," he complains, as he coughs messily into a handkerchief.)[6] Meanwhile, figures who might more readily be identified as "Victorian" drift around in the story's margins, each one showing how easily a life we take for granted might have ended up as a stunted or distorted version of itself. In a world where making up stories is far less important than other kinds of invention, Disraeli writes trashy romances and is a "bit of a madcap," though "he's steady enough when he's sober." Laurence Oliphant is a dapper journalist who drips condescension as he goes about the business of the Royal Geographical Society. And Dickens? He does not appear as a named character at all. Perhaps he is the "King of the Bill Stickers" (a sharp-talking Cockney who was the subject of a *Household Words* essay written by the real Dickens in 1851), who remembers "Hard times" in the past. Perhaps he is a member of the "clock-watching" class "who read the *Dictionary of Useful Knowledge* and the *Journal of Moral Improvement* and [look] to get ahead." Or perhaps he is just an anonymous face in the crowd, like the pedestrians who get in the way of a steam-gurney in the novel's opening pages and "[scatter] sulkily before the vehicle's advance."[7]

The absence of Dickens is surprising. No Victorian writer is harder to make vanish through a counterfactual conjuring trick. In fact, no writer of any period is more closely identified with the time and place in which he lived, which is why "Victorian" and "Dickensian" have become more or less interchangeable terms. "Genius" may be overused as a form of praise, but it is one that his original reviewers increasingly resorted to as his career started to fill out the word's full implications—meaning not just an unusually brilliant individual, but someone who came to embody the defining values of his age: its irresistible energy, its self-divisions and self-doubts, its urgent striving for something beyond the present.[8] For R. H. Horne, Dickens was "manifestly the product of his age" (1844); for Alfred Austin, "he was the man of his epoch, and had the spirit-time throbbing within him" (1870).[9] Although regularly marginalized or patronized by the critics, for countless thousands of readers he became the standard against which all other novelists should be judged. Anne Ritchie recalls her little sister looking up from a book in which she had been absorbed and "saying, in her soft childish voice, 'Papa, why do you not write books like *Nicholas Nickleby?*'"[10] Her father was William Makepeace Thackeray. It is not known how Thackeray responded to this sweetly innocent suggestion, but he was painfully aware that there was no point in trying to write books like the man who styled himself "The Inimitable." Dickens was at once the most central and most eccentric literary figure of the age. Nobody could write like Dickens. Even Dickens sometimes found himself unable to reproduce his earlier styles: every novel was an experiment in form, every sentence an exploration into what it meant to write as himself.

But if we are to understand why Dickens made such an impact on the period, and why the aftershocks of this impact continue to reverberate, we need to unlearn much of what we know about his career. We need to remember that he was Charles John Huffam Dickens long before he earned the distinction of being referred to by his surname alone, and that he was one of hundreds of ambitious young writers swept along by the uncertain currents of the 1830s, who bobbed into view or sank without trace in ways that baffled prediction. One of the reasons he described London's crowds so brilliantly was that he wrote about them with an insider's knowledge. He too was a member of the nameless hordes before he achieved, and to a large extent invented, a new form of literary "celebrity." The word was first adopted in its modern sense in 1849, the same year he published the first installments of *David Copperfield,* a novel constructed around thick struts of autobiography; but Dickens's name had been a familiar literary trademark ever since it appeared on the title page of *Oliver Twist* in 1838. It was the clearest sign yet that it would be this name, rather than one of Dickens's earlier pseudonyms—"Boz," "Tibbs," "Timothy Sparks," "W"—that would come to be associated with an imagination so rich it made the real world seem like a pale and flimsy imitation of its fictional rival. We need to remember this, but by now his life is so well known that it is much easier to forget it. No writer seems to hold fewer surprises. No subject seems better suited to the reassuring certainties of biographical hindsight.

It isn't difficult to nudge the events of Dickens's life into a neat narrative shape. A miserable childhood, soured by poverty and traumatized by work in a rat-infested blacking factory, is followed by dull periods as a shorthand writer in the courts and the House of Commons. Then, in 1836, while he is still in his early twenties, he bursts onto the literary scene with the *Pickwick Papers,* a work that rapidly develops into a public craze. By the time of Queen Victoria's coronation in 1838, he is well on the way to becoming the most famous writer in the world. Summarized so baldly, it sounds less like a career path than the plot of a romance, and, as with any other kind of story, once we know how Dickens's early struggles end, it is tempting to read his life backwards as well as forwards. As the future loses its potential for surprise, so everything that happens to him starts to acquire the same even sheen of inevitability. Every chance event becomes a stepping-stone that fate drops into his path.

Actually, this is a version of his life that Dickens himself sometimes enjoyed promoting. In *David Copperfield,* the hero tries to explain how he became a successful novelist, and concludes that "I could never have done what I have done, without the habits of punctuality, order, and dili-

gence, without the determination to concentrate on one object at a time
. . . which I then formed." That sounds like an impressively independent-
minded way of going about things, but elsewhere in the novel David cannot quite shake out of his voice the idea that he became a success because
it was written in the stars. "I had no idea you were such a determined
character, Copperfield!" exclaims his friend Traddles, but several episodes remind us that the narrator exists within a world where, like all fictional characters, he acts in a way that is "determined" by the plot rather
than his own free will—as when he explains that he "never entertained a
more determined purpose in my life" than when running away to his Aunt
Betsey, or points out that "I was determined to keep apart" while walking
alongside the clammy and clinging Uriah Heep.

To some extent such ambiguities reflect the inevitable compromises
involved in any attempt to give life's uncertainties the biographer's coher-
ing touch. We might compare Samuel Smiles's best-selling 1859 guide
Self-Help, which similarly finds itself being drawn back to words like
"determined" as it discusses the secrets of success: Edward Bulwer is
described as one who was "determined to succeed"; Dr. Johnson is approvingly quoted for his definition of "genius"—a powerful mind "accidentally determined in some particular direction."[11] As these biographical sketches mount up, so each life falls into the same narrative groove, in
which hard knocks are always overcome by hard work, and good fortune
always comes to those who seek it out. And once this pattern is set, it can
seem rather harder to escape success than achieve it. Because Smiles is interested only in people whose lives have happy endings, everything they
do appears to be tugged on by a kind of comic fatality. Even their most
embarrassing early failures are subject to the gravitational pull of their
later successes. They are doomed to fame.

Real life is far harder to predict. Philip Larkin's poem "I Remember,
I Remember" fondly mocks the tendency to invent moments in the past,
non-memories, which now seem pregnant with significance:

I'll show you, come to that,
The bracken where I never trembling sat,

Determined to go through with it; where she
Lay back, and "all became a burning mist."
And, in those offices, my doggerel
Was not set up in blunt ten-point, nor read
By a distinguished cousin of the mayor,

Who didn't call and tell my father *There*
Before us, had we the gift to see ahead—[12]

Such defining moments rarely announce themselves at the time. It is only when reading a novel that we can flick forward a few pages to see how the story ends, or look again at events our eyes may have skimmed over too quickly the first time. Indeed, one of the satisfactions of well-crafted fiction is that it creates a parallel world in which every detail, no matter how trivial or seemingly inconsequential, is part of a meaningful whole; even accidents turn out to be part of an overall design. Making up stories is, among other things, a way of making up for the contingencies of everyday life, cluttered as it is with promising moments that are abandoned, or avoided, or that fail to lead anywhere important.[13]

David Copperfield recognizes as much in the way he chooses to begin his account. His first sentence—"Whether I shall turn out to be the hero of my own life, or whether that station will be held by anybody else, these pages must show"—sets the scene for a novel that is full of speculation about how many possible lives are contained within each human life. Haunted by the idea that he might have died instead of his brother, David is repeatedly reminded not to take his own identity for granted; the reminders range from Aunt Betsey's sad dreams about the life he might have led if he had been born a girl, to Steerforth's casual inquiry about whether or not he has a sister. ("That's a pity," he replies, when David answers in the negative; "I should think she would have been a pretty, timid, little, bright-eyed sort of girl." He makes up for his disappointment by renaming David "Daisy.") As the novel continues, phrases such as "might have" and "could have" produce an insistent counterfactual rhythm, conjuring up a series of shadow plots in which his characters end up elsewhere and things happen otherwise. These alternative versions of *David Copperfield* reach a crisis point at the end of the novel, when David's first wife, Dora, dies, and he recalls her shyly asking him "what might have happened" if he had married the saintly Agnes instead. His conclusion is that "the things that never happen, are often as much realities to us, in their effects, as those that are accomplished."

Dickens might have been writing about his own early career. During the 1830s, before he settled on—or settled into, or settled for—life as a novelist, he tried several other jobs on for size, including actor, stage manager, journalist, and clerk. At one point he even considered emigrating to the West Indies. It is tempting to ignore these other branches of Dickens's life, by assuming either that great novelists are born rather than made, or that choosing a career is as straightforward as picking a card from the pack. Both views were popular among Dickens's contemporaries. Romantic ideas about the writer as a special type of being, inspired by the muse, remained enticing to many Victorian readers, despite coming under increasing pressure from no-nonsense utilitarians, while William James pointed out that once somebody chooses one career over another, little by little the alternative disappears from his mind. "At first," he admitted, "he may sometimes doubt whether the self he murdered in that decisive hour might not have been the better of the two; but with the years such questions themselves expire, and the old alternative ego, once so vivid, fades into something less substantial than a dream."[14]

For Dickens, the decisive hour came one evening towards the end of 1833, as he walked up Fleet Street with a thin package in his hand. Some of the addresses he walked past had already achieved a certain notoriety, such as the pastry-cook and confectioner's shop where, in 1827, William Corder met his first wife, soon after he had killed his lover in a case that became known as the "Murder in the Red Barn." Others were still waiting for their chance to enter the public consciousness, such as Hen and Chickens Court, a dark alleyway leading off No. 185, where Sweeney

Todd would later set up his fictitious barber's shop.[15] Fleet Street also had more private associations for Dickens. It contained some of his favorite childhood haunts, including Mrs. Salmon's waxworks at No. 17 and the church of St. Dunstan's-in-the-West, which reopened in 1833 after being rebuilt in fashionable Gothic Revival style. So as he walked along the crowded pavement Dickens was also treading in his own earlier footsteps, traveling back in time.

Then he made a turning that took him away from the crowd. As he recalled in his 1867 preface to the *Pickwick Papers,* the package he was carrying was a copy of his first story, "Mr. Minns and His Cousin" (later published as "A Dinner at Poplar Walk"), which he "dropped stealthily one evening at twilight, with fear and trembling, into a dark letter-box, in a dark office, up a dark court." The "dark letter-box" belonged to the *New Monthly Magazine,* and the "dark court" was Johnson's Court, although the vaguely portentous air of Dickens's account makes it sound more like a fairy-tale quest or creation myth than the story of just another would-be author clogging up the magazine's letter-box. (An echo of the biblical injunction to "work out your own salvation with fear and trembling" adds a particular edge to Dickens's sense that in dropping off his story he was literally taking his fate into his own hands.)[16] A later drawing by James Stephenson (Figure 1) captures Dickens's emergence from the shadows. He appears confident, even cocky, as he stands in a shaft of light, feeding his manuscript into a slot marked "EDITOR'S BOX." Far from trembling with fear, he seems happily aware that he is on the verge of making a name for himself, just as "BOX" is only a pen stroke away from transforming itself into "BOZ."

Written just three years before his death, Dickens's description was undoubtedly influenced by what happened next, starting with the magazine editor's decision to publish the story. This was the moment at which he stopped being just another clerk and instead became, to borrow one of his favorite words, *somebody.* It was an idea that cheered and worried him in roughly equal proportions. In many of his later writings, such as the essay "Nobody's Story," or *Little Dorrit* (which he originally planned to call *Nobody's Fault*), he observed that thinking of yourself as "some-body," a person of consequence, made sense only if your actions them-selves had meaningful consequences. "Thou art still Nothing, Nobody," observes Teufelsdröckh in Carlyle's *Sartor Resartus;* "who, then, is Something, Somebody?" Dickens spent much of his career trying to an-swer that question, as he satirized politicians who ducked responsibility for their fellow human beings, while writing in a way that bound him ever more closely to his readers. (A coldly furious essay he published in 1856, "Nobody, Somebody and Everybody," tried to do both at once, by attack-ing the public inquiry that had absolved from blame every one of the se-nior figures involved in the "intolerable misery and loss" of the Crimean War.) But the hope that his writing might turn him into a "somebody," in this sense, was always trailed by the worry that he might not reach people, or might not touch them. He might even end up worse than when he started. One of the most mysterious characters in *Bleak House* is a clerk, a member of Dickens's former profession, who lives in a room "nearly black with soot, and grease, and dirt," and scratches out a living by copy-ing legal documents. After he dies, it turns out that his past is the center on which the plot pivots, but while he is alive nobody other than Jo the crossing-sweeper knows or cares anything about him. He responds by calling himself Nemo: Nobody.[17]

❧❧

Nemo is probably the most extreme example of the "alternative egos" that haunt Dickens's fiction, embodying his fear that although he had success-fully come out of the shadows, they were always ready to welcome him back. But even in his more optimistic moods Dickens often found himself thinking, like Mr. Dombey, of "what might have been, and what was not." Just as he enjoyed inventing different characters for himself in his letters—in addition to the Inimitable, he was the Sparkler of Albion, or Revolver, or the Great Protester, or frequently just plain Dick—so his fiction teems with surrogate selves.

Sometimes these emerge as fragments of disguised autobiography.

Towards the end of his life, Dickens confessed that he was "accustomed to observe myself as curiously as if I were another man," and his fiction frequently includes moments when he looks at himself with fresh eyes.[18] Many of his characters strike a playful balance between the self-revealing and the self-concealing. The most obvious example is David Copperfield, whose initials reflect Dickens's in reverse, like a mirror image, and who in the course of his novel encounters a mad old secondhand clothes-dealer named Charley, an ineffectual flute-playing schoolteacher, also named Charley, and a character named Mr. Dick who is writing a "Memorial" in which King Charles keeps rearing, and then losing, his head. But Dickens's autobiographical reflections started much earlier and lasted much longer than this. Oliver Twist drifts away from his delicate pauper friend Dick and joins a gang of London pickpockets which features a young joker named Charley. Another Dick appears as the hero of Dickens's contribution to *The Seven Poor Travellers,* a collection of stories published in the 1854 Christmas edition of *Household Words.* Supposedly a relative of the storyteller, he enlists in the army under the name "Doubledick," after he has "gone wrong and run wild" following a love affair that, in an unhappy echo of Dickens's own youth, ends in rejection and despair. (The mixture of self-pity and self-mockery generated when Dickens came to write about characters called Dick was not limited to his fiction: the garden of Gad's Hill Place, Dickens's final home, contained a small tombstone that he had erected over the grave of his daughter's pet canary, named after Tim Linkinwater's blind blackbird in *Nicholas Nickleby,* and that bore the inscription "This is the Grave of DICK The Best of Birds.")[19] More complex still is *A Tale of Two Cities,* which revolves around physical doubles whom Dickens originally wanted to call Charles Darney and Dick Carton, so that even their initials would reflect each other—CD:DC.

What remains unclear is how far these refracted self-images were the result of deliberate choices, as opposed to unconscious drives: we could see Dickens as a writer fond of private jokes or, just as plausibly, as one whose creativity largely depended on his "not examining what went on in his own mind."[20] More straightforward is the frequency with which his characters act as ethical sounding boards for each other. In *Dombey and Son* the prostitute Alice Marwood is described as a "faded likeness" of Edith Dombey, who is bought and sold on the marriage market, while in *Great Expectations* Trabb's boy provides a glorious caricature of the snobbish Pip, as he struts down the street drawling, "Don't know yah, don't know yah, pon my soul don't know yah!" Even when they inhabit different novels, Dickens's characters often present themselves as complements or rivals to each other: *Oliver Twist*'s leering Fagin (bad Jew) is offset by *Our Mutual Friend*'s saintly Riah (good Jew); *The Old Curiosity Shop*'s Quilp (clever, evil dwarf) is posthumously trumped by *David Copperfield*'s Miss Mowcher (clever, kindly dwarf).

Dickens's awareness of "what might have been, and what was not" can be seen still more sharply in his methods of composition. A surviving memorandum book, dating from 1855, contains dozens of embryonic characters and stories:

> Talk, Talk, Talk.
> . . . . .
> "The family's Legs"
> . . . . .
> *We* must emigrate to China.
> . . . . .
> The Invisible One.[21]

Such narrative doodles occupy a strange twilight existence, frozen on the page before they could either grow into fully formed stories or vanish back into the silence of the mind. Few of them give any clues about how they might have developed; in some ways they are only a level up from inkblots in which we can see whichever stories we choose.

Given how many of these seeds Dickens planted, and how few of them flourished, he would probably have agreed with a letter published in the *Morning Advertiser* on April 19, 1838, which pointed out how unlikely it was that works such as *Sketches by Boz* or the *Pickwick Papers* should have been written at all. "Some will believe that when an author displays himself to be a genius, and produces certain works," the correspondent explained, "that these were inevitable—that he being a genius *must* have of necessity produced these very works. To an author this will at once appear an absurdity."[22] Dickens takes this idea a stage further. His published narratives typically include the stubs of rival stories that are gradually overwhelmed by what emerges on the page, as if a novel were a Darwinian environment in which only the fittest ideas survived. In novel after novel, we are led to expect outcomes that remain unrealized, and instead drift around in the background like a set of counterfactual ghosts. Sometimes this involves major structural ironies: *Dombey and Son* turns out to be about Dombey and Daughter; the hero of *Great Expectations* belatedly recognizes that he has horribly misunderstood the kind of story he is in. At other times, these alternative outcomes are temptingly dangled before our eyes and then removed, as when Scrooge is forced to confront a miserable and lonely future, but is afterwards granted the opportunity to change his fate.

Even when Dickens's narratives follow a more predictable path, they tend to include elements that comment satirically on each other, working to remind us of how differently each story might have been told. *The Mystery of Edwin Drood* is the star example here: a murder mystery in which the key question became not whodunnit, but how Dickens would have done it—how he would have completed a novel that hints at so many possible narrative outcomes. The novels Dickens did complete, similarly, incorporate a ready willingness to imagine supplementary or alternative versions of themselves, as when *Bleak House* ends with Esther poised on the brink of a revelation she never makes: "even supposing—." The same quality of "just suppose," that founding principle of all fiction, informs everything Dickens wrote. It even affects his more factual writings, whether he is urging the readers of his journalism to make a future that will live up to their hopes and dreams, or imagining how differently things could have turned out in the past.

History books describing what did not happen were something of a nineteenth-century specialty. Thomas Carlyle's study *The French*

Revolution (1837), for example, the "wonderful book" that Dickens joked he had read five hundred times, offers several tantalizing glimpses of un-realized futures—"and the whole course of French History different!"—even as it is pointing out that the past is "simply and altogether what it *is*."[23] In *A Child's History of England*, Dickens plays these rival approach-es off against each other. Thus, "if Canute had been the big man" when challenged to single combat by Edmund Ironside, "he would probably have said yes, but, being the little man, he decidedly said no"; afterwards, Ironside's sons are packed off to Sweden, where "if the King of Sweden had been like many, many other men of that day, he would have had their innocent throats cut." Repeatedly, Dickens deploys the little word "if" as a passport to a series of alternative futures; repeatedly, he shows that the facts of history can be seen clearly only when viewed against a back-ground of counterfactuals.

This biography offers a critical account of Dickens's early years as a writ-er: a period when his mind was especially preoccupied by supposing, as he tried to come to terms with the events that had made him into the person he was, and to work out what kind of writer he might yet become. Although I do not attempt an exhaustive account of everything that hap-pened to Dickens in these years, I do begin with some of the key events of his childhood, not least because he continued to return to them in his later life with all the wary fascination of someone touching a bruise. I end with the events that, in 1838, prompted him to start signing his work as "Charles Dickens," a label that was both a statement of intent and a way of gathering together everything he had experienced in the previous years. Throughout, my aim is to re-create the texture of his life as it was lived: ambitiously, uncertainly, and full of loose ends.

Dickens's biographers have usually presented a far neater picture than this. Dickens the philanthropist, the inventor of Christmas, the campaign-ing journalist, the creator of vivid comic grotesques, the fierce protector of children: such characterizations have been repeated so often that they have become indistinguishable from historical facts. There is little space in these accounts for the other Dickens we occasionally glimpse in the cracks of his letters or in stray corners of contemporary accounts: a sad, strange figure who was always on the move, but never seems to have been sure whether he was searching for something or running away from it. His early writing was equally unsettled. As Dickens grew older, he enjoyed promoting a view of his fiction as deliberate and artful: the postscript to his last completed novel, *Our Mutual Friend*, describes the novelist as "the story-teller at his loom," and this reflects his growing attachment to the idea that in a good writer's hands every sentence is part of an intricate design, no part of which can be removed without the whole fabric unraveling. Yet his first full-length attempts at fiction, such as the *Pickwick Papers*, were not seen as novels at all. They reveled in muddle and mess; many of their most memorable scenes and characters emerged only in the process of writing. Even when Dickens moved towards more carefully organized stories, he remained uneasily aware of how difficult it was to construct a plot without bullying its events into place. There is a good deal of fellow-feeling in his later description of an inmate of Lancaster Lunatic Asylum, who is absorbed in studying a small piece of matting and trying to find a pattern in its fibers.[24] Dickens treated his own life in a similar fashion. If some parts were planned, others were dizzying flights of improvisation: the process of learning how to be a novelist was also one in which he was discovering what it meant to be himself. What he would eventually discover was that, if his life involved weaving many strands together, the image presented to the public depended on another side that was hidden from view, or what Tennyson's early play *The Devil and the Lady* describes as "The dark reverse of it, / The intertwining and rough wanderings / Of random threads and wayward colourings."[25]

This is a very different Dickens to the one we are used to, not least because our image of him tends to come from the stage of his life that is closest to us. Ask people to think of Dickens, and the picture that usually comes into their heads is the grizzled beard and deeply creased face of the Victorian sage, rather than the youth who achieved fame before he needed to start shaving. This image has an intellectual as well as a physical aspect to it. In his last years, Dickens encountered the young Henry James, who noticed the "merciless *military* eye" he kept beadily trained on what was going on around him.[26] That was certainly one side of Dickens: the rigidity and absolute self-certainty that made him a ruthless negotiator when dealing with his publishers, and in every sense a hard man to live with. Yet it is a sign of Dickens's greatness that there is almost nothing one can say about him of which the opposite is not also true. His writing is full of fixed obsessions, but also has a restless experimental quality that allowed his early works to surprise everyone, including himself. He became an author through "nature and accident," like David Copperfield, but he was also good at cultivating useful friends, and had a happy knack of being in the right place at the right time. He is the quintessential Victorian, yet he first achieved fame in the years before Victoria came to the throne—that period of transition in the 1830s when the future seemed to be a blank sheet just waiting to be written on. His early career was held up as a model of how far anyone could get via talent alone, yet the metaphors used to describe his rise—fireworks, balloon—also contained veiled warnings about how easily he could be buffeted off course. Even Dickens's eyes are not straightforward. Merciless and military they may have been, but there was little agreement on what color they were: "clear blue intelligent eyes" (Thomas Carlyle), "a distinct and brilliant hazel" (Thomas A. Trollope), "black" (an anonymous American writer), "a dark steely warm grey, looking at a little distance like brown eyes" (William P. Frith).[27] He is not the only literary figure to have created such doubts—Julian Barnes's 1984 novel *Flaubert's Parrot* plays a set of tongue-in-cheek variations on the kaleidoscopic qualities of the heroine's eyes in *Madame Bovary*—but they seem especially appropriate for a writer whose early life had so many different aspects that his name might easily have been mistaken for a plural noun.

The editors of Dickens's correspondence point out that the period covered by their first volume, from 1820 to 1839, is one in which he often experimented with his signature.[28] The capital letters attract extra twirls and flourishes; the line underneath his name starts off as an elaborate scroll, and ends up looking more like a bouncy spring bursting into life or a twister ready to carry him away (Figure 2). In this book, I would like to explore what lies behind that signature. How did the child who in later life claimed that "I might easily have been, for any care that was taken of me, a little robber or a little vagabond" become the novelist Charles Dickens?[29]

CHAPTER ONE

❦❦❦❦❦

Lost and Found

"When I was a very small boy indeed," Dickens recalled in his 1853 essay "Gone Astray," "I got lost one day in the City of London." It is hardly an unusual childhood memory, especially at a time when the churning crowds of Britain's cities made it all too easy for individuals to lose their moorings and be set adrift in a sea of strangers. In 1849, commenting on the number of children "left inefficiently attended" in Manchester, the journalist Angus Reach claimed that every year "more than 4,000 go annually astray and get 'lost' in the streets," while newspapers like the *Times* regularly carried notices pleading for information about those who had gone missing.[1] They included a nine-year-old boy last seen with a man who had promised him "lots of sugar—a great many basins full," and a seven-year-old who disappeared wearing "a blue jacket, black trousers, blue waistcoat, old brown pinafore, cloth cap and hob-nailed boots"— a heartbreakingly precise description of clothes so common they would have worked like a cloak of invisibility in the bustling city streets.[2]

Such stories were usually told from the perspective of the adult whose grip or attention had momentarily slipped: a sadly familiar plot that started with shock, developed into heaving panic, and ended in the frantic scanning of a scene that had suddenly become punctuated by tantalizing human fragments—the same hat here, a similar profile there—as if the child had not merely vanished but had somehow been scattered into the crowd. Dickens's version is different. In the first place, he tells it from the perspective of his own boyhood self who is treated to an outing by "Somebody." They start at St. Giles's Church, before moving on to view the celebrated lion statue over the gateway of Northumberland House in the Strand, where "in the act of looking up with mingled awe and admira-

·[19]·

tion at that famous animal I lost Somebody." At this point the second key difference emerges: after a paragraph lamenting the child's "unreasoning terror of being lost," Dickens recalls how quickly he dried his tears and started to imagine possible futures for himself.

With one shilling and four pence in his pocket, a "pewter ring with a bit of red glass in it" given to him by his six-year-old sweetheart, and a head full of stories, he sets out to seek his fortune. "When I had found it, I thought I would drive home in a coach and six, and claim my bride," but the prospect of being a modern-day Dick Whittington is soon chased away by the thought of becoming a drummer-boy in the army, and after a day wandering the streets he ends up in a theater, the natural home of identities that are unstable and provisional. Here actors throw themselves off the summit of "a curious rock, presenting something of the appearance of a pair of steps," while a pretty young actress returns in a different play as a boy, as if becoming someone else were as simple as pulling on a new pair of trousers. If that was the only strand of thought in Dickens's essay, it would be little more than a cheerful counterweight to the usual distraught stories about lost children, one in which a child drifts through the dirt and gloom of the city without being touched by it, like a scene from *Babes in the Wood* that had been dropped into real life. The story even has a happy ending, as the boy hands himself over to a watchman and is reunited with his father. The seeds of tragedy refuse to sprout.

But the outcome could easily have been different—sadder, nastier, bloodier—which is why Dickens shadows the day's events with dangers that the child is only dimly conscious of but are intended to make adult readers squirm. At one stage he encounters a stray dog, to whom he gives the optimistic name Merrychance, and who seems happy to play, "frisking about me, rubbing his nose against me, dodging at me sideways, shaking his head and pretending to run backwards, and making himself good-naturedly ridiculous, as if he had no consideration for himself, but wanted to raise my spirits." Given a taste of the boy's "small German" sausage, however, he quickly decides that a small boy would be even better: "his mouth watering, and his eyes glistening . . . he sidled out on the pavement in a threatening manner and growled at me." The dog's behavior is a model of the essay as a whole, which playfully romps around in its description of the child's mini-odyssey, but switches into a far more menacing tone whenever it notices figures who pose a risk to his safety, such as a chimney-sweep who "looked at me as if he thought me suitable to his business," or theatergoers whose swearing makes Dickens wonder "how long it would take, by means of such association, to corrupt a child."

Such questions were especially pressing at the time of the essay's publication. In 1850–1852, Henry Mayhew had published a series of investigative articles, later reprinted in *London Labour and the London Poor* (1861–1862), that anxiously circled back to the topic of street children, and in particular to how easily a new recruit could end up joining the small army that scrambled for a living by begging pennies, stealing handkerchiefs, or turning cartwheels to amuse passers-by. Orphans and runaways composed a sizable percentage of this group, but some of the most troubling cases had found themselves swelling its ranks after falling through the cracks of their previous lives. They included a wealthy jeweler's son nicknamed "The Kid," like an early prototype of Charlie Chaplin's lovable scamp, who had discovered to his cost how rarely the events of real life fell into the groove of sentimental comedy. Befriended by a bunch of crooks, and later imprisoned, he was now reduced to begging beside a sign that read "I AM STARVING" chalked on Waterloo Bridge.[3] Another eighteen youths who attended one of Mayhew's rowdy public meetings similarly confessed that they had been "led astray by bad companions," just as Oliver Twist joins a gang of pickpockets once he falls in with the Artful Dodger.[4]

Other possible fates awaiting the lone child included abduction and theft. Kidnapping was a popular theme in contemporary novels; in 1837, the year Dickens began writing *Oliver Twist*, in which abduction is a constant threat, it also featured in novels by, among others, Harrison Ainsworth, Edward Bulwer, Captain Marryat, and Charlotte Adams.[5] Such fiction was based on a real anxiety; the final volume of *London Labour and the London Poor* included a category of thieves known as "child strippers," who would "watch their opportunity to accost children passing in the streets, tidily dressed with good boots and clothes," and entice them away "for the purpose, they say, of buying them sweets."[6] Fifteen years earlier Dickens had offered a fictional version of these thieves in the shape of *Dombey and Son*'s Good Mrs. Brown, who not only robs Florence Dombey of her clothes after the child gets lost in the London streets, but has also effectively sold her own daughter into prostitution. The same idea also took less extreme forms in Dickens's writing. In *Mrs. Lirriper's Lodgings,* one of his many bumbling policemen tries to cheer Mrs. Lirriper with the thought that, although her adopted son has gone missing, "people ain't over-anxious to have what I may call second-hand children." The worst that will happen, he observes reassuringly, is that he will be "found wrapped up in a cabbage-leaf, a-shivering in a lane."

But children who fell into the wrong hands could lose far more than their clothes. They could also lose their innocence, their liberty, and sometimes even their lives. The philanthropist Edward Pelham Brenton, who helped to organize the Society for the Suppression of Juvenile Vagrancy, estimated in 1832 that there were around 15,000 boys sleeping rough on the streets of London. One Covent Garden gang styled themselves the Forty Thieves, a dimly remembered homage to the *Arabian Nights,* and identified themselves by numbers that were tattooed into the palms of their hands with a needle dipped in gunpowder.[7] In September 1828, numbers 5 and 8, both around twelve years old, were arrested for theft and committed for trial—a sudden irruption of reality into a world that had hitherto teetered on the edge of fantasy, like a game of cops and robbers that had somehow turned into a real shootout. For campaigners like Brenton, their fate was as inevitable as the aging process: boys who were denied a family home, he argued, would eventually end up as "the inmates of workhouses, of prisons, of dark cells, of tread mills, pursuing an uninterrupted course through all the gradations of misery and infamy, to the hulks [prison ships] and the gibbet."[8] Some did not even make it as far as the gibbet. G. M. W. Reynolds's lurid collection of stories *The Mysteries of London* (1845–1848) opens with a scene in which a youth becomes lost in a maze of alleys, is abducted by two men, and is finally flung through a trapdoor into a well that empties into the stagnant filth of the Fleet River—a fictional echo of the real-life revelations in 1831 that children were among the victims of London's body-snatchers, whose favorite methods of killing included lacing the child's drink with laudanum, and then lowering his or her head into a well until the water stopped bubbling.[9] Such details add an extra edge to the haunting moment in "Gone Astray" when young Dickens rests in the churchyard and wonders what it would feel like to be buried there. It is a quiet warning that while some losses might be temporary—the same hope that would later animate J. M. Barrie's fantasy of the "lost boys" in *Peter Pan*—others might not.

The fate of a lost child largely depended on where he or she ended up. The area around St. Giles's Church, where Dickens had started his journey, was one of the most notoriously seedy parts of London, and if he had tried to retrace his steps from Northumberland House he would quickly have found himself in the adjacent district of Seven Dials. This was a honeycomb of slum dwellings centered on a star-shaped pattern of streets, and according to his friend and biographer John Forster, visiting it made Dickens "supremely happy": "'Good heaven!' he would exclaim, 'what wild visions of prodigies of wickedness, want, and beggary, arose in my mind out of that place!'"[10] Its hollow-eyed children, seemingly held together only by their rags, were trapped in the district's squalid courts and blind alleys like flies in a web. In one of his earliest articles for *Bell's Life in London,* in 1834, Dickens described the situation of "the stranger who finds himself in 'The Dials' for the first time and stands . . . at the entrance of seven obscure passages, uncertain which to take" ("Seven Dials"). It sounds less like a piece of urban geography than a fragment of fairy tale or myth, in which the number seven carries quasi-magical properties (seven sons, seven leagues, seven dwarfs), as if each road from "Seven Dials" led not just to a different destination but to a different destiny altogether. Looked at the other way round, though, "Seven Dials" was also where these roads met—a center that drew the poor and lonely towards it like fingers clenching themselves into a fist. Once there, these lost souls might be unable to extricate themselves. Worse still, they might come to think of life there as the only kind they could ever presume to lead. The saddest parts of *London Labour and the London Poor* are Mayhew's interviews with slum-dwellers who no longer notice the squalor of their surroundings, like the "pure-finder" (collector of dog's dung), a "poor old woman resembling a bundle of rags and filth stretched out on some dirty straw," who claimed that she would rather starve than leave her accustomed way of life: "I'm so used to the air, that I'd sooner die in the street, as many I know have done."[11]

Such encounters add a new sense of threat to Dickens's boast in "Gone Astray" that he was good at "adapting myself to the circumstances in which I found myself." After all, this essay first appeared in his journal *Household Words* alongside the serialization of *Bleak House,* and only a few months had passed since he'd introduced a child into the novel who had perfectly adapted himself to life on the streets—so perfectly, in fact, that Jo the crossing-sweeper knows "nothink" other than how to sweep crossings.[12] He is like an emanation of his environment, a clump of dirt brought to cringing life, and Dickens appears to have had some doubts over whether someone so detached from the rest of society had a proper claim to being thought of as human at all. When a band strikes up, he and a waiting dog listen to it "probably with such the same amount of animal satisfaction," and the contrast with "Gone Astray" is striking. While young Dickens is attacked by a dog, Jo is viewed as little more than a dog—one that can walk on its hind legs and perform a trick with a broom, but a dog nonetheless. Shuffling around on his crossing, he is not lost, because he has never been missed. He is merely a stray.

※ ※ ※

The figure of the child who is lost and found again haunted Dickens like a restless ghost. "Keep the child in view" he reminded himself when composing the final stages of *The Old Curiosity Shop;* and as his career developed, what had been a local warning not to lose track of Little Nell in the dense weave of his plot gradually emerged as a more general template for his fiction.[13] Oliver Twist, Smike, Jo—the pages of Dickens's novels are crowded with children who wander away from their old lives and need to be rescued from danger, usually much later than Dickens was, and sometimes too late altogether. Whenever he seemed to have exorcised this ghost it reappeared in ever stranger forms, as when Arthur Clennam, light-headed from want of sleep and food, worries that his mind is "going astray," and is revived by the appearance of Little Dorrit ("Your own poor child come back!"), or when the imprisoned Dr. Manette in *A Tale of Two Cities* tries to make sense of his daughter's sudden reappearance by touching her hair ("In the midst of the action he went astray, and, with another deep sigh, fell to work at his shoemaking"), and is recalled to his senses only when he is taken in her arms and "rocked . . . on her breast like a child."

Dickens was equally haunted by the irrevocable consequences that one wrong turning in life might have, as it does for the anonymous lad in *The Old Curiosity Shop* who is sentenced to transportation after being "led astray" by wicked companions. To some extent he was voicing much broader fears of the period, especially in London, where dreams of upward mobility were forever shadowed by fears of the opposite movement downwards. His phrasing suggests how often such stories were treated like parables, because it recalls the biblical story about the need to become as little children in order to enter the kingdom of heaven: "If a man have a hundred sheep, and one of them be gone astray, doth he not leave the ninety and nine, and goeth into the mountains, and seeketh that which is gone astray? . . . Even so it is not the will of your Father which is in heaven, that one of these little ones should perish."[14] The idea that we all have the potential to go astray is one that Dickens often returned to, although "idea" is probably too strong a word for the loose bundle of hopes and fears it gathers up in his writing. Dr. Manette is only one of many characters who discover that their previous selves remain nested inside them like the figures of a Russian doll, forever ready to be called upon in a moment of crisis, whether this be the joy of Scrooge at being given a chance of redemption ("I'm quite a baby. Never mind. I don't care.

I'd rather be a baby") or, in *Bleak House,* the moment when the dying Sir Leicester Deadlock is picked up "like a child" by Trooper George. And yet, for all the commitment Dickens shows to these biblically inspired ideas of return and redemption, he seems to have accepted that they were of little practical help when it came to making day-to-day decisions and then living with the consequences. Once we have chosen one path over another, or over many others, he admits, we can never retrace our steps and recover the opportunities we have lost. "Pause you," Pip urges the reader in *Great Expectations,* "and think for a moment of the long chain of iron or gold, of thorns or flowers, that would never have bound you, but for the formation of the first link on one memorable day." It is good advice, although not especially helpful for Dickens's other characters, who, in one of those strange paradoxes we tend to overlook when entering the parallel world of fiction, seem never to have read anything by Dickens. Accordingly, his fiction echoes with the sound of doors slamming shut behind his characters, and the past being dragged around like Marley's clanking chains. Near the end of *Our Mutual Friend,* the scheming Lammles walk out of the novel arm in arm, as if "linked together by concealed handcuffs." They are like an unhappy embodiment of the terse note in Dickens's memorandum book which reads "WE—fettered together."[15] No other writer is quite as good at making marriage vows about remaining together "till death us do part" sound more like a suicide pact. In fact, by the time he wrote this note Dickens had good personal reasons for feeling aggrieved at the way a marriage might turn out, but the larger idea about being bound by previous events started much earlier and cut much deeper.

The past almost always turns out to be a constraining force in his writing, hobbling any attempt to move freely towards the future. Whenever Dickens tried to be more optimistic he was rarely so convincing, as he found himself giving voice to ideas about freedom and self-determination that were impeccably progressive in tone but had nothing like the same imaginative power. "Whatever we once were (which I hardly know) we ceased to be long ago, and never can be any more," says Little Dorrit;

but the context of her remark is a conversation about how accustomed her family has become to life in the Marshalsea debtors' prison—so accustomed to it, in fact, that when they move away they continue to carry the shadows of its bars around with them. The prison expands to fit the size of the world, and the world contracts to fit the size of the prison. Even Dickens's syntax gets in on the act, with sentence after sentence uncoiling across the page, as if seeking an escape into a different kind of story, before ending up in the same place: "The fair little face, touched with divine compassion, as it peeped through the grate, was like an angel's in the prison." There is more than one sense in which *Little Dorrit* is a novel of prison sentences.

Some readers have felt that Dickens overplays the metaphor of the prison in this novel, but it would be hard to overstate its importance to him. For when it came to writing about the lingering taint of prison life, or the grinding routines of poverty, he already had the best research resource available to any writer: memory. The story of Dickens's childhood, and in particular the period in which he was obliged to work in a blacking warehouse while his father was imprisoned for debt, is now so familiar that it is tempting to assume it was equally well-known during his lifetime. Nothing could be further from the truth. Although Dickens occasionally dropped clues, they were only of the most teasingly oblique kind, and otherwise the period was a sad and shameful secret he kept to himself. His son Henry recalled how the family once played a memory game the Christmas before Dickens's death, in which each player had to repeat a list of words ("Beefsteak, Caligula . . .") and add another to the growing tail. When it came to Dickens's turn, "There was a pause for a while, and then, with a strange twinkle in his eye and a curious modulation in his voice, he gave it as '*Warren's Blacking, 30 Strand.*'"[16] Dickens gave a less twinkle-eyed version of the same response in 1847, when Forster mentioned in passing that Charles Wentworth Dilke claimed to have seen the young Dickens working in a warehouse near the Strand, and in return for a half-crown had received "a very low bow." "He was silent for several minutes," Forster reports, and not for several weeks did he say anything more about "a time of which he never could lose the remembrance, while he remembered anything, and the recollection of which, at intervals, haunted him and made him miserable, even to that hour."[17] The pause and the silence both hint at how close Dickens came to losing his voice as a novelist for good.

The fragment of autobiography Dickens went on to write showed how skillfully he could turn his experiences into a story that kept one foot in the humdrum world of fact and another in the more tempting world of fiction. Seen through his eyes, Warren's was at once an ordinary place of business, which employed boys to paste labels onto pots of shoe polish, and a "crazy, tumble-down old house" transplanted from a fairy tale, in which the hero was forced to undertake tasks as cruel and pointless as those of Cinderella, who must separate out piles of lentils and ashes. Perhaps this is why, when Dickens came to write down his experiences, what Forster describes as "the story of the author's childhood" often takes on the vivid coloring of a story for a child, rather than one merely about a child. The sound of the rats "squeaking and scuffling" in Warren's cellar, for example, might have been unnerving for anyone aware of urban legends recounted in contemporary articles such as "The Natural History of Rats," which tells of a watchdog's skeleton discovered in the sewers after being licked clean by "the insatiable rats," or James Rodwell's later study *The Rat: Its History and Destructive Character,* with its bloodthirsty promise of "A Child's Fingers eaten off by a Rat" and "A Child's Toe gnawed by a Rat."[18] But they would have been even more worrying for a small boy like Dickens, who vividly remembered his nurse's story ("Chips") of a man who is driven mad by talking rats, drowns, and ends up floating to shore with an immense rodent sitting on his corpse and laughing. Other details sound less like the clutter of ordinary life than like clues planted for future biographers. When we read that he used to take a piece of bread to work "wrapped up in a piece of paper like a book," the scene is close to toppling over into a fable of wasted potential, in which this poor child will eat out of books but never earn a crust by writing them. That is certainly how Forster presents it: the Household Edition of his *Life of Charles Dickens*

(1880) includes a title-page vignette (Figure 3) that shows young Dickens in a dark corner of the warehouse, turning his head away from the viewer as he succumbs to misery, or shame, or simply sheer exhaustion. The child seems pathetically young and frail, and this reflects Dickens's tendency to exaggerate how small he was at the time, as if only by reducing his size could he show how little he meant to the grown-ups. The drawing also reflects Dickens's later sense that this episode was a crossroads as well as a crisis. The closer one looks at the table on which his head rests, the more it starts to resemble a mocking imitation of the writer's desk: the stack of labels is indistinguishable from a bundle of documents; the glue brush looks like a pen resting perkily in its inkpot. In this context, it is not hard to see why the tone of Dickens's autobiographical fragment finds itself swinging unpredictably between accusation and self-pity, or why it sometimes sounds as if Dickens is taking the witness stand, as when he complains that the period was one in which he received "no advice, no counsel, no encouragement, no consolation, no support, from any one that I can call to mind, so help me God." It is the response of a successful writer to a set of circumstances that nearly prevented him from becoming a writer at all.

Dickens's own view of the memoir was revealed by his later decision to incorporate large chunks almost verbatim into *David Copperfield*. (The sole "memorandum" for this episode, in which David joins Murdstone and Grinby's warehouse, was: "What I know so well.") It was a story, shaped and colored by the skill of a storyteller, which ended up turning into a form of authorial mythmaking. These were the events, Dickens implies, that would later encourage him to write novels like the one he called his "favourite child," as if wanting to prove to himself how well a child could develop if it received the right kind of loving attention. These were the events that had permanently shaped his imagination.

❦❦

Despite these biographical false trails and dead ends, it is possible to reconstruct the true sequence of events with some accuracy. Born on

February 7, 1812, Dickens experienced a childhood that for the first few years was nothing out of the ordinary. His father was a clerk in the Navy Pay Office, moving from Portsmouth to London, then to Chatham, and finally back to London; and although the family finances had trembled on the edge of comfort for some time, John Dickens had always managed to bargain and borrow his way out of trouble. Then came disaster. The precise cause remains a matter of conjecture—Dickens's stern fictional treatment of drink and gambling have been noted by critics, though sheer financial ineptitude on the part of his father seems more likely—but by the start of 1824, as the family's latest rented home, 4 Gower Street North in Bloomsbury, was slowly stripped of anything that could be sold or pawned, the inevitable could not be postponed any longer. Arrested on February 20 for failing to pay £40 he owed to the local baker, John Dickens was forced to move into the Marshalsea prison for debtors, followed at staggered intervals by his wife, Elizabeth, and their younger children, who lodged with him while he tried to make arrangements with his creditors and lobbied his mother for yet another advance on his inheritance. Some half-hearted attempts to solve the problem had already failed, notably the efforts of Elizabeth Dickens to launch a school for young ladies, which announced its arrival with a shiny brass plaque on the house in Gower Street and the distribution of some flyers. But "MRS. DICKENS'S ESTABLISHMENT" failed to attract a single pupil, and the family had to face up to the fact that the luxuries they could no longer afford included young Charles's childhood.

James Lamert, a distant relative of Dickens who had previously lodged with the family when they lived at 16 Bayham Street, Camden Town, probably thought he was pulling helpful strings when he suggested employing Charles in the blacking warehouse he was currently running on behalf of his cousin and brother-in-law George.[19] The business had recently been taken over from the founder, Jonathan Warren, who had split from his brother Robert after they quarreled over which of them owned the original family recipe to "Warren's" boot blacking. Consequently, there were two "Warren's" warehouses within shouting distance of each other: Robert Warren's large and well-situated premises at 30 Strand, and Jonathan Warren's more tumbledown operation, located in a creaky wooden building at Old Hungerford Stairs, just off the Strand, which he carefully advertised as:

WARREN'S BLACKING
30 HUNGERFORD STAIRS STRAND

—in the hope of piggy-backing on the popularity of his brother's brand. Although the dates are uncertain, Dickens probably started work in late 1823 or early 1824, shortly before his twelfth birthday, at a salary of six shillings a week. At first, James separated him from the rest of the working boys, putting him in the counting-house on the first floor, and promised to give him some schooling during his meal breaks, but Dickens soon found himself being moved downstairs. There he formed part of a human production line, whose job it was to cover small earthenware bottles of Warren's product with pieces of oiled paper, tie them round with string, and then paste on a printed label. It was routine labor of a kind familiar to anyone who has worked in a factory, where the satisfaction of finishing a job quickly and neatly (Dickens reports with a sad pun that he soon reached "a pitch of perfection" at the work) was immediately crushed by the need to do another one exactly the same. WARREN'S BLACKING, WARREN'S BLACKING, WARREN'S BLACKING, again, and again, and again.

The Dickenses' move into the Marshalsea anticipated the trajectory of many other families in the following months. A banking and stock market crash in December 1825, the first and worst of the century, became notorious for having struck down "the innocent and the guilty" alike, leading to a further 1,650 bankruptcies in the first half of 1826 alone.[20] In an atmosphere of growing financial suspicion, where steady economic growth was being replaced by cycles of boom and bust (during Dickens's lifetime, there were further crashes in 1837, 1847, 1857, and 1866), the country reverberated with anxious whispers about who might be the next to fall.

Such anxiety was especially fueled by the knowledge that one's financial security and social identity were as intimately connected as a check and its signature: when bankruptcy came, "The erasure of the name from the doors and the memory of the firm from their friends were almost simultaneous."[21]

The social ambitions of Dickens's parents may have caused them to feel the shame of debt especially keenly. On Monday, February 10, 1812, three days after Charles's birth, readers of the *Hampshire Telegraph* and the *Hampshire Courier* would have noticed a small, proud advertisement that announced "BIRTHS—on Friday, at Mile-End Terrace, the Lady of John Dickens, Esq., a son"—an awkward mixture of grandeur and ordinariness that said far more about the couple's capacity for self-invention than it did about their new baby. John Dickens claimed to be related to the Dickenses of Staffordshire, and (without permission) used their family crest of "a lion couchant, bearing in his dexter paw a Maltese cross," while his son would later broadly hint that Mrs. Nickleby's clumsy airs and graces ("We used to keep such hours! . . . Balls, dinners, card-parties") were based on his mother's affectations.[22] There was, one acquaintance in Chatham later recalled, "more than a ghost of gentility hovering in their company."[23] Whether this ghost was the echo of a more prosperous past, or the outline of a more prosperous future, was far from clear. Many of John Dickens's mannerisms were capable of being viewed as signs of either confidence or doubt. His orotund manner of speaking, for example, which Dickens enjoyed parodying, producing sentences that were rich with sub-clauses and self-qualifications, did not necessarily indicate someone puffing out his chest. They might equally have revealed his nervousness at reaching out into the world, unsure how far his speech would take him. Later in life, Dickens adopted his father's sham heraldic device, having it engraved on his silver plate and using it as a bookplate; and his recollection that he was known at Warren's as "the young gentleman," reflecting his superior "conduct and manners," seems similarly in keeping with his parents' hopes about their true, albeit temporarily disguised, social standing. So does his assumption that this nickname was offered as the linguistic equivalent of a tradesman respectfully touching his cap, rather than being intended as a sneer or a slur. Like father and mother, like son. What had become painfully evident, though, was that these ambitions were as fragile as one of Warren's bottles. As Dickens settled into the rhythms of his new life, in which regular hours of drudgery alternated with periods of aimless wandering and staring in through shop windows, calculating what he could afford to eat, the possible futures he had been encouraged to dream about gradually thinned and disappeared. "No words can express the secret agony of my soul as I sunk into this companionship," he wrote, "compared these every day associates with those of my happier childhood; and felt my early hopes of growing up to be a learned and distinguished man, crushed in my breast."

There was a telling occasion when Dickens suffered an attack of side spasms, and another of the boys, Bob Fagin, offered to walk him home. Too proud to let him know about the prison, Dickens led him to a street near Southwark Bridge, pretending that he lived there, and when they reached the house he identified as his family's, "in case of his looking back, I knocked at the door, I recollect, and asked, when the woman opened it, if that was Mr. Robert Fagin's house." Dickens tells the story as a comedy of errors, retrospectively winking at his own resourcefulness, but the substitution of Fagin for himself also suggests his nervousness about the increasingly close alignment of their lives. Not until he came to write *Oliver Twist* would he lay that particular ghost to rest, by making his pure-souled hero triumph over the villain to whom he gave Fagin's name, thereby proclaiming to the world that a "young gentleman" would always be more than a match for his common associates. Worse still, his older sister Fanny had not been forced to make the same sacrifices, and despite an embarrassment of unpaid fees was still being kept on as a pupil at the Royal Academy of Music. At one point, Dickens attended a ceremony where she was awarded a prize, and the contrast between brother and sister caused the tears to run down his face. "I never had suffered so much," he recalled, adding: "There was no envy in this." Perhaps young Dickens was indeed saintly enough to be thrilled at his sister's success, but the fragment in which he describes being a "poor little drudge" suggests rather different feelings about the apparent divergence of their paths. "I might easily have been, for any care that was taken of me, a little robber or a little vagabond," he writes, where the stress on his littleness manages to combine a routine touch of pathos—small creatures are easily crushed—with the grim recognition that size was not everything when it came to London's "prodigies of wickedness, want and beggary." Out of little acorns wild things could grow. (That Dickens was not alone in worrying about these "prodigies" is clear from the formation of a Society for the Rescue of Boys Not Yet Convicted of Any Criminal Offence, a name that circled around "Yet" like someone nervously checking his pockets in a crowd.)[24] And what of his parents' feelings? "My father and mother were quite satisfied," Dickens frostily recalled; "They could hardly have been more so, if I had been twenty years of age, distinguished at a grammar-school, and going to Cambridge."

Dickens's fall was a temporary one, but it would not have seemed so at the time, and his later uncertainty over how long the period at Warren's lasted, "whether for a year or more, or much less," accurately reflected his childhood sense that, like his father in the Marshalsea, he had been given an indeterminate sentence that was largely beyond his own power to bring to an end. G. K. Chesterton, who was never slow to pick up on religious significances, once pointed out that because children lack a clear sense of historical perspective, there can be a "dreadful finality" to any disaster that befalls them: "a lost child can suffer like a lost soul."[25] The idea that Dickens's experiences were hellish rather than merely miserable may be overstated, but it is one that he was equally keen to promote. "My rescue from this kind of existence I considered quite hopeless," he writes, "and abandoned as such." The echo of the inscription over the gate of Dante's Hell, "Abandon all hope, ye who enter here," is subtly introduced; presumably we are supposed to put the routine of sticking labels on jars in the same category as tortured souls endlessly gurgling in mud or being dunked in boiling pitch. The parallels were equally strained when Dickens explained that, after a tearful outburst directed at his father, he was allowed to move into lodgings in the attic of a house in Lant Street, "and when I took possession of my new abode, I thought it was a Paradise." Perhaps he was filtering his memories through what happens in his later fiction, which frequently situates itself on the same boundary between allegorical and literal-minded ways of looking at the world. The pattern reaches a powerful climax in the seesawing fortunes of the characters in *Our Mutual Friend,* where Jenny Wren has a garden on her roof from which she looks down on "the people who are alive, and crying, and working, and calling to one another in the close dark streets," and as her guests go down the stairs she shouts out, "Come back and be dead, Come back and be dead!" The idea that the state of one's soul can be given precise spatial coordinates is an odd one for a child to have, as Dickens recognizes by making Jenny Wren into a curious hybrid of bright-eyed girl and sharp-eyed adult. The implication in his memoir that working at Warren's involved his soul in a spiritual tug-of-war, by contrast, sounds much less like the feelings of a vulnerable child than those of his appalled adult self. As in many autobiographies, the real struggle seems to be between his reliving the past and relieving himself of it.

And yet, to a twelve-year-old in Dickens's position, it might well have been difficult to make a clear distinction between his physical place of work and the more abstract idea of his place in society. James Lamert had already gone back on his word by bringing him down from the upper floors to work among the other common boys. Now, as his dirty hands automatically snipped and slapped the labels on pots of blacking, he could stare out of the window at the mudlarks foraging for scraps in the ooze of the riverbank and wonder how much further he had to fall.

❦⸱⸱❦ ❦⸱⸱❦

Dickens's fragment breaks off without discussing what happened next, but perhaps he did not need to say any more. By this stage he had already said it in his novels, which replay the story so often that he sometimes appears to be struggling to prevent them from turning into a huge serialized autobiography. "I know how all these things have worked together to make me what I am," he admitted, and the sense of an ongoing process ("*have* worked together" rather than simply "worked together") indicates that he did not think of the Warren's episode as merely one step in his passage through life. It was the fixed center around which his imagination continued to revolve.

Describing the dark underside of London in *The Uncommercial Traveller*, Dickens writes that "I can find—*must* find, whether I will or no—in the open streets, shameful instances of neglect of children": he seems uncertain whether he could not help stumbling upon these poor wretches or could not prevent himself from seeking them out. A reader might wonder much the same about his fiction. Even if it is turned into rueful comedy, as when *David Copperfield*'s Tommy Traddles tearfully draws skeletons over his slate each time he is thrashed, there is a vague sense of threat hanging over all of Dickens's fictional children. Many of them seem doomed from the start. Here Little Dick in *Oliver Twist* sets the stage and the tone for Dickens's later novels. Introduced to us as Oliver's "little friend and playmate," who had been "beaten, and starved, and shut up" with him "many and many a time," his first appearance comes as Oliver is running away, at which point Dick explains that the doctor must be right to think that he is dying, "because I dream so much of heaven, and angels, and kind faces that I never see when I am awake." Clearly he is not long for this world, and is duly sacrificed to show the fate Oliver narrowly escapes. The mixture of sentimental regret and ruthless efficiency is typical of what later children could expect from Dickens's pen. His working notes for *Bleak House* include a brisk decision on what to do with the crossing-sweeper: "Jo? Yes. Kill him."[26] Dickens's attachment to his fictional offspring did not always prevent him from observing them with the cool eye of a farmer sizing up his livestock.

In his autobiographical fragment, Dickens explained that "even now, famous and caressed and happy, I often forget in my dreams that I have a dear wife and children; even that I am a man; and wander desolately back to that time in my life." His fictional characters are similarly unable to let the past be. In *Master Humphrey's Clock*, Dickens relates the story of a man who kills his nephew and buries him in the garden, but is then haunted by visions of the victim's hand or foot sticking out of the grass, and ends up placing his chair over the grave to prevent the corpse from being disturbed or bursting vengefully out of the ground. (The fear that the dead might not stay dead is one that ripples uneasily through Dickens's fiction: in *Great Expectations,* Pip watches Magwitch picking his way through the brambles of the churchyard "as if he were eluding the hands of the dead people, stretching up cautiously out of their graves, to get a twist upon his ankle and pull him in.") Jonas Chuzzlewit is equally fixated on the scene of his crime, and after murdering Montague Tigg imagines himself creeping back through the undergrowth to peer at the corpse, "startling the very flies that were thickly sprinkled all over it, like heaps of dried currants." We know that Dickens got a similar thrill from standing in places where people had died, as if needing to reassure himself from time to time about the difference between the living and the dead. Writing about a tour of the prison in Venice, he recalled that "I had my foot upon the spot, where . . . the shriven prisoner was strangled," while in Cambridge, Massachusetts, he inspected the scene where Professor Webster of Harvard had murdered and dismembered a colleague, sniffing at the reeking furnace and offering the suggestion that there was "some anatomical broth in it, I suppose."[27] At the same time, Dickens was aware that some parts of the past cannot be returned to. The fragility and vulnerability of a child's innocence, in particular, obsess him, and he has a straightforward if somewhat romantic view of its purity. For Dickens there are no degrees of innocence, any more than there are degrees of virginity. Once compromised, it is gone forever. Perhaps this is why the moment in *Paradise Lost* when Adam and Eve are forced to leave Eden reverberates so unhappily across his career. The move to Warren's came "in an evil hour for me, as I often bitterly thought," he explained, recalling how Adam in a reproachful pun talks of "Eve in evil hour," and the idea was extended further in his published works, where attempts to depict lost innocence often produce quiet echoes of Milton.[28] In *A Child's History of England,* a description of Henry II dying "distressed, exhausted, broken-hearted" is followed by the legend of Rosamund, whose fellow nuns dress her tomb with flowers in remembrance of the time when she had enchanted the young king and "his life lay fair before him," recalling Milton's "The way was all before them," while Pip and Estella walk away from the ruined garden of Satis House at the end of *Great Expectations* "hand in hand," again like Adam and Eve leaving Paradise, although both recognize that a possible future together hardly compensates for what has been left behind.

Yet Dickens was far too resilient a human being, and far too good a writer, to let his private obsessions get the better of him on the page. Frequently, when he returned to these most painful of memories, he also found himself wondering how they might look from a perspective that was more detached and skeptical—in other words, more comic. Just as the clowns in Shakespeare's tragedies supply a wry commentary on the dreadful events unfolding around them, so Dickens introduces the voice of a heckler ready to mock everything the rest of his writing takes most seriously. When *Nicholas Nickleby*'s Mrs. Kenwigs bursts into tears at the sight of her children, for example, and cries out, "Oh! they're too beautiful to live, much too beautiful!" she sounds suspiciously like a parody of Dickens's attitudes elsewhere, given the average life-expectancy of his fictional offspring. Even the death of Little Nell—a scene that was widely reported to have brought the nation to its knees when first published in 1841—is given a refreshingly unsentimental gloss in *The Old Curiosity Shop* itself, which concludes with Kit describing to his children how Nell used to laugh at him, "at which they would brush away their tears, and laugh themselves to think that she had done so, and be again quite merry."

Viewed in this context, Dickens's habit of making fleeting references to Warren's Blacking in his writing starts to look less like a form of repetition compulsion than a running gag or creative itch he enjoyed scratching, like the cameo appearances of Alfred Hitchcock in his own movies. In *Great Expectations,* the first thing Joe does when he gets to London is to go and look at the "Blacking Ware'us," though he is disappointed when comparing it to the printed advertisements, where "it is drawd too architectooralooral." In *Barnaby Rudge,* the old house "mouldering to ruin" where the secrets of the past are buried is called "The Warren," while in the *Pickwick Papers* Tony Weller declares that "Poetry's unnat'ral; no man ever talked in poetry 'cept a beadle on boxin'-day, or Warren's black-in." He is referring to the poems that appeared on handbills promoting Warren's wares, like an early form of advertising jingle, and it seems that Dickens had first-hand experience of the genre. With a masterful blend of overstatement and understatement, his journalist uncle John Barrow told John Payne Collier, the scholar and forger of Shakespeare, that at one time his nephew "had assisted Warren, the blacking-man, in the conduct of his extensive business, and, among other things, had written puff-verses for him." Such rhymes usually appeared alongside a picture showing the daz-zling efficacy of the product: a cat spitting at its own reflection in a boot, or a man using the highly polished surface of his footwear as a shaving mirror. (In *Hard Times,* Bounderby, who tells stories about his supposed childhood poverty like someone auditioning to be included in *Self-Help,* boasts that as a boy the only pictures he possessed were "of a man shaving himself in a boot on the blacking bottles.") Collier quoted as an example some lines that accompanied the picture of a dove cooing over her own reflection after mistaking it for her mate:

> I pitied the dove, for my bosom was tender,
>> I pitied the sigh that she gave to the wind;
> But I ne'er shall forget the superlative splendour
>> Of Warren's Jet Blacking, the pride of mankind.[29]

The advertisement's mixture of public sentiment and private glee is some-thing that Dickens would continue to play on throughout his career. As late as 1868, just two years before his death, he wrote a spoof piece of sporting journalism, in which he described a walking race to a village "with no refreshments in it but five oranges and a bottle of blacking."[30] Sometimes the laughter is so muffled as to be almost inaudible, as when he describes the "sickly bedridden hump-backed boy" in *Nicholas Nickleby* who sits apart from other children, "watching the games he is denied the power to share in," and whose only pleasure is some hyacinths "blossoming in old blacking-bottles." The memory bobs to the surface of Dickens's writing like a message in a bottle. But even this suggests some optimism about the future, and a confidence that what is small and hidden can contain powerful latent energies, as when Pip notices the "tied-up brown paper packets" in Mr. Pumblechook's shop and wonders "whether the flower-seeds and bulbs ever wanted of a fine day to break out of those jails, and bloom." The insinuating associative chain of seed, bulb, and pip offers a densely packed image of Pip's ambition. It also hints at something else Dickens may have recognized when reflecting on his time in the blacking warehouse: a seed needs darkness in order to germinate.

What would have happened to Dickens if he had remained in the same line of work? Perhaps he would have scrambled to the top of the pile, like the industrialist Charles Day, founder of the rival blacking manufacturers Day & Martin, who left some palatial "architectooralooral" premises in Holborn and the huge sum of £450,000 when he died in 1837. Or perhaps he would merely have ended up as one of the freelance copywriters who turned out chirping slogans like that rhyme about the lovesick dove. Such a fate clearly haunted Dickens from early on. In the 1837 sketch "Seven Dials," we are told of a "shabby-genteel man" who is "an object of some mystery," but as he never buys anything apart from cheap food and ink, "his fellow-lodgers very naturally suppose him to be an author; and rumours are current . . . that he writes poems—for Mr. Warren." An even sadder case is Mr. Slum, the traveling poet in *The Old Curiosity Shop*, who is dressed in once-smart but now threadbare clothes, and tries to talk himself into a job: "Ask the perfumers, ask the blacking-makers, ask the hatters, ask the old lottery-office-keepers—ask any man among 'em what my poetry has done for him, and mark my words he blesses the name of Slum." Like all good satire, the portrait winces with fellow feeling.

⁂

The end of Dickens's time in the blacking factory came about through a combination of good luck and good judgment. John Dickens was released from the Marshalsea under the provision of the Insolvent Debtors' Act on May 28, 1824, a month after his mother, with impeccable timing, had died, leaving him £450 in her will. Part of the legacy was used to pay off outstanding debts, though not Fanny's bills from the Royal Academy, which received instead an IOU in John Dickens's usual swollen style, as if he were hoping that the generosity of his language might somehow compensate for the absence of actual money: "A circumstance of great moment to me will be decided in the ensuing term," he wrote, "which I confidently hope will place me in comparative affluence, and by which I shall be enabled to redeem the order before the period of Christmas Day."[31] Nothing could have been more typical of his character, a Micawber in the making, than that awkward stutter from "confidently" to "hope," nor the way in which he smoothly rolled over this local embarrassment towards the dream of "comparative affluence."

Unusually, perhaps uniquely in his case, this time it proved to be an accurate prediction. Neatly sidestepping the fact that he was writing from the Marshalsea, two weeks after being jailed he had also sent a letter to the Treasurer of the Navy, requesting early retirement; he enclosed a medical certificate, signed by a surgeon, stating that "infirmity of body, arising from a chronic infection of the Urinary Organs, incapacitated [him] from attending to any possible duty."[32] It was a suspicious-sounding medical complaint, but it appears to have been rooted in fact: the official cause of John Dickens's death in 1851 was "Rupture of the Uretha from old Standing Stricture and consequent Mortification of the Scrotum from infiltration of Urine," which strongly suggests that his earlier medical problems were timely rather than merely opportunistic.[33] The request slowly ground its way through the cogs of government machinery, until, despite some murmuring in the Navy Pay Office about the propriety of helping a declared bankrupt, on March 9, 1825, it was approved. After nearly twenty years of service, he was to be granted a pension of £145 per year. (To put this figure into context, the family had been paying less than £26 annually for rent and other charges on their house in Bayham Street.) It was scarcely riches, but "comparative affluence" is a good summary of how it would have appeared to a family that had grown used to living on less than nothing. As for their dutiful and unhappy son, after roughly a year of drudgery, his prayers of being "lifted out of the humiliation and neglect in which I was" had finally been answered. John Dickens and James Lamert quarreled, in a scene that may have been stage-managed by the father, and soon Charles was walking away from Warren's Blacking for the last time. A generous financial settlement, accompanied by a recognition that the boy with nice manners had been deserving of something better all along: it was like a romance brought vividly to life, and Dickens never forgot it, playing variations on the same plot in novel after novel, from *Oliver Twist* to *Great Expectations* and beyond.

Not everyone prospered in these new circumstances. A servant girl who had originally been engaged from the Chatham workhouse had her employment terminated by the Dickens family, like the Orfling in *David Copperfield* after Micawber's release from prison; and just as the Orfling disappears from the pages of Dickens's novel ("going back, I suppose, to Saint Luke's workhouse"), so this servant—faceless, nameless, untraceable—melted into London's crowded streets. Other than some faint echoes of her "sharp little worldly and also kindly ways" in *The Old Curiosity Shop*'s Marchioness, Dickens never mentions her again.[34] Perhaps he felt no need to, given how common it was to "let a servant go" without worrying about where she would end up. But it is hard to read about Dickens's preparations for school without seeing her as one of the saddest and quietest of the shadows that trailed his life: the child who was lost and not found again.

CHAPTER TWO

The Clerk's Tale

The school John Dickens chose for his son had a predictably grand name: Wellington House Classical and Commercial Academy. The reality was, equally predictably, only a shabby imitation of what such a name promised. Housed in a small building on the Hampstead Road, it was run by a podgy, bullying schoolmaster named William Jones, whose pleasure in beating the weaker and poorer pupils was matched only by his skill at fawning over the wealthy. In later years Dickens was briskly dismissive of the whole operation, describing Jones as "by far the most ignorant man I have ever had the pleasure to know," whose only interest was in "ruling," an appetite he satisfied by using his "bloated mahogany ruler" as both a scepter and an instrument of torture. When Dickens returned as an adult to this "pernicious and abominable humbug" of a school, he discovered that it had been razed for the construction of the London and North Western Railway, and although he was usually wary of the destruction wrought by railway lines, as their steel fingers stretched greedily across the landscape, in this case he warmly approved.[1] "The Railway had cut it up root and branch," he reported, clearly energized by the thought that some corrupt establishments could be "reformed" only by being smashed into pieces and rebuilt as something else.[2]

It was not Dickens's first school. He had previously attended a "Preparatory Day-School" in Chatham, about which he recalled little other than the baleful presence of a "puffy pug-dog" that had been trained to balance a piece of cake on its nose while the teacher counted to twenty. Dickens then spent two years at a more impressive establishment run by an intelligent nonconformist, William Giles, who had a reputation as "a cultivated reader and elocutionist."[3] No doubt his entry to Wellington

House in June 1824 felt like a fresh start. But his recent experiences had left their mark. This is hardly surprising: even in a period before compulsory secondary education, the standard practice was for children to start with school and then enter the world of work, not the other way round. Dickens's topsy-turvy progress, however, meant that—like the traces of blood Pip discovers outside Satis House in *Great Expectations*—his past had a nasty habit of "starting out like a stain that was faded but not gone."

A schoolfellow who sat at the next desk recalled that Dickens was one of the contributors to "Our Newspaper," a handwritten weekly publication circulated among the pupils and lent out in return for marbles and pieces of slate pencil.[4] Its "sundry bits of boyish fun" included a column of mock "Lost and Found" advertisements:

> *Lost.*   Out of a gentleman's waistcoat pocket, an acre of land; the finder shall be rewarded on restoring the same.

> *Lost.*   By a boy with a long red nose, and grey eyes, a very bad temper. Whoever has found the same may keep it, as the owner is better without it.[5]

Such in-jokes rarely translate well, humor being one of the hardest things to pass through the fine mesh of a social network, and the same is true of the made-up nonsense language called "gibberish" that Dickens and his friends employed to bamboozle and irritate adults—another bit of boyish fun, and just as unlikely to raise a smile on the face of anyone who wasn't part of the gang. But even his closest school friends were probably unaware of why speculating on what had been lost and found had such resonance for Dickens. The idea continued to resound in the more serious journalism of his adult life, when as the editor of *Household Words* and then *All the Year Round* he wrote or commissioned numerous articles on the same topic, from the serious ("Lost and Found in the Snow," or "The Lost Arctic Voyagers," which defended the survivors of John Franklin's 1845 expedition against rumors that they had engaged in cannibalism), to further spoof paragraphs in an "Occasional Register" of items "Wanted,"

"Missing," or "Found," so proving that as far as he was concerned the old jokes were often the best. He who laughed first laughed longest.[6]

A patchwork production, cobbled together from spare scraps of paper, "Our Newspaper" had an excellent chance of succeeding with its—admittedly captive—audience, given the popularity of published miscellanies at the time. Dickens's favorite was *The Portfolio,* a cheap and cheerful magazine that brought together the pleasures of storytelling with the reassurance of self-improvement. The full title gave a good indication of what potential purchasers could expect for their twopence: *The Portfolio of Entertaining and Instructive Varieties in History, Science, Literature, the Fine Arts, &c.* The first issue, in 1823, amply lived up to the promise of that "*&c,*" with articles on "Female Revenge," "The Mutiny," "The Dwarf and His Three Brothers," "The King's Cottage at Windsor," and ten other items, including "On Women Having No Beards" and "Anecdotes, Bon-Mots, Epigrams &c," all crammed into sixteen small and tightly printed pages. Other articles in the first few issues included:

> "Astonishing Deliverance from Danger"
> "Account of Cat-Eaters"
> "Custom of Pressing to Death"
> "Advantages of Early Rising"
> "Inconveniences of Early Rising"
> "Hindoo Theatricals"
> "Account of the Mammoth"
> "Wholesomeness of Potatoes"
> "Sailor's Receipt for Tying a Pig-Tail"

Moving from page to page was like watching a variety show being put through its paces in double-quick time, although such publications were designed to be dipped into rather than read all the way through—an introduction to the pleasures of skipping and lingering.

An alternative model for "Our Newspaper" was *The Terrific Register,* another of Dickens's regular purchases, which brought together crudely violent woodcuts with the sort of stories guaranteed to make the mouth of *Pickwick*'s fat boy water:

> In the month of June, 1803, Mr. Isaac Evans, of Ashover, Derbyshire, was thrown from his horse, and received such injury as occasioned his death in a few hours.—One of his sons, some time before, unthinkingly placed the butt-end of a loaded gun between a wall and a tree, which went off instantly and killed him.—Another of his sons, shooting rooks at Alfretton a few days preceding the death of his father, the gun burst, and so violently shattered his hand, that it was obliged to be immediately amputated.—And about ten months since, his daughter (an infant) was scalded to death by falling into some hot liquor.

The title of this tragicomedy was "An Unfortunate Family." One can easily see the appeal of such black humor to schoolboys, especially when it is spiced by gloating details such as "(an infant)," and the accretive style of the narrative may have been equally attractive to the newspaper's contributors. Just as each dash in this story ratcheted up the level of horror another thrilling notch, so Dickens and his friends could add new fragments to each issue as they passed it from hand to hand, either feeding off what had come before or attempting to trump it.

Whatever they chose to write about would have been a welcome holiday from the usual routine of the school day. Like most schools of the time, however enticing Wellington House Academy's prospectus may have sounded, its students found themselves surviving on little more than a thin and predictable diet of copybook exercises. The system had its advantages, though, which for Dickens meant freeing his imagination to soak up the details of his surroundings, including the sort of human oddities that always struck his mind with photographic exactness. In the essay "Our School," he recalled some of them: a mysterious young man who stayed for only a short while, "during which period, though closely observed, he was never seen to do anything but make pens out of quills, write small-hand in a secret portfolio, and punch the point of his sharpest blade in his knife into his desk"; "a fair, meek boy, with a delicate complexion and rich curling hair," whose mother was rumored to carry "a silver pistol . . . always loaded to the muzzle" in order to shoot the wicked viscount who had deserted her; and a Latin master with a crutch who was "always putting onions into his ears for deafness" and had bits of flannel peeking out from under his clothes.

The other students remembered Dickens far less vividly, as one might expect of a boy who had good reasons for not wanting to draw attention to himself. Despite Dickens's later idealization of childhood, all real children know how sensitive the antennae of their peers are to the slightest hint of difference, and how skilled they are at lobbing questions primed to exploit any weakness. Confessing where he had spent the previous year would have been about as sensible as attaching a target to the seat of his pants. "What would they say," asks David Copperfield after his release from Murdstone and Grinby's warehouse, "if they could know how I have scraped my halfpence together, for the purchase of my daily saveloy and beer, or my slices of pudding? How would it affect them, who were so innocent of London life and London streets, to discover how knowing I was (and ashamed to be) in some of the meanest places of both?" Good questions, which the young Dickens would almost certainly have preferred to leave unanswered. Such questions were especially troubling at the time he was writing this section of *David Copperfield:* his twelve-year-old son, Charley, had recently enrolled at Eton College, and the contrast between Charles then and Charley now seems to have left Dickens unusually torn between feeling pleased with himself and feeling sorry for himself. Yet, to a suspicious eye, his attempts to fit in at school were precisely what might have made him stand out. "He was very particular with his clothes," a contemporary remembered, and "appeared always like a gentleman's son, rather aristocratic than otherwise."[7] A world of fear and possible exposure lurks in "like" and "otherwise." Later on, when Dickens had become a successful novelist, people noticed how much care he continued to take of his appearance, always ensuring that his clothes were bright and clean, and whipping out a comb whenever he noticed a stray hair out of place. These days we might label him with a mild form of obsessive-compulsive disorder; although he may not have been consciously trying to distance himself from dirt and disarray, his neatness was undoubtedly less a preference than a fundamental need.

The same contemporary who noticed his clothes added that, as a schoolboy, Dickens walked with his head held "very upright, almost more than upright, like leaning back a little," as if only by staying perfectly erect could he convince anyone that he was "upright" in ways that went beyond his posture. Yet it is hard to concentrate on staying upright without coming across as uptight, and further recollections of Dickens at the time suggest that although, as Gladys Storey nicely puts it, the secret of the blacking warehouse remained "bottled up" inside him, he could not always keep himself in check.[8] Another school friend, Henry Danson, remembered Dickens leading a posse of boys on a fake begging expedition, targeting old ladies in particular, and "when the old ladies were quite staggered by the impudence of the demand, Dickens would explode with laughter and take to his heels."[9] John Forster cites these stories as examples of Dickens's "irrepressible vivacity" and bubbling good spirits, but one might see his laughter as something other than the merely carefree.[10] It was a controlled explosion. Getting laughs out of childhood poverty allowed him to transform his hidden fears into nightmare's comic alternative: farce.

One danger in relying on explosions, of course, is that they cannot always be kept under control. Another of Dickens's schoolboy pursuits was staging plays in his toy theater—a structure about the size of a dollhouse which allowed children to perform cut-down versions of popular plays for a select audience of family and friends, who would gather around the brightly colored opening and watch the young impresario pushing his wobbly cardboard characters around the stage. One of Dickens's favorite plays was Isaac Pocock's *The Miller and His Men* (1811), a creaky melodrama that ends with a mill being destroyed in a satisfying rush of flames. Such fiery spectacles were standard fare in the major theaters: *The Siege of Gibraltar* (1804), staged in the huge water tank constructed at Sadler's Wells, climaxed with the burning of the Spanish fleet and the rescue of small children in sailor costume from the waves; *Masaniello* (1829) depicted Vesuvius as "a terrific explosion ensues from the mountain, the lava impetuously flows down its side, and extends itself into the sea"; while in the final scene of *The Cataract of the Ganges* (1823) "burning trees fall on all sides" as troops appear, "pouring down the rocky heights around the Cataract in every direction."[11] These were scenes of carefully choreographed chaos, in which the buckling of trees and rending of mountains gave audiences the excitement of a world collapsing around their ears, along with the reassurance that such events were as phony as the villain's glued-on moustache. The stage effects in Dickens's toy theater offered similar thrills on a much-reduced scale. Henry Danson reported that the mill was constructed so that it would fall to pieces "with the assistance of [fire]crackers," and in one performance the fireworks "were so very real that the police interfered, and knocked violently at the doors."[12]

Staging theatrical mini-spectaculars was a common enough pastime, but few boys would have had as much personal history accumulated in their toys as Dickens, whose theater had been built for him by James Lamert, the man responsible for his introduction to Warren's Blacking factory. Even fewer would have found as much to reflect on in the opening scene of *The Miller and His Men,* in which a gang of robbers pose as harmless millworkers as they set about the daily grind. Later in life, Percy Fitzgerald recalled how Dickens still "dwelt on it with affectionate interest," and "cherished all the varied images, quoting with gusto 'More sacks to the mill!' . . . He knew it all by heart."[13] But it is not only through memory that one might know something "by heart," and Dickens's recent experiences had left him peculiarly vulnerable to a play in which little robbers are exposed and their ramshackle place of business is blown to pieces.

If we wanted a picture of Dickens at this stage of his life—and Dickens often thought of the different "stages" of life as theatrical in nature—we can imagine him crouching over the homemade scenery of his toy theater, practicing the moves of his characters while doing all the voices, until he was confident that he could spring surprises on his audience while remaining coolly in control. Such a balance between gaining control and losing it would become central to his fiction, in which the centrifugal force of his imagination, which could never resist spawning extra characters and narrative details, is always on the verge of escaping from the centripetal force of his plots. But already there were clues that this balance might be hard to maintain without either sticking the story in a straitjacket or allowing it to flail around unchecked.

"Our School" explains that the boys used to keep white mice, and trained them to do tricks involving an elaborate collection of costumes and props: "We recall one white mouse, who lived in the cover of a Latin dictionary, who ran up ladders, drew Roman chariots, shouldered muskets, turned wheels, and even made a very creditable appearance on the stage as the Dog of Montargis. He might have achieved greater things, but for having the misfortune to mistake his way in a triumphal procession to the Capitol, when he fell into a deep inkstand, and was dyed black and drowned."[14] Dickens's facetious tone is properly in keeping with his mixture of cruelty and carelessness at the time, just as his deft deployment of the journalistic "we" reminds his readers that this is routine behavior for small boys, whose comparative powerlessness often leads them to stage compensatory fantasies in which they transform themselves into a dashing combination of ringmaster and god. Tennyson's friend Arthur Hallam showed how far this activity could go, confessing to his fiancée that "when a child I used to entrap flies into water for the pleasure of taking them out again," a process which was "seldom so satisfactorily completed, but two or three of them perished by the way."[15] That stutter over "two or three" is perfectly true to the child's hearty indifference to the suffering of other creatures—he is much more interested in his own feelings than the precise number of flies he has drowned—just as "by the way" hovers between being a simple statement of fact ("in the process") and a nonchalant shrug of the shoulders. Presumably he would not have expected his fiancée to be especially shocked by what was, after all, just another episode in the same old story: "As flies to wanton boys are we to th' gods;/They kill us for their sport."[16] In the case of Dickens's mouse, the stakes were raised along with the size of the victim, because although the tone of the story remains resolutely jocular, in the context of Dickens's recent history the detail about drowning in black ink carried far more troubling associations. The mouse that might have achieved greater things was like a small dark shadow of the boy who might have achieved far less if his life had taken a different turn.

The end of Dickens's time at Wellington Academy came in 1827, when he chose—or was asked—to leave. It was so predictable a disappointment that it may have come as something of a relief. For all John Dickens's confidence that his future would be one of "comparative affluence," two years later he still had creditors snapping at his heels; and if he withdrew his son voluntarily, this at least prevented the embarrassment of having him expelled for nonpayment of fees. Their dealings with various landlords indicate that the Dickens family had become good at knowing when they had outstayed their welcome. In the years 1825–1831 they occupied five different addresses, and Dickens's departure from Wellington Academy coincided with their eviction from a house in Somers Town for failing to keep up with the rent. Clearly it was time for their son's holiday from the world of work to be brought to an end. Earlier that year, Elizabeth Dickens had befriended her aunt's lodger, Edward Blackmore, a junior partner in the solicitors' firm of Ellis & Blackmore, situated at 1 Holburn Court, Gray's Inn, and now she persuaded him to employ her son as a junior clerk. The move from blacking to Blackmore was only a coincidence, one of the chance encounters that are built into the English language, but it may have contributed to Dickens's sense of how easily such small things can seem to add up. Although, as David Copperfield observes, "trifles make the sum of life," it is not always obvious at what point they start to take on a sense of momentum or group themselves into a pattern. Dressed in "a Prussian jacket and a soldierly young cap," Dickens took up his position in May.[17] He was fifteen years old, and if he shared David Copperfield's dreamy excitement that "life was more like a great fairy story, which I was just about to begin to read, than anything else," then his next job brought him down to earth with a bump.

"It was a poor old set of chambers," recalled George Lear, who had been articled two years previously to the senior partner, Edward Ellis, and Dickens soon slipped into the sleepy routines of office life: copying papers, dealing with clients, and carrying legal documents to and from some of London's 150-odd "public offices."[18] Many of their names sounded like the inventions of a satirist: the Alienation Office, the Dispensation Office, the Six-Clerks Office, the Prothonotaries' Office, the Sixpenny Receivers Office. From January 5 to March 16, 1828, Dickens was responsible for keeping the petty-cash book; and although the surviving entries are no more exciting than those of any other office ledger ("Dickens, Coachhire to get will registered 2 shillings" is about as memorable as "Sandra, biscuits for staff tea-room £1.40"), his signature on the flyleaf is shyly revealing.[19] There is a blot on the name itself, suggesting a young clerk's struggle to control his spurting quill pen, but for someone who would go on to be a professional writer, the swirling flourish underneath has all the swagger of someone practicing his autograph.[20] Other names in the book show how easily people's lives could be shrunk into just a handful of words—Mrs. Bardell, Corney, Rudge, Newman Knott—just as the reappearance of these names later in Dickens's fiction would reveal the vivid human dramas that could emerge out of even these seemingly unpromising raw materials.

A surviving anecdote in which Dickens drops cherry stones on the heads of passers-by from the window of the solicitors' office, after it had relocated to 1 Raymond Buildings, suggests that he was not exactly thrilled by his work. It was a steady job with regular pay, eventually rising to 15 shillings per week, but it was not quite a career, and the prospects for self-advancement were slim. The example of George Lear provides an instructive parallel. He later identified himself as the original of *Pickwick*'s "Articled Clerk," who has paid a premium to train under an experienced solicitor, and "runs a tailor's bill, receives invitations to parties, knows a family in Gower Street and another in Tavistock Square, goes out of town every Long Vacation to see his father, who keeps live horses innumerable; and who is, in short, the very aristocrat of clerks." By contrast, Dickens was one of the "office lads," who sneer at schoolboys and club together to buy sausages and porter, possibly on the way to becoming a "salaried clerk," like his friend Charles Potter, who "repairs half-price to the Adelphi [Theatre] at least three times a week, dissipates majestically at the cider cellars afterwards, and is a dirty caricature of the fashion, which expired six months ago." The two classes of clerk could mingle quite happily at work—Lear recalled Dickens's brilliant powers of mimicry, indicating that he shared the office lads' jokes, if not their sausages—but neither was under any illusion as to who would eventually be more successful within the legal profession. Whereas Lear went on to develop a prosperous practice in Sussex, Dickens could look forward to inching his way up a ladder that had a pronounced dearth of rungs.

Edward Blackmore, looking back with rosy hindsight in 1870, recalled that his former clerk Dickens was "a universal favourite," and was almost poached by another Sussex solicitor: "had I consented, it is more than likely the boy's thoughts and pursuits would have been diverted into a different channel, and the world have lost the benefit of his wonderful genius."[21] In fact, any such diversion is likely to have been purely geographical in nature. Even if Dickens had relocated to Sussex, his career prospects would have remained more or less identical. At worst, he might have settled into the seedy dullness of *Pickwick*'s middle-aged copying clerk, "who is always shabby, and often drunk." At best, he might have turned into a real-life version of Charles Pooter in *The Diary of a Nobody*, the middle-ranking bank clerk whose struggles to achieve gentility are repeatedly sabotaged by his social clumsiness: "I left the room with silent dignity but caught my foot in the mat."[22] Either way, he would have had every chance of swelling the ranks of the respectable lower-middle class, and practically none of advancing any further.

What Charles Potter, Charles Pooter, and Charles Dickens have in common is that, whether by choice or default, all were members of the growing army of clerks that was needed to copy and organize the paperwork of a developing economy. The history of the Bank of England shows how the working conditions of clerks were changing. Over the course of the nineteenth century, they were gradually deprived of the license to bring liquor into the office, smoke cigars at work, accept tips, and even grow moustaches, as they were (according to social optimists) turned into a decent professional body, or (so gloomier observers said) ruthlessly purged of their individuality. In 1834, a member of the staff wrote a set of verses that lamented the reduction of bank holidays to a mere four per year, down from a peak of forty-seven in the eighteenth century, and complained that it would no longer be possible for clerks to see the cornfields or the sea, or to breathe anything other than the "smoky London air."[23] He was swimming against the tide of history. Soon the sight of clerks pouring into the city in the morning, and draining from it at night, would become one of the defining rhythms of the age, and increasingly what would distinguish clerks as a social group would be, paradoxically, how difficult it was to tell one from another. They were the drones whose lives were, however grudgingly, dedicated to serving a society that revolved around an increasingly large and powerful queen.

In this context, Dickens's decision to pack his fiction with clerks was a canny business decision, as well as a way of drawing on his own experience. The pages of his novels were like funfair mirrors that allowed a burgeoning group of readers to see flattering or comically grotesque reflections staring back at them. Even within the small world of lawyers' clerks, there was enough variety among what *Our Mutual Friend* lists as "the managing clerk, common-law clerk, conveyancing clerk, chancery clerk, every refinement and department of clerk" to give Dickens's readers pleasurable jolts of recognition. They include the first-floor clerk in Jaggers's office who looks "something between a publican and a rat-catcher," and "the flabby terrier of a clerk with dangling hair" on the second floor; the cheeky assistants Mr. Pickwick finds at Dodson & Fogg's, who ignore their clients in favor of relating their adventures the previous night ("I was so precious drunk, that I couldn't find the place where the latch-key went in"); young Smallweed, "of small stature, and weazened features"; and Mr. Guppy, who spends his time spinning around on one leg of his stool and gazing into space, and eventually puts his head in the office safe "with a notion of cooling it." It is a long and inglorious cast list, featuring a life cycle that was like a reversal of the natural order, in which the clerk started off as a flashy butterfly before degenerating into a seedy caterpillar. It is also noticeable, however, that not one features as more than a comic walk-on or a supporting actor. Dickens is happy to let his clerks amuse us for a few minutes, as they show off their achingly fashionable clothes or smoke a halfpenny cigar; but with the possible exception of Dick Swiveller in *The Old Curiosity Shop,* whose character turns in so many different directions he risks making the reader giddy, he takes care to hurry them off the page before they get too interesting. The clerk is perfect as a clown, it seems, but unsuitable as a hero.

Dickens's contemporaries largely agreed, although there was an important exception to the rule of "Once a clerk, always a clerk." He could become a writer. The hero of G. H. Lewes's *Ranthorpe* (1847) is an attorney's clerk, earning 10 shillings per week, who is impatient "to set himself fairly afloat upon the wide sea of literature," and ends the novel, still only twenty-five years old, firmly settled "amongst the literary men of England." "The poor attorney's son has become an honoured author," Lewes concludes, in exemplary *Self-Help* fashion, but the fact that he probably had Dickens's career in mind indicates how much work went into that shift from "poor" to "honoured." The social status of professional authors was far from assured at the time in which *Ranthorpe* is set, and although Dickens's success would make writing a more respectable choice of career, suspicions lingered that even if it was reasonable to expect payment for one's work, only hacks really needed the money. Proper authors wrote out of fine feelings and the need for self-expression; anyone who picked up a pen in order to pay the rent was little better than a clerk with pretensions to grandeur.

The alternative was hardly much more alluring. In his *Uncommercial*

Traveller essay "Chambers," Dickens nervously described the fate that could await someone whose life became snarled up in the legal profession. Starting with a description of Gray's Inn as "one of the most depressing institutions in brick and mortar known to the children of men," he goes on to give some of the stories that lay behind its general air of decay. These include a "man of law" who hangs himself in his chambers, only to be discovered when his letter-box is too "choked" to receive any more letters, and "a certain elderly gentleman" who dies on Christmas Eve after falling over and groping around on the floor while some young people are playing Blindman's Buff in the rooms above him. "Hark!" one of them cries. "The man below must be playing Blindman's Buff by himself tonight!" and they listen as he bangs against the furniture, before going on with their game, "more light-hearted and merry than ever." Finally, Dickens tells the story of "Mr. Testator," who discovers some furniture stored in the cellar of his chambers, and gradually shifts the "blue and furry" items into his apartment, feeling "as wicked as a Resurrection Man." One night another man turns up and recognizes the furniture, whispering "Mine!" as he lovingly examines it piece by piece, then drinks a decanter of gin and stumbles away down the stairs. "From that hour he was never heard of," Dickens writes. "Whether he was a ghost, or a spectral illusion of conscience, or a drunken man who had no business there, or the drunken rightful owner of the furniture . . . he never was heard of more." All three stories share the theme of loneliness, and the way in which lives can overlap without having any meaningful point of contact. Such a theme would become central to Victorian fiction, especially in its investigations of life in London, where feelings of isolation and alienation seemed to increase in direct proportion to the size of the crowds. What Dickens points out in this essay is that the Inns of Court offered not a refuge from this trend, but a concentration of it. A small, self-contained world set at a deliberate angle to the rest of London, the Inns may have given the illusion of a united purpose, but many of their inhabitants had little in common other than a tendency to cut themselves off from each other.

Later in his fiction Dickens would give short shrift to those who, like

Miss Havisham in *Great Expectations* or Mrs. Clennam in *Little Dorrit*, deliberately chose a life of isolation, but his experience in Gray's Inn had revealed that in some professions it crept up unbidden, like a slow-acting trap. The law generated loneliness, just as it generated paperwork or dust, and the camaraderie of fellow clerks was no defense against its power to grind down anyone who stayed in its echoing courts too long.

Dickens worked at Ellis & Blackmore for around eighteen months, by which time his appearance had been transformed. Not all of this was his own doing—puberty had its part to play—but he had happily embraced one of the habits for which London's clerks were famed: following fashions as closely as a stockbroker followed share prices. "I remember his having a new suit of clothes, brown all alike," wrote George Lear, his "coat cut like a dress coat, and with a high hat; he seemed to grow into a young man at once."[24] Dickens had a far sharper eye for detail than Lear ("brown all alike" doesn't greatly distinguish this particular outfit from a sack), and in his description of David Copperfield he recalled his taste for equally sharp fashions. With his long-tailed coat, straw-colored kid gloves, toe-pinching shoes, neatly slicked hair, and a flower in his buttonhole ("pink camelia japonica, price half-a-crown"), David sometimes takes two hours to prepare before he can leave the house. In many ways Dickens never outgrew this taste for clothes that teetered between the exquisitely tasteful and the vulgar. A few years later he was spotted wearing "crimson velvet waistcoats, multi-coloured neckties with two breast pins joined by a little gold chain, and yellow kid gloves," and as late as 1851 he appeared at a banquet in honor of the actor William Charles Macready "in a blue dress-coat, faced with silver and aflame with gorgeous brass buttons; a vest of black satin, with a white satin collar and a wonderfully embroidered shirt."[25] "The beggar is as beautiful as a butterfly," sniffed Thackeray, "especially about the shirt-front."[26]

If there are hints of fancy dress in this outfit, other reports of Dickens's bright waistcoats and loud accessories, which he persisted with even as public tastes shifted to a more muted palate, make it sound as if in middle age he was still dressing the part of a prosperous clerk. It is only a short step from this to the characters in his fiction who grimly try to hang onto their youth, like the elder Turveydrop in *Bleak House,* who has "a false complexion, false teeth, false whiskers, and a wig," or Mrs. Skewton in *Dombey and Son,* a simpering old woman whose girlish looks are constructed every morning out of false hair and cosmetics, and who is finally discovered struck down by paralysis, "arrayed in full dress, with the diamonds, short sleeves, rouge, curls, teeth, and other juvenility all complete." Such characters are effectively parodies of Dickens's usual attitude towards clothes, which is that they are not so much costumes as second skins we choose for ourselves. In *Bleak House,* Mr. Vholes takes off his black gloves "as if he were skinning his hands," and "lifts off his tight hat as if he were scalping himself," while one of Barnaby Rudge's fantasies is that clothes hanging on the line talk to each other as the wind blows them about. John Carey has written well about this aspect of Dickens, and in particular Dickens's interest in the idea that clothes take on aspects of their owners' personalities.[27] The clothes of drowned men in the Paris morgue, for example, mimic the fate of their owners in having a slimy appearance with "puffed arms and legs," while Kate's clothes in *Nicholas Nickleby* have "that indescribable air of jauntiness and individuality which empty garments—whether by association, or that they become moulded, as it were, to the owner's form—will take." Such a lively confusion between people's insides and outsides is central to Dickens's imagination, and it has usually made his critics uneasy, as if reading his novels was like opening up a textbook of psychology and discovering a fashion magazine hidden inside. Henry James shrewdly identified the problem: "It is one of the chief conditions of his genius not to see beneath the surface of things," he wrote. "If we might hazard a definition of his literary character, we should, accordingly, call him the greatest of superficial novelists."[28] For James, Dickens's superficiality can be put down to his relative lack of interest in human character, which is why James's article, which starts off as a review of *Our Mutual Friend,* rapidly escalates into an attempted literary coup, as the clever young novelist (aged just twenty-two when this piece was published) sets out to demonstrate a need for novels to deal with the superfine textures of human life, rather than just the cut of its trousers—a need, that is, for the novels of Henry James.

James was mistaken to think that Dickens's interest in people was limited to their surfaces, although it is true that Dickens can appear to skimp on his characters' personalities, and even what they look like from the neck up, when compared to the loving attention he lavishes on their outfits. In the *Pickwick Papers,* we are told that Sam Weller is "habited in a coarse-striped waistcoat, with black calico sleeves, and blue glass buttons: drab breeches and leggings. A bright red handkerchief was wound in a very loose and unstudied style round his neck, and an old white hat was carelessly thrown on one side of his head," and although there are plenty of clues here about his class and character, he could be a midget or a luxuriously bearded amputee for all the attention the rest of him gets. Similarly, when Mr. Jingle makes his first appearance, Dickens's writing is rich with detail about his green swallowtail coat, black trousers, mended shoes, pinched hat, and so on; the fact that his face is "thin and haggard" is given almost as an afterthought.[29]

Dickens's keen interest in clothes reflected his love of the theater, a world where the identity and status of a play's characters were conferred by the evidence of their boots or stockings long before they opened their mouths. As late as 1878, *The Actor's Handbook* was advising would-be actors that "to have a good stock of tights, boots, hats, swords, &c., &c., often procures a young man an engagement when he could not obtain one on his merits." A tragedian, for example, will require "two or three embroidered and plain shirts, a few wigs of different kinds, ringlets, at least three swords, a cross-sword, a Roman sword, a claymore, pantaloons and tights of different colours, russet boots, black and russet shoes, old English shoes with buckles, gauntlets, plain and embroidered collars, ruffles, sword carriages, belts, and various feathers and fur ornaments, the royal garter, a jewelled collar, &c., &c." The advice for clowns is much simpler: "a Low Comedian cannot have too many wigs; some who have been eminent in the profession have owned a complete gallery."[30] And what about a clerk? Dickens's appearance in 1828 was no less theatrical, but he was also a teenager, and teenagers have always used fashion as a way of working out who they are, like someone who learns to swim by throwing himself into a fast-flowing current. Perhaps this accounts for the suspicion that, in his dress coat and high hat, Dickens was not just being a clerk, but having fun in playing the part of a clerk, even if his later appearance showed that he could not simply drop this disguise once a more interesting role came along.

Dickens left Ellis & Blackmore in November 1828. "Why he left I do not remember," Edward Blackmore wrote, "but fancy he disliked the drudgery of the office, and felt, perhaps, equal to a better occupation."[31] If that was a polite way of saying that young Dickens was bored and restless, it is fully in keeping with Dickens's own interest in ambition and the importance of developing it in the right direction. As Garrett Stewart has observed, many of the most sympathetic characters in Dickens's earlier fiction are escape artists, whose powers of imagination allow them to slip the leash of reality and disappear into an alternative world of their own creation.[32] Sometimes this escape mechanism is relatively straightforward, as when the Marchioness in *The Old Curiosity Shop* sits in a dank basement and pretends that slices of old orange peel dipped in water are as delicious as fine wine. More complicated are instances in which characters like Lizzie Hexam in *Our Mutual Friend*, or Louisa Gradgrind in *Hard Times*, stare into the fire and see images of a possible future flickering there. Yet although such fire gazing can suggest the creative power to forge one's own destiny, it also has the potential to turn into a viciously destructive force. *Barnaby Rudge*'s Simon Tappertit, for example, muses to himself about the "ignoble existence" into which he has been born: "A voice within me keeps on whispering Greatness. I shall burst out one of these days, and when I do, what power can keep me down?" The answer comes shortly after he joins "the very scum and refuse of London" fanning the flames of the Gordon Riots, when he ends up "burnt and bruised, and with a gun-shot wound in his body; and his legs—his perfect legs, the pride and glory of his life, the comfort of his existence—crushed into shapeless ugliness." The moral is plain: admiring one's legs is not the same as using them to get on in life.

By the time Dickens came to write *Barnaby Rudge*, he had long been practicing what he preached. While he was still a clerk at Ellis & Blackmore, during the evenings when he was not at the theater, he had tried to advance his career prospects by studying shorthand. His father, in an unusual burst of determination, had already mastered its intricacies, and was now being employed as a journalist. Although Dickens was still too young to be taken on in the same line of work, he set himself the same challenge by purchasing Gurney's *Brachygraphy; or, An Easy and Compendious System of Short-Hand*. It was probably the fifteenth edition, published in 1825 by William Gurney, who was the grandson of the original author and had been official shorthand writer to the Houses of Parliament since 1813. Though a slim book, it carried a fat price tag of half a guinea, reflecting the semi-official status of Gurney's system, which over the course of its long publishing history (eighteen editions in the years 1750–1884) did not have any serious competition until Isaac Pitman brought out his *Stenographic Sound-Hand* in 1837.[33] Gurney's subtitle was something of a tease. His system was certainly not easy, comprising several lists of more or less arbitrary points, circles, straight lines and curves that substituted for particular sounds; and at seventy-six pages it was hardly compendious, although Dickens's edition bulked up its advice with a series of gushing verses:

> The nice-wrought acorn (say the learn'd) contains
> The oak's vast branches in its little veins!
> Each leaf distinct, and every fibre line,
> Mark'd unentangled in the small design:
> Nor less the wonders of the pigmy scene,
> That live the miniature of GURNEY's pen.[34]

Learn shorthand, the verses promise, and you will enjoy magical powers to contract the world into a span. Turning words into symbols, however, was only half the battle. The other half was turning the symbols back into words, because when taking dictation at speed, certain sounds were simply elided, leaving the writer to piece together the speech later. It was like trying to work out the design of a jigsaw puzzle when half the pieces were missing: recalling how he wrestled with shorthand as a young man, Joseph Crowe ruefully noted that he "made fair progress in writing, though but slow progress in reading my own hieroglyphics."[35] Gurney offers the example of a shorthand speech to Parliament translated back into ordinary English, in which each sentence gradually emerges like the picture on an opening fan. A literal expansion of the "brachygraphic" symbols into letters ("mst al dply afd w so s los") is followed by the addition of any words or sounds missed out in the shorthand transcription (*"but you* mst al *have been* dply af*ct*d w*th* so s*ver a* los"), and is finally expanded into a complete sentence: "but you must all have been deeply affected with so severe a loss."

Learning how to "concertina" writing in this way appealed to the side of Dickens that enjoyed extrapolating stories from tiny clues, such as the mysterious stone tablet over the door of Staple Inn in Holborn:

Dickens suggested several humorous glosses for this inscription, including "Perhaps John Thomas," "Pretty Jolly Too," and "Possibly Jabbered Thus."[36] Eventually he would make writing's capacity to expand or contract human experience central to his style, as he paused over selected fragments of the world that caught his attention, from door-knockers to bits of old newspaper, while having the confidence to skim over those parts of it that did not merit a second look. At this stage, though, he was concerned only to master Gurney's symbols, and despite the anonymous poet's enthusiasm for shorthand's miniaturized world in which oceans "slumber in a shell," Dickens, like David Copperfield, found that he had "plunged into a sea of perplexity":

> The changes that were wrought upon dots, which in such a position meant such a thing, and in such another something else, entirely different; the wonderful vagaries that were played by circles; the unaccountable consequences that resulted from marks like flies' legs; the tremendous effect of a curve in the wrong place; not only troubled my waking hours, but reappeared before me in my sleep. When I had groped my way, blindly, through these difficulties, and had mastered the alphabet, which was an Egyptian Temple in itself, then there appeared a procession of new horrors, called arbitrary characters; the most despotic characters I have ever known; who insisted, for instance, that a thing like the beginning of a cobweb, meant expectation, and that a pen-and-ink sky-rocket stood for disadvantageous.

Those last two jokes contained elements of serious reflection. The idea that expectations can become cobwebs, snaring the unwary, would recur in *Great Expectations*, where Pip finds himself caught between the spidery embrace of Satis House and life on the marshes (pronounced "meshes"). Here, even the moisture hanging on twigs and grass, "like a coarser sort of spider's web," acts as a subdued warning about being stuck in a world in which everything appears "coarse," from the convict's gray uniform to his own hands. Closer to home, and also to the autobiographical trajectory of *David Copperfield*, the "pen-and-ink sky-rocket" that stands for "disadvantageous" may be a squib aimed at the critics, and in particular a famous review in 1837 that had looked forward with gloomy satisfaction to the young novelist's fate unless he mended his ways: "he has risen like a rocket," Abraham Hayward noted, "and he will come down like the stick."[37] But if Gurney's system had taught Dickens anything, it was how alike "advantageous" and "disadvantageous" could appear to an aspiring writer. The trick now was to keep them apart.

After a spell spent with another solicitor, Charles Molloy of New Square, Lincoln's Inn, Dickens had learned enough shorthand to attempt a change of career, and by the end of 1829 he was sharing an office in Doctors' Commons as a freelance stenographer. Although he could not yet choose his own words, for the first time he was earning an independent living as a writer.

※҉⁕ ※҉⁕

Doctors' Commons was one of the most mysterious addresses in London. Steerforth gives the official version of its function in *David Copperfield*, albeit with some satirical topspin, when he explains: "It's a little out-of-the-way place where they administer ecclesiastical law, and play all kinds of tricks with obsolete old monsters of Acts of Parliament. . . . It's a place that has an ancient monopoly in suits about people's wills and people's marriages, and disputes among ships and boats." His sprawling summary accurately indicates the eclectic nature of the activities for which Doctors' Commons was responsible. Officially incorporated in 1768 as "The College of Doctors of Law, exercent in the Ecclesiastical and Admiralty Courts," over the course of Dickens's lifetime its powers were gradually stripped away, but in 1829 its team of advocates and proctors (loosely equivalent to modern barristers and solicitors) still handled a wide range of legal disputes involving probate, divorce, and shipping, or "wills, wives, and wrecks," as well as investigating charges of misbehavior in church or at parish meetings.[38] It was located in a set of old buildings that contained legal chambers, a library, a dining hall, and another large hall where the courts held their sittings, all squeezed into two sleepy quadrangles near St. Paul's Cathedral. To a casual eye, it closely resembled an Oxford or Cambridge college—which was probably not surprising, given how many lawyers had gone directly from one to the other, although outsiders had even less understanding of Doctors' Commons than they did of what went on inside the mysteriously inward-facing buildings of the ancient universities. "Do you know—what's a-name—Doctors' Commons?" asks Jingle in the *Pickwick Papers*, to which Sam Weller, with his intimate knowledge of London's alleys and byways, immediately replies, "Paul's Church-yard, Sir; low archway on the carriage-side, bookseller's at one

corner, hot-el on the other, and two porters in the middle as touts for licenses." The precise external detail instantly draws attention to how little
he knows about what goes on inside.

As a place of business, Doctors' Commons was at once self-consciously genteel and crammed with intrigue. Even as the proctors glided through
its hushed corridors, presenting themselves as models of respectability,
their touts lurked in doorways ready to ambush "all persons in mourning, and all gentlemen with anything bashful in their appearance," along
with any other potential clients ready to supply them with a juicy fee. The
fact that the same small group of professionals had to deal with so many
different kinds of disputes, squeezing the business of several courts into
a single hall, and swapping roles and robes as they acted as judge in one
case and then advocate in another, meant that in Dickens's eyes its proceedings were little more than a pompous game of charades. "They are
like actors," Steerforth complains, in a straightforward piece of authorial
ventriloquism; "now a man's a judge, and now he's not a judge; now he's
one thing, now he's another; now he's something else, change and change
about; but it's always a very pleasant, profitable affair of private theatricals, presented to an uncommonly select audience."

Dickens's role in this affair was far less performative: he simply waited to be hired by one of the proctors to record the judgment of particular cases, hopefully more accurately than the clerk who compiled the
1831 *Law List*, where, under the heading "Shorthand Writers," we find
"C. Dickins, 5, bell-yard, doctor's commons."[39] A copy of one judgment
in Dickens's hand is preserved from a case heard in the ecclesiastical
Arches Court in November 1830.[40] It seems to have been the basis of the
Bumple v. Sludberry case in *Sketches by Boz,* where we are given an explanation in toe-curling legalese of why a charge of "brawling" or "smiting"
in a church has been brought:

> . . . that on a certain night, at a certain vestry meeting, in a certain
> parish particularly set forth, Thomas Sludberry, the party appeared
> against in that suit, had made use of and applied to Michael Bumple,
> the reporter, the words "You be blowed"; and that on the said Michael

Bumple and others remonstrating with the said Thomas Sludberry on the impropriety of his conduct, the said Thomas Sludberry repeated the aforesaid expression, "You be blowed"; and furthermore, desired and requested to know whether the said Michael Bumple "wanted anything for himself," adding, that if the said Michael Bumple did want anything for himself, he, the said Thomas Sludberry "was the man to give it him"; at the same time making use of other heinous and sinful expressions, all of which, Bumple submitted, came within the intent and meaning of the Act.[41]

Like most of Dickens's references to the law, this is both appalled and amused (each of those semicolons looks like a raised eyebrow combined with a wink), as the self-extending syntax neatly skewers the way in which Doctors' Commons lawyers drew out such proceedings as expansively and expensively as possible. The satire hardly oversteps the reality. One of the real cases tried in the years 1827–1829 had originally been heard in the Archdeacon's Court at Totnes, and had then been subject to an appeal at the Court of Exeter; this was followed by a hearing at the Arches Court, and was finally settled by the Court of Delegates. It concerned which of two people had the right to hang his hat on a particular peg. Creaky and painfully slow, Doctors' Commons was like a medieval time capsule that had somehow been preserved into the modern age. Even the jokes surrounding it were dusty:

DOCTORS' COMMONS WIT

A farmer from the country, going into the Will Office in Doctors' Commons, and observing the large volumes ranged along the wall, inquired if they were all Bibles. "No," replied an attendant, "they are all *testaments* though."[42]

It is the sort of pun guaranteed to make Mr. Pooter roar with laughter. But working in Doctors' Commons did have two major advantages, when compared to Dickens's previous life as a clerk: it was better-paid and less demanding. It also rewarded precisely the talents he had been most assiduous in cultivating: accuracy, patience, and a willingness to listen closely to other people. He had time to join the British Library in February 1830, immediately after his eighteenth birthday, and set about an eclectic program of reading: everything from the works of Shakespeare to Arthur Austin's *Lights and Shadows of Scottish Life,* and Hans Holbein's *Dance of Death.* More generally, he now had an opportunity, like Herbert Pocket in *Great Expectations,* to "look about" him.

When it came to looking about him, to someone with Dickens's curious eyes the sense of weighing up his options was indistinguishable from the more literal sense of scrutinizing his surroundings. As "the place where they grant marriage licenses to love-sick couples, and divorces to unfaithful ones; register the wills of people who have any property to leave, and punish hasty gentlemen who call ladies by unpleasant names," the quadrangles of Doctors' Commons were full of people in search of the one piece of paper that they believed would complete, or extend, or alter the direction of their lives.[43] The Prerogative Office, in particular, where wills were stored, provided the setting for dozens of small human dramas every day. A near-contemporary description of how the Prerogative Office worked isolates a couple of figures from the busy-fingered crowd. A sailor tracks down "the object of his hopes and fears," and as he reads through the will, "line by line you can see his face grow darker and darker—a grim smile at last appears—he has not been forgotten—there is a ring perhaps—or five-pounds to buy one, or some such trifle"; meanwhile, a lady, "dressed in a style of the showiest extravagance," meets another in the doorway "with so low a curtsy, and with such an expression of malice in the countenance, as at once tells the story confirmed by their respective appearances. The successful and the unsuccessful have met."[44] They are close imaginative relatives of the figures in Dickens's "Doctors' Commons" sketch who are discovered poring over Prerogative Office papers, including a "dirty-faced man in a blue apron" who is left in despair by the complexity of the will he unearths, and a "hard-featured old man, with a deeply wrinkled face," who discovers what he is looking for and hobbles away looking ten years younger.

Dickens treats his targets with a rancor bred by intimacy. As a freelancer working within Doctors' Commons, he found himself straddling the line that divided insiders from outsiders, which is where the best satire always dwells. What is surprising is that, although he continued to poke exasperated fun at the legal profession for the rest of his life, it was not until 1855 that he finally gave up the ambition of joining it as a barrister or serving as a police magistrate.[45] In 1857, Doctors' Commons were abolished as a separate set of courts, and ten years later the buildings themselves were pulled down to make way for Queen Victoria Street. If that seems neatly emblematic of the way in which the legislature gradually reformed itself during the nineteenth century, Dickens's lingering hopes of a legal career are equally emblematic of an aspect of the law that remained largely unchanged: its reputation as a profession where clever young men were rewarded with security and status. The fact that Dickens retained his rooms in chambers long after he had become the most famous author in the country indicates how uncertain authorship was, or at least how uncertain he felt it to be, when compared to the solidity of the law. It may have been fussy, arcane, and dull, but it was also a world he knew inside out, and his writing about it accordingly took especially savage glee in treating it either with plain disrespect or, even more witheringly, a sarcastically inflated respect. Like Edward Carson, the prosecutor of Oscar Wilde, who had studied alongside the beleaguered defendant at Trinity College, Dublin, when Dickens criticized the law he did so "with all the added bitterness of an old friend."[46]

Dickens's "Doctors' Commons" sketch ends with his falling into "a train of reflection," as he walks home, "upon the curious old records of likings and dislikings; of jealousies and revenges; of affection defying the power of death, and hatred pursued beyond the grave," which the Prerogative Office's "worm-eaten old books" contain: "silent but striking tokens, some of them, of excellence of heart, and nobleness of soul; melancholy examples, others, of the worst passions of human nature."[47] It is a good example of Dickens's interest in lives that survive only in haunting fragments, whittling down the noisy past to a few stray cries and whispers. Coming from an ambitious young writer, though, it sounds less like a summary of "old records" than like a prospectus.

CHAPTER THREE

Up in the Gallery

"In spite of Dickens's assertion that he had no friend or companion to help him when he commenced literature," James Friswell observed shortly after the novelist's death, "the lonely and unaided young author seems to have been peculiarly happy in the number and influential character of his friends."[1] Friswell's assessment is strangely thin-lipped, especially coming from a writer whose own pages reverberate with the steady thud of names being dropped. It also fails to point out that Dickens's happy fortune started much closer to home. Dickens was undoubtedly good at making friends, and equally good at making the most of his friendships, but in the earliest stages of his career it was his relatives who were of more immediate use. His uncle, John Henry Barrow, was a successful journalist who had previously reported the proceedings of Doctors' Commons for the *Times,* and in January 1828 had established the *Mirror of Parliament,* a weekly newspaper that offered verbatim reports of parliamentary debates. The first commercial rival to *Hansard,* which published the official transcripts of these debates, it was far more accurate than the summaries contained in the popular press, and a regular window onto a previously strange and distant world. It was Barrow who had first helped John Dickens to find work as a journalist, and in 1831 he agreed to take on the younger Dickens as one of his team of shorthand reporters.[2] Whether he viewed this as a way of helping out his nephew (nepotism) or extending his family's influence (self-protection), it was a turning point in Dickens's career.

The public gallery of the old House of Commons in St. Stephen's Chapel was hardly a glamorous working environment. Cramped, gloomy, and stuffy, it required the reporter to squeeze himself onto one of the benches provided for visitors, and then balance his notebook on his knees while he strained to hear the speeches drifting up from the floor of the chamber. Barrow's "sixteen or seventeen picked reporters" worked in shifts that were relatively short and well-paid ("guinea turns of three-quarters of an hour each"), as they were given the ear-sapping and eye-scrambling task of trying to keep up with the speeches and then puzzling out their stenographic squiggles.[3] But in being invited to join this group, Dickens had been given the key to one of the most exclusive and influential clubs in London.

Newspapers had been around for many years, of course, but this period marked the birth of modern "journalism" (the word itself was a recent invention), and Dickens was at the heart of the process. Although it had long been fashionable to sneer at newspapers for coarsening the tone of political debate, the reading public was more reliant on them than ever as a source of information and opinion once the pace of reform started to quicken, with new legislation on topics as diverse as Catholic emancipation, the abolition of slavery, amendments to the Poor Law, and dozens of other proposals that would help to shape the nation's future. This public included the very MPs whose activities were being scrutinized, a fact that made their lofty dismissals of the press especially disingenuous. "The tone in which newspapers are usually mentioned in the House of Commons is absurd," wrote Robert Stephen Rintoul in the *Spectator*. "Men who cannot breakfast without one, in the evening pretend to be hardly cognizant of the existence of such things."[4] As the influence of the press grew, so did this sort of double dealing, whereby statesmen furtively courted the very journalists they attacked in public, and even wrote articles themselves—a complex game that eventually produced spectacles such as the one in which Lord Henry Brougham, who was paid a retainer of £100 a month by the *Times,* was discovered with a piece intended for the *Morning Chronicle* that refuted a *Times* article written earlier by himself.[5] No wonder politicians and journalists were on the way to becoming the two least trusted professions. What was becoming increasingly clear, though, as they variously colluded and collided, was how much they needed each other.

Gallery reporters, in particular, were establishing themselves as the censor or conscience of a political system that was starting to examine its own workings with new vigor. One sign of this was the House of Lords' decision to allot reporters a separate row of seats in 1831; another was Charles Barry's 1835 design for the new Palace of Westminster, which gave them permanent galleries of their own. "The gallery in which the reporters sit," Thomas Macaulay argued in 1828, "has become a fourth estate of the realm."[6] Just as significant, particularly for someone as class-conscious as Dickens, was the fact that these reporters enjoyed a standing that was considerably higher than that of ordinary hacks. During a debate in 1833, one MP pointed out "he had good reason to believe that they were gentlemen of education and integrity," and his views were more than just a way of sucking up to the men writing them down.[7] Even though other journalists were routinely mocked for their ability to reconcile high-flown rhetoric with down-at-heel morals, parliamentary reporters were widely thought to be an exception to the rule: they were deemed more trustworthy, better educated, better connected.[8] In 1810, eighteen out of the twenty-three working in the gallery had a university education, many of whom were reading for the Bar; and when their credentials as serious writers were questioned, it was pointed out that their predecessors had included Joseph Addison, Richard Steele, and Samuel Johnson.[9] Similar thoughts float through the mind of Thackeray's fictional hero in *The Adventures of Philip* (1862), when he resolves to learn shorthand in order to earn some extra money as a reporter: "Why should not Mr. Philip Firmin, barrister-at-law, bethink him that he belonged to a profession which has helped very many men to competence, and not a few to wealth and honours?"[10] It is a question Dickens may also have pondered when he joined the staff of the *Mirror of Parliament*. Clearly he had been given an opportunity to rise in the world. Equally clearly, for all the stories later in the period about powerful figures who were "self-raised," Dickens's elevation to the gallery, like that of many other reporters whose potential had first been spotted by members of their immediate family, required a significant leg-up from his uncle.[11]

John Barrow had promised that the *Mirror of Parliament* would offer "the greatest talent and experience that have ever been applied to parliamentary reporting."[12] Employing his nephew, whose time in Doctors' Commons had left the young man's ear rather better attuned to the drone of legal arguments than to the cut and thrust of political debate, might have strained the definition of "experience," but Dickens undoubtedly had talent. "There never *was* such a reporter," wrote his friend and fellow journalist Thomas Beard, and Dickens rapidly established himself among "the very highest rank" of the press.[13] One proof of his success was that before long he was combining the roles of reporter and "a sort of sub-editor" on the newspaper. "It was a great object to get it before the public in advance of its rival," a contemporary recalled, "and by means of the good system the new hand established it was usually done."[14] That reference to "system" rings true: if Dickens's new career demonstrated his capacity to master other people's systems, even Gurney's baffling "System of Short-Hand," his later career would reveal a fondness for systems of his own. Whether this involved elaborate rehearsal schedules for his amateur theatricals, or speeches which he claimed to have memorized by filing each topic into a separate mental cubbyhole, the underlying impulse was the same: a pleasure in subduing the clutter of everyday life to principles of method and order.

While commercial competition undoubtedly sharpened the skills of Barrow's reporters, the "great object" of the *Mirror of Parliament* involved more than just professional rivalry. Though neutral in tone, and therefore less likely to appeal to readers who preferred newspapers that told the truth but told it slant, its success depended on the unprecedented appetite for political discussion that had been stimulated by the passage of the first Reform Bill. With its declared aim of taking "effectual Measures for correcting divers Abuses that have long prevailed in the Choice of Members to serve in the Commons House of Parliament," the Reform Bill in effect set out to reorganize the lines along which the country was run, by granting seats to the new industrial cities, increasing the numbers eligible to vote, and decreasing the chances that an MP would be elected by only a handful of voters in one of the so-called "rotten boroughs." Introduced by Lord John Russell, the first major debate took place on March 1–9, 1831, and a letter from Dickens dated March 7—the earliest that survives from his adult life—in which he apologizes for breaking an engagement because "I was so exceedingly tired from my week's exertions that I slept on the Sofa the whole day," indicates that he was there from the start.[15] For the next fifteen months, as the bill slowly inched its way through Parliament, he occupied one of the best seats in the House.

A great deal was written at the time, and a great deal more has been written since, about whether or not the Reform Bill was a genuinely radical piece of legislation, but that does not blunt its significance. In many ways it was the pivot on which the century turned. This was not only because of the practical changes it sought to make, but also because it was the first official acknowledgment that things could no longer carry on as they were. Not that popular feeling always divided neatly along party lines: memories of the French Revolution, with its rapid slide from high ideals to scenes of indiscriminate butchery, were still fresh enough for many people to want both continuity *and* change, a measured re-forming of old institutions rather than a radical overthrow of them. Tennyson, whose anxieties about the Reform Bill produced some of his most nervous political poems, was hardly alone in believing explicitly in progress, while also believing implicitly, as T. S. Eliot observed, that progress consisted in things remaining much as they were.[16] Wordsworth went further still, declaring that if the bill passed he would retire to a "safe and conservative government like Austria."[17] Faced with such diverse, and potentially divisive, views the prime minister's response was strangely muted. On November 2, 1830, just a few months after the July Revolution in France, and amid signs of social unrest that included riots against the newly formed Metropolitan Police, an attempt by six thousand working men to invade the Tower of London and the Bank of England, and huge public meetings at which tricolor ribbons and cockades were openly sported, the Duke of Wellington made a speech in Parliament in which he declared his implacable opposition to reform, on the grounds that "Britain possessed a Legislature which answered all the good purposes of legislation, and this to a greater degree than any Legislature ever had answered in any country whatever."[18] It was an oddly Panglossian gloss on the situation, and when he sat down a colleague congratulated him on announcing the fall of his government. How could anyone defend a system in which local landowners arranged for their tenants and cronies to elect up to two MPs in some boroughs, while major cities including Manchester, Leeds, Sheffield, and Birmingham had no parliamentary representation at all? It did not require a very radical imagination to conclude that there was something rotten in the state, and that only some fairly urgent surgery would prevent the cancer from spreading.

By March 1, 1831, more than a thousand petitions had been presented in favor of reform, with only two against. Sensing an opportunity to ride the mood of the nation, a new Whig government, having originally taken up the cause of reform with some diffidence, found itself not only introducing the bill, but then forcing it through a long series of spoiling motions, votes, dissolutions of the government, and new elections. For more than a year, as the progress of the bill stalled, there was a whiff of revolution in the air. After the House of Lords rejected the first bill, the night of April 27, 1831, brought a "General Illumination," in which Londoners placed lit lamps and candles in their windows to show their support for reform. The city was ablaze with light, and the fact that the police had to disperse a crowd of up to three thousand protesters intent on throwing stones at any darkened windows made many wonder how close London was to being set ablaze in a more destructive fashion. Meanwhile, social discontent rippled across the country. When the Lords rejected a second version of the bill on October 8, the bells in Birmingham were muffled, and there were riots in Derby, Nottingham, and Bristol, where the prisons and the bishop's palace were burned to the ground and a cavalry charge was needed to restore order. It was only after further threats of public violence in May 1832 that a third version of the bill was finally passed by the Lords, on June 4.

At this distance, it is hard to know how close the nation was to collapsing into a full-blown civil war. Even at the time, nobody seemed quite sure—and it is this fact that gave their forecasts such gloomy power, whether they were offered in the service of reformers, who hoped to scare waverers into action, or of conservatives, who hoped to scare them back into inaction. One of Dickens's early poems describes the Devil laughing gaily as he stalks through "a scene of desolation" in Bristol—a sign that even those who supported reform were nervous about the excesses to which it might lead.[19] The situation was complicated still further by the fact that the London mob, which had been the stuff of nightmares ever since the Gordon Riots of 1780, did not always seem to take the issues—or themselves—entirely seriously. In October 1831, for example, a huge crowd gathered to cheer the carriages of the bill's supporters and jeer those of its opponents. A piece of orange was thrown at the Duke of Wellington, but no soldiers were needed to control the protesters, and there was laughter when they realized that they should have been cheering rather than jeering Lord Ellenborough. Even on the night of the General Illumination, the crowd that was stoning the windows of Wellington's London home on Park Lane withdrew as a mark of respect when they were told that his wife had just died and was lying inside.

All the same, one should not underestimate how intently the stuttering progress of the Reform Bill was followed, or how carefully the MPs chose their words, knowing that their speeches would be pored over for hidden clues and nuances. On both sides of the debate, political soundbites were brandished like flags. "We shall be bound to proceed further" (Robert Peel); "We live in the days when men are industrious and desire to be free" (Henry Brougham); "Renew the youth of the State. . . . The danger is terrible. The time is short" (Thomas Macaulay).[20] Understandably, the high political stakes meant that MPs were especially keen not to be misquoted; equally understandably, the pressures on reporters to reproduce their speeches as quickly as possible made misquoting almost inevitable. This could also be done with deliberately mischievous intent. When Thomas Hansard was summoned before a Select Committee investigating the standard of parliamentary reporting, he was asked, "So, it might happen that you put into a Member's mouth what he ought to have said, rather than what he said?" And he replied, "That would not be a very great evil." More surprisingly, he went on to claim that reshaping the speeches of MPs should be seen as "literary work."[21] Dickens would later refine this work for maximum comic effect. "A Parliamentary Sketch" (1836), for example, notes of the eccentric ultra-Tory Colonel Sibthorp (lightly disguised as a "ferocious-looking gentleman" with "a large black moustache"): "He is very punctual in his attendance at the House, and his self-satisfied 'He-ar-He-ar' is not infrequently the signal for a general titter." The real joke here is that Sibthorp had complained that Whig journalists willfully misrepresented his parliamentary speeches by inserting "laughter" and "cries of 'oh, oh' and 'question, question'" into their reports. On the contrary, Dickens observes, it was Sibthorp's own interruptions that had helped to make him into such a diverting figure of fun.[22]

However tempting it might have been to filter or flex the politicians' words, there is no evidence that Dickens ever succumbed. "Reporting is certainly not *sine arte*," advised an 1830 article in *Fraser's,* "but for the rest a young beginner must frequently be scrupulous as to truth."[23] The ambiguity of this would not have escaped Dickens, but working for a newspaper that advertised its commitment to "the principle of absolute and uncompromising impartiality" would have made exploiting it inadvisable. Dickens's accuracy is indicated by the fact that, of the large *Mirror of Parliament* team which covered Edward Stanley's marathon six-hour response to the first reading of the Suppression of Disturbances Bill in February 1833, his contribution was singled out by Stanley as the one that stuck most closely to the original speech. As a result, Dickens was brought to Carlton House Terrace to transcribe the whole thing, with Stanley pacing up and down in his study, declaiming for "hour after hour, to the end, often becoming very much excited, and frequently bringing down his hand with great violence upon the desk."[24]

Soon Dickens's growing reputation had secured him another appointment. This time it was on the *True Sun,* a new evening newspaper, launched on March 5, 1832, which prided itself both on its radical political stance and the speed with which its reports on the Reform crisis were distributed to the provinces. (The issue of April 14, 1832, devoted twenty of its twenty-four columns to the question of Reform, and on April 18 it boasted that a full account of a House of Lords debate that had finished at 7:00 P.M. reached Sheffield, 160 miles away, "in the incredibly short space of about twelve hours.")[25] It is not known exactly what Dickens's duties were, but here too he established a position as "one of the most ready, rapid and reliable of its reporters."[26] Although the enthusiastic alliterative rattle of this description does not suggest that Dickens ever rewrote material hostile to the paper's political agenda, he would certainly have had more opportunities than before of blurring the line between "truth" and "literary work." Indeed, one poetic squib published in the *True Sun* at the time draws explicit parallels between politicians and journalists, both of whom suspected the other of twisting facts to suit the occasion, and scoffs at the MPs' vision of themselves as "virtuous, gifted, lofty, libelled martyrs / To that most horrid clique—the base Reporters."[27]

Dickens's own political views can be inferred from his position on a paper that was strenuously anti-Tory, as they can from his later blunt assessment of the Tories as "people whom, politically, I despise and abhor."[28] But whether or not he had a party allegiance, the passage of the Reform Bill is an event in which he might have been expected to take a keen personal interest. The decision to extend voting rights to all male householders living on properties worth at least £10 a year was widely seen as an attempt to reward and encourage the growing ranks of the respectable middle class. Lord Grey argued along these lines when he called for "a greater influence to be given to the middle classes, who have made wonderful advances in property and intelligence," and "who form the real and efficient mass of public opinion"; so did Lord Palmerston when he pointed out that they were "distinguished by morality and good conduct—by obedience to the laws—by the love of order," and added that the main purpose of the bill was to include more of them in the Constitution. Both were responding to Macaulay, who had followed up his call to "renew the youth of the state" by explaining that in the ongoing "struggle between the young energy of one class, and the ancient privileges of another," it was "the middle classes of England" who were best placed to give the nation a shot of youthful vigor.[29] Dickens was certainly youthful, just twenty years old when the bill was passed in 1832, but he was far from secure in this class. As his parents lurched from one financial crisis to another, and as he juggled various freelance reporting jobs, he was at best a probationary member. But his ambition was not in doubt. The sinuous course of the Reform Bill was being tracked in his own search for security and respectability; and in reporting its plans to change society, he was also projecting a more personal future for himself.

For the rest of his life, Dickens's interest in politics went hand in hand with his distrust of politicians, especially the MPs sitting in "that great Dust Heap down at Westminster."[30] "Night after night," David Copperfield remarks of his stint in the gallery, "I record predictions that never come to pass, professions that are never fulfilled, explanations that are only meant to mystify. I wallow in words." Dickens was sometimes even less complimentary. When he had some dummy book spines made for his study at Tavistock House, he commissioned a set entitled *Hansard's Guide to Refreshing Sleep:* "As many volumes as possible."[31] He was irritated by Lord Grey's "fishy coldness" and "insufferable though most gentlemanly artificiality," mocked Lord Derby as "the Honourable Member for Verbosity," and even cooled towards Brougham, "by far the greatest speaker he had ever heard."[32] He was especially fond of mimicking Brougham's telescopic syntax, which extended sentences in a way that made them sound both urgent and self-indulgent; and when he recalled the famous climax to Brougham's defense of reform ("I solemnly abjure you—I warn you—I implore you—yea, on my bended knees, I supplicate you—Reject not this Bill!"), he pointed out that in fact Brougham had to be picked up off his knees, having polished off four bottles of port during his speech.[33] His fictional MPs are equally ludicrous. In *Sketches by Boz,* he describes one who has "a great idea of his own abilities, which must have been a great comfort to him as no one else had" ("Sentiment"), where the lurch from "great idea" to "great comfort" nicely captures the self-serving nature of political rhetoric; while Mr. Gregsbury in *Nicholas Nickleby* has "a pompous manner, a tolerable command of sentences with no meaning in them, . . . a senatorial gravity, and a statesmanlike habit of keeping his feelings under control."

The implied criticism of speakers who exercise self-control reads oddly when we learn that Dickens had earned a reputation among other gallery reporters for being "exceedingly reserved."[34] The difference, perhaps, is that whereas MPs seemed able to switch their feelings on and off like a tap, Dickens's "reserve" was more like a reservoir, a facility for storing up feelings that were worryingly vulnerable to overflow. During one speech by the Irish MP Daniel O'Connell, which eloquently described the sufferings of the Irish poor, Dickens "put down his pencil . . . and declared he could not take notes of the speech, so moved was he by its pathos."[35] O'Connell would later repay the compliment, being so touched by Dickens's description of Little Nell's death in *The Old Curiosity Shop* that he burst into tears, flinging the book out of the window of the train in which he was traveling. The difference, of course, is that the Irish really were suffering, whereas Little Nell was made out of paper and ink, and thus immune to genuine pain—a distinction that suggested a certain lack of proportion on O'Connell's part. The parallel shows why Dickens was so suspicious of politicians. It went beyond their tendency to defend privilege rather than seek proper social change. Even if they managed to tap deep and genuine feelings in their listeners, their rhetoric was often as phony as an 11-shilling note. Put simply, they behaved like a company of actors playing to the gallery.

The idea that Parliament resembled a theater was a standard complaint of the time. Walter Bagehot's famous distinction later in the century between the "efficient" elements of the Constitution and its more ceremonial or "theatrical" side was anticipated in many earlier descriptions of parliamentary debates, which make them sound like scenes from a play in which members of the chorus kept trying to hijack the role of the hero.[36] In *David Copperfield,* Dickens has David remark of his time as a parliamentary reporter that "I am sufficiently behind the scenes to know the worth of political life," while "A Parliamentary Sketch" describes MPs with all the professional detachment of a stage manager making a backstage inventory of props and costumes. One MP is reduced to being a hoarse-voiced man dressed in a "blue coat, queer-crowned, broad-brimmed hat, white corduroy breeches, and great boots"; another wears a "costume" of a "loose, wide, brown coat, with capacious pockets on each side," together with a silver watch chain dangling below an "immensely long waistcoat," and a "white handkerchief tied in a great bow, with straggling ends sticking out beyond his shirt frill." "The Pantomime of Life" goes even further in this satirical direction, describing MPs as clowns who are capable of performing night after night, "playing the strangest antics, and giving each other the funniest slaps on the face that can possibly be imagined, without evincing the smallest tokens of fatigue." Such antics, Dickens concludes, produce the sort of roaring and confusion that "would put to shame the most turbulent sixpenny gallery that ever yelled through a boxing-night."

Dickens would have been especially alert to the theatricality of such characters at the time of the Reform Bill. Not only was this the period of his most enthusiastic theater attendance, but his movements between the reporters' gallery and the theater gallery also coincided with a far more widespread interest in the overlap of politics and the stage. At a time when political discussion was frequently clogged by uncertainty, the theater was a place where everything was more clearly expressed, more brightly colored, more sharply illuminated than in everyday life. Not everyone was happy about the idea of political debate being staged for the general public. Giving evidence to the Select Committee on Dramatic Literature in 1832, George Colman, the "Examiner of Plays" (i.e., censor) in the Lord Chamberlain's office, was asked whether he would strike out the word

"Reform" if it appeared in a script. "No," he replied, "I should say, 'I think you had better omit it; I advise you to do so for your own sakes, as you will have a hubbub.'"[37] As one might expect from someone whose ears quivered professionally at the slightest hint of danger, his own word was carefully chosen: "hubbub" could mean simply the confused noise of a crowd, but its origins lie in an Irish word used as a battle-cry, suggesting how easily murmurings of dissent might swell into the howling of a mob. Looking at some of the other words that made the Lord Chamberlain's office nervous, including "angel" ("it alludes to a scriptural personage") and "gammon" (objected to by a Mr. Gammon of Hampshire, whose feelings had been hurt by a previous play that referred to "the Hampshire hog"), it is tempting to conclude that Colman was being oversensitive.[38] "Better locked in a safe than sorry," seems to have been his motto. On the other hand, contemporary descriptions of theater audiences make his caution appear wholly understandable.

When John Payne Collier was asked by the Select Committee about the "gross immorality seen in the larger theatres," he agreed that it was "a most decided objection to any man carrying his wife or sister to the theatre."[39] Although his language did not greatly distinguish between his relatives and a pair of gloves, his listeners would have been aware of the problem to which he was obliquely alluding: the prostitutes who were attracted to the bright lights of the theater like gaudy moths, and whose growing numbers were making it ever harder to pretend they did not exist. Other social problems were equally difficult to miss, particularly at the larger theaters that were being built to entertain London's rapidly expanding working class. The Surrey Theatre (1810), Whitechapel Pavilion (1828), the Garrick Theatre (1831), and others were technically "minor" theaters, as they were licensed to play only drama accompanied by music; but each seated up to three thousand spectators, who packed themselves in at 6:00 P.M. and stayed for hours, "quarrelling and fighting, cheering, hissing, clapping, booing, stamping and stinking to the very rafters."[40]

Audiences in the cheap gallery seats, occupied mostly by domestic servants, apprentices, costermongers, and laborers, were famous for behaving especially badly. Far from being happy to tuck themselves away at the top of the theater, they were keen to put themselves at the heart of the action. A German who visited England in 1826, and who attended an opera at the King's Theatre, recorded his disgust when they repeatedly interrupted the singers by shouting catcalls and tossing bits of orange peel onto the heads of spectators in the pit below.[41] Slightly later in the century, Henry Mayhew described a night in the threepenny gallery of the Coburg Theatre (opened in 1818, renamed the Royal Victoria Theatre in 1833, and now known as the Old Vic) as a riot of noise and spectacle equal to anything occurring on the stage. Starting with the rush of spectators to their seats, a process that is "peculiar and almost awful," his account exhibits the wariness of an anthropologist worried that the savage tribe he is studying may turn on him at any moment. Seen from below, the "vast slanting mass of heads" is a "huge black heap, dotted with faces," which start to perspire as the temperature rises: "Recognitions take place every moment, and 'Bill Smith' is called to in a loud voice from one side, and a shout in answer from the other asks 'What's up?' Or family secrets are revealed, and 'Bob Triller' is asked where 'Sal' is, and replies amid a roar of laughter, that she is 'a-larning the pynanney.'" Eventually the whole gallery joins together in a rousing chorus, and "the throats of the mob burst forth in all their strength," with Mayhew's shift from plural to singular nouns neatly enacting the process whereby individual voices are gradually absorbed into the shared identity of the crowd.[42]

Mayhew's anxiety was widely shared by his contemporaries. George Cruikshank's etching *Pit, Boxes, and Gallery* (Figure 4) shows the audience of the Surrey Theatre in 1836 dividing neatly along class lines, like a human three-layer cake: sturdy middle-class spectators in the pit, showily dressed aristocrats in the boxes, and finally the blowsy and boozy gallery.[43] But there is something that breaks the clear lines of the picture: a cudgel hangs over the edge of the gallery, in a perfect visual echo of the lines of the trumpet and lute molded onto the balcony. The moral is clear: theaters are places where high culture knocks up against far lower urges; they are an expression of civilization and its discontents. More alarming still, the cudgel-wielder is seated in the section known as "the gods," so named because of its height from the stage—but anyone familiar with the theater would have known that in tragedy the gods are also the beings responsible for sudden and violent interventions in human affairs. Tucked away in the corner of the picture, he is like an imp capering in the margins of an illuminated manuscript: an amusing doodle, safely kept in his place, but always on the verge of taking over the main story.

This nervousness about the mixing of classes was rarely reflected on stage. The most popular theatrical form was melodrama, which tended to celebrate a world in which character and status were as fixed as the hero's upper lip. However fiercely dramatists competed to attract audiences with new and thrilling spectacles ("LAKE OF TRANSPARENT ROLLING FIRE!" "THE SKELETON MONK!" "TERRIBLE DEGRADATION OF AGNES!" "DESTRUCTION OF THE MURDERER BY THE FANGS OF THE FAITHFUL DOG"), they united in offering a view of the world that had an appealing cartoon-like simplicity.[44] In real life, new arrivals to London during the 1820s and 1830s found themselves being buffeted by economic forces and chance events that were usually beyond their control, and sometimes even beyond their comprehension. Melodrama, by contrast, presented life as it ought to be. However cunning the villain's plans, and however close the hero came to being shot or sliced up, virtue always triumphed. It was a dream world, crafted from papier mâché and cardboard, in which characters reliably behaved as they were expected to, without any possibility of real change. The indestructible hero would always be true to his sweetheart, and the cackling villain would always seek to drag her off to his lair. It was, in other words, a stubbornly conservative art form, which allowed its largely working-class audience to entertain the fantasy that truth and justice were on their side, but without encouraging them to make the real world more like its brightly colored alternative. On the rare occasions that politics crept into the dialogue, it proved far less successful than the standard formula of swapping stagey one-liners. John Walker's play *The Factory Lad,* for example, first staged in October 1832 at the Surrey

·[83]·

Theatre, revolves around an evil factory-owner who replaces his workers with machines, and it reaches a cliff-hanger climax in which the crazed hero shoots him, "laughing hysterically" as he cries out, "Justice shall have its due. Die, tyrant!" It lasted six performances.[45] Even W. T. Moncrieff's *Reform; or, John Bull Triumphant* (1831), a one-act drama performed at the same Coburg Theatre that would later so alarm Mayhew, opens by looking forward to the "host of evils" that will disappear once the "wise measure . . . of a fair and equal representation" has been introduced, but it ends with a tableau of national unity and a patriotic chorus of "Rule Britannia."[46]

Few theatrical productions of the time were this keen to engage in political debate; the Reform Bill was usually a background murmur rather than the subject of dramatic speeches. That indefatigable theatergoer Henry Crabb Robinson chats away to his diary about the plays he saw in 1831–1832, including farces (such as *My Wife—What Wife?*), melodramas, a modern opera entitled *Fra Diavolo* ("most dull and fatiguing"), and pantomimes such as *Aladdin* and *Tom Thumb;* but when he felt in need of some "political gossip" on May 14, 1832, he left the theater to go to the Athenaeum Club.[47] Yet there was one actor—Dickens's favorite solo performer—whose work undoubtedly did reflect the ambitions of social reformers, albeit disguised by a series of wigs and funny voices. In the years 1824–1834, Charles Mathews's "At Home" residencies at Covent Garden and the Adelphi Theatre became as much a part of the theatrical season as a trip to the pantomime. These one-man shows took the form of a loosely connected jumble of comic songs, recitations, and impressions, and always concluded with a "Monopolylogue," a farce in which Mathews used his skills as a ventriloquist and quick-change artist to play all the roles. It was a brilliant demonstration of the idea that personal identity was largely a matter of self-invention. In 1830, Mathews's characters included Miss Never-end, "who despises colons and semi-colons, and never in her life could be induced to make use of a full stop"; Squire Sadjolly, "a gentleman who rides forty miles a day, swallows continents of beef, lakes of gravy, and rivers of port," even though his lungs are "worn out," his liver is "shrivelled," and his stomach is "in tatters"; and Mr. Acid, who takes his children to Vauxhall Gardens "to make them happy," but ends up beating them "a hundred times an hour."[48] Part of Mathews's perennial appeal can be attributed to his personal warmth, which allowed him to poke fun at his characters while remaining affectionately tolerant of their eccentricities. The other part can be put down to his social inclusiveness: every member of the audience recognized a friend or colleague in his comic gallery, and Mathews was able to change roles—say, from squire to French housemaid—with only a slight twist of his features.

Many aspects of Mathews's "At Home" performances appear to have lodged firmly in Dickens's head. While some were very specific, such as the rambling sentences of Miss Never-end, which can be heard behind the gushing syntax of *Little Dorrit*'s Flora, others were more general: the public reading tours Dickens undertook towards the end of his life not only echoed Mathews's rubber-faced, rubber-voiced performance style, but also borrowed Mathews's set—a simple writing desk placed squarely center stage. During this early part of his life, however, Dickens was more likely to have been struck by another part of Mathews's act: his fondly mocking descriptions of young men seeking to get ahead. *Travels in Air, on Earth and Water,* an early "At Home" from 1822, begins with Mathews dismounting from a hot-air balloon on stage, and informing the audience that, knowing of the world's misfortunes, "the only way in which I could effectually rise in life, was to go up in a Balloon." He sings:

> I once did trot, but now do not,
> > Long spurs and pantalooning—
> But since I've got a proper spot:
> > To fly my air-balloon in,
> I now will make my pony wait
> At Charing Cross, or Grosvenor Gate—
> > Once in the air, they gape and stare
> And much astound, for miles around,
> > The folks with air-ballooning.[49]

Jokes about being full of hot air flicker briefly, but the song is fully in tune with one of Mathews's favorite themes: the ambitious young man who tries to move in a more rarefied social atmosphere and quickly discovers that he is out of his element. One episode in the first "At Home" entertainment had featured a youth of recent education and wealth, but no social graces, committing a series of faux pas at a dinner party. In time, this would become useful source material for one of Dickens's best comic routines, as Pip and Herbert in *Great Expectations* hold their first dinner, and hire a waiter who has "wandering habits of putting the covers on the floor (where he fell over them), the melted butter in the arm-chair, the bread on the bookshelves, the cheese in the coal-scuttle, and the boiled fowl in my bed in the next room"—a suitably messy reflection of the way in which Pip feels himself to be equally out of place in London society. But Mathews's song was more encouraging than this, because it was sung by a man who, despite being almost entirely self-taught, had emerged as one of the most successful and popular actors of the age. The celebrated "mobility" of Mathews's acting offered another model of how an ambitious young man might rise in the world.

❦❦❦

Dickens's practical theatrical experience at this time was mixed. George Lear, his fellow clerk at Ellis & Blackmore, reported that Dickens had acted in one of the small private theaters that offered stage-struck amateurs the opportunity to perform in public, on payment of a fee, in order to show off to their friends or try out a new career.[50] Whether or not Dickens performed, he had certainly witnessed another clerk from the office, Thomas Potter, doing so at the City Theatre, and in his sketch "Making a Night of It" he borrowed Potter's name for a character who seems keen to get in on the action even when he is officially a member of the audience, calmly receiving insults such as "Give that dog a bone" and "Throw him o-ver" while he cocks his hat and stands "with his arms a-kimbo, expressing defiance most melo-dramatically."

Another early sketch, "Private Theatres," is even less complimentary.

Beginning with the price list of various roles written up in the green room ("RICHARD THE THIRD.—DUKE OF GLO'STER, 2*l.*; EARL OF RICHMOND, 1*l.*; DUKE OF BUCKINGHAM, 15*s.*"), Dickens goes on to suggest that private theaters are little more than a confidence trick designed to exploit people with more money than talent. The audience is composed of "a motley group of dupes and blackguards," the backstage area is draped with cobwebs and reeks of a "damp, mildewy smell," and the actress singled out as Lady Macbeth has been chosen to play the part "because she's tall and stout, and *looks* a little like Mrs. Siddons—at a considerable distance." Like most of Dickens's satirical sketches, this one has an inward understanding of its target that teeters on the edge of sympathy, reflecting his more general fascination for the shabby and dingy that John Forster characterized as "a profound attraction of repulsion."[51] In this case, so early in Dickens's career, his lofty moral tone may also have been a way of flattering his audience, by reflecting their prejudices back at them with an authorial nod of approval. Private theaters were widely viewed with a suspicion that bordered on hostility, not only because they set out to part fools from their money, but also because of their lingering radical associations. They had emerged out of the late eighteenth-century fad for "spouting clubs," which attracted "'prentices and clerks, and giddy young men, all intoxicated with plays," who paid a small fee to gather in taverns and perform.[52] By 1771, the *Oxford Magazine* was claiming that the contagion of acting among the lower orders required government intervention, since the "ignorance and want of education" among the clubs' members "can only be equalled by the mad ambition they have to become actors."[53] The spectacle of grubby youths strutting around on stage pretending to be kings or dukes was especially troubling after the French Revolution, and public unease over how far such "mad ambition" might stretch rumbled on well into the next century. Frequently this was bound up with fears of immorality. In July 1829, the Catherine Street theater that features in Dickens's sketch was cited by a policeman giving evidence to the Mansion House magistrates' court, who had witnessed "romping . . . and very indecent conduct" among its patrons, and went on to claim that "the mischiefs produced in society by places of this kind were incalculable."[54] The vagueness of the threat would only have increased its lurid appeal to respectable middle-class readers.

The less flashy alternative to private theaters was private theatricals. Acting plays at home had long been a staple of country house entertainment—in the late 1780s the glittering theatricals at Richmond House had caused a sitting of the House of Commons to be postponed so that MPs could attend—and although not everyone approved of their tendency to encourage showing off (the rehearsals in Jane Austen's *Mansfield Park* turn out to be especially divisive in this respect), their genteel associations made them a popular choice for ambitious middle-class families. And yet, as Dickens's second published sketch demonstrates, even though the participants in private theatricals did not have to sponsor their parts, there could still be a price to pay.

The setting for Dickens's tale "Mrs. Joseph Porter, 'Over the Way'" is Rose Villa, Clapham Rise, the home of Mr. Gattleton, "a stock-broker in especially comfortable circumstances," and of his wife, "a kind, good tempered, vulgar old soul." As the house is turned over to satisfy "the mania for Private Theatricals," Dickens examines the family's social pretensions with all the cool professional detachment of a scientist dissecting a frog. Nothing is beneath notice, from the vague enthusiasm of the stage manager ("in the market-scene we can walk about in cloaks and things"), to the provisions ordered in as refreshments, as greedily observed by the Gattletons' nosy neighbor: "'There!' said Mrs. Porter, looking out of the window; 'there are two rounds of beef and a ham going in, clearly for sandwiches; and Thomas, the pastry-cook, says there have been twelve dozen tarts ordered, besides blanc-mange and jellies. Upon my word! think of the Miss Gattletons in fancy dresses, too!'" Later in the sketch, Mrs. Porter sabotages the play, and triumphantly tells the rest of the audience that it has been "a complete failure"; but the real social drama is contained in small scenes like this one, in which her living-room window becomes a small proscenium arch opening onto the lives of her neighbors, and her twitching curtains announce a longing to meddle in their lives. It could be the blueprint for a hundred sitcoms.

It could also be another fragment of disguised autobiography. The first part of the evening's entertainment in "Mrs. Joseph Porter, 'Over the Way'" is *Othello*, a tragedy in which local gossip takes on a ruthless momentum, and Dickens's sketch was published in the same year (1834) that his family held a similar evening to put on his version of the play. But here the differences are as significant as the parallels, because whereas the Gattletons' *Othello* aims at high seriousness and disintegrates into farce, Dickens's *O'Thello* was deliberately written as a burlesque. The theatrical selections of both families reflect their relative social standing. Emerging as a distinct genre with the success of John Poole's *Hamlet Travestie* (1810), burlesque's mixture of broad humor and songs offered a comically distorted reflection of the tragedies performed at the patent theaters.[55] *Othello* was an especially popular choice of play to spoof, perhaps because it already contained so many elements of black farce that it did not require more than a few alterations in language and tone to twist it in a new direction. Recent versions had included *Othello, the Moor of Fleet Street*, by "William Brakespeare" (Charles M. Westmacott), first performed at the Adelphi Theatre on January 28, 1833, which translated the action to Blackfriars and recast the hero as a crossing-sweeper; and Maurice Dowling's *Othello Travestie*, performed at the Strand Theatre in 1834, in which Othello performed a solo to the tune of "King of the Cannibal Islands" and Desdemona rose from her deathbed to sing a cheerful ditty about being smothered.[56] Dowling's play may also have given Dickens the impetus to adopt the stage convention of the comic Irishman, as the original cast list of *Othello Travestie* had included "IAGO, Othello's Officer, once a native of the Gaultree Mountains, County of Tipperary, Province of Munster, and Kingdom of Ireland."

The few surviving sheets of *O'Thello* work to a standard burlesque formula of quick-fire plotting, groaning puns, and clunky gear-changes between speech and song: "Good! There's no more business now to bore us,/So I propose we have a jolly chorus."[57] Yet two features of this early production are worth pausing over. The first is the choice of play. If putting on private theatricals implied a certain kind of gentility, burlesque carried far more raffish associations. It is hard to imagine real-life versions of the Gattletons belting out some of the song lyrics Dickens wrote, such as "Let's be happy,/Lots of baccy,/Let the cheerful smoke abound." Perhaps this accounts for the note of envy in Dickens's description of their "large drawing room," which has enough space for a stage, an orchestra, several rows of seats, and "a strange jumble" of scenery and props, especially when compared to the line he gives to his own Desdemona: "Our house is rather small." (His family's lodgings at the time, 18 Bentinck Street, to which they moved in January 1833, were located above the premises of an upholsterer and cabinetmaker.) The second feature worth pausing over is why so little of *O'Thello* survives. This can be attributed partly to Dickens's habit of seizing and burning copies of his earliest productions, claiming to be embarrassed by their literary clumsiness, but also to the fact that as soon as he had achieved a measure of fame, his father, who ironically had taken the role of "The Great Unpaid" in the play, appears to have sold off his own acting copy one page at a time.[58] Like all the best memorabilia, the first page even carries a certificate of authentication:

> This Manuscript is in the handwriting of Mr. Charles Dickens, giving a portion of one of the "Parts" in a Burlesque Burletta on "Othello," written by him for representation in his own family in the year 1833.
>
> —John Dickens[59]

Such sprightly opportunism hardly comes as a surprise from a man who would continue to lean on his son's name financially for many years to come. Yet it is hard to imagine a form of behavior better guaranteed to alarm the other family Dickens was involved with at the time. Throughout the period that he had been engaged in these private theatricals, he had been courting a young woman named Maria Beadnell, and her father was a long way from being a debtor, a bankrupt, or "The Great Unpaid." George Beadnell was a City banker.

CHAPTER FOUR

Mr. Dickin

It is not known who introduced Dickens into the Beadnell family circle; possibly the connection was made by his friend Henry Kolle, a bank clerk who was courting another of the daughters, Anne, at the time. What is certain is that by the second half of 1831 he was intimate enough with the family to have been invited to a dinner party at their house on Lombard Street. Dickens's way of thanking them was to perform a long piece of doggerel, "The Bill of Fare," loosely based on Oliver Goldsmith's poem "Retaliation," which he made by sticking together a series of food-based character sketches and mock-epitaphs inspired by the other guests.[1] Part of a tradition of nonsense writing that would later produce Lewis Carroll's talking "Mock Turtle," Dickens's choice was in some ways a sophisticated one. Goldsmith's original subtitle, "A Poem, Including Epitaphs on Some of the Most Distinguished Wits of the Metropolis," had advertised the roots of his piece in the competitive good humor of eighteenth-century coffeehouses, and Dickens's version modernized its source by domesticating the scene, lightening the tone, and, crucially, opening it up to women. He may also have had more personal reasons for thinking that a recitation would impress the assembled company. As a child, John Forster recorded, Dickens had "told a story offhand so well, and sang small comic songs so especially well, that he used to be elevated on chairs and tables, both at home and abroad, for more effective display of these talents." Recalling those occasions in later years, Dickens had the grace to admit that his childhood voice now tingled in his ears, "and he blushed to think what a horrible little nuisance he must have been to many unoffending grown-up people who were called upon to admire him."[2] Presumably he did not feel the same way about "The Bill of Fare," but the poem risked producing similar fixed smiles in its audience, as it slowly ground out more than three hundred lines of quips and allusions. His witty variations on phrases such as "no more" and "never again" were especially vulnerable to mockery. The harder Dickens tried to entertain the assembled company, in fact, the more obvious it became that they were being invited to sit back and enjoy the spectacle of him entertaining himself. "Arthur Beetham—this dish has cost me some pains—/Is a tongue with a well made garnish of brains": even his rhymes sound as if they are patting themselves on the back.

Dickens's pen portraits range from hopeful flattery to laddish banter, and the unevenness of his tone reveals an awkwardness that was as much social as literary. It is as if he could not decide whether he wanted to suck up to his new friends or put them in their place. Nor is it clear how seriously he intended some of his jokes to be taken. The mock-epitaph on his host, for example, having praised George Beadnell's pro-Reform stance as "a good politician" who was "to ballot and freedom a friend," concludes: "And if he be fairly, and all in all ta'en,/'We never shall look upon his like again.'" The allusion is to Hamlet's summary of the qualities that will be missed now that his father is dead: "Take him for all in all,/I shall not look upon his like again."[3] If one wonders how the "hospitable, friendly, and kind" Mr. Beadnell felt about being compared to a murder victim, one wonders still more how he would have regarded Dickens's implicit self-promotion to the position of his bookish, lovesick son.

Any doubts Mr. Beadnell may have had about the poem's real purpose would have been removed by the central section, in which Dickens abandons parody and falls into a pattern of genuine sentiment, like a clown whose greasepaint tears turn out to have been real all along:

> Has Maria left this world of trouble and care
> Because for us she was too good and too fair,
> Has heaven in its jealousy ta'en her away
> As a blessing too great for us children of clay[?]
> All ye fair and beautiful sadly come here,

And Spring's early flowers, Strew over her bier . . .
My bright hopes and fond wishes were all centred here[,]
Their brightness has vanished, they're now dark and drear.
The impression that mem'ry engraves on my heart
Is all that I have left, and with that I ne'er part.

It is a strange piece of writing. Telling a new girlfriend what you would feel like if she were dead is certainly an unusual seduction technique, and here the conceit of the lover luxuriating over his loss drifts dangerously close to the idea that love itself is retrospective, as if true devotion could be exercised only on someone safely removed from a world where hearts can change. In time, this idea would become central to Dickens's fiction: his lines are also a rehearsal of Little Nell's deathbed scene, just one of the occasions on which Dickens's writing, like Mrs. Gamp's fingers, seemed unable to resist the urge to rearrange sleeping limbs into the attitude of a corpse. On this occasion, however, he had a more immediate aim. These high-minded and somewhat heavy-handed verses announced to every-one present that Dickens was in love; or, as the poem put it, that he was a young cabbage who had "lost his heart." It was an uneasy but charac-teristic overlap of food and love. John Payne Collier recalled how, as they passed through Hungerford Market together in 1833, Dickens bought a bag of cherries and then popped them one by one into the mouth of a "grimy child" slung over his oblivious father's shoulder: "He informed me, as he walked through it, that he knew *Hunger*ford Market well, laying unusual stress on the two first syllables."[4] Looking back at his childhood, Dickens recognized how intimately children can link a hunger for food with other kinds of hunger—for security, acceptance, love—that are far less easily satisfied. "The Bill of Fare" was the first sign that this nagging sense of want would become as central to his adult life as it would to his career as a writer. It is no coincidence that the most famous scene he ever wrote would be the one in which Oliver Twist asks for more.

In the meantime, few women seemed to offer more than Maria. She was small, blonde, and pretty. She was also well educated, having recently returned from a finishing school in Paris, and she dressed with fashionable good taste—Dickens never forgot how the first sight of her "in a sort of raspberry coloured dress with a little black trimming at the top" pinned his heart "like a captured butterfly."[5] In fact she would have been perfect, if only she had not treated him with an amused tolerance that bordered on indifference. Their relationship was an unhappily lop-sided affair, involving as it did a young man who was desperate to fall in love and a slightly older woman who was unwilling to commit to anything more than a protracted flirtation. Biographers have usually taken Dickens at his word when he claimed that he had been "horribly in earnest" and set himself to win her with "all the energy and determination of which I am the owner"—a process he later characterized as one of "the maddest romances that ever got into any boy's head."[6] The collision between "earnest" and "romances," however, provides a clue that this relationship may have been as much indebted to fiction as it was to real life.

Dickens would later show just how dangerous it was to think that life fell into the reassuring patterns of old stories. In *Great Expectations,* Pip is so enchanted by Estella that he assumes he is living out a fairy tale in which he has been chosen to "do all the shining deeds of the young Knight of romance, and marry the Princess." The discovery that he is part of a rather different story turns out to be a frustration of his narrative expectations as well as his hopes for gentility. Young Dickens, too, seems to have thought that he had entered a storybook world in which Maria was a Rapunzel pining away in her Lombard Street tower, but unfortunately they appear to have disagreed on what kind of story they were in. Doomy romantic tragedy? Frothy social comedy? A farce of mistaken identities? Dickens may have enjoyed casting himself and Maria as Romeo and Juliet, star-crossed lovers denied happiness by their families (in 1831, with unfortunate timing, John Dickens's name had again appeared in the *London Gazette* as one of those being sued in the Insolvent Debtors' Court), but in truth Maria was more like Rosaline, the reported object of Romeo's first crush, who cares so little about his lovesick verses that she does not even bother to appear on stage. Having cast himself in the role of hero, Dickens was disappointed to discover that the woman he adored apparently had not read the same script.

Maria's personal album contains a good deal of evidence about Dickens's attempts to woo her, as it does about the rivals who stood in his way. Bound in green leather, and presented to her on November 17, 1827, its 140-odd pages include paintings, drawings, music, and verses from many of the young men who were also jostling for her attention in real life.[7] In some cases they were prepared to cooperate in order to tease her into a response. A couple of Dickens's poems appear alongside watercolors painted by Henry Austin, a friend who would later become his brother-in-law, and for both of them flattery was closely aligned with fantasy. For example, alongside a poem of ten lines transcribed by Dickens, entitled "Written in an Album by T. Moore" ("But could I thus within thy mind,/One little vacant corner find"), is a watercolor by Austin that depicts Maria as a simpering milkmaid. Dressed in dainty shoes and a snow-white pinafore, her coquettish expression implies that there may not have been a shortage of vacant corners to choose from. She is about as convincing a pastoral figure as Marie Antoinette playing on her toy farm, although the costume itself is ambiguous: it might be taken as evidence that she enjoyed adopting different guises, or that her suitors enjoyed treating her as a doll they could dress up. Far more earnest is an acrostic in which Dickens spells out the words of her name:

> My life may chequered be with scenes of misery and pain,
> And 't may be my fate to struggle with adversity in vain:
> Regardless of misfortunes tho' howe'er bitter they may be,
> I shall always have one retrospect, a hallowed one to me,
> And it will be of that happy time when first I gazed on thee.
> Blighted hopes and prospects drear, for me will lose their sting,
> Endless troubles shall harm not me, when fancy on the wing
> A lapse of years shall travel o'er, and again before me cast
> Dreams of happy fleeting moments then for ever past:
> Not any worldly pleasure has such magic charms for me
> E'en now, as those short moments spent in company with thee;

Life has no charms, no happiness, no pleasures, now for me
Like those I feel when 'tis my lot[,] Maria, to gaze on thee.

As in many acrostics, the verse staggers and sags as the concertinaed syntax and strained rhymes struggle to keep the first letter of each line in
place. But the most jarring moment is kept until last, where the stuttering
rhythm means that "Maria" fails to fit into the poem that is trying to con-
jure her up. At the very last moment the spell is broken, and the effect is of
scales falling from the poet's eyes. It is hard to know how deliberate this
was, but it does not suggest that Dickens had a particularly hopeful view
of their future together.

Another of his contributions, "Lodgings to Let," was based on the
conceit of the album as a boarding-house that welcomed new lodgers. It
wasn't an especially funny joke, and the lines that urged "I'll settle here,
no more I'll roam / But make this place my happy home" sounded suspiciously like a personal plea. It was unlikely to be answered. Maria's mother
even made a point of getting his name wrong. Dickens later remembered
how he once escorted them "with native gallantry" to a dressmaker's,
where they were going to order some clothes for the eldest daughter's
marriage to a prosperous tea and coffee merchant, at which point Mrs.
Beadnell, "seized with an apprehension . . . that I might come in, said
emphatically, 'And now Mr. Dickin'—which she always used to call me—
'We'll wish *you* good morning!'"[8]

❧·❦·❧·❦

Mrs. Beadnell's caution was understandable, particularly in the context
of buying wedding dresses. Though charming and keen to impress, Mr.
Dickin was hardly an attractive prospect as a son-in-law. The attentions
he had been paying to Maria were those of a courtly lover rather than a
cad—wooing her with verses, buying her small favors such as a new pair
of gloves, and so on—but they might easily have been misinterpreted. His
tendency to think of women as moral elevators, in particular, in the way
that David Copperfield perceives the saintly Agnes, "ever leading me to

something better; ever directing me to higher things," to suspicious eyes might have been hard to distinguish from a form of social climbing. What is more, he was young, and looked it. A miniature painted by his aunt Janet Barrow when he was eighteen (Figure 5) shows a fresh-faced youth standing very erect, with one eyebrow slightly cocked, as if commenting ironically on the absurdity of the whole enterprise. If "the very essence of a good portrait is, that it must be either serious or smirking," as the portraitist Miss La Creevy observes in *Nicholas Nickleby,* then Aunt Janet's attempt placed itself firmly on the side of the smirk. Even with the benefit of hindsight, it is hard to reconcile this image of the young man with later photographs of the novelist; it is scarcely possible to blame anyone at the time for failing to foresee how one would morph into the other.

His immediate prospects were not impressive. As a parliamentary reporter, he earned on average 15 guineas per week—a healthy sum, particularly when supplemented by freelance shorthand work at Doctors' Commons; but he was paid only when the House was sitting, which in 1833 amounted to a mere 142 days. Having already tried two professions, the law and journalism, he was still unsettled, and even briefly considered emigrating, closely questioning a relative about "the prospects for pushing his fortune in the West Indies," and "wanting but a little encouragement to try his luck there."[9] He did not even have a private address, as he was still living with his parents after an attempt to move into private lodgings had failed. "The people at Cecil Street," he told Henry Kolle, "put too much water in the hashes, lost the nutmeg grater, attended on me most miserably, dirtied the Table Cloths, etc., etc."; and so, "detesting petty miseries," he moved his possessions back to the family home on Bentinck Street.[10] The letter manages to make glum comedy out of the situation, but it is not hard to detect an element of smiling through gritted teeth. Kolle would soon marry his fiancée, the second Beadnell daughter, his acceptability no doubt boosted by his father's thriving calico-printing business, and in many ways he offered Dickens a distorted or inverted image of his own prospects. Indeed, although they were not rivals for the same woman, there are the first stirrings here of a pattern that would eventually develop into one of the strangest and saddest in Dickens's fiction: the would-be lover, in novels such as *A Tale of Two Cities* and *Our Mutual Friend,* who is forced to witness another's success, and finds himself living on as an unnecessary alternative, the superfluous man.

Clearly "energy and determination" alone would not be enough to persuade the Beadnells that Dickens was a suitable match. Accordingly, over the course of 1832 and 1833, he took a number of steps to improve his eligibility. The only problem was that these steps did not seem to be leading in any particular direction. In March 1832, according to Forster, Dickens wrote to George Bartley, the stage manager at Covent Garden, announcing that his close study of Charles Mathews had led him to believe that he too had "a strong perception of character and oddity, and a natural power of reproducing in his own person what he observed in others." Bartley replied offering "an appointment to do anything of Mathews's before him and Charles Kemble, on a certain day at the theatre."[11] There was no shortage of material to choose from: Mathews's scripts had been published, as had cheap reprints of extracts such as *Sketches from Mr. Mathews at Home!* This pamphlet included a song entitled "Trade Choosing" (sung to the tune of "When a Man Weds") that listed some of the occupations a poor family might consider for their son:

Then reads list
Of plumbers, glaziers,
Printers, braziers,
Basket-makers,
Undertakers.
Undecided are all O;
Barber, tailor,
Blacksmith, sailor,
Poulterer, gunner,
Bow-street runner,
Slater, furrier,
Joiner, currier,
And now on one they fall O.[12]

Unfortunately, before Dickens could fall on the profession of actor, he fell ill. When the day of his audition came, he was laid up in bed with a bad cold and inflammation of the face, and so was unable to keep the appointment. He never repeated his application, later explaining: "I had a little distinction in the world of the newspaper, which made me like it; began to write; didn't want money; had never thought of the stage, but as a means of getting it; gradually left off turning my thoughts that way; and never resumed the idea. . . . See how near I may have been to another sort of life."[13]

That was at best an approximation of the truth. A famous story told by his daughter Mamie, describing how she once observed him in the process of composition, indicates that Dickens did not so much abandon acting as incorporate it into his daily routine:

> My father wrote busily and rapidly at his desk, when he suddenly jumped up from his chair and rushed to a mirror which hung near, and in which I could see the reflection of some extraordinary facial contortions which he was making. He returned rapidly to his desk, wrote furiously for a few moments, and then went again to the mirror. The facial pantomime was resumed, and then turning toward, but evidently not seeing, me, he began talking rapidly in a low voice.[14]

At the time of his audition he was fully prepared, having prescribed for himself a special "system for learning parts" and rehearsed them with typical thoroughness.[15] As he pointed out to Forster, some of the actions he chose to polish, such as walking in and out and sitting down on a chair, "often four, five, six hours a day," indicated a robustly "business-like" understanding of show business.[16] A whole career might hang on the actor's physical prowess (Mathews himself had secured his first role because of his fencing skills), and Dickens was leaving nothing to chance.

But even if he had rearranged his audition at Covent Garden, any ambition Charles Dickens might have had to become the new Charles Mathews had two serious flaws. The first is that there already was a new Charles Mathews—namely, his son. Having attended public school and "been made a pet of in many aristocratic families," Charles Mathews the younger would make his debut in December 1835 in a farce entitled *The Old and Young Stager,* and would soon establish a reputation as an elegant, charming, light (some said lightweight) comedian.[17] Originally celebrated as "a sort of aristocratic prototype of Sam Weller,"[18] and later an unhappy victim of bankruptcy, he was another Charles whose life was played out in the wings of Dickens's life. The more serious flaw, however, is that, with the exception of a handful of star names, most actors lived in a world that was considered bohemian only by its most starry-eyed admirers. More often it was thought to be crawling with vice. William Charles Macready, an actor who was also viewed as an intellectual and a gentleman, was an exception even in his own eyes. In 1836, having just returned from a performance that was drunkenly slurred through by one of the actors, he wrote despairingly in his diary about being "compelled to be a party to the blunders, the ignorance, and wanton buffoonery, which . . . degrade the poor art I am labouring in."[19] A more recent survey is even blunter in its assessment of the theatrical profession at the time of Dickens's aborted audition: "It would be no exaggeration to say that, in general, the actor of 1830 was a social and artistic outcast."[20] Short-term liaisons between well-to-do young men and poor actresses were common enough, but it is hard to imagine the Beadnells being thrilled with a reversal of the gender roles.

Most of Dickens's other attempts to find work were extensions of what he was already doing. In December 1832 he was in Lambeth, helping his uncle to organize the election campaign for Charles Tennyson, the prominent Liberal MP, and crowing that he had been asked to find "no less than *Eighteen* young men" to serve as polling clerks. In the same letter he promised his correspondent some work on the *Mirror of Parliament* "when the Session commences."[21] Evidently he was gaining influence among his fellow journalists: Forster, who became the *True Sun*'s drama critic in 1832, the same year its staff went on strike, noted that it was Dickens who "had been spokesperson for the recalcitrant reporters, and conducted their case triumphantly."[22] Yet for all his growing reputation, Dickens was canny enough to realize that there were occasions on which he might need to disguise his ambition, and that sometimes the best way to get ahead is to bow one's head. Accordingly, during the next parliamentary recess, in June 1833, he wrote to Richard Earle, private secretary to Edward Stanley, who had earlier been so impressed by his accuracy as a reporter, asking to be considered if any opportunity arose in which "the services of a Short Hand Writer are required." The letter concluded: "I will not detain you further than by again apologising for writing to you, and venturing to express a hope that you will not consider my application impertinent, and consequently unworthy of notice"—a sentence whose stiff politeness comes close to collapsing into the 'umble writhing of Uriah Heep.[23] Finally, John Barrow tried to raise his nephew's professional profile by holding a dinner party, on July 27, 1833, at which he introduced Charles to the well-connected *Morning Chronicle* journalist John Payne Collier. Once again Dickens was prepared to sing for his supper, this time literally, the invitation to Collier having been sweetened by the promise that the young reporter "was cheerful company and a good singer of a comic song." The evening turned out to be "merry," Collier wrote in his diary, with Dickens being pressed to sing "The Dandy Dog's-Meat Man" ("then much in vogue with the lower classes"), and a composition of his own entitled "Sweet Betsy Ogle." Though Dickens was still so young that "he had no vestige of beard or whiskers," Collier had reason "to think so well of his abilities . . . that I had little hesitation in recommending him to the proprietor of the *Morning Chronicle*."[24] Whether these "abilities" included Dickens's journalism or his social skills, he does not say; perhaps the fog of a merry evening had made it hard to tell them apart. In any case, he was a powerful friend to make.

Sadly, in terms of enhancing his eligibility as a suitor for Maria, by then it was too late. From the evidence of Dickens's letters, in which he wavered between wanting to pick over the bones of old quarrels and the more generous impulse to forgive and forget, their relationship unraveled with painful inevitability. The process was hastened by some gossipy meddling by her friend Mary Anne Leigh, and was punctuated by a series of unhappy social occasions. On February 11, Dickens's parents held a party (the invitation fashionably promised "Quadrilles / 8 o'clock") to celebrate his twenty-first birthday. The account of the evening he later published as "Birthday Celebrations" may have massaged the truth for dramatic effect, but in terms of the main events it appears to have been written from the heart. "Behind a door," he wrote, "in the crumby part of the night when wine-glasses were to be found in unexpected spots, I spoke to Her—spoke out to Her." She replied with a "short and dreadful word of three letters, beginning with a B—which, as I remarked at the moment, 'scorched my brain.'" Presumably the word was "Boy," a particularly hurtful thing to say to someone on the day he could legally marry, although Maria might have felt her stance was justified by how Dickens went on to demonstrate his maturity, which was to get blindingly drunk. That signaled the first break.

Shortly afterwards, Dickens threw himself into organizing an evening of amateur dramatics at Bentinck Street to celebrate Shakespeare's birthday on April 23. It was an ambitious program: J. H. Payne's *Clari; or, The Maid of Milan* (a two-act opera that featured the hit song "Home, Sweet Home!"), followed by P. P. O'Callaghan's one-act farce *The Married Bachelor,* and finally R. Brinsley Peake's two-act musical *Amateurs and Actors.* For someone whose eligibility as a suitor had come under scrutiny, Dickens's choice of parts was brave and somewhat surprising: in the final piece, for example, he played a poor actor who sings a plaintive ballad about being the victim of Cupid's tyranny, which was hardly likely to endear him to Maria or her family. The rules he laid down as company stage manager suggest that the process was causing him a certain amount of strain:

1. Mr. Dickens is desirous that it should be distinctly understood by his friends that it is his wish to have a Series of Weekly Rehearsals for some time, experience having already shewn that the Rehearsals are perhaps the most amusing part of private Theatricals . . .

2. It is earnestly hoped that Ladies & Gentlemen who may have somewhat inferior parts assigned them in any piece will recollect the impossibility of giving any performer a principal character, and that

they will be consequently induced rather to consult the general convenience and amusement than individual feeling upon the subject.[25]

Dickens may have been sending himself up, but for the joke to work he must already have earned a reputation for being no less exacting. Presumably the other Ladies and Gentlemen would not have been surprised by the playbill he had printed that announced: "Private Theatricals. Stage Manager, Mr. Charles Dickens. On Saturday Evening, April 27, 1833, *At Seven o'clock precisely.*"[26] It would be some years before a standardized time was introduced across the country, largely as a response to the development of railway timetables; but nobody receiving one of Dickens's playbills would have been in any doubt that for him time was measured in absolute rather than relative terms.

Some of this twitchiness can be explained by the sheer difficulty of producing three plays to a high standard within such tight limits of budget and location. Reading Dickens's letters, as he describes how "the *Corps dramatique* are all anxiety, the scenery is all completing rapidly, the machinery is finished, the Curtain hemmed, the Orchestra complete," it is easy to forget that he was referring to a scene taking place in his front room rather than Covent Garden.[27] But his mood also seems to have been influenced by the letters he was writing to Maria, which are shot through with the difficulty of knowing whether he was a "principal character" in the drama of her life or merely one of the "somewhat inferior parts." Having originally depicted himself in "The Bill of Fare" as a dashing young hero, a Hamlet-in-waiting, he seems finally to have realized that within the fixed social hierarchy of Lombard Street he was destined to be no more than an early prototype of T. S. Eliot's Prufrock, "one that will do / To swell a progress, start a scene or two, / . . . / At times, indeed, almost ridiculous— / Almost, at times, the Fool."[28]

Perhaps this is why his letters of the time are so theatrical in tone. Or perhaps using such language was simply the most honest way in which he could detach himself from a relationship that had been rooted in performance from the start. Repeatedly, they drift into blank verse ("I have but one word more to say . . ."), stiffen into melodramatic poses ("the miser-able reckless wretch I am"), and even enlist the help of Shakespeare. The last surviving letter was sent via Kolle, who was acting as intermediary and buffer, with a note explaining that it had been written "sans pride, sans reserve sans anything but an evident wish to be reconciled."[29] The allusion is to Jacques's "seven ages of man" speech in *As You Like It,* and at a first glance one might assume that Dickens was borrowing the ex-ample of "the lover," but that is not the case. He is echoing the last line of Jacques's speech, describing the final scene of life: "Sans teeth, sans eyes, sans taste, sans everything."[30] As a way of summing up his relationship with Maria, Dickens's letter was less an appeal than a death rattle.

Looking back in 1845, Dickens had a more balanced view of this early infatuation. "If any one had interfered with my very small Cupid," he told his friend Thomas Powell, "I don't know what absurdity I might not have committed. But having plenty of rope he hanged himself, beyond all chance of restoration."[31] Such sturdy common sense was certainly one way of dealing with rejection. The other was to cling to Maria all the more tightly once she was available only as a memory.

Over the years that followed, his lines in "The Bill of Fare" turned out to be oddly prophetic: "The impression that mem'ry engraves in my heart/Is all I have left, and with that I ne'er part." The idea is a com-mon one in Dickens's writing, from *Great Expectations'* Joe musing over an epitaph for his father's gravestone ("Whatsume'er the failings on his part, Remember reader he were that good in his hart") to the essay "First Fruits," which, along with many other "firsts" in life, including "the first pair of trousers" and "the first oyster," gives pride of place to the lingering sweetness of first love: "You may have loved Fanny, Maria, Louisa, Sarah, Martha, Harriet, or Charlotte, or fancied that you loved them since then; but in your heart of hearts you still keep the portrait of your first love, bright."[32] Perhaps it is just a coincidence that in this list Maria's name comes directly after that of Dickens's sister, whose success at the Royal Academy had caused him so much pain. In any case, it was in fiction that Dickens kept the memories of his first love brightest. Sometimes this involved small acts of comic revenge. The middle-class young ladies in his early novels, in particular, are routinely exposed as monsters of vanity and snobbery, however hard they try to hide their ruthless competitiveness behind little giggles and pouts. The enchanting Miss Snevellicci in *Nicholas Nickleby* even has Portsmouth lodgings "in a place called Lombard Street," a double private joke that brought together where Dickens had come from and where he had once dreamed of ending up. When he came to writing about David Copperfield's first love, on the other hand, he endowed Dora with everything that had so charmed him in Maria, from her curly hair to her yappy lapdog. Killing her off in the novel then allowed him to preserve her on the page, as if his ink were actually a form of embalming fluid, keeping her as fresh and fragile for his readers as when he had first met her.

But that was not the end of the story. In 1855, at a time when Dickens was "altogether in a dishevelled state of mind," haunted by "one happiness I have missed in life, and one friend and companion I have never made," Maria wrote to him out of the blue.[33] The sight of her handwriting had an astonishing effect. "Three or four and twenty years vanished like a dream," he told her, "and I opened [your letter] with the touch of my young friend David Copperfield when he was in love."[34] It was a telling parallel. In *David Copperfield*, Dickens's hero explains that he, too, suffers from an "old unhappy loss or want of something," but in his case it turns out that this something is actually a someone. It is Agnes, David eventually realizes, the companion of his youth, who is the only person capable of filling the aching void in his heart. Was Dickens's own old flame similarly capable of smoldering back into life? They exchanged further letters that were chattily intimate on her side and almost desperately needy on his. "I know that the Dream I lived in did me good, refined my heart, and made me patient and persevering," he explained; and in response to her warning that she had become "toothless, fat, old, and ugly," he reassured her that his feelings for her had not changed. "You are always the same in my remembrance," he told her. "You ask me to treasure what you tell me, in my heart of hearts. O see what I have cherished there, through all this time and all these changes!"[35] Exclamation marks are usually a bad sign in Dickens, working like little distress flares to warn the reader that his rhetoric has pitched itself higher than his thought, and in this case he genuinely seems not to have considered the possibility that his memory of her might no longer fit the reality. Their reunion was a crushing disappointment. She had indeed become "*very* fat! and quite common place," Georgina Hogarth tartly observed, and her tinkling voice had become a vehicle for nervous prattle.[36] Everything had changed—everything, that is, except for her yappy little dog. In the hallway Dickens calmly contemplated his old rival, and noted how well Maria's pet had managed to defy the aging process. It had been stuffed.

Dickens's first response to the altered Maria was to recoil in alarm, as can be seen in his remaining letters to her, which swerve away from the heartfelt to the merely hearty, and eventually peter out into a series of limp excuses for not seeing her, as he is "going off, I don't know where or how far, to ponder about I don't know what"—a sad collapse from his previous protestations of constancy. His more lasting response, a year later, was to introduce the character of Flora into *Little Dorrit*, whose hefty approximation of her earlier girlishness, and machine-gun delivery of conversational odds and ends, so alarm her former lover Arthur Clennam:

> "If we talk of not having changed," said Flora, who, whatever she said, never came once to a full stop, "look at Papa, is not Papa precisely what he was when you went away, isn't it cruel and unnatural of Papa to be such a reproach to his own child, if we go on in this way much longer people who don't know us will begin to suppose that I am Papa's Mama!"
>
> That must be a long time hence, Arthur considered.
>
> "Oh Mr. Clennam you insincerest of creatures," said Flora, "I perceive already you have not lost your old way of paying compliments, your old way when you used to pretend to be so sentimentally struck you know—at least I don't mean that, I—oh I don't know what

I mean!" Here Flora tittered confusedly, and gave him one of her old glances.

In this exquisitely painful scene, it is little words like "old" that carry the burden of the years, because Flora's "old glances" are her former glances, but they come out of a face that has indeed become old. More painful still is the way in which the pair's awkward negotiation of the passage of time is dramatized by Dickens's own perfect comic timing. Like a ventriloquist's dummy, the more Flora's speech seems to be careering out of control, the more energetically Dickens can be seen pulling her strings and making her mouth clatter up and down. It is a brilliantly achieved piece of writing. It is also a good example of Dickens's skill at translating his private experience into fiction. After all, if Flora resembled Maria in 1855, she was also painfully close to himself in 1833, when his letters to Maria had been full of equally breathless confidences. "Our meetings of late have been little more than so many displays of heartless indifference on the one hand while on the other they have never failed to prove a fertile source of wretchedness and misery," he wrote, in one unpunctuated burst of feeling, "and seeing as I cannot fail to do that I have engaged in a pursuit which has long been worse than hopeless and a further perseverance in which can only expose me to deserved ridicule."[37] Clearly Flora wasn't the only one who didn't know when to stop.

Dickens's skill at turning such memories into the fuel for comedy allowed him to do more than shake his head over his failure to anticipate how much Maria had changed. It also reassured him, secure in the new social position that his writing had won him, that the Beadnells had been equally lacking in foresight. In her later years, drink-soaked and sentimental, Maria would kiss the spot on the couch where Dickens used to sit, and refer to him as the "poor reporter" whom her father "would not tolerate."[38] But by then Dickens had shown how wrong her father was—and had done so not only by becoming successful, which has always been a good way of answering one's critics, but by writing novels that gave sympathetic attention to the very people and ideas he found most disagree-

able. A novel like *Little Dorrit* is a model of toleration. It even manages
to find a place for Mr. F's aunt, a grim old woman who startles Arthur
Clennam by delivering herself of implacably hostile observations such as
"the Great Fire of London was not the fire in which your uncle George's
workshops was burned down," or "When we lived at Henley, Barnes's
gander was stolen by tinkers." Her comic liveliness far outlasts her function in the plot; as so often in Dickens's best writing, when she enters a
scene the center and margins of the novel swap places. Ultimately she
serves a double purpose. In the context of *Little Dorrit,* her gnomic exclamations offer a dark commentary on the spectacle of old lovers fondly
reminiscing; with her habit of making observations such as "There's mile-
stones on the Dover road!," she is like a tragic chorus shrunk to the dimensions of one scowling widow. In the context of Dickens's life, though,
her interruptions stretch much further back. They are like a grotesque
caricature of Mrs. Beadnell's conversation-ending snubs. Still trying to
break the couple up, but now reduced to blurting out random one-liners,
Mrs. Beadnell reappears in the novel as Mr. Dickin's final revenge.

Yet Dickens had been rewriting the events at Lombard Street long before *Little Dorrit.* "The Bill of Fare" may not have fared especially well
as a literary calling-card, but on December 3, 1833, only a few months
after his separation from Maria, he wrote to Kolle to announce that "A
Sunday Out of Town," the story he had submitted anonymously to the
Monthly Magazine, had appeared in the latest issue, retitled "A Dinner
at Poplar Walk." "Knowing the interest (or thinking I know the interest) you are kind enough to take in my movements I have the vanity to
make this communication," he wrote coolly, before dropping the mask
in a postscript that revealed how significant this moment was: "I am so
dreadfully nervous, that my hand shakes to such an extent as to prevent
my writing a word legibly."[39] It was his first published piece of fiction,
and the most important sign yet that there might be other ways to "rise in
life," as Charles Mathews had sung, than by taking a hot-air balloon. As
for Maria Beadnell, who would by a cruel coincidence of fate end up in
the same cemetery as Dickens's later mistress, Ellen Ternan, she deserved

better than to be turned into a figure of fun. In many ways, Dickens had her to thank for sharpening and directing his ambition. He acknowledged as much himself. In 1855, at the point when his memory was still flushed with romance, he wrote to John Forster to explain that his original pursuit of her had been successful in one way: it had given him "a determination to overcome all the difficulties" that stood in his path.

The events of those years may not have been out of the ordinary—there has never been a shortage of teenage boys keen to impress girls who are socially out of reach—but in this case they had far-reaching consequences. For as Dickens later admitted, it was this relationship, and the anxiety it gave him about being "low" (an idea that would continue to nag away at him), that "lifted me up into that newspaper life, and floated me away over a hundred men's heads."[40]

CHAPTER FIVE

"Here We Are!"

Anyone who picked up the December 1833 issue of the *Monthly Magazine* and turned to "A Dinner at Poplar Walk" on pages 617–624 would have been forgiven for scanning it quickly and moving on. At first glance, there was little to suggest that a major talent was being incubated in these eight compact pages. Even after Dickens had secured his reputation, the story remained largely unread, creating a pattern of neglect that has continued to the present day. "A Dinner at Poplar Walk" is the ugly duckling of Dickens's career. But it is worth examining carefully, not only for what it reveals about his state of mind at the end of 1833, but also for the clues it offers about the direction his pen would continue to travel in for several years to come.

The story begins cautiously, even coyly, with a description of the central character:

> Mr. Augustus Minns was a bachelor of *about* forty, as he said—of about eight-and-forty, as his friends said. He was always exceedingly clean, precise, and *tidy,* perhaps somewhat priggish, and the most "retiring man in the world." He usually wore a brown frockcoat without a wrinkle, light inexplicables [trousers] without a spot, a neat neckerchief with a remarkably neat tie, and boots without a fault; moreover, he always carried a brown silk umbrella. He was a clerk in Somerset House, or, as he said, he held "a responsible situation under Government." He had a good and increasing salary, in addition to some 10,000*l.* of his own (invested in the funds), and he occupied a first floor in Tavistock-street, Covent Garden, where he had resided for twenty years.

At first the writing seems to side with the hero, by using many of the same words he might choose to describe himself. As the story develops, however, it becomes clear that this is merely a pose designed to set him up for the events that follow. His peaceful breakfast is interrupted by "an appalling creaking of boots on the staircase, accompanied by a pattering noise," and soon afterwards his cousin Octavius Bagshaw bursts in, preceded by a pink-eyed poodle "dressed in a suit of fleecy-hosiery," like a canine parody of Minns's own elegant attire. What follows is a comedy of manners that depends upon Bagshaw's blithe disregard for manners. After dusting his boots with a table napkin, he coolly observes his dog ruining the curtains, after which he relents and locks it outside the door, where it sets up "a most appalling howling" and vigorously scratches the paint off the bottom panels. Worse still, Bagshaw invites Minns to dinner, in the secret hope of gaining a legacy for his son—a proposal that results in a miserable journey there, a painfully tedious meal, and an even more miserable journey home. Viewed in this light, almost every detail in the opening description turns out to be a veiled warning. Minns's prudence makes him a target for greedy relatives; his neat clothes are vulnerable to grimy children—first a spoiled brat on the coach, who "rubbed its shoes on his new drab trowsers," and then his nephew, who paws at him "after dabbling half-an-hour in raspberry jam and custard"; even his favorite brown silk umbrella is lost. And throughout, Minns tolerates these abuses with just the occasional grimace and groan, which together give a good indication of the kind of story he reluctantly finds himself in. It is a modern pantomime.

Dickens, who adored pantomime, would later claim that it was "a mirror of life"; and in "The Pantomime of Life," an article he published in *Bentley's Miscellany* shortly before he edited the great clown Grimaldi's *Memoirs* in 1838, he pointed out that its irresistible spirit could not always be confined to the theater. Observe an old gentleman stumbling in the street, Dickens writes, and you will see how the crowd that gathers roars with laughter as they cuff him about: "Every time the elderly gentleman struggles to get up, his relentless persecutors knock him down again.

The spectators are convulsed with merriment! And when at last the elderly gentleman does get up, and staggers away, despoiled of hat, wig, and clothing, himself battered to pieces, and his watch and money gone, they are exhausted with laughter, and express their merriment and admiration in rounds of applause."

Presumably Dickens does not intend his readers to find this as funny as the participants. The carefully judged disparity between weighty subject matter and airy tone is a technique he would develop throughout the 1830s, largely as a way of shocking his readers out of automatic responses to serious social problems. His decision in *Nicholas Nickleby* to write some of the most repulsive of the Dotheboys Hall scenes in a vein of light comedy, for example, dares us to laugh at or ignore child abuse in much the same way that his description of the old gentleman being beaten up dares us to laugh at or ignore mob violence. On each occasion, he warns us away from thoughtless reactions by seeming to expect them so fully. Even the *Pickwick Papers,* which is usually assumed to take place in a world far removed from the grim reality of elder abuse, reminds us on several occasions how vulnerable comedy is to real life. As early as the third chapter, Dickens tells the story of "a low pantomime actor" who rises up from his deathbed to perform, despite the fact that his "grotesquely ornamented head" is "trembling with paralysis." He begs for money, and as the narrator turns away after putting a few shillings in his hand, "I heard the roar of laughter which followed his first tumble on to the stage." It is an early warning, in a book that on the surface seems so sunny and upbeat, that the victims of slapstick violence can bruise like anyone else.

Clearly Minns belongs to some other category of clown. This is not only because he lives in much more comfortable circumstances, but also because nothing that happens to him goes any deeper than the surface. His greatest misfortunes are jam and custard stains rather than bloodstains, the custard being a playful nod to the tradition from which he comes, where the only thing funnier than a man getting a custard pie in the face is the same thing happening to one who is inordinately proud of his appearance. Here, too, Minns's prissy horror at the dog snuffling round his flat is funny not because Dickens outwardly pokes fun at him, but because he seems to sympathize with him so fully. Thus, when Minns casts "a diabolical look at the dog, who, with his hind-legs on the floor, and his fore-paws resting on the table, was dragging a bit of bread-and-butter out of a plate, which, in the ordinary course of things, it was natural to suppose he would eat with the buttered side next to the carpet," the finicky syntax illustrates Minns's tidy-mindedness, and draws out the sentence to show these messy events unfolding in his eyes with almost hypnotic slowness; but in purposefully driving on to its conclusion, it also dramatizes how unavoidable they are. For in a slapstick world the fact that the bread falls butter-side down is not simply bad luck; it is as inevitable as what happens when one pantomime clown has the bright idea of tapping a fellow clown on the shoulder just as he bends down to pick up a plank of wood. Minns is funny, that is, not just because he is routinely humiliated, but because he attempts to retain his dignity in a world where chance has been replaced by a form of malign necessity—one where every dog is guaranteed to misbehave, and every child has sticky fingers. It is a world that entraps him ever more tightly the harder he fights to escape it.

If Minns is one type of clown, the long-suffering stooge, his cousin is another type altogether: the wise-cracking comedian, whose theatrical entrance ("enter Octavius") marks him out as a character who is used to playing to the gallery. "He always spoke at the top of his voice," the narrator explains, "and always said the same thing half-a-dozen times." The first thing he repeats, "How are you?," may not be much of a catchphrase, but it is no worse than Grimaldi's cheery "Here we are!"; and everything else he does suggests that he, too, is the representative of a class.[1] A former corn-chandler who has "realised a moderate fortune" through his trade and retired to *"the country"* (i.e., the suburbs), he is the epitome of the lower-middle-class man made good.

That social category, "lower middle class," would not be formally identified until the early 1850s, but as early as the 1820s it was widely understood to be a growing sector of the population, consisting largely of shopkeepers and small businessmen, who were frequently depicted as shabby or vulgar and almost always as figures of fun.[2] In fiction they were sometimes given dreams of upward mobility, although their very names, like that of "Snooks" the grocer in a *New Monthly Magazine* sketch from 1822, indicated that such dreams existed primarily to be smiled at by an indulgent reader.[3] Dickens was far more sympathetic, in part because, as George Gissing observed, it was to this class, "a social status so peculiarly English, so rich in virtues yet so provocative of satire, he by origin belonged," and in part because he was keenly aware of the difficulties confronting anyone who hoped to leave it behind.[4] A novel like *Little Dorrit* offers an epic version of this struggle, reflected in Fanny Dorrit's lofty conviction that she is superior to her surroundings, and in painfully comic scenes such as John Chivery's proposal to Little Dorrit—a scene in which Chivery dresses up in a plum-colored coat, embroidered vest, striped trousers, and "a cane like a little finger-post," and makes a speech that launches itself at gentility ("I know very well that your high-souled brother, and likewise your spirited sister, spurn me from a heighth") but that never gets beyond the swagger of an East End swell.

"A Dinner at Poplar Walk" is far less ambitious in scale, but it, too, shows how sensitive Dickens was to the fine calibrations of class. Minns's complaint that his cousin is a "vulgar fellow" is duly borne out in Bagshaw's behavior: "'Don't you think you'd like the ham better,' interrupted Minns, 'if you cut it the other way?' as he saw, with feelings which it is impossible to describe, that his visitor was cutting, or rather maiming, the ham, in utter violation of all established rules." The 1830s saw a marked increase of interest in etiquette manuals designed to explain these rules. Most were aimed at the same people who bought other kinds of improving literature, and they exploited a similar mixture of ambition and fear. The vogue had reached its peak by 1850, when the "Copperfield Advertiser," a tear-out pamphlet that surrounded each monthly installment of *David Copperfield*, was including advertisements for such guides as *The Good Boy Henry; or, The Young Child's Book of Manners* and *Manners and Customs in Ye England in 1849*. Dickens's novel, too, offers a crash course in dining etiquette, largely by describing meals at which it is sorely lacking. David's "little housewarming," for example, turns into a drink-sodden disaster, while a dinner at the Waterbrooks', though undeniably genteel, runs to the other extreme by being too dull to be enjoyable.

Meals were important to Dickens, serving as useful reminders of the fundamental physical needs shared by everyone, regardless of birth or breeding; but in his fiction they are more often occasions for making social distinctions, table manners being as much an index of class as flashy clothes or dropped aitches. Minns's agonies as he watches his cousin hacking at the ham anticipate Herbert Pocket's interventions in *Great Expectations,* as he offers Pip good-natured tips such as "a dinner-napkin will not go into a tumbler," and "in London it is not the custom to put the knife in the mouth—for fear of accidents." Both stories make comic capital out of their readers' fears that they might fit into new company no more comfortably than a knife in someone's mouth. Even though there was nothing intrinsically wrong with them, in more refined social circles they might still feel like—to borrow Mary Douglas's famous definition of dirt—"matter out of place."[5]

As "A Dinner at Poplar Walk" picks up momentum, Dickens can be seen turning these feelings of social awkwardness into a style. The brat that Minns encounters on the coach not only rubs its shoes on his new trousers, but also kicks him throughout the journey; Dickens describes how "the interesting infant, . . . with its agreable countenance, contrived to tax Mr. Minns's ingenuity, in the 'art of self-defence,' during the ride." Words such as "interesting" and "agreable" are thick with irony, but they also provide Minns with a suitable linguistic environment. Like Minns, who is forced to travel alongside a vicious child and an indulgent mother, they do not fit into the company in which they find themselves. They, too, appear to be out of place. At Minns's cousin's house, similarly, Dickens is keen to open up a gap between the high ideas his hosts have of themselves, and the far less impressive reality of their situation. His story was written at a time when it was a common tactic to treat the idea of the *petite bourgeoisie* with comic literalness, by describing them as small in stature, small-minded, and so on; and Dickens goes a stage further by making the little and the large repeatedly knock up against each other. In effect, Minns is a modern Gulliver, who has landed in an unfamiliar social world but cannot work out whether he is in Lilliput or Brobdingnag, and Dickens joins in the joke by describing the "garden" of Minns's hosts as "a small, loose bit of gravelled ground," and the Cupid on either side of their front door as "perched upon a heap of large chalk flints." Similar disparities of scale extend indoors, where Minns is taken by a "stumpy boy" in "high-lows" [ankle-boots] into "a small drawing-room" packed with a dozen people waiting for dinner. The same double perspective is reflected in the name of Minns's cousin, Octavius Bagshaw, which neatly splices classical grandeur with down-to-earth Britishness; and the joke is taken even further in the name of his nephew, Alexander Augustus Bagshaw, which manages to bring together two world-conquering leaders in the shape of one grubby little boy.

Yet Augustus Minns is hardly in a position to sneer at the pretensions of his relatives. For all his respectable address and "responsible situation," the fact remains that he is a clerk, and in making his prized possession an umbrella Dickens hints that he may be no less vulgar than the matching Cupids outside his cousin's door. In Dickens's imaginative world, umbrellas are almost exclusively working-class or lower-middle-class accessories. (By the time E. M. Forster wrote *Howards End,* the thought had hardened into a truism: Forster's plot turns on the umbrella lost at a classical-music concert by Leonard Bast, a clerk who is engaged in a dogged struggle to improve himself.) The pattern stretches across his career, from the "shabby-genteel" men in *Sketches by Boz,* who hang around in the City "leaning on great, dropsical, mildewed umbrellas," to Silas Wegg in *Our Mutual Friend,* whose umbrella, when furled, looks like "an unwholesomely-forced lettuce." Perhaps Wegg shares a supplier with Mrs. Gamp, whose huge umbrella in *Martin Chuzzlewit* is "in colour like a faded leaf."[6] Augustus Minns's version may be made out of brown silk, but it is still an umbrella, and is therefore little more than a snobbish enhancement of an everyday object, like gold faucets or a diamond-encrusted toothpick. To put this another way, Minns is presented as a character who has ideas above his station, and Dickens's writing implies that perhaps we should expect nothing less from someone whose name brings together the making and breaking of empires with far more modest associations: the minor, the minion, the minnow. His story responds with all the cruel logic of caricature. What does a caricaturist do to subjects who are not especially intelligent? He reduces their brains to the size of a pea. What about people who are fat? He makes them ripple and spread lardily across the page. So what does Dickens do with a character who is vulnerable to being demeaned and diminished? He ruthlessly cuts him down to size.

A number of ideas in Dickens's first story would become central to his later fiction. Minns's shuttling between his apartments and his cousin's house dramatizes an interest in unwelcome relations that would climax with the plot of *Bleak House,* which asks "What connexion can there be?" between people and places that at first appear wholly distinct, and eventually reveals that those at the top of the social world are as unavoidably connected to those at the bottom as a body and its shadow. There is also room in "A Dinner at Poplar Walk" for some of Dickens's quirkier imaginative obsessions. The fact that Octavius Bagshaw announces his arrival with "an appalling creaking of boots," for example, has nothing to do with the main thrust of the story, but everything to do with Dickens's interest in boots, which he seems to have thought of as intrinsically comic objects, and frequently described as if they had lives independent of their owners. When Dombey approaches Edith in *Dombey and Son,* Dickens explains how he "betook his creaking boots towards her," while in *Great Expectations* Jaggers wears "great, bright, creaking boots" which seem to laugh "in a dry and suspicious way." The notion that somebody's personality resides in his boots is closely connected to Dickens's interest in theater, where an actor trying to establish a character might decide to work from the bottom up but not get much further than choosing the right kind of footwear. Alternatively, it could be a relic of Dickens's childhood, given that children are much closer to the ground than adults, and so might be expected to have a correspondingly greater sensitivity to objects usually found on that level. Or perhaps it is a combination of the two: in an *Uncommercial Traveller* paper, Dickens recalls being taken as a child to the Theatre Royal at Chatham, where he observes how the wicked Richard III sleeps on a sofa that is much too short for him, "and how fearfully his conscience troubled his boots."

More recent associations may also have played a part in Dickens's choice of subject matter. Mocking a middle-class dinner party is likely to have been especially satisfying after his experiences at the Beadnells', and it is possible that his own father makes a cameo appearance in the form of "a little smirking man with red whiskers" who keeps interrupting the dinner with theatrical anecdotes and puns. The story was also carefully pitched to appeal to the tastes of its readers. Short comic tales of urban life had become a popular staple of journals—so popular, in fact, that they had recently become the targets of satire. In October 1833, at about the time that Dickens submitted his story to the *Monthly Magazine,* a rival journal, the *Metropolitan,* ran a comic dialogue in which the editor lamented the quality and quantity of contributions sent to him. The "pyramids of papers" included "a host of 'Uncles Rogers, Cousins Bobs,'— 'Aunt Deborah's Spectacles,'—'Brother Tom's Nose' . . . and other *light* papers, as they are called; the light papers, *entre nous,* being the *heaviest* of the whole set."[7] When Dickens republished his story in *Sketches by Boz,* he retitled it "Mr. Minns and His Cousin," so he was certainly aware of the market for such subjects.

A more particular influence was John Poole, whose hit farce *Paul Pry* (1825) had featured a character with an umbrella he deliberately leaves behind as an excuse to return for a snoop around; his catchphrase "I hope I don't intrude" was still making audiences chuckle at the end of Dickens's life. Dickens thought well enough of Poole to be instrumental in securing a series of grants for him from the Royal Literary Fund, and in 1847 he donated some of the profits from his amateur theatrical performances at Liverpool and Manchester to the now impoverished author. In addition to borrowing Paul Pry's umbrella as a comic prop, Dickens also remembered Poole's chatty stories, two of which can be seen flickering behind "A Dinner at Poplar Walk." Both stories discover rich comedy in the heirs and graces of ordinary people struggling to gain some personal advantage in an increasingly crowded social world.

The direct source is "The Inconvenience of a Convenient Distance," which Isaac Pocock adapted for Covent Garden in 1830 as the farce *The Omnibus; or, A Convenient Distance,* taking Poole's initial situation of a fussy old bachelor tormented by his greedy relatives and adding an obnoxious young nephew, who unwittingly reveals his mother's scheming when he cries out, "You mean to leave us all you have, you know, when you hop the twig."[8] A more oblique but equally funny line of influence can be traced back to "My Aunt's Poodle," which features a poodle with a limp, scalded skin, mangy fur, and damaged eyes. It answers not to the name of Lucky, as the old joke has it, but Lovely, and Poole's story revolves around the attempts of a group of relatives to ingratiate themselves with its doting owner, who threatens to disinherit anyone who upsets her beloved pet. Invited to dinner, they fawn over the evil old mutt, who responds by getting as muddy as possible in the rain and then jumping into their laps. There are faint stirrings here of Dickens's Alexander "fixing the print of his paws on Minns's trowsers" and tactlessly crying out, "Do stop, godpa—I like you—Ma says I am to coax you to leave me all your money!" although Dickens's ending, in which Minns decides not to leave his relatives a penny, is far more decisive than Poole's, which ends tantalizingly and somewhat menacingly with the observation: "My Aunt Margaret's property is all funded; and of her twelve hundred a-year, she regularly lays by two-thirds. This we happen to know."[9]

The other vein of periodical publication Dickens was tapping might initially seem less promising, but it would ultimately prove just as important in defining the trajectory of his career. This was the educational writing that became especially popular after the Reform Bill, and that was principally aimed at readers with a little spare income and a large appetite for self-improvement. Instrumental in this shift away from high-brow journals were the publishers William and Robert Chambers, whose success with *Chambers's Edinburgh Journal,* launched in 1832, was followed by a string of cheap magazine titles, starting with *Information for the People,* and extending to include the *Miscellany of Useful and Entertaining Information, Papers for the People,* the *Pocket Miscellany,* and the *Repository of Instructive and Amusing Tracts.* Although they might not sound like much fun to modern ears, they proved hugely successful. While some of their rivals, such as the *Penny Magazine,* refused to print anything as frivolous as fiction, the Chambers brothers insisted on including short stories to sweeten the pill of knowledge—"a nice amusing tale," as William put it, "no ordinary trash about Italian castles, and daggers, and ghosts in the blue chamber, and similar nonsense, but something really good."[10] The strong implication was that really good stories were of the kind that did some good, adopting the ancient classical notion of instruction through entertainment for a self-consciously new class of readers.

The aims of the Chambers brothers were initially more democratic than this. On the *Journal's* second anniversary, in 1834, William outlined a model of distribution in which "one shepherd, upon a tract of mountain land, receives his copy, perhaps from an egg-market man or a travelling huckstry-woman," and after reading it he places it under a stone for a neighboring shepherd to read, while at the other end of the social scale copies would reach the most refined drawing rooms in the land. "In short," William wrote with urgent italics, "it *pervades the whole of society.*"[11] There is evidence to suggest that this, or something like it, did happen in a few isolated cases. In one Cambridgeshire village, five poor boys clubbed together to buy their weekly copy of *Chambers's,* while the workers of a cotton mill near Glasgow purchased a total of eighty-four copies of each issue.[12] For the most part, though—as one witness flatly stated in 1851 to a parliamentary inquiry into the general population's reading habits—the sale of publications like *Chambers's* was "almost exclusively confined to the middle classes . . . chiefly among small shopkeepers."[13] Working-class readers usually preferred their instructive entertainment in other forms, the cheaper and bloodier the better. In 1828 James Catnach, a publisher of street ballads and "true confessions," reputedly sold over a million copies of the "Last Dying Speech and Confession" of William Corder, the perpetrator of the notorious "Murder in the Red Barn"; and in 1837 the "execution papers" of James Greenacre, who killed and dismembered his fiancée, Hannah Brown, scattering her body parts around London, reached sales of 1.65 million copies.[14] To possess an issue of *Chambers's,* by contrast, was a badge of belonging, a sign that the reader was attempting to elevate himself out of the class in which he had been born—a reader like Dickens's Octavius Bagshaw, in fact, the former grocer who in later life spends his time earnestly discussing the education of his son and "disputing whether the classics should be made an essential part thereof."

The *Monthly Magazine* appears to have had a circulation of around six hundred copies, which was hardly a serious threat to the fifty thousand copies of *Chambers's,* let alone Catnach's hot presses. It did, though, contain a similar mixture of instruction and entertainment, albeit with a sharper political edge and a more generous slant towards fiction. The issue in which "A Dinner at Poplar Walk" appeared included twenty-eight other items, ranging from weighty economic commentary ("The Operation of Monopolies"), to popular science ("The Phenomena of Magnetism," "Progressive Degeneracy of the Human Race"), together with rousing episodes from military history, miniature romances, theatrical gossip, and much more. In effect, it was a sophisticated version of the miscellanies Dickens had enjoyed as a child, a fact that may have accounted for part of its appeal.

The December 1833 issue also included two further clues as to why Dickens may have chosen the *Monthly* to launch his writing career. The first was prestige: an editorial directed "To Our Subscribers" points out that the title was nearly fifty years old, during which time it had distinguished itself for "the continuation of talent" in its pages; indeed, the editor concludes, "there are few writers of our own century, that have been venerated or respected in letters, but whose sentiments may be traced through the pages of this periodical."[15] It was a shameless piece of self-promotion, but the notion of "continuation of talent" may have been especially attractive to a writer like Dickens, so concerned with his place in the literary order of things. Second, the *Monthly*'s politics were unapologetically radical: in November 1832 it noted with approval that nearly three thousand people had assembled in a tavern "in aid of the fortunes of the *True Sun*," which "in its short career has established itself in an unprecedented degree in the confidence and attachment of the working classes."[16] Dickens was contributing to the *True Sun* at the time, and the *Monthly* took a parallel political line; in its article on monopolies, it scoffed at "the aristocratical tone of our government, which has been the curse of our country for so many years," and concluded with the hope that "it will not be long ere talent will be freed from Tory trammels, fit only for an ignorant and barbarous age."[17] A note in "The Editor's Letter-Box" of the next issue, published in January 1834, made the point even more forcefully: "The MONTHLY MAGAZINE was founded upon the principle of political freedom and reform. We have faithfully pursued the path of its founders—eschewing the bondage of fashion, but supporting to the best of our belief the cause of Truth and Liberty."[18]

Despite its political idealism, or perhaps because of it, the *Monthly* was a precarious, shoestring operation. For all the attentions of its colorful editor, Captain Holland, a former mercenary who had bought the journal for £300 upon his return from Simón Bolívar's campaign in South America, it was never more than an issue or two ahead of the bailiffs, and eventually folded in 1843. The nearest recent parallel might be the small literary magazines of the 1960s, some of which enjoyed only a mayfly existence of an issue or two, while others scratched around for readers a little longer. Ian Hamilton has memorably described how he ran his poetry magazine, the *Review,* from a "poky, freezing and superbly squalid" flat in Soho, occasionally interrupted by a crumpled stranger he found on the stairs opening the magazine's mail and pocketing the stamped addressed envelopes.[19] It would be surprising if some of the smaller nineteenth-century magazines were run more efficiently. The basic equipment was the same, principally scissors and paste; and even though the emergence of steam presses in the 1820s had speeded up methods of production, Captain Holland's plaintive editorials in the *Monthly*, in which he apologized for having fallen behind with his correspondence, suggest that the day-to-day management was equally bohemian—a word soon to enter the language (the first recorded use is in 1848) to describe that densely populated artistic territory where idealism rubbed shoulders with ineptitude.[20] The fact that Holland could not afford to pay his contributors indicates that the *Monthly* was scarcely better off than a publication like *Holt's Journal*, whose editor, Thomas Lyttleton Holt, issued an advertisement in 1836 in which he complained about the "host of troubles" he was facing: "Beset by bailiffs, hunted by vindictive creditors, harassed by the harpies of the law, who will have their bond, or else no small number of pounds of flesh in the shape of my body, I am compelled to throw myself upon the good feeling of my readers, to raise the price of the magazine one halfpenny as the readiest means of relieving myself."[21] It collapsed shortly afterwards.

Compared to the impact Dickens had in the reporters' gallery, where he'd made "a great splash," his first foray into fiction created barely a ripple.[22] There were, however, three encouraging signs that "A Dinner at Poplar Walk" had touched a popular nerve. The first was a positive review in *Bell's New Weekly Messenger*, which described the sketch as "a choice bit of humour," albeit "somewhat exaggerated."[23] The second was its almost immediate reappearance in the *London Weekly Magazine*, a journal founded in 1832 by Henry Mayhew and originally entitled *The Thief*, which filled most of its pages with extracts pilfered from other publications.[24] (Dickens observed that the editors "have done me *the honor* of selecting my article," smartly balancing pleasure and pique at being singled out in this way.)[25] The third and most important sign, as Dickens wrote to Henry Kolle, was that "I have had a polite and flattering communication from The Monthly people requesting more papers."[26] He was being given the opportunity to show that a "continuation of talent" could rest in a single writer's hands.

In the years that followed, Dickens's critics were often tempted to treat him in a way that echoed Minns's reception of his cousin. To many he seemed as out of place in the house of fiction, a pushy *arriviste*, as Octavius Bagshaw in Minns's elegant Covent Garden apartments. Variations on the theme were still being offered towards the end of the century, when Lady Emily Lytton observed in a letter to the Reverend Whitwell Elwin that Dickens was "dreadfully vulgar," and that his characters fell far short of being "real ladies and gentlemen." This was evident, she concluded, from the fact that they generally "seem to do nothing but drink." Her *de haut en bas* comments were hardly significant as literary criticism, but they reflected a widely held prejudice about Dickens which usually had less to do with what he wrote than where he had come from. "Like the perpetual drinking," her correspondent pointed out, "the vulgarity belonged to the class from which Dickens sprung and was deeply ingrained in him. He never got rid of it. He could not even relish the company of gentlemen."[27]

That might have come as a surprise to Lady Lytton's grandfather, Edward Bulwer, who had become one of Dickens's closest literary advisers, and in whose stately home, Knebworth, Dickens had discussed the conclusion to *Great Expectations,* a novel intended to show that gentlemanly qualities were available to everyone regardless of the accident of birth. "O God bless him!" Pip penitently whispers to himself once he has discovered that the dull-witted but kindly Joe has paid off his debts. "O God bless this gentle Christian man." That placing of "Christian" between "gentle" and "man" is one of the subtlest interventions Dickens ever made in the period's social debates, where it forms a piece of shorthand for all the ingredients he considered necessary to make a true gentleman: honesty, humility, politeness, courage, and self-respect.[28] Such radical thinking was clearly lost on readers like Lady Lytton and the Reverend Elwin, but their suspicions accurately reflected how little Dickens had to say to them, or about them, compared to the material he had to work with lower down on the social scale. For more refined readers, who sometimes seemed to take it as a personal slight that he was not Thackeray, reading Dickens could be like a dialogue between two people speaking different languages. His early work offered even less encouragement to those who preferred fiction that dwelt on idealized models of conduct rather than on examples of ordinary human behavior. For instead of writing a country house comedy, or a society piece full of noblemen arching their eyebrows at each other, he decided to follow up "A Dinner at Poplar Walk" by doing what all fiction writers are routinely advised to do. He would write from experience.

From January 1834 to February 1835, starting with "Mrs. Joseph Porter, 'Over the Way,'" Dickens published eight more tales in the *Monthly Magazine,* and one ("Sentiment") in the racier pages of *Bell's Weekly Magazine.*[29] While they occupied the same geographic and imaginative terrain as "A Dinner at Poplar Walk," they dealt with the lives of an even wider range of ordinary Londoners, whose delicate social maneuverings in many cases reflected the vulnerability of their position. (The fact that Dickens was not paid for any of the stories may have increased his sensitivity towards the financial struggles of his characters.) Trapped in the growing no-man's-land between the lower and middle classes, these characters interact in ways that take on a noticeably dramatic air. This is not just a reflection of Dickens's own love of the theater. Historians of the period have noticed how, in a society where dreams of self-advancement encouraged people to reinvent themselves, even if this meant tidying up or ignoring their real situation, "public life became a site on which individuals and groups negotiated roles."[30] Eventually this culture of display would produce fictional characters like the Spangle Lacquers in *Punch,* a socialite couple who are so achingly fashionable that they buy a particular kind of ice because they believe it is "much colder" than its rivals, or the Veneerings in *Our Mutual Friend,* whose social origins are obscured by the dazzle of their possessions.[31] At this stage of Dickens's career, the outlines of the idea are blunter, but his treatment of it is also much funnier, as he plays a set of comic variations on what was increasingly being seen as one of the most painful problems confronting the lower middle class: the need to keep up appearances.

Fear of social humiliation is not intrinsically funny, of course, and it was not thought to be so at the time. In *The Great Metropolis* (1836), James Grant pointed out how many Londoners felt obliged to spend their money on lodgings in a "respectable" neighborhood, as if fitting in was only a matter of choosing the right place to live, even if as a result they might have nothing to eat but dry crusts for days on end. "They are finely dressed," he observed, "and everything appears respectable, as it is called, to the eye of visitors. Little do those visitors know the struggle they have to keep up appearances; little do they suppose they are kept up at the sacrifice of many of the necessaries of life." But even in these appalling circumstances some people remained vulnerable to humor. Grant describes one such individual: a "gentleman of some commercial note," who travels regularly from the east end to Westminster, wears cotton gloves for the first part of his journey, not anticipating any awkward meetings with the "fashionables" in that part of town; but as soon as he reaches Charing Cross, "he doffs his cotton ones, stows them in his pocket, and replaces them by a white kid pair."[32] He joins a list of comic examples that stretches from Dickens's Minns back to Shakespeare's Malvolio, all of whom are carefully dressed up by their creators in finery that actually exposes what it is trying to conceal. The idea that London forced a kind of double life onto its inhabitants is one that Dickens would later develop. In *Great Expectations,* as Wemmick walks into the city from his house in the suburbs, he gets "dryer and harder" and tightens his mouth into an inscrutable letter-box slit. Here, the change in Wemmick's appearance is a shell he grows every day to protect himself from the demands of his work in Jaggers's office. Dickens's early stories, by contrast, show that leading a double life might be more than just a way of coping with the pressures of London. It generated a protective bubble of fantasy, a way of blurring the distinction between how things were and how they ought to have been.

The best example, and one of the funniest stories Dickens ever wrote, is "Horatio Sparkins," published in the *Monthly* issue of February 1834. The most famous literary Horatio until then was to be found in *Hamlet,* where he is the hero's friend and confidant, his tragic sidekick, and Dickens's story plays on this knowledge by creating a farce of mistaken identities in which a modern Horatio attempts to step into the limelight. Sparkins is introduced into the household of Mr. Malderton, whose "successful speculations" in the City have "raised him from a situation of obscurity and comparative poverty, to a state of affluence." The members of the family quickly convince themselves that Sparkins must be a man of property and influence—in short, an eligible suitor for their frumpish daughter, and an excellent opportunity for further social leap-frogging. Over the course of two meetings, "the young man with the black whiskers and the white cravat" is transformed in their eyes from "the most gentleman-like young man I ever saw" to "a very genteel young man, certainly," even though he does little more than look mysterious and make gnomic observations such as "What is man? . . . I say, what is man?" The fact that this sounds like a botched line from *Hamlet* fails to rouse the family's suspicions. Nor does his "theatrical air," or the romantic speculation that "he must be somebody in disguise."

Delighted with their new social conquest, the Maldertons invite Horatio to join them at the pantomime, and the next day they go shopping for suitable clothes to wear, revealing their own true colors by stopping at a "dirty-looking" draper's that sells shoddy fashions at bargain prices. Serving behind the counter is the "mysterious, philosophical, romantic, metaphysical Sparkins," who is "suddenly converted into Mr. Samuel Smith . . . the junior partner in a slippery firm of some three weeks' existence." The joke is that the Malderton family has been treated to a pantomime slightly sooner than they were expecting, given that pantomimes were famous for scenes in which ordinary people and objects were transformed into more enchanting alternatives: a pumpkin swells into a glass coach; Cinderella's rags froth up into a ball gown. Here the process happens in reverse, as the family's dreams are brought crashing down to earth; but the real comedy of the situation is that they and their guest have been playing the same game of bluff all along. Their social affectations, Dickens implies, are no less ridiculous than the fantasies of a shop assistant in a flashy new business, as they force their groom-cum-gardener "into a white neckerchief and shoes" to play the role of a foot-man, and snobbishly refuse to acknowledge that Mr. Malderton's brother is a grocer. The moral is plain: it takes a special kind of social climber not to recognize another social climber. Their own ambitions couldn't be any more obvious if they had gone shopping for crampons and ropes.

Dickens's attitude towards such targets, while gently mocking, is far from hostile. Perhaps this is to be expected, given that his writing exploits several aspects of their worldview, albeit in a far more knowing way. He, too, is drawn to surface appearances, and lovingly describes the jumble of everyday life in clustering lists—a style of writing which, G. K. Chesterton suggested, embodied Dickens's "democratic optimism," because under-lying it was the conviction that everything is potentially interesting.[33] At the same time, Dickens is quick to penetrate surfaces and expose what is really going on, like a stagehand lifting the curtain while the scenery is still being shuffled into place. So, when he describes a ladies' finishing school in "Sentiment," the opening page draws attention to windows that are de-liberately left open in order to "impress the passer-by with a due sense of the luxuries of the establishment"; a front parlor that is stuffed with maps and books to give a "very deep appearance to the place" when parents visit; and one of the owners, who enters with her false hair in curling pa-pers "in order to impress the young ladies with a conviction of its reality." It is the perfect environment, in other words, for a plot in which a lover tries to elope with his sweetheart before his disguise is rumbled—another revelation, like that of Horatio Sparkins, which suggests that young men who faked new identities for themselves were merely one symptom of a world in which everyone and everything was in disguise.

We might expect a satirist like Dickens to be keen on exposing such pretense, given how often satire is drawn to ideas of delving and strip-ping away; but taking on new identities is also something to which his own writing is indebted. Repeatedly, in these stories, he holds ideas up to the light and turns them round until they reveal unexpected new angles, as when he describes in "The Bloomsbury Christening" how the miserable Dumps attends the christening of his much-loathed godson, "feeling about as much out of place as a salmon might be supposed to be on a gravel-walk"; or in "The Steam Excursion" how, as the pleasure boat lurches in a storm, "the pigeon-pies looked as if the birds, whose legs were stuck outside, were trying to get them in." These are not important parts of either narrative, but they are key moments in Dickens's development as a writer, as he discovers how to make the most ordinary parts of life seem magically strange, even as he is ruthlessly exposing everything that people only pretend to be true. Much later in his career, in the preface to *Bleak House,* he pointed out that he had "purposely dwelt upon the romantic side of familiar things." What distinguishes these early stories is his skill at showing how quickly the romantic and the familiar can exchange places, like the two sides of a spinning coin.

Dickens's transformations of everyday life in these stories extend to the use they made of his own life. There are several glints of autobiography, such as the preparations made for Horatio Sparkins, which include Marianne's plan to "request the favour of some verses for her album," a detail which draws out his memories of Lombard Street, just as "Marianne" extends "Maria"; but each time, Dickens refuses to dwell on the moment and quickly pushes the narrative in a different direction. The young heroine in "Sentiment," similarly, has been sent to a finishing school to remove her from "some ridiculous love affair, with a person much her inferior," as was rumored to have happened to Maria when she was being courted by Dickens. Within the safe experimental conditions of fiction, however, Dickens allowed himself to contemplate a different ending to the story. It is not a happy one. The young intellectual with whom she elopes "writes incessantly," but "none of his productions appear in print," and his wife begins to think that "a marriage contracted in haste, and repented at lei-

sure, is the cause of more substantial wretchedness than she ever anticipated." It is a curious reflection on one of the possible futures Dickens
narrowly avoided, like a way of taking revenge upon an absent enemy. It
also indicates his growing dissatisfaction with the scaled-down demands
of these short stories.

"Passage in the Life of Mr. Watkins Tottle" reveals some of the ben-
eficial effects this dissatisfaction had on Dickens's writing. The small and
sweetly inoffensive Watkins Tottle is arrested for debt, in another echo of
Dickens's father; and by attempting to marry a woman with money, he
unwittingly ends up helping her marry someone else. The final paragraph
describes how Tottle quits his lodgings, and soon thereafter a body is
found floating in the canal, with nothing in its pockets but a handful of
change, a lonely-hearts advertisement, a toothpick, and a card case containing "nothing but blank cards"—a nastily appropriate end for a man
who was fairly anonymous even before he was dragged from the water.
More important, though, is the fact that this story was extended over two
parts, published in successive issues of the *Monthly Magazine* in January
and February 1835. In fact, Dickens seems to have contemplated extending Tottle's life even further: the *Monthly* version included a paragraph,
later cut when the story was republished in *Sketches by Boz*, which explained that when Tottle died, he "left a variety of papers in the hands of
his landlady—the materials collected in his wanderings among different
classes of society—which that lady has determined to publish, to defray
the unpaid expenses of his board and lodging. They will be carefully arranged, and presented to the public from time to time, with all due humility, by BOZ."[34] The idea of miscellaneous stories centered on a single
character would later be picked up in the *Pickwick Papers*, and in some
ways the "plump, clean, and rosy" Tottle, who "stood four feet six inches
and three-quarters in his socks," is like an unhappy prototype for Mr.
Pickwick, another character who gets involved in an ill-fated, if unwitting,
marriage scheme.[35] Even more significant is the conjunction of a landlady
with the name of "Boz," because the first time Dickens had used this literary alias was at the conclusion of "The Boarding-House," a two-part story

published in the *Monthly* in May and August 1834. It was a key moment in his career.

"The Boarding-House" brought together several key ingredients of Dickens's fiction to date, including social scrambling, theatrical posturing, and a style that is full of unexpected sideways connections. Even when describing something as humdrum as a letter, Dickens tackles the task with comic brio: the writing looks like "a skein of thread in a tangle," the address is "squeezed up into the right-hand corner, as if it were ashamed of itself," and the ink-stained seal bears "a marvellous resemblance to a black-beetle trod upon." Like Mr. Tomkins, one of the boarding-house lodgers, such descriptions demonstrate "a great character for finding out beauties which no one else could discover." The figure Dickens most resembles, however, is the boarding-house owner, Mr. Tibbs—not in his appearance (like many of Dickens's human grotesques, Tibbs brings together competing physical features in the same body, in his case "very short legs" and a "peculiarly long" face), but in his way of starting stories but never finishing them. He is, Dickens observes, "a melancholy specimen of the story-teller." Dickens himself wraps things up neatly enough—a series of farcical events involving overheard whispers and misunderstood motives results in Tibbs's separation from his bullying wife—but he cannot resist hinting that he could say much more, were it not that his readers "prefer leaving it to be imagined." On the evidence of this story, they are unlikely to have an imagination with anything like his force and stamina. Every aspect of "The Boarding-House" indicates that its two parts could easily become three, or five, or twenty, as each incident locks onto the next, and each character spawns a host of eccentric offspring.

In describing a boarding-house, Dickens not only found himself sketching the outlines of characters he would plump out in his later work—Mrs. Tibbs, in particular, is a comic prototype for *Martin Chuzzlewit*'s Mrs. Todgers, who runs a dingy "Commercial Boarding-House" populated chiefly by spiders and funny smells—but he had also discovered the perfect model for his early fiction. Like a boarding-house, each of his stories offered a space for social encounters, but also one in which individuals could withdraw from each other into eccentric worlds of their own. The theatrical influence is unmistakable: Dickens's characters engage in dialogue, and sometimes in crowd scenes, but are always tempted to retreat into soliloquy. Equally unmistakable is Dickens's interest in the idea of constructing a literary dwelling for his characters, like an early version of Henry James's house of fiction, albeit one more suitable for the lonely widows, shabby respectables, and other inhabitants of the lower middle class. The idea can be traced back to "Lodgings to Let," one of the poems he wrote in Maria Beadnell's album, and it reaches forward to *Mrs. Lirriper's Lodgings,* a set of Christmas stories published in 1863, in which he developed the idea of people sharing a house, and did so by including several episodes, written by various collaborators, which were supposedly told by or about each of its inhabitants. Dickens himself adopted the voice of Mrs. Lirriper, which shows that he was still intrigued by the comparison of running a boarding-house to the act of writing a book, in which the different characters needed to be carefully handled if they were to coexist harmoniously. Perhaps this is why he signed himself "Tibbs" when he contributed a set of twelve sketches to *Bell's Life in London* in the period from September 1835 to January 1836: it was an in-joke designed to alert his readers to the fact that his stories, like Tibbs's, were still going.

Names were important to Dickens. When he planned his novels, often it was the names that came first: they offered keyholes into his characters' minds, blueprints for their behavior, even clues about what they looked like. In this context, it would be surprising if he had chosen his own pseudonym without some careful thought. "Tibbs," for example, may have been a private joke, a tip of the hat to Beau Tibbs, who appeared in Oliver Goldsmith's essays, given the resonance that Goldsmith had for Dickens. A copy of Goldsmith's *Bee* had been given to him by his schoolmaster, William Giles, as a keepsake when he left Chatham for London—a book "which I kept for his sake, and its own, a long time afterwards."[36] Now, as he completed "The Boarding-House," he chose another pseudonym that brought together Goldsmith and childhood associations: "Boz."

According to John Forster, "Boz" was the nickname of Dickens's brother Augustus, "whom in honour of the *Vicar of Wakefield* he had dubbed Moses, which being facetiously pronounced through the nose became Boses, and being shortened became Boz."[37] The origin of "Boz" in an eighteenth-century writer may also have been in Dickens's mind, given how carefully his early novels try to find some middle ground between his childhood reading of Smollett and Fielding and the demands of the modern age. In 1829, Carlyle had identified one of the key "signs of the times" as "the boundless collision of the New with the Old," and in this sense Dickens's calling himself "Boz" was the first sign of how far he would make the times his own.[38] He was a modern Moses who, so far as the development of the novel was concerned, had glimpsed the Promised Land. But Dickens also seems to have chosen this pseudonym for more private reasons. His own explanation has usually been taken at face value: "Boz was a very familiar household word to me, long before I was an author, and so I came to adopt it."[39] Of course, long before Dickens was an author he had also been a laboring drudge in Warren's blacking warehouse, and his interest in *The Vicar of Wakefield* may have been concentrated by the novel's inclusion of a character named Dick who is sent out to work when his father is put into a debtors' prison. Some years later, Dickens tried to develop the idea of "familiar" speech in his journals *Household Words* and *All the Year Round,* in both of which he treated his readers like a set of close relations; and his choice of "Boz" can be seen as a first attempt to reconstitute an idealized family around him. But one can adopt children as well as names, as Mrs. Lirriper takes on a child left behind by a dead lodger, and it is hard to escape the feeling that in giving himself the name of his younger brother, Dickens was trying to recapture, if not his own childhood, then some of the qualities he associated with childhood: unconditional love, uncompromising trust, and the power to transform what other people accept without question. That, and an ability to laugh at the silliest things.

Dickens placing his first literary contribution in the editor's box.

1. Robert Herbert, after James Stephenson: *Dickens Placing His First Literary Contribution in the Editor's Box* (mid-nineteenth century). National Portrait Gallery, London.

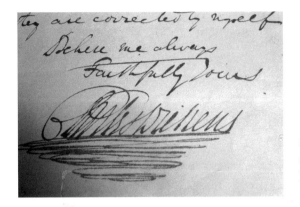

2. Sample of Dickens's early signature. Charles Dickens Museum, London.

3. Fred Barnard: *Dickens in the Blacking Warehouse* (1880). The Bodleian Library, University of Oxford.

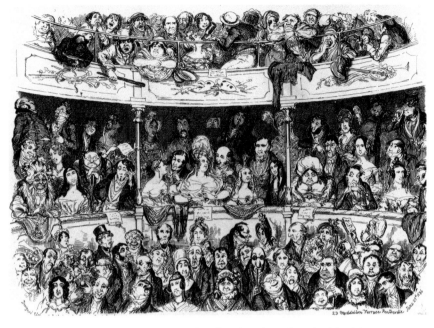

4. George Cruikshank: *Pit, Boxes, and Gallery* (1836). Hulton Archive / Getty Images.

5. Janet Barrow: Miniature of Dickens as a young man (1830). Charles Dickens Museum, London.

6. John Orlando Parry: *A London Street Scene* (1835). Alfred Dunhill Museum and Archive, London.

7. George Cruikshank: *Public Dinners,* from *Sketches by Boz* (1836). The Bodleian Library, University of Oxford.

8. George Cruikshank: *Early Coaches,* from *Sketches by Boz* (1836). The Bodleian Library, University of Oxford.

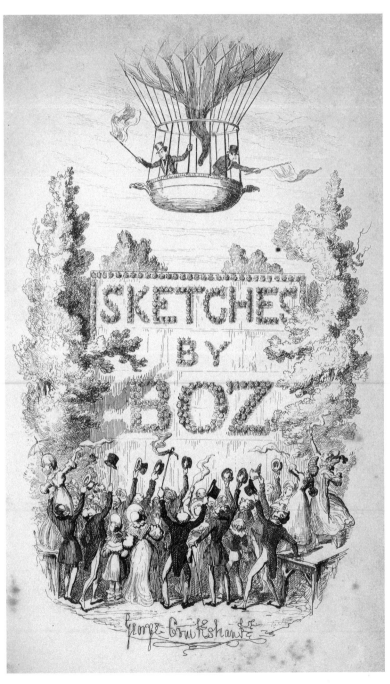

9. George Cruikshank: Title page from *Sketches by Boz, Second Series* (1836). The Bodleian Library, University of Oxford.

10. George Cruikshank: *London Going Out of Town—or—The March of Bricks and Mortar* (1829). Copyright © The Trustees of the British Museum.

11. Paul Pry (William Heath): *The March of Intellect*. Published by Thomas McLean, London, c. 1829. Copyright © Museum of London.

12. Robert Seymour: *Locomotion*. Published by Thomas McLean, London, c. 1835. City of London, London Metropolitan Archives.

13. B. R. Haydon: *Waiting for the "Times"* (1831). Copyright © *The Times* / NISyndication.com.

MR BOZ   MR TINTO   Mr MAC.   Mr PROUT.

Drawn by W. M. Thackeray
at St James's Square 1836.

14. W. M. Thackeray: *Mr. Boz* (1836). Reproduced from *The Library of the Late Ogden Goelet* (auction sales catalogue), American Art Association, 1935.

15. George Cruikshank: The rejected "Fireside Plate" for *Oliver Twist* (1838). The Bodleian Library, University of Oxford.

16. George Cruikshank: *Fagin in the Condemned Cell,* from *Oliver Twist* (1838). The Bodleian Library, University of Oxford.

17. George Cruikshank: *Rose Maylie and Oliver,* from *Oliver Twist* (1838). The Bodleian Library, University of Oxford.

18. No. 48 Doughty Street:
exterior view. Charles Dickens
Museum, London.

19. No. 48 Doughty
Street: drawing room.
Charles Dickens
Museum, London.

20. George Cruikshank: Sketch Portrait of Dickens (1837). Charles Dickens Museum, London.

21. Etching of Dickens from the *Court Magazine and Monthly Critic* (1837). The Bodleian Library, University of Oxford.

22. Daniel Maclise: Sketch of Dickens, Mary Hogarth, and Catherine (1837). V&A Images / Victoria and Albert Museum, London.

23. Cartoon inspired by Dickens's final reading tour of America (1867–1868). Charles Dickens Museum, London.

24. Samuel Laurence: Drawing of Dickens (1837). National Portrait Gallery, London.

25. George Cruikshank: *Sketch of Charles Dickens* (1837). Henry W. and Albert A. Berg Collection of English and American Literature, The New York Public Library, Astor, Lenox and Tilden Foundations.

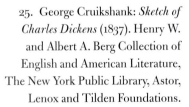

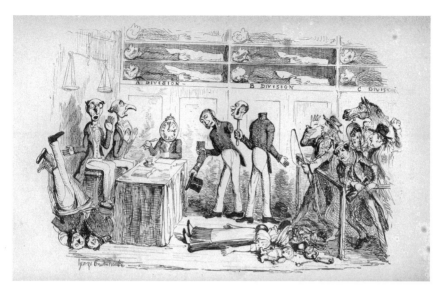

26. George Cruikshank: Illustration for Dickens's final Mudfog paper in *Bentley's Miscellany* (1838). Charles Dickens Museum, London.

EXTRAORDINARY GAZETTE.

SPEECH OF HIS MIGHTINESS
ON OPENING THE SECOND NUMBER OF

BENTLEY'S MISCELLANY,

27. Hablot K. Browne: *Publishing Day of "Bentley's Miscellany"* (1837). Charles Dickens Museum, London.

28. R. W. Buss: *Dickens's Dream* (1875). Charles Dickens Museum, London.

CHAPTER SIX

Becoming Boz

Early reviews of Dickens's *Monthly Magazine* stories ranged from warm ("a capital quiz") to tepid ("a choice bit of humour, somewhat exaggerated"), while some critics hedged their bets by resorting to terms of praise—"clever" was the choice of the *Sun* reviewer—that looked more like insults in disguise.[1] The British may admire intelligence, but they have always been suspicious of anyone thought to be "clever," and the *Sun* reviewer's comment that Dickens was "too ambitious of saying smart things . . . too much on the strain" sounded like the reproach of a teacher telling the class clown to stop showing off. Yet Dickens soon had even better reasons for feeling pleased with himself. Although his uncle's first attempt, in 1833, to secure him a job on the *Morning Chronicle* had failed, in 1834 Dickens continued to press his case: in person, by writing to the long-serving editor John Black; through his father, who followed up Dickens's approach by contacting the influential Whig parliamentary agent Joseph Parkes to promote his son's "competence in every respect for the duties he will be required to perform"; and via his old friend Thomas Beard, who had recently moved to the *Chronicle* from the *Morning Herald*.[2] Eventually this triangulation of forces broke through, and in August 1834 the *Chronicle* appointed the twenty-two-year-old Dickens as a full-time reporter at a basic salary of 5 guineas per week.

It was an important time for the newspaper, which had been bought in January 1833 by three businessmen with the ambition of turning it into a major Whig rival to the Tory-supporting *Times,* and Dickens was doubly fortunate to have been taken on during its reorganization. In the first place, he was joining a newspaper that was closely aligned with his own political sympathies, and would become increasingly popular after

November 1834, when it declared its support for the ousted government of Lord Melbourne and "Liberal principles generally."[3] Better still, he found himself working for an editor who had spotted his talent and was keen to encourage it. For an aspiring fiction writer, John Black's notorious eccentricity was probably an added perk of the job; in fact, if he hadn't already existed Dickens might well have invented him. A serious-minded individual who turned out somewhat ponderous leading articles, Black was quick to take offense (he was rumored to have issued no fewer than twelve challenges to fight a duel before he was twenty-four), and wandered the streets holding a cudgel with a mastiff trotting menacingly at his heels. In his dusty office he hid behind piles of books, which he borrowed from friends and then clung to "with a death-like tenacity of grasp."[4] Presumably his friends were too scared to ask for them back. But though famous for "not having the slightest sense of humour," he appreciated those who did, or at least recognized their value in attracting and retaining readers.[5] In January 1834 he had printed an article about two thieves in Billingsgate Market named Catsmeat and Winkles, one of whom had attempted to conceal four or five plaice under his shirt "and disposed of several eels in the seat of his breeches, which were made tight at the knees, no doubt for the purpose of preventing any stray fish from escaping at such outlet." In Dickens, Black had found a writer capable of mapping out the same imaginative terrain.[6]

The newspaper's subeditor, Charles Mackay, recalled that Black tried to save Dickens from ordinary reporting duties when he was not working in Parliament, "having the highest opinion of his original genius." That is a somewhat rose-tinted retrospect—the number of theater reviews and other routine column-fillers Dickens produced shows that he was hardly kept "in reserve for great occasions," as Black later claimed—but Dickens was certainly encouraged to continue his original work and extend its range.[7] In the next twelve months, he published five "Street Sketches" in the *Morning Chronicle,* and twenty "Sketches of London" in its sister paper the *Evening Chronicle,* a tri-weekly publication launched in January 1835 that was "conducted upon the political principles of THE

MORNING CHRONICLE . . . for a Metropolitan as well as a Country circulation."[8] These were followed by twelve "Scenes and Characters" contributed to *Bell's Life in London* on a freelance basis, from September 1835 to January 1836.[9] In effect, Dickens was turning out a feature of at least two thousand words every fortnight, in addition to his regular reports. No wonder so many of his letters record the time, in a voice pitched somewhere between incredulity and resignation. In June 1835 alone, he found himself writing on "Thursday Morng. ½ past 3," "Saturday Morning / 6 O'Clock," and "Saturday Morning 5 O'Clock"; by "Saturday Morng. ½ p 4" on August 8, he was reduced to a plaintive postscript: "(half-asleep)."[10]

The same letters also show Dickens widening his social circle. Some of his correspondents, such as the two Thomases (Mitton and Beard), were old and lasting friends, while others flickered only briefly in the margins. "My dear Longhurst," one letter begins, but he was not so dear that the usually indefatigable editors of Dickens's correspondence can be sure who he was: "Possibly George Longhurst, translator and shorthand writer, of Clarendon Square; or Thomas Longhurst, solicitor, of Lincoln's Inn."[11] So far as the written record is concerned, the friendship splutters briefly into life and then fizzles out. Dickens was also starting to seek out new contacts in the world of print: his correspondence from this period includes an invitation to Eugene Nugent, parliamentary reporter with the *Times,* "to meet half a dozen friends"; a note, probably to another editor, offering "a suggestion to you for consideration"; and tactful exchanges with the popular illustrator George Cruikshank and the ambitious young publisher John Macrone.[12] Such letters provide the firmest evidence yet that he was settling into London's literary life and learning its rules of engagement, where the line between enjoying genuine friendship and seeking professional advantage was less a barrier than a well-trodden path.

Many years later, at a public dinner held shortly before his second visit to America in 1867, Dickens claimed that he had chosen a rather different way of life: "I have in my day at odd times heard a great deal about literary sets, and cliques, and coteries . . . and mutual admiration societies, and I know not what other dragons in the upward path. I began to tread it when I was very young, without influence, without money, without companion, introducer, or adviser."[13] That was a reassuringly romantic version of his past, which allowed Dickens to cast himself in the role of the lone author who sets up base camp in his garret before setting out to conquer posterity, but it bore only a glancing relationship to the truth. Not only had he started by following in the footsteps of his uncle, but he then energetically set about gathering every additional companion, introducer, and adviser he could. Nor is this particularly surprising. "We pretend that success is exclusively a matter of individual merit," Malcolm Gladwell points out in his study of the factors that lie behind rags-to-riches stories, when actually "successful people don't do it alone. Where they come from matters. They're products of particular places and environments"—New York's garment district in the 1890s, for example, or Silicon Valley in the 1970s—where their particular talent is given the opportunity to flourish.[14] To this list of miniature lands of opportunity we might add London in the 1830s, the creative seedbed of Dickens, Thackeray, Disraeli, and many of the other writers who would go on to dominate the Victorian literary scene, with the slight adjustment that for professional writers the "environment" in which they found themselves included everyone else working in the city of words. Nowhere was Carlyle's assessment of modern life more eagerly demonstrated: "To understand man . . . we must look beyond the individual man and his actions or interests, and view him in combination with his fellows. It is in Society that man first feels what he is; first becomes what he can be."[15]

Writing on the state of London's newspaper industry in 1829, the editor Gibbons Merle estimated that it employed approximately 1,100 people full-time, in addition to countless penny-a-liners waiting for scraps of work to be thrown their way.[16] By 1834 the numbers had increased still further, as newspaper offices in the area that included Fleet Street and the Strand expanded to keep up with burgeoning literacy rates (by 1840 just over half the population could read) and a seemingly insatiable appetite for news.[17] Journalists continued to occupy an ambivalent position: geographically central, but socially on the edge of things, they were professional outsiders who were still some way from shaking off their reputation as a swell mob whose good opinion could be bought for the price of a drink. (This is the period when waggish insiders started to refer to Fleet Street, not always apologetically, as "the street of drink.") The views of polite society were summed up by Walter Scott's declaration in 1829 that "nothing but a thorough-going blackguard ought to attempt the daily press. . . . I would rather sell gin to the poor people and poison them that way," although his assumption that there was a neat distinction between the shabby morals of journalism and the high ideals of literature was increasingly being muddled by the number of writers who had a foot in both camps.[18]

Some managed to combine raffish lifestyles with impeccable social credentials. The hero of Thackeray's *Pendennis*, a novel rooted in the 1830s, is the Cambridge-educated son of a country squire who on his first day in London joins an expensive club, is quickly introduced to the proprietor of the *Pall Mall Gazette* (a fictional version of the journal founded in 1865) and various other "literary gentlemen," and when commissioned to write his first book review "flings himself" into an "easy chair" for the day.[19] He is a thinly disguised version of Thackeray himself, who by 1833 had managed to rise to the position of editor of the *National Standard of Literature, Music, Theatre and the Fine Arts*, at the impressively early age of twenty-one, by the simple but effective means of buying the business outright. (The previous year, his bills for four months spent in Paris had come to nearly £350, considerably more than Dickens's annual salary; the sum included £160 to his tailor and £66 spent on gloves.)[20] Yet while literary London was still far from being a meritocracy, the relative value placed on education and breeding was shrinking: in a pioneering piece of research into the social origins of literary figures, Raymond Williams notes that of the novelists born in the years 1780–1830, "the contribution of women and men from the poorer social groups is especially marked."[21]

Also receding in importance was the notion that writers were a special breed, more fragile and sensitive than ordinary people, who needed to be protected from the rigors of the marketplace by patronage or a large private income. Much more popular was the no-nonsense view expressed by Pendennis's friend Warrington: "There are thousands of clever fellows in the world who could, if they would, turn verses, write articles, read books, and deliver a judgment upon them."[22]

The connections these writers made for themselves were far more significant than any number of letters of introduction. The son of Dickens's later illustrator, Hablot Knight Browne ("Phiz"), remembered literary London in the 1850s as a comparatively small and intimate place—a village within a city—and his comments about "those who were in the business of amusing the public" at midcentury holds equally true for the 1830s: "News spread mysteriously, as it is said to do amongst the Indians, but we must remember that there was a constant communication between authors, artists, engravers, printers, and the like, and anything interesting was continually carried to and fro by a mob of subordinates."[23] This communication could take many forms, from accidental encounters in the street to swelling waves of gossip; even negative reviews could be helpful, given how close the connections were between getting known and getting on. The mixture of planning and chance that lay behind many successful careers is vividly depicted in a novel illustrated by "Phiz," Thomas Miller's *Godfrey Malvern: or, The Life of an Author* (1843), in which the poet hero bumps into an impoverished author, one of "the writers who contribute to cheap periodicals, and now and then, get an article inserted into the magazines, too often without their name being affixed to it." Within a few pages Malvern has been introduced to the editor of the *Monthly Magazine,* where Dickens's first stories were published; the editor glances at a small poem while enjoying a strategically ordered bottle of wine, and promptly takes Malvern on as a freelance reviewer. On the basis of his work for this editor, Malvern sells an unwritten volume to a publisher, and is then commissioned to write a series of articles with guaranteed payment by the sheet. His career develops, in other words, as his chain of social connections lengthens. Conscious that "very few authors become famous all at once," he eventually finds himself venturing into the "LITERARY RAT-TRAP" of a soirée based on the glittering parties of the Countess of Blessington, with its chattering clump of the vain, the stupid, the needy, and the deservedly unread, all of them pursuing the next link in the chain.[24] Such scenes give an authentic flavor of the delicate social maneuvering required of authors who were aware that the "upward path" to fame was a jostling thoroughfare. Becoming an author involved competition as well as collaboration, and ambitious individuals had to strike a tricky balance between social networking and shouldering their way through the crowd.

One way in which these impulses could be reconciled is suggested by George Colman's popular miscellany *Broad Grins,* which was among Dickens's favorite books as a child. It opens with a poem showing Dick and two close friends engaged in literary conversation:

> Tom, Dick, and Will, were little known to Fame;—
>   No matter;—
> But to the Ale-house, oftentimes, they came,
>   To chatter.
>
> It was the custom of these three
>   To sit up late;
>   And, o'er the embers of the Ale-house fire,
>   When steadier customers retire,
> The choice *Triumviri,* d'ye see,
>   Held a debate.[25]

The topic of this debate—the state of literature in general, and the decline of the modern novel in particular—may strike modern ears as a familiar one, but for Dickens its substance would have been less important than the social situation in which it unfolds. However large his circle of acquaintance grew, especially after he was welcomed into the padded opulence of places like the Athenaeum Club and the Garrick Club, he continued to think that the ideal literary club would have a strictly limited number of members, preferably no more than three, in the same way that "Tom, Dick, and Will" allows Dick to be buttressed by the other two members of the *Triumviri*. His early attempts in this direction, such as the Trio Club or the Cerberus Club, "Ainsworth, Forster, and myself, the only members," were as earnest as those of a small boy forming secret societies with passwords and special handshakes.[26] They became even more important once his growing reputation meant that far more people knew about him than could ever know him personally. Yet from the start he was aware that some kinds of literary debate could not be restricted to such a select audience. For in the eager push and pull of 1830s London, professional networking was not restricted to pubs and soirées. It could also happen on the page.

Ambitious young writers, in addition to complimenting or criticizing each other, also borrowed freely from each other's works, using their pens as sensitive antennae that twitched in response to every passing trend. Even a relative unknown like Dickens was vulnerable to being annexed or gazumped. Not only was his first publication, "A Dinner at Poplar Walk," smuggled into the pages of Henry Mayhew's journal *The Thief,* but in October 1834 he was sent to review *The Christening* at the Adelphi Theatre, advertised as a new farce by J. B. Buckstone, only to discover that it was in fact a rewriting of his own sketch "The Bloomsbury Christening."[27] Dickens pointedly welcomed Buckstone's characters as "old and very particular friends of ours," and followed up his review with a letter in the *Chronicle* protesting against the "kidnapping" of his "offspring."[28] It was the first serious warning that success brought powerlessness along with influence. The more popular "Boz" became, the less he could control what others made of him.

Dickens's amused tone in both review and letter suggests he was aware that taking such liberties was an inevitable part of the literary game, although he may have felt that he could afford to be generous to a writer who was not a direct rival. The fact that he was reviewing the play, rather than nervously awaiting the audience's applause, indicated that he had chosen to stay on the other side of the footlights for now. In any case, his sense of the possible lives opening up before him was not limited to the theater. "See how near I may have been to another sort of life," his response to an earlier turn away from the theatrical profession, was starting to take on an additional set of implications.[29] The idea resonated in his new sketches, many of which circled anxiously around the large differences there could be between lives separated by only a few inches, like the pedestrians who walk past the walls of Newgate Prison "with a light laugh or a merry whistle," oblivious to the fact that they are "within one yard of a fellow creature, bound and helpless, . . . whose miserable career will shortly terminate in a violent and shameful death" ("A Visit to Newgate"). Equally powerful was Dickens's sense of how near he might be to another version of his current life. In such a competitive literary marketplace, where there were always fewer pages to fill than pens eager to fill them, it was hard not to see the line between success and failure as a seesaw, where one writer's rise inevitably meant another writer's fall.

The idea is given material expression in John Parry's 1835 watercolor *A London Street Scene* (Figure 6), which depicts the temporary wooden hoardings surrounding one of London's many building sites. Primarily the scene draws attention to how rapidly London was renewing itself during the 1830s, as old buildings were knocked down and fresh ones put up in their place; but the tangle of posters—evidence of an "epidemic of bill-posting" at the time—also offers a neat pictorial representation of the intense competition between writers, whose rise and fall could be even quicker.[30] Just visible above the group of street traders is a poster advertising *The Christening* at the Adelphi, which shows that Dickens's ideas (albeit in secondhand form) were still in the public eye when this watercolor was completed. At the same time, the fate of other Adelphi attractions such as *The Last Days of Pompeii*, the poster for which is gradually being crowded out by newer rivals, shows how short-lived such success could be.[31]

G. K. Chesterton put his finger on the problem when he pointed out that "the greatest mystery about almost any great writer is why he was ever allowed to write at all": "The first efforts of eminent men are always imitations; and very often they are bad imitations. The only question is whether the publisher had . . . some subconscious connection or sympathy with the public, and thus felt instinctively the presence of something that might ultimately tell; or whether the choice was merely a matter of chance, and one Dickens was chosen and another Dickens left."[32] For Dickens, this question would have been sharpened by the sheer number of failed writers who drifted through London, bobbing in and out of sight among the crowds like the victims of a shipwreck. They included Angus Reach, who worked sixteen hours a day as a shorthand reporter, comic writer, and novelist, and who died of "softening of the brain" at the age of thirty-five.[33] Further away from Dickens's line of work, but even closer to the trajectory of his life, there was Robert Bowles, an out-of-work law writer who starved to death in a freezing apartment in Johnson's Court, just off Fleet Street, in January 1827. When his body was found, it was "completely covered with vermin. He had scratched the skin off almost every part of his body, and consequently the sheets and bed were nearly soaked with blood."[34] It was only a few feet away from the editor's box where Dickens would deposit his first story in 1833. Perhaps one Dickens had been chosen because no other Dickens was left.

However much sympathy Dickens had for these victims of the literary marketplace—and his later efforts to support the families of figures like Reach suggests that it was a great deal—he was quick to exploit them for his own ends. One of his later sketches, "Our Next Door Neighbours," concludes with the deathbed scene of a young man from the country who earns a pittance "by copying writings, and translating for booksellers." Sentence by sentence Dickens ratchets up the pathos, until the starving figure raises himself up to curse London with his dying breath: "bury me in the open fields—anywhere but in these dreadful streets. . . . they have killed me." Clearly the glamor of the garret had been overstated. Although this writer was only a fictional creation, killing him off showed precisely the ruthless streak Dickens would need if he was to avoid a similar fate in his own life. "Recollect, we must scrunch or be scrunched," Mr. Boffin memorably observes in *Our Mutual Friend,* the novel where Dickens's interest in rivalrous doubles and uncanny twins reaches its strange climax.[35] "It is questionable whether any man quite relishes being mistaken for any other," the narrator remarks early on, but the rest of the novel is dedicated to characters who either are or hope to be mistaken for each other: John Harmon and his look-alike George Radfoot, Lady Tippins's husband who was "knighted in mistake for somebody else," and especially Bradley Headstone, whose schoolmaster clothes "usually looked as if they were the clothes of some other man," but who, when dressed in imitation of Rogue Riderhood, looks, "in the clothes of some other man or men, as if they were his own."

Dickens's attitude towards such ideas in the 1830s was far more positive, largely because he had friends who understood that literary rivalry did not have to topple over into enmity. The most important of these was William Harrison Ainsworth, a Manchester-born writer who had given up a career in the law after coming to London, and whom Dickens seems to have met shortly after his Dick Turpin novel *Rookwood* had caused a sensation in 1834. Soon Dickens's letters were dropping Ainsworth's name with a shy pride, expressing how "highly gratified" he was by "Ainsworth's opinion," and subsequently referring to him with greater confidence once their friendship had developed into a routine of walks and dinners.[36] He had good cause to be grateful. Known for his dashing good looks and achingly fashionable clothing, both of which led to his being mistaken for the celebrated dandy Count D'Orsay, Ainsworth was well connected in literary circles and a famously generous host. At his Kensal Lodge home, Dickens was introduced to most of the people who would help to shape the next stage of his career, including his first publisher, John Macrone, his first illustrator, George Cruikshank, and his future biographer, John Forster. Ainsworth's impact on Dickens's life cannot be overstated. Perhaps that is why Dickens's later friends were so tempted to underplay it. The first published work by Ainsworth had been a tragicomedy in rhyming couplets entitled *The Rivals*, and Forster in particular seems to have cast him retrospectively as a rival to his own billing as chief supporting actor, or even co-star, in the story of Dickens's life.[37]

Within a year of meeting Macrone, Dickens had arranged to republish his *Chronicle* sketches as a book, and he continued to update Ainsworth on his progress like a student sending letters to his former tutor. There may have been a degree of self-interest in this: although they had become good friends, Ainsworth was undeniably the senior partner, and even if Dickens was not initially attracted to him for his reputation, he seems to have been happy enough to accept the fringe benefits. For several years they resembled a body and its shadow, although after Dickens's success with the *Pickwick Papers* Ainsworth was increasingly obliged to follow at his heels rather than the other way round. In 1839 Ainsworth published *Jack Sheppard,* his powerful tale of a small boy sinking into the criminal underworld, directly after Dickens had concluded *Oliver Twist,* his slightly more original exercise in the same genre. In the same year Dickens resigned from the editorship of *Bentley's Miscellany,* where both novels were serialized, and recommended Ainsworth as his replacement, with the sort of generous condescension one might use to pass on an unwanted Christmas present to a needy relation. As late as 1844, Daniel Maclise's portrait of Ainsworth, exhibited at the Royal Academy and used as a frontispiece for the recently launched *Ainsworth's Magazine,* depicted him sitting in an armorial wooden chair in an attitude "almost identical with that of Dickens in the portrait painted by Maclise in 1839."[38] In defiance of chronology, his career was starting to resemble a crude copy of a Dickensian original. The turning point came in 1838, when he accompanied Dickens and Forster to Manchester on a research trip for *Nicholas Nickleby,* and generously invited them to a civic banquet arranged to celebrate his return as the city's prodigal son. Unfortunately, by the time they arrived at the reception, there was no doubt who Manchester's citizens had primarily turned out to see. Dickens had been moved center stage, like a real-life version of *Broad Grins* in which Dick was to be supported by John and Will. It was the strongest evidence yet that, while Dickens continued to enjoy Ainsworth's company, he no longer needed him.

Thereafter their careers took different directions, as Dickens's reputation continued to rise at roughly the same rate that Ainsworth's declined.

John Sutherland summarizes the change in their fortunes: "Many would have backed Ainsworth's talent against Dickens's in 1840. In the 1860s Dickens was earning £10,000 a novel, Ainsworth a hundredth of that sum; Dickens was buying Gad's Hill, Ainsworth was forced to sell his property piecemeal."[39] Timing as well as talent had its part to play, or its spanner to throw into the works. Had Ainsworth died in 1840, he would have stood a good chance of being immortalized as the Byron of the young Victorians: a literary star who shone brightly but briefly and left his readers wanting more. His tragedy was that with each novel he wrote (some forty altogether) he left them wanting less. He outlived his fame. The period contains no more powerful warning about the need to manage a writing career carefully, rather than let it drift uncontrolled across the decades, than the story Robert Browning told Forster at a dinner party in the 1860s. Describing how he had just met "a sad, forlorn-looking being" who "reminded me of old times," Browning recalled how this shabby figure gradually "resolved himself into—whom do you think?—Harrison Ainsworth!" To which Forster replied, "Good heavens! is he still alive?"[40]

In December 1834, four months after his arrival at the *Morning Chronicle,* Dickens moved into a "three-pair back" at 13 Furnival's Inn, Holborn: a three-room apartment, with cellar and lumber room, on the third floor of a blandly respectable building that had formerly been an Inn of Chancery. Whether or not he had planned for this new degree of independence, circumstances had forced his hand. In November his father was again arrested for debt, this time because of a wine merchant's unpaid bill, and was extricated from Abraham Sloman's detention house only after Dickens and his wallet intervened. Clearly the family's budget would have to be trimmed, and on December 4 John Dickens wrote to Thomas Beard to explain that the family had decided to break up their home in Bentinck Street, "Mrs. Dickens, my daughters[,] Alfred & [Augustus] going into more economical apartments somewhere in the vicinity of Fanny's engagements, Charles (taking Frederick with him[)] into Chambers . . . and your humble Servant 'to the winds.'"[41] His flighty metaphor was not the happiest choice; within a fortnight he was writing to Beard again, this time asking for a loan of two sovereigns to have his shoes repaired. Dickens's response to this latest financial crisis, while loving and dutiful, amounted to little more than a long sigh. Once again the child was proving to be father to the man. After managing to secure John Dickens's release, at a time when he was himself "most desperately hard up," there may even have been a note of quiet satisfaction in his comment that "my father I apprehend will not re-join his family for some time."[42] A letter to Beard making arrangements for a housewarming party on December 20, in which he boasts that "I have got some really *extraordinary* french brandy," sounds like somebody rubbing his wrists after the removal of a set of handcuffs.[43]

Dickens's other letters from this period offer few clues as to how he was spending his time away from work. There are occasional overlaps between his private life and his sketches: a proposal "to get one or two young men together for the purpose of knocking up a song or two," for example, echoes his description of a "harmonic meeting" (a tavern-based forerunner of the music hall) in "The Streets—Night," and connects even more intriguingly with the antics of the "stout, good-humoured looking gentleman" who rents an apartment in "Our Next Door Neighbours" and starts to bring home friends, who express their good spirits in the early hours of the morning by singing songs with long choruses "to be shouted forth by the whole strength of the company, in the most enthusiastic and vociferous manner, to the annoyance of the neighbours."[44] Most of his leisure activities were less noisy affairs: dinners, trips to the theater, or relaxing with friends over "a Glass of Punch and a Cigar."[45] There is little evidence he was taking advantage of the more unusual sights and sounds London had to offer.

A full list of the attractions that were new in 1834 would take up several pages. They included the serious, such as a plaster-of-Paris model of the proposed redevelopment of Charing Cross at the exhibition rooms in King William Street; the bizarre, such as an entertainer who styled himself "THE MUSICAL PHENOMENA" and who, at the Quadrant in

Regent Street, "performed as a musical snuffbox, producing popular airs from a throat that could utter the treble and bass lines simultaneously"; and the risibly kitsch, in the shape of a mechanical figure of Napoleon, on display at the Cosmorama Rooms, which reclined on a coach in full uniform "and breathing as if asleep." Over in Leicester Square, Robert Burford's famous panorama was offering an Arctic scene ("Boothia") hastily assembled to celebrate the return of the explorer Sir John Ross after three years trapped in the polar ice: the *Times* singled out for special praise its representation of the aurora borealis and stars of "refulgent brightness." At the Adelaide Gallery—or, more officially, the National Gallery of Practical Sciences, "Blending Instruction with Amusement"— new inventions on display included a gas mask, a shower bath, a cattle stomach pump, a "hand grenade for human defence," a steam-powered machine gun, a tiny glass diving bell operated by a mouse, and a "model of the bust of a human figure" so sophisticated that "by a mechanical contrivance a knife can pass through the neck without detaching the head; and at the same time a faint cry will be heard, and the eyes will move."[46]

A number of attractions that now sit somewhere between the traditional and the timeless still carried the shine of novelty. The Zoological Gardens in Regent's Park were only six years old. Madame Tussaud's exhibition of waxworks and historical curiosities, including Napoleon's toothbrush and one of his teeth, had just arrived at the Royal London Bazaar in Gray's Inn Road after a nationwide tour like that of Mrs. Jarley's boldly advertised "stupendous collection of wax-work" in *The Old Curiosity Shop*.[47] Most startling of all was the Colosseum, a pleasure dome in Marylebone that first opened its doors in 1832, featuring a vast panorama of London to be viewed from a 112-foot-high rotunda modeled on the dome of St. Paul's Cathedral.[48] (The central column also contained an "ascending platform," the world's first passenger elevator.) In 1835, after disappointing attendance figures, the attraction was relaunched, with the addition of "Illuminated Terraces," an "Indian Supper Room . . . overlooking the waterfalls," and a "Grand Reception or Banqueting Room of Mirrors, supported by Crystal Columns, and Lined with Looking

Glass." If those self-important capital letters suggested a certain pride in the Colosseum's attractions, a ticket price of 25 shillings for the opening charity fête in July also indicated the sort of clientele the organizers were hoping to keep away, loftily characterized by the *Times* as "persons who had no pretensions to respectability."

The *Morning Chronicle*, as might be expected from a more radical newspaper, was far less enthusiastic about the spectacle of society figures approvingly observing themselves in a hall of mirrors. Dickens was chosen to report on the reopening, and while applauding the elegance of the Colosseum ("a perfect scene of enchantment"), he was quick to undermine the "respectable" credentials of those attending: "matchmaking mammas in abundance—sleepy papas in proportion—unmarried daughters in scores—marriageable men in rather smaller numbers —greedy dowagers in the refreshment room . . . and envious old maids everywhere." Together they made up a reasonable cross-section of the class of "nobles and fashionables," but only a tiny proportion of society as a whole, so there is an element of ironic ventriloquism in Dickens's summary of the occasion as "everybody was there." Only when he ventures outside the Colosseum's grounds are his sympathies fully engaged, as he describes the good-natured mob of ordinary people hanging around the gates, "who beguiled the time and enlivened the occasion, as the different carriages set down, by urgently entreating the visitors to 'flare-up' [have a good time]; imploring smartly-dressed gentlemen 'not to cut it too fat, but just to throw in a bit of lean to make weight,' and similar *facetiae*." Clearly they beguile and enliven Dickens, too; only when they barge their way into his report does it crackle properly into life.[49]

This is the "everybody" that not only enjoyed Dickens's *Chronicle* sketches ("His excellence," noted an 1837 review, "appears indeed to lie in describing just what everybody sees every day"), but also starred in them.[50] Poor parish schoolmasters, sharp street-traders, disappointed linen-drapers, stage-struck apprentices, aggressive cab drivers, "attenuated cats, depressed dogs, and anatomical fowls": everybody is there. And as Dickens shows how these people spend their time, "there" turns out to be just as unpredictable as "everybody." In his first sketch, Boz can be seen taking an omnibus on his "daily peregrination from the top of Oxford-street to the City" ("Omnibuses"); in the second, he has shifted his ground to the south bank of the Thames, "a little distance beyond the Marsh-gate," where his regular beat includes a shop that is falling into decay as different tenants move in, fail, and move out again ("Shops and Their Tenants"); by the third, he is at the Old Bailey, examining the faces of criminals for clues about what has brought them to their current plight ("The Old Bailey"). No place is off limits to his roving, rummaging consciousness, as he exercises his omnivorous enthusiasm for "amusement." This is a key word for Dickens, not just because he returns to it so frequently, but because, in a more radical sense, amusement is the key by which he unlocks London's secret life, unleashing figures who tumble into the spotlight of his curiosity.

Attempts to capture London's restless quality in print were nothing new. In fact, readers in the 1830s seeking entertaining depictions of city life were spoiled for choice. Dickens's *Evening Chronicle* sketch "Greenwich Fair," for example, was pitched at precisely the same audience that might also have enjoyed Thomas Hood's imitation of a rustic visitor open-mouthed at the fair's "fore theatres besides a Horseplay A Dwarft A She Giant, a fat Child a prize ox five carriboo savidges, a lurned Pigg . . . a real see Murmaid a Fir Eater and lots of Punshes and Juddies"; or Theodore Hook's satirical squib in which his killjoy narrator bemoans the "deplorable state" of a fair that was once a glorious annual treat.[51] Indeed, when Dickens points out that the road to Greenwich on Easter Monday "presents a scene of animated bustle," one wonders how much of the commotion was being caused by other writers eager for good copy.

Dickens's most important precursor in this genre was Pierce Egan, whose bestseller *Life in London* (1821), illustrated by George Cruikshank, had featured the first popular double act named Tom and Jerry, comprising a sophisticated Regency buck who accompanies his greenhorn friend in a series of romps through a London that is busy with slang and pockmarked by vice, keen to satisfy his "impatient ardour to join in the *fun*—to enjoy the *larks*—to laugh at the *sprees,* and to be alive in all his RAMBLES."[52] Egan was still a household name in the 1830s, largely because of a long-running theatrical adaptation at the Adelphi (it forms part of an advertised double bill with *The Christening* in Parry's painting *A London Street Scene*), and many found his glee at uncovering "the tricks and fancies of London" infectious, not least the young men who treated his stories more like a guidebook than a piece of fiction.[53] The diary Thackeray wrote in 1832, for example, frequently gives the impression of a young swell trying to live out Tom and Jerry's antics in uncensored form, although by the time he came to record his larks and sprees he was usually consumed by remorse: "Took a lesson in dancing, & dined in chambers with Caldwell played ecartè till four o'clock in the morning & lost eight pounds 7 shillings—before I knew where I was, so much for reform" (April 5); "The day spent in seediness repentance and novel-reading. . . . I did nothing else all day except eat biscuits, a very excellent amusement & not so expensive as some others" (June 5).[54]

Where Dickens differed from these other writers was in recognizing that London was not only a celebration of sociability. It was also a place that magnified loneliness. Although many people feel isolated from time to time, London seemed especially adept at transforming such moods into a way of life, like that of the pinched man Boz observes walking mechanically up and down in St. James's Park, "unheeding and unheeded; his spare, pale face looking as if it were incapable of bearing the expression of curiosity or interest" ("Thoughts about People"). This was not a new concern: as early as *The Prelude* (1805), Wordsworth had been "baffled" by the thought of "how men lived / Even next-door neighbours, as we say, yet still / Strangers, and knowing not each other's names."[55] Nor was it solved by a growing population. William Booth arrived in London from Nottingham in 1849, and when he came to write his autobiography, the notes he made under the heading "London" amounted to a solitary word: "Loneliness!"[56] "There is no place," James Grant observed in 1836, "in which the injunction, 'Mind your own business,' is so scrupulously attended to as in London."[57] More optimistically, there is nobody who more scrupulously ignores this injunction than Dickens. Whether he is describing in *The Old Curiosity Shop* those "who live solitarily in great cities as in the bucket of a human well," or showing in *Bleak House* how Charley Neckett "melted into the city's strife and sound, like a dewdrop in an ocean," his writing repeatedly zooms in on isolated individuals and keeps them company on the page.

What reconciles London's two-faced potential for sociability and loneliness in Dickens's early sketches is his narrator. In many ways Boz is easy to mistake for Dickens himself, from his pinhole-sharp vision to his unpredictable turns between humor and pathos; but as he developed in the years 1834–1836, Boz started to take on the independent life of a fictional creation. In fact, he became as hard to pin down as London itself, less a human being than the city's conscience given legs and a voice. At times he is merely a mouthpiece for the lower middle classes; at other times he holds himself at an angle to the rest of the world, the perfect embodiment of a way of life that encouraged proximity while discouraging intimacy. The way he refers to himself shuttles between the two. "We," his usual choice of pronoun, gestures towards democratic inclusiveness, by inviting readers to see London through his eyes ("We maintain that hackney coaches . . . belong solely to the metropolis"), but it is also capable of turning into an editorial "we" ("We have grown older since then") as he turns his gaze inwards. He is both an anonymous face in the crowd, just below the threshold of visibility, and the self-crowned king of the streets. Though he is occasionally noticed, as when "a bulky lady of elderly appearance" interrupts his reverie in Monmouth Street by calling out "Hope you'll know me agin," he never bumps into a friend or an acquaintance. If anything, he seems more likely to encounter some of Dickens's other alter egos, like the "clerk of the lowest description" or the "contributor to the press of the same grade" whom he numbers among the "shabby-genteel" class. And as he wanders, he wonders, using the city as raw material for speculation on everything from door knockers to wife beating.

Yet Boz is not quite a prototype of the flâneur, the middle-class dilettante who would later become such a familiar figure in Baudelaire's

Paris. Although he characterizes himself as a drifter, most of the time he walks with the coordinates of the city securely in his mind. "We had been lounging, the other evening, down Oxford-street, Holborn, Cheapside, Coleman-street, Finsbury-square and so on, with the intention of returning by Pentonville and the New-road" ("The Parlour"): the names fall into place like an address book, supplying precise grid references for Boz's route across the impersonal scatter of the city. The same names also show Dickens starting to mark out his own imaginative terrain. By supplying a set of directions to anyone wishing to follow in Boz's footsteps, an invitation which would later be taken up enthusiastically by the many books offering walking tours of "Dickens's London," he was making his first experiment in a form of writing he would go on to perfect in his novels. In *Bleak House,* for example, his readers are plunged into street-level confusion while also being given tantalizing glimpses of an overview— whether attained through Inspector Bucket's mounting "a high tower in his mind," or the narrator's describing a crow soaring over the muddled patchwork of the city—that shows how everyone and everything is connected. Boz's list of place names is far less sophisticated than this, but it offers a distilled version of the same narrative process. London is gradually converted from a maze into a map.

If Boz is a prototype of any figure who would come to characterize urban experience, it is not the flâneur but the detective. Boz is like a young Sherlock Holmes in training. In Arthur Conan Doyle's story "A Case of Identity," Watson exclaims, "You appeared to read a great deal in her which was quite invisible to me," and receives Holmes's cool reply, "Not invisible but unnoticed."[58] Just as Holmes can penetrate disguises by zooming in on details such as a character's limp or a scuffed toecap, producing a whole narrative from the human equivalent of a footnote, so when Boz explains that there are many cab drivers he has the honor of "knowing by sight" he is gesturing towards a much more radical claim about his powers of observation. There is very little Boz does not know by sight. He can retrieve whole biographies at a glance. A boy and his weeping mother are seen emerging from the Old Bailey, and having scanned

them for clues Boz concludes that "their little history was obvious"—
one he proceeds to unpack with the detached professionalism of a social
worker writing up a set of case notes ("The Old Bailey"). Somebody who
owns a house with green blinds is instantly pinned down to a job in a public office: "we know the fact by the cut of his coat, the tie of his neckcloth
and the self-satisfaction of his gait—the very green blinds themselves have
a Somerset-house air about them" ("The New Year"). No object is free
from the force of Boz's curiosity, not even an unusually large gooseberry
produced by the tree of a neat suburban couple which is "carefully preserved under a wine-glass, on the sideboard, for the edification of visitors" ("London Recreations")—a detail which looks trifling until we are
reminded that often it is the smallest things that become the focus for human lives, their unexpected center of gravity. In sketch after sketch, single
details swell into a whole personality, and real life rearranges itself into
the reassuringly simple outlines of a cartoon. As Boz passes the secondhand clothes in Monmouth Street, London's largest "burial place" for
decayed fashions, his imagination is quick to fill each item with its former
owner, until "whole rows of coats have started from their pegs . . . lines
of trousers have jumped down to meet them . . . and half an acre of shoes
have suddenly found feet to fit them, and gone stumping down the street"
("Meditations in Monmouth-street"). Even figures who are usually invisible to their fellow city-dwellers, such as the friendless man who tries to
"revive" his threadbare clothes by dyeing them a glossy black ("Shabby-
genteel People"), are briefly thrust center stage and revealed to be just as
interesting to us as they are to themselves. Boz's eyes waste nothing.

The future itself is not safe from his searching gaze, as he projects possible entanglements and outcomes for the people he encounters. In "The
Prisoners' Van" he joins a crowd to watch two young female prisoners arriving handcuffed together at Bow Street police station. They are sisters,
and to judge from the clues dropped about their "depravity" and "gaud-
ily dressed" appearance, they are almost certainly prostitutes. While the
younger one, who is about fourteen years old, is "weeping bitterly" and
trying to hide her face in her handkerchief, her older sister responds with

a "flaunting laugh," yanking her companion into the van with the cry, "Come down, and let's show you the way." Boz seizes on the line as a model of how a way of life can be passed down from generation to generation like a curse: "What the younger girl was then the elder had been once; and what the elder then was, she must soon become. A melancholy prospect, but how surely to be realised: a tragic drama, but how often acted! Turn to the prisons and police-offices of London—nay, look into the very streets themselves. These things pass before our eyes day after day, and hour after hour—they have become such matters of course, that they are utterly disregarded." Such scenes once again lend Dickens's writing a self-consciously theatrical air, this time by drawing on the sense of "sketch" as a "short play or performance."[59] The younger sister's life may still be a rough outline waiting to be filled in by events (another sense of "sketch" Dickens is quick to activate), but there is an irresistible narrative momentum drawing her on to her doom.[60] She is like an understudy waiting to step into the leading lady's shoes.

Dickens's career provides a more optimistic version of this process, because several of his sketches resemble working notes for ideas and characters that would later be developed in his novels. Some are only stray fragments caught out of the corner of Boz's eye: the youth at Astley's who self-importantly busies himself "rubbing the place where [his] whiskers ought to be," for example, is in effect practicing for the role of Fledgby in *Our Mutual Friend,* who after years of smooth-chinned disappointment still finds himself jealously contemplating other, hairier men, "and considering which pattern of whisker he would prefer to produce out of himself by friction, if the Genie of the cheek would only answer to his rubbing." Other hints are scattered across different sketches like a set of dots waiting to be joined into a meaningful pattern: put together the thirteen-year-old pickpocket who blames his "twin brother . . . vich is so exactly like me, that no vun ever knows the difference atween us," the young woman viciously beaten up by a "powerful, ill-looking young fellow" ("The Old Bailey"), the vividly imagined last night of a condemned man ("A Visit to Newgate"), the broad-shouldered brute who "seldom walked forth without a dog at his heels" ("Meditations in Monmouth-street"), and the pompous beadle who glares at some parish urchins ("The Beadle"), and the cast for *Oliver Twist* is starting to assemble. (Since Dickens began *Oliver Twist* as a follow-up to his "Our Parish" sketches, before it outgrew itself and turned into a novel, the connections may have been strategic rather than accidental.) Add the rowdy young men in "Our Next Door Neighbours," who amuse themselves by "counterfeiting the shrieks of females in distress," and we even hear the first stirrings of the public reading in which Dickens acted out Nancy's murder. It is like an echo in reverse.

Of course, reading Dickens's early sketches as windows that open onto his future risks falling into a form of critical doublethink, in which the early writing is praised as promising, but only because we know that its promise was subsequently fulfilled. Yet if there is a strand of thought which links Dickens's sketches together, it is the ease with which lives can be stymied or knocked off course. In one sketch, an old lady returns from her trip to the seaside to discover that an admirer has "completely effaced the name from her brass door-plate" in his eagerness to polish it ("Our Parish: The Old Lady"). In another, the brass plate of one tenant replaces that of his failed predecessor ("Shops and Their Tenants"). Both sketches pause over how easily a life in the city can vanish or be overwritten. Even figures who remain in view often find their lives branching off unexpectedly. Sometimes this is done with comic literalmindedness, in the manner of the omnibus conductors who take a mischievous pleasure in snaring passengers and then merrily rattling away in the wrong direction ("Omnibuses"). Elsewhere, Dickens's interest in these biographical tipping points creates a narrative structure in which he describes his characters' attempts to break out of the looping returns of their daily routines—by falling in love, for example, or holding a party—and then shows the unhappy consequences. And throughout, he is developing a style of writing designed to involve his readers in this world, by encouraging us to imagine the likely outcome of a line of thought and then giving it an unexpected twist. Just as there is "no saying how long" a character like Amelia Martin "might have continued [in the same] course of life," had an accidental encounter not sprung the trap of her singing ambitions ("The Vocal Dress-maker"), so in reading these sketches we cannot say how long Boz will stick to the same way of describing anything. As comedy gives way to pathos, or potential tragedy collapses into farce, we, too, repeatedly find ourselves being knocked off course.

Amateur detective, but also anthropologist, sociologist, tour guide, and master of ceremonies, Boz, with his many faces, accurately reflects a city that has always seemed to be one step ahead of our efforts to secure it in our minds. What struck Dickens's original readers with even greater force was that, even after Boz had finished with London, it stubbornly refused to settle back into its old way of life. Instead it took on what Dickens later called, in a memorandum note, "an odd unlikeness of itself."[61] In a curious reversal of cause and effect, the more attention Dickens devoted to London, the more it seemed to imitate him. "When I got to London," Francis Parkman wrote in 1843, "I thought I had been there before. . . . The hackney coachmen and cabmen . . . the walking advertisements . . . and a hundred others seemed so many incarnations of Dickens's characters."[62] Such responses gave the strongest indication yet that here was a writer who was not content simply to reflect the world. Through an eccentric character here, or a flourish of syntax there, he was making the world seem increasingly "Dickensian."

By the beginning of 1836, Dickens found himself far closer to the heart of literary London than he had been only a year or two before. J. C. Hotten provides an interesting piece of evidence when he recalls Dickens's love of practical jokes:

> When Charles Dickens first became acquainted with Mr. Vincent Dowling, editor of *Bell's Life* . . . he would generally stop at old Tom Goodwin's oyster and refreshment rooms, opposite the office, in the Strand. On one occasion, Mr. Dowling, not knowing who had called, desired that the gentleman would leave his name, to be sent over to the office, whereupon young Dickens wrote:

> **CHARLES DICKENS,**
> RESURRECTIONIST,
> *in search of a subject*

Some recent cases of body-snatching had then made the matter a general topic for public discussion, and Goodwin pasted up the strange address-card for the amusement of the medical students who patronised his oysters. It was still upon his wall when "Pickwick" had made Dickens famous.[63]

This has been described as an "unwitting prophecy" on Dickens's part, the first sign of his interest in locating the dead that would eventually produce results as diverse as Jerry Cruncher in *A Tale of Two Cities,* a Fleet Street porter whose enthusiasm for funeral processions is explained by the fact that he moonlights as a body-snatcher, and Dickens's own obsessive returns to the Paris morgue.[64] It may also have been an unwitting prophecy on the part of Tom Goodwin, who little knew how famous Dickens's name would become when he pasted up the card in his bar. But Dickens must still have been known well enough for the joke to have made sense at the time; the pun on "subject" could only have been activated if the other customers—presumably fellow journalists as well as medical students, given Tom Goodwin's location on the Strand—recognized his name as a writer keen to dig up good stories. Like a more sophisticated version of his "sundry bits of boyish fun" at Wellington House, this was an in-joke from a member of the in-crowd.

Dickens's letters demonstrate the care with which he was plotting the next steps of his "upward path." They included some tactful correspondence with the famously prickly George Cruikshank, who had been persuaded to illustrate a two-volume collection of his sketches, and some watchful notes to Macrone on the need to keep up momentum after Macrone had earlier told Dickens "most imperatively and pressingly to 'get on.'"[65] (When Cruikshank delayed sending a batch of his etchings, Dickens judiciously asked Macrone if he would write on his behalf, "impressing the necessity of dispatch upon him," a joke that gave way to a glint of menace in his next comment: "I think he requires the spur.")[66] Macrone's sense of urgency was understandable. Only three years older than Dickens, he had set up business as an independent publisher in September 1834 with a loan of £500 from a hopeful female admirer, despite his limited experience and doubtful qualifications for the job. (In 1848 Dickens recalled that "poor Macrone" could not even spell the word "book," his various stabs at it including "buke, "boke," and "booke.")[67] Having recently purchased the rights to reprint Ainsworth's novel *Rookwood,* this "young and spirited publisher" (Ainsworth's description) was impatient to forge a reputation as a promoter of new talent, and was prepared to invest in Boz: £100 for the copyright of the first edition, a fair sum for a publisher with such meager resources, together with an aggressive advertising campaign.[68]

Dickens was far less confident over how best to promote himself. Though he had carefully revised his original newspaper and journal sketches, sharpening up some bits of phrasing and toning others down (a winking joke about the aphrodisiac qualities of oysters was cut, as were some of the racier bits of slang, once he realized that broad humor would not necessarily appeal to a broad public), he was caught between the desire to remain self-effacing and a competing desire to announce his arrival with a fanfare of publicity.[69] The first impulse led him to a title (*Sketches by Boz, Illustrative of Every-day Life, and Every-day People*) that was, he hoped, "unaffected and unassuming—two requisites which it is very desirable for a young author [not] to lose sight of."[70] Yet one needn't be a committed Freudian to notice that the word helpfully supplied by Dickens's editors—"not"—was originally missing from his sentence, an omission indicating a degree of uncertainty over whether he really was humble, or whether, like Uriah Heep in *David Copperfield,* he had realized that declarations of humility could provide useful cover for his ambition. He was far less reticent when inserting an advertisement into the *Morning Chronicle* on February 2, 1836, which promised the republication of some popular sketches, together with "a variety of original papers by the same versatile author," all accompanied by "numerous etchings in GEORGE CRUIKSHANK's best style." "A more entertaining miscellany cannot well be imagined," it concluded, "and we most earnestly wish it the success which we are quite certain it will deserve." The editorial "we" cannot wholly disguise Dickens's hand behind this "modest paragraph."[71]

Such "puffing" was standard publishing practice at the time, despite grumbles from within the industry about "extravagant self-publicity," but Dickens was understandably nervous about how to present himself to a public that knew him principally through a pseudonym.[72] Sometimes nervousness was indistinguishable from gloom. Having already written several sketches on how easy it was to fail in London, and the terrifying vulnerability of anyone who attempted to change his or her life, the three "original papers" he now added were all concerned with the prospect of impending death, whether seen through the lens of reportage ("A Visit to Newgate"), comedy ("The Great Winglebury Duel"), or melodrama ("The Black Veil"). That hardly suggested an optimistic frame of mind. A similar struggle between self-assertion and self-restraint can be seen in the first series of *Sketches by Boz*, published in two volumes on February 6, which opened with a preface in which the first adjective was "humble": "In humble imitation of a prudent course, universally adopted by aeronauts, the Author of these volumes throws them up as his pilot balloon, trusting it may catch some favourable current, and devoutly and earnestly hoping it may *go off well*." "Author" signaled the existence of an identity separate from Boz, and one who was far warier than his spirited alter ego, as Dickens went on to announce that he had hitched himself and "all his hopes of future fame, and all his chances of future success" to this balloon. Explaining that he was too scared to make "so perilous a voyage, in so frail a machine, alone and unaccompanied" (so much for his boasts about traveling "without companion, introducer, or adviser"), he introduced Cruikshank as his ballooning companion: "this is their first voyage together, but it may not be their last." The preface concluded with an announcement that if these "little pictures of life and manners" should prove a success, the Author "hopes to repeat his experiment with increased confidence, and on a more extensive scale." It was an enticing rhetorical performance, at once masterful and halting, like watching a high-wire act in which the skill of the artist is nowhere near as exciting as the thought that he might plummet at any moment.

The process was helped by Cruikshank's illustrations, one of which depicted himself and Dickens among the ushers conducting guests into a public dinner (Figure 7).[73] It closely reflected Dickens's hope that the *Sketches* would make an equally swaggering entrance into the world of print; and by the time he found himself introducing a second edition of the first series in August, he was prepared to give his writing a slightly more ambitious edge. Once again, though, he was careful to give the impression that anything else he might produce would be a shared project, this time with his readers. Having acknowledged the "unlooked-for success" of the first edition with "deepest gratitude," he noted that "if the pen that designed these little outlines, should present its labours frequently to the Public hereafter; if it should produce fresh sketches, and even connected works of fiction of a higher grade, they have only themselves to blame." If, if: though Dickens was starting to work out a strategy to retain his readers' loyalty—flatter them, tease them, make them his friends—he was not getting carried away just yet.

An alternative image of the author had already been provided by Cruikshank's illustration, in the first series, for *Early Coaches* (Figure 8). A figure readily identifiable as Dickens, with floppy hair and neat traveling clothes, is arranging to take a coach while his trunk, marked "Mr. Boz London," is being handed across the counter. Packed with realistic details of early-morning coach travel—sleepy porters, pools of gaslight, an air of barely organized clutter—it is a knowingly accurate portrait of Dickens at the time he was putting together both series of *Sketches by Boz*. A writer who was starting to be identified with a single location (if London was indeed one place rather than many), he was also part of a world that seemed to be spinning faster than ever before. As he pointed out in "Hackney Coach Stands," the urge to "keep moving" was becoming unstoppable.

❧❧❧❧❧❧❧❧

CHAPTER SEVEN

The Moving Age

Sketches by Boz was not the only title Dickens contemplated for his first book. A letter to his publisher John Macrone, written in October 1835, showed him trying out alternatives that would suit the volume's miscellaneous contents and sit invitingly on the page:

—What do you think of

Sketches by Boz
and
Cuts by Cruikshank

_____

or

Etchings by Boz
and
Wood Cuts by Cruikshank.

_____

I think perhaps some such title would look more modest—whether modesty *ought* to have anything to do with such an affair, I must leave to your experience as a Publisher to decide.[1]

Dickens's deferential tone cannot conceal some nervous coughing and shuffling, which was understandable given that Macrone's original suggestion seems to have been something along the lines of *Bubbles from the Bwain of Boz and the Graver of Cruikshank.*[2] An ambitious but inexperienced publisher, Macrone had taken his lead from the marketplace: his title was a spoof of Sir Francis Bond Head's *Bubbles from the Brunnens of Nassau, by an Old Man,* a collection of sensible pieces about a trip to drink the spa waters, published in 1834. Presumably Macrone was aiming to nudge the book-buying public's memory, as well as poke them in the ribs: *Bubbles from the Bwain of Boz* would be a way of complimenting his young author's fizzing intelligence, while tapping into a ready-made audience for travels that lay far closer to home. Dickens was right to be grateful, and even more right to be wary. Choosing such a modish title would have meant that, like many parodies (*Bored of the Rings, The Da Vinci Cod,* and so on), his book would have been uncomfortably dependent on the longevity of its source, parasitically tangled up with a literary organism that was already starting to wither, and Dickens's letter reveals that his ambitions were working on a far longer timescale than those of his publisher. While "bubbles" are fun but inherently ephemeral, the direction of thought that saw "Sketches" sinking into "Etchings" demonstrated his hope that these early pieces, for all their lightness of touch, would make a lasting mark.

Despite some reviews of the first series that vied with each other to find the best superlative—a good-natured skirmish won by the *Metropolitan Magazine*'s choice of "perfect"—the second series, launched in December 1836 (ten months after the first), revealed that Dickens was still trying to find a suitable balance between self-confidence and self-doubt.[3] Even Cruikshank's title-page illustration (Figure 9) is more ambivalent than first meets the eye. On the face of it, this depiction of Dickens and himself is a scene of mutual appreciation, as they flourish their little flags and the crowd urges them on by waving everything from a parasol to a hat on a walking stick. The balloon that hovers over the main title looks far too small to lift two people off the ground, but it is a comically outsized version of the only sort of bubble that does have some staying power: a speech bubble. Perhaps Cruikshank was recalling the cartoons he had drawn earlier in his career, which made fun of the latest political scandal or fashionable intrigue in the shape of caricatures whose speech ballooned grotesquely out of their mouths and lingered gleefully in the air; perhaps he simply found his pencil falling into the old style. In effect, it made the words "Second Series" into an announcement from Dickens, whose arms are raised in greeting, and maybe a hint of triumph, as the tail of the balloon curls gently away from his head. Yet a reader who investigated the sketches in this new collection would quickly have discovered another reference to balloons. The climax of "Vauxhall Gardens by Day," after Boz has walked around this once-fashionable pleasure garden and "met with disappointment at every turn," involves the final preparations for an ascent by one of Mr. Green's commercially operated balloons, as "the aërial travellers stood up, and the crowd outside roared with delight, and the two gentlemen who had never ascended before, tried to wave their flags, as if they were not nervous, but held on very fast all the while." Soon the balloons are distant specks, and the crowd dissipates "perfectly satisfied" with what they have seen, but Dickens concludes by noting that Mr. Green will be making "another ascent next Wednesday." Short-lived, routine, yet fraught with peril, a balloon flight was at best an equivocal model for writing. Dickens was practically inviting the accusation that he needed to be brought back down to earth.

Cruikshank's illustration was perfectly in keeping with the restlessness of the time. Dickens's earliest *Morning Chronicle* sketch, "Omnibuses," had singled out a feature of London life introduced as recently as 1829—the first attempt at a public transport system that had started to thread its way through the city's streets—and his choice was especially revealing about the territory he was marking out as his own. Dickens's London was a city on the move. The opening sketch in his second series, "The Street—Morning," provided a carefully staged introduction to its bustling energy. Starting with a deserted nightscape, distinguished by an "air of cold, solitary desolation" after the last drunk has staggered home and the last "rakish-looking cat" has slunk away down its alley, Dickens slowly adds the movement and noise needed to bring London back to life, building up the "busy, eager crowd" one group at a time, like a film director gradually populating his set with extras. A "long straggling line" of market traders snakes its way towards Covent Garden, weighed down by baskets of fruit and vegetables; a few schoolboys "rattle merrily over the pavement" as they set off in a different direction to their school; a young chimney sweep arrives at his first house and patiently waits on the front step. Soon there is so much going on that Dickens finds himself resorting to swelling lists, where "men [are] shouting, carts backing, horses neighing, boys fighting, basket-women talking, piemen expatiating on the excellence of their pastry, donkeys braying"—a scene in which all those present participles flow naturally out of "morning" as a time when everything seems to be happening at once. Finally, "the streets are thronged with a vast concourse of people—gay and shabby, rich and poor, idle and industrious," and within half a sentence the sketch draws to a close. It ends, in other words, just at the moment when the scene is set, but without any threat to its cheerfully democratic tone. No event is promoted from the background to become the mainspring of a plot; no figure emerges from the throng to announce himself or herself as the hero.

Put another way, the sketch is halted before it has the opportunity to develop into a novel like *Little Dorrit*. This begins with a description of London as seen through an indiscriminate wide-angle lens ("Nothing to see but streets, streets, streets"), before zooming in to notice Arthur Clennam as he sits in a coffeehouse surrounded by ten thousand "responsible houses" and fifty thousand stinking "lairs," and eventually, in the final sentence of the novel, zooms out again as Clennam and his new wife, Amy Dorrit, rejoin the world of their readers: "They went quietly down into the roaring streets, inseparable and blessed; and as they passed along in sunshine and shade, the noisy and the eager, and the arrogant and the froward and the vain, fretted and chafed, and made their usual uproar." In a brilliantly staged narrative dissolve, Dickens's characters sink back into the anonymous crowd, like two swimmers disappearing under the busy waves, albeit with a comforting echo of the marriage service to remind us that, although the city threatens to replace genuine community with mere contiguity (all those *and*'s look like a set of hands reaching out and grasping thin air), it is still possible to make lasting and meaningful connections. Dickens's description of the "gay and shabby, rich and poor, idle and industrious" at the end of "The Street—Morning," by contrast, does not make any attempt to unpick that dense social weave, a task to which *Little Dorrit* devotes many hundreds of pages. Instead, the question is left hanging thoughtfully in mid-sentence.

One social group that Dickens singles out deserves special mention: "the early clerk population of Somers and Camden Towns, Islington, and Pentonville," who "are fast pouring into the City, or directing their steps towards Chancery-lane and the inns of court." Dickens's special interest in clerks is again evident here, and this allusion to London's new suburbs was also a timely reminder that the city's energy could no longer be contained by what was happening at its center. London was spreading outwards in a way that was perfectly in keeping with the habits of its population: a mixture of purposeful movement and aimless wandering. Photographs and drawings from later in the century have produced a composite image of nineteenth-century London that is hard to shake off: a world dominated by a forest of smoking chimneys and muffled by fog; a city so dirty, with its mud-spattered streets and soupy air, that from a distance it resembled a huge brown stain spreading across the countryside. The truth is slightly less compliant—in 1838 Dickens could describe Chelsea as being "in the country," and as late as 1888 Henry James reported that it was possible to walk from Notting Hill to Whitehall, a journey mimicking the daily route of many clerks, "altogether on soft, fine turf, amid the song of birds, the bleat of lambs, the ripple of ponds, the rustle of admirable trees"—but it was impossible to avoid London's greedy sprawl for long.[4] Within a century, a population of some 960,000 in 1801 had expanded to over 6.5 million, in a process that was both unprecedented and unparalleled. London overwhelmed comparisons. By 1901 it was more than twice the size of New York, its nearest rival for the unofficial title of capital of the world, and there were more Londoners than there were inhabitants of Edinburgh, Glasgow, Dublin, Belfast, Cardiff, Birmingham, Manchester, Liverpool, Newcastle, Bradford, Bristol, Leicester, Nottingham, Sheffield, and Leeds put together.[5] It is not surprising that this period saw the first sustained attempts at statistical analysis, and even less surprising that when confronted by the challenge of London even the best statisticians quickly retreated into the consolations of romance. Henry Mayhew's fact-gathering in *London Labour and the London Poor,* for example, often takes on a strange fairy-tale quality, as when he calculates the number of cigar-ends thrown away each week as thirty thousand, and estimates that if one-sixth of this "refuse tobacco" is picked up and recycled by the cigar-end finders, then some proportion is forever in circulation, like a gritty version of Hans Christian Andersen's silver shilling.

What none of these figures revealed was the sense of almost visceral shock felt by those who witnessed London's ragged creep outwards, and in particular its sudden growth spurts, as speculative builders created a no-man's-land between country and city in which new houses seemed to spring up like mushrooms overnight. Dickens's description of Holloway in *Our Mutual Friend* is equally representative of the landscape created by the first building boom, lasting roughly from the turn of the century to the end of the 1830s: "a tract of suburban Sahara, where tiles and bricks were burnt, bones were boiled, carpets were beat, rubbish was shot, dogs were fought, and dust was heaped by contractors." Cruikshank's 1829 etching *London Going Out of Town—or—The March of Bricks and Mortar* (Figure 10) vividly captures the alarm caused by such unregulated growth, as kilns belch threatening black smoke into the air, and some puny haystacks flee a shower of bricks forming a broken rainbow in the sky. The invading army of chimney pots, in particular, adds a disturbing military gloss to popular phrases of the time, such as "the march of mind" or "the march of intellect."[6] Such phrases would soon stiffen into clichés (explaining that refined audiences "won't have no ghosts, no coffin, and no devil," a Punch and Judy performer complained to Mayhew that "it's the march of hintellect wot's a doing all this ere"), but Cruikshank's etching tapped a public mood that was still too raw to have settled into a particular shape.[7] Like his black smoke and brick shower, such questions were in the air indistinctly, menacingly.

Another etching from 1829, *The March of Intellect* (Figure 11) shows equally radical social changes at work: in the foreground a workman delicately eats an ice cream and his companion gnaws at a hothouse pineapple, both happily oblivious to traditional class divisions, while steam-powered machines whisk people across the ground and through the air. Like many satires on the shape of things to come, its scoffing has largely been silenced by the passage of time: only a batlike snout and wings prevent the imaginary flying machine from resembling a modern airliner, while a few decades later Londoners would think nothing of entering a "tube" to carry them across the city. Even in 1829, the idea that people might travel in little motorized vehicles of their own was not completely outlandish: for eighteen months in 1827–1829, Goldsworthy Gurney's prototype steam-powered road carriage could be seen puffing around London at speeds of up to twenty miles per hour. But the fears expressed by this etching were real enough, and they took on added momentum after the passage of the Reform Bill. If this was indeed "the moving age," as Dickens later christened it in *Bleak House,* then where was it heading?

In any battle between tradition and modernity, there is no doubt which side Dickens would take. "Dickens was a pure modernist," John Ruskin wrote in 1870, "a leader of the steam-whistle party *par excellence*—and he had no understanding of antiquity except a sort of jackdaw sentiment for cathedral towers."[8] Not even Dickens's architectural sentiments could restrain his enthusiasm if there was an opportunity to reduce dirty and rotten aspects of the past to rubble. Reporting from Paris in 1853, he applauded Baron Haussmann's remodeling of the city's historic core, and declared the demolition of thousands of houses to be "wonderfully improving." Presumably the inhabitants of these houses might have felt rather differently, but that did not prevent Dickens from asking the "ridiculous" City of London authorities why they refused to follow Paris's lead.[9] (Dickens seems to have forgotten the ironic tone he had adopted only a few years earlier, in *Dombey and Son,* when describing the wholesale destruction wrought by the railway's "mighty course of civilisation and improvement," not to mention his pointed observation that the development of New Oxford Street, while it produced a grand sweep of chunky

Victorian buildings, had also ruthlessly swept away the slums where many of the most deprived Londoners lived: "Thus, we make our New Oxford Streets, and our other new streets, never heeding, never asking, where the wretches whom we clear out, crowd.")[10] In Rome, he reported in *Pictures from Italy,* he was drawn to the crumbling grandeur of the Coliseum, where he was struck by the "whirl of strife, and blood, and dust" that lingered in the empty arena like a bad smell. Though he was briefly tempted into standard guidebook-speak, declaring it to be "the most impressive, the most stately, the most solemn, grand, majestic, mournful sight, conceivable," he quickly betrayed his true feelings, observing that the people of modern Rome remained as "fierce and cruel" as ever, and concluding that "there is scarcely one countenance in a hundred, among the common people in the streets, that would not be at home and happy in a renovated Coliseum to-morrow." Not until his second visit to Italy, in 1853, did he see something to convince him that the forces of progress had enlightened Rome's dark heart: a telegraph line that went through the arena "like a sun beam—in at one ruined arch, and out at another."[11]

Dickens was equally uncompromising in his fiction. The false book spines he had made for his study in Gad's Hill included a set of volumes entitled *The Wisdom of Our Ancestors:* "I.—Ignorance. II.—Superstition. III.—The Block. IV.—The Stake. V.—The Rack. VI.—Dirt. VII.—Disease," and he sometimes found it hard to convince himself they were altogether out of date. He is notably tough on characters who seem stuck in the past, such as *Great Expectations*'s Miss Havisham or *Little Dorrit*'s Mrs. Clennam, and even tougher on those who would be happier to return there, such as the sleekly complacent Mr. Filer in *The Chimes,* who repeats "the good old times!" like a refrain whenever he wants to wag his finger in the face of the present. The moral of *The Chimes* is given by the Phantom, who instructs Trotty Veck that "The voice of Time . . . cries to man, Advance!"—and for all his fears about stagnation or regression, Dickens was generally quick to take his own advice. Although he was often tempted back to the period of his childhood, and became increasingly interested in psychological phenomena such as flashbacks and déjà vu, he seems to have been even more attracted by the simple fact that his narratives allowed him to push off from the past and move inexorably forwards in time. Each sentence unspooling across the page was a little model of how civilization could build on its past and reach confidently into the future. Even novels that dealt with the bloodiest excesses of the previous century, such as the French Revolution *(A Tale of Two Cities)* or the Gordon Riots *(Barnaby Rudge),* show him recoiling from their horrors in narratives that are designed to outrun the brutal events of the past.

Dickens was similarly keen to heed the call of "Advance!" in his private life. "It was one of Mr. Dickens's maxims," the journalist George Sala reported, "that a given amount of mental exertion should be counteracted by a commensurate amount of bodily fatigue; and for a length of years his physical labours were measured exactly by the duration of his intellectual work."[12] Balancing this equation could involve activities from horseback riding to vigorous dancing, but for most of Dickens's life it was concentrated into walking through the London streets, often for miles and hours at a stretch. These were research trips, as well as escape routes. "For a week or a fortnight I can write prodigiously in a retired place," he explained in 1846 while working on *Dombey and Son* in Lausanne, but "my characters seem to want to stand still if they do not have a London around them."[13] What he also seems to have shared with his characters is a vague but powerful sense that physical movement was bound up with more abstract ideas of progress. David Copperfield confesses that, a week after resolving to learn shorthand in order to become a parliamentary reporter, "I continued to walk extremely fast, and to have a general idea that I was getting on." All that distinguishes this from Dickens's own general idea is a slight tweak of parody, together with a worrying echo of Steerforth's advice about how to succeed in life: "Ride on! Rough-shod if need be, smooth-shod if that will do, but ride on! Ride over all obstacles, and win the race!" These are standard mid-Victorian sentiments, in which life becomes an obstacle course to be won, whether by nimbly skipping around impediments or ruthlessly crushing them underfoot; but while Dickens strongly approved of the need to keep moving onwards, he remained troubled by who or what might get damaged in the process. A particularly nasty scene in *A Tale of Two Cities* features the haughty Marquis, whose carriage experiences "a sickening little jolt" as it runs over a child, and who responds by remarking coolly that "One or the other of you is for ever in the way." While Dickens is clearly excited by the "wild rattle and clatter" of the carriage, he is quick to condemn a character willing to take Steerforth's advice quite so literally.

In this context, an element of serious reflection can be detected underneath Dickens's joke about the speed with which he was riding around the country on newspaper business in 1835: "I have a presentiment, I shall run over an only child before I reach Chelmsford."[14] For by the time he joined the reporting staff of the *Morning Chronicle,* the potential human cost of "the moving age" had already become clear. While road traffic accidents were common in towns long before the arrival of the internal combustion engine—in 1803 two pedestrians were trapped between coal wagons on the Strand and crushed to death "notwithstanding their screams and shrieks"—the emergence of the railway brought a new fear that it was not just in metaphorical terms that people were being ground down by the gears and pistons of a mechanical age.[15] In 1830, the first passenger train had also resulted in the first widely reported railway fatality, as the local MP William Huskisson tumbled under the wheels of Stevenson's Rocket at the opening of the Liverpool and Manchester Railway, while the unreliability of early steam locomotives meant that there was no guarantee of safety even if one stayed inside the carriage. A colored etching published as part of a set circa 1835 (Figure 12) contains some imaginative satires on future forms of *Locomotion* (steam-powered boots, some more batlike flying machines, a huge passenger-carrying kettle), but the happy fantasy is disrupted by what is happening in the background: a steam engine exploding discreetly behind a bush. The so-called railway boom might be a noisy and messy affair.

"Bless railroads everywhere," Thackeray sardonically makes one of his speakers in "The Speculators" say, "and the world's advance."[16] Dickens was similarly ambivalent: being a leader of the steam-whistle party did not blind him to the fact that whistles had been introduced to warn people of the danger coming their way. Yet although he worried about the destruction wrought by railway construction, and was irritated by an enthusiasm that could be as thoughtlessly mechanical as its object (in *The Old Curiosity Shop*, Miss Monflathers sternly advises Little Nell to improve her mind "by the constant contemplation of the steam-engine"), he could never entirely extinguish his excitement at the thrusting power and speed of a train in full flight. The most celebrated example comes in *Dombey and Son*, as the "remorseless monster" gobbles up everything in its path: "Away, and still away, onward and onward ever: glimpses of cottage-homes, of houses, mansions, rich estates, of husbandry and handicraft, or people, of old roads and paths that look deserted, small, and insignificant as they are left behind: and so they do, and what else is there but such glimpses, in the track of the indomitable monster, Death!" Dickens's sense of alarm is palpable, but so is his complicity with the engine's relentless advance, as the rhythms of his sentence support the democratic vistas glimpsed through the carriage window, and push on towards that final and wholly democratic word "Death!"

Dickens often enjoyed drawing parallels between himself and a steam engine, envisaging his imagination as a container of energy that needed to be directed along precisely engineered lines. Of course, the analogy was slightly hampered by the fact that, unlike a poet working within previously calibrated forms, as a prose writer Dickens was creating his lines in the act of moving along them. Perhaps he thought of the novelist as a creature like those heroes of twentieth-century cartoons who cheat disaster on runaway trains by frantically scattering lengths of track ahead of themselves. Certainly, on the evidence of *Sketches by Boz*, he had experimented long before *Dombey and Son* with a form of writing in which it was impossible to say whether plot generated style or the other way round. As early as 1835, he explained that in order to "get on" with his writing he had to build up a head of steam: "My composition is peculiar; I can never write with effect—especially in the serious way—until I have got my steam up, or in other words until I have become so excited with

my subject that I cannot leave off."[17] Over time, this would have damaging consequences on Dickens's health (this is the period in which he
starts to complain about feeling exhausted, although nobody was driving
him harder than himself), and possibly also on the health of those around
him: in January 1836, "The Butcher" wrote "to say that his boy was going
to take out a warrant against me for an assault."[18] Whether Dickens had
lashed out, or the butcher's letter was a piece of opportunistic blackmail,
it served as a timely warning of what could happen if he overheated or
came off the rails. The death of Carker in *Dombey and Son*, who is caught
under the train's wheels and thrown into the air as a confetti of "mutilated
fragments," also shows the possible fictional consequences of not being
able to leave off. Officially it is an accident, but as far as the novelist is
concerned every accident is deliberate; and earlier sentences like the one
about the engine's monstrous appetite show Dickens not merely observing events as they unfold, but actively forcing them on to their conclusion.
Carker may be crushed by a train, but he is also a victim of his creator's
narrative momentum.

   Sometimes this momentum took far longer to build. On December 2,
1835, Dickens reported for the *Morning Chronicle* on a fire at the
Elizabethan mansion known as Hatfield House, in which the eighty-five-
year-old Marchioness of Salisbury had died. Although Dickens's report
occasionally broke out into atmospheric details, imagining "the fury and
rapid progress of the flames" and noting that the "ruins were still smoking
when I visited them," he was tactfully imprecise about the fire's victim,
concluding that "there appears every reason to suppose that the ill-fated
lady suffered little from burning, and that she was most probably suffo-
cated by the dense smoke at a very early period of the fire." The truth
was far more unpleasant, as Dickens implicitly acknowledged by insisting
once more that "the aged lady . . . escaped the torment of being burnt to
death,"[19] thereby conjuring up the very image he seemed so determined
to quash. In fact, it seems that the Marchioness had been writing when
"the feathers in her high-piled hair—she still wore it in the fashion of
her youth—had caught in the candle and so started the fire."[20] Privately,

Dickens's response had all the briskness of an account by a seasoned hack, announcing that "here I am, waiting until the remains . . . are dug out from the ruins of her Ancestor's Castle. I went over the place this morning, and shall 'flare' briefly in the Chronicle tomorrow,"[21] the editors of his correspondence helpfully glossing "flare" as "to appear in print, from its meaning 'to burst into a sudden and temporary blaze' *(OED).*"[22] It was one of Dickens's favorite pieces of contemporary slang, which he used to refer to anything that lit up everyday life, from a "flare at the English Opera House last night with the ladies" (September 3, 1834) to "a slight flare" of electoral scuffling "just stopping short of murder and a riot" (December 16, 1835), and his cruelly funny use of it in this context shows its longer-term importance to his imaginative habits.[23] His newspaper report was a briefly satisfying "flare," like a match being struck, but it would continue to smolder away inside his imagination.[24] Another twenty-five years would pass before it burst into life again in *Great Expectations,* where the same ingredients—an eccentric old woman, a creaky old house, outdated fashions, a personal inferno—came together once more in the fiery demise of Miss Havisham, whose cobwebbed appearance indicated just how long she had been locked away in Dickens's mind.[25]

Yet at the time he was filing this report, Dickens, like most of his readers, had far more pressing concerns. For most of 1834 and 1835, he had to squeeze his sketch writing into the gaps between assignments as a *Morning Chronicle* reporter, involving stints in Parliament, theater reviews, news reports like that of the Hatfield House fire, and anything else that needed his sharp eye and rapid shorthand. In particular, he was regularly sent out around the country to report on elections and other political events—a task that, after passage of the Reform Bill, had assumed even greater importance for a newspaper with the *Morning Chronicle*'s radical stance. The temptation for a biographer is simply to join these dots together and then tidy up the edges, but that would not be true either to Dickens's experience or to the sense of uncertainty nagging away at his readers during the period of transition that followed the Reform Bill. "There never was anybody connected with newspapers, who, in the same space of time, had so much express and post-chaise experience as I," Dickens told John Forster, and in many ways he embodied "the moving age."[26] Traveling from town to town, he had to deploy his pen like a compass needle, establishing the overall drift of public opinion while remaining sensitive to every local mood.

Dickens's first assignment outside the South of England came in September 1834, when he and Thomas Beard were sent to Edinburgh to cover the "Grey Festival," a civic celebration held in honor of the Whig politician widely praised as the man responsible for steering the Reform Bill through Parliament. When Lord Grey stepped down as prime minister in 1834, after the controversy surrounding the Irish Coercion Bill that Dickens had been reporting on from the gallery, many saw it as the end of an era; as one recent biographer has pointed out, "Few Prime Ministers have retired to such a chorus of tributes."[27] Nowhere was the applause more enthusiastic than in Scotland, which had been one of Reform's major beneficiaries, with the creation of eight new parliamentary seats and an electorate increased from 4,500 to 65,000, so there was plenty of support for the decision of the Edinburgh authorities to thank Grey with a grand public dinner and the Freedom of the City. The importance that the *Morning Chronicle* placed on the event is indicated by the fact that it devoted eleven columns to a detailed report of Grey's triumphal progress from Oxenfoord Castle to Edinburgh, followed by the proceedings of the dinner itself on September 17. Dickens traveled there via a ship to Leith, which left him "prostrated" by seasickness, though he had been put in a good mood by the sight of a fellow passenger laughing out loud at something he had written in the *Monthly Magazine*. Scanning through the reports he and Beard sent back, one sees little to catch the eye: the erection of a temporary pavilion, some confusion over tickets, lengthy speeches, much cheering. So why had he been selected? To some extent, John Black's choice was based on purely practical considerations: he needed someone who could report quickly and precisely, and nobody was quicker or more precise than Dickens. He and Beard were "the two best reporters of the time," one of the paper's subeditors recalled, and were chosen for any "great occasions" on which "the *Chronicle* desired, as it always did, to beat all competitors . . . in the priority of its intelligence and in the fullness and accuracy of its reports."[28]

But Black also seems to have given Dickens license to roam in another sense: "having the highest opinion of his original genius," and enjoying the sketches that Dickens was producing alongside his routine reporting work, Black, unusually, allowed him to spice up the facts with occasional flourishes of style.[29] One paragraph in particular stands out. A guest who had patiently waited for the official party for a couple of hours eventually decided to tuck into the buffet, leading to a general scramble of plates and a "clatter of knives and forks" punctuated by cries of "Shame!" from "several gentlemen, who were not hungry," echoed by "several other gentlemen who were hungry [and] cried 'Shame!' too, eating nevertheless, all the while, as fast as they possibly could." At this point, "one of the stewards mounted a bench and feelingly represented to the delinquents the enormity of their conduct, imploring them for decency's sake, to defer the process of mastication until the arrival of Earl Grey. This address was loudly cheered, but totally unheeded; and this is, perhaps, one of the few instances on record of a dinner having been virtually concluded before it began."[30] The passage contains an authentic glimpse of young Dickens at work, as he pretends to give a neutral report of events while each sentence is creasing into an ever wider smile. Overpitched phrases such as "enormity of their conduct" and "process of mastication" are especially well-chosen to skewer the steward's pomposity, and Dickens's gleeful tone reveals his sneaking respect for anyone who refused to be bound by the rules of petty officialdom: his cheerfulness is the literary equivalent of their "loud cheers."

The connection is only lightly hinted at, but for Dickens's original readers this story about loyal citizens waiting "with exemplary patience" for their share of beef and lobsters may have sounded oddly like a political fable. More than two years after the Reform Bill, the optimism it had generated was starting to evaporate; disappointingly little had changed. In 1831, 478,000 men had been eligible to vote in Great Britain and Ireland; after 1832, the figure had almost doubled to 874,000, but this was still no more than one in seven of the adult male population.[31] (The number of female voters remained stable at precisely zero.) Parliament was still dominated by the traditional landed interest, which boasted nearly 500 MPs in 1833, 217 of whom were the sons of peers or baronets; and the self-perpetuating nature of this clique meant that distinguishing among Buffy, Cuffy, and Duffy was no easier than before. Many MPs, like Sir Leicester Dedlock in *Bleak House,* were still elected unopposed by a handful of voters within the boroughs they controlled, and even the increased number of radicals was no guarantee that political representation would also be socially representative: their numbers included William Molesworth, who had once challenged his Cambridge tutor to a duel, and Edward Wakefield, who had been imprisoned for abducting an heiress.[32] Indeed, the suspicion remained that, for all their carefully staged quarrels at the dispatch box, MPs continued to have far more in common with one another than with the country they were supposed to be serving. Hazlitt's comment that the two main parties were like rival stagecoaches which splashed each other with mud, but went by the same road to the same place, seemed more accurate than ever.[33]

In such an unsettled atmosphere, accidents were swiftly adopted as omens. On October 16, 1834, a few weeks after Dickens's return from Edinburgh, the old Houses of Parliament burned to the ground, and although the official report described it as a "melancholy catastrophe," the feeling among most eyewitnesses was that the politicians had it coming.[34] "The crowd was quiet," Carlyle reported, "rather pleased than otherwise," and they "whewed and whistled when the breeze came, as if to encourage it. 'There's a flare-up for the House of Lords!' 'A judgment for the Poor Law Bill!' 'There go their *Hacts!*' Such exclamations seemed to be the prevailing ones: a man sorry I did not see anywhere."[35] (As the flames rose higher, one spectator cheered and was instantly arrested.) The conflagration had started when bundles of wooden splints called "tallies," formerly used to keep accounts, had been stuffed into a stove in the basement of the House of Lords, where they had set fire to the ancient paneling. For Dickens, the events were neatly emblematic of the worm-eaten traditions on which British society was built; as he recalled in a speech made in 1855, the fact that these now-useless sticks had been hoarded rather than distributed to the poor as kindling was a dreadful warning of "that all-obstinate adherence to rubbish which the time has long outlived" and which will inevitably "some day set fire to something or other."[36]

Dickens's clearest contribution to the debate was "The Story without a Beginning," which appeared in the *Chronicle* on December 18, 1834, a month after William IV had summarily dismissed the Whig government of Grey's successor, Lord Melbourne, and invited the Duke of Wellington to form a Tory administration in its place. It was the last time in British history a monarch tried to exercise that prerogative, and Dickens's response, under the guise of a fairy tale "Translated from the German by Boz," dripped with satirical venom. Starting with a blithe child (the king), who walks on soft carpets and feasts on delicacies, the story shows him being corrupted by the buzzing advice of "insects and reptiles that bask in sunshine" (the Tories). As a result, he neglects his flowers (the people), including those of "a bright, bright green" (the Irish), which duly wither and rot. Only the plucky efforts of some bees (the Whigs) save the rest of the flowers, which respond by coldly ignoring the child's plea for forgiveness, "and the child found, to his grief and sorrow, that the appeal had been made too late." It wasn't the subtlest of allegories, and details such as the child and insects crying "like slimy crocodiles" occasionally disrupted Dickens's tone of injured innocence, breaking through the surface of his writing like a shark's fin; but two aspects of the story stand out as especially significant. The first is Dickens's experiment with a narrative structure that grafted an old-fashioned fairy tale onto contemporary society, a process he would later adopt in many of his novels, which organize themselves around a fragile truce between needing to face up to everyday life and wanting to gloss it with a sense of enchantment.[37] The second is that, although Dickens offered this as "The Story without a Beginning," the real-life events that followed the king's unhappy intervention made it clear that many of his contemporaries were plotting for something rather different: a story with an alternative ending.

Forced into a general election in January 1835, the Tories gained nearly a hundred seats but failed to secure an overall majority. After suffering six parliamentary defeats in six weeks, Robert Peel resigned on April 8, and the Melbourne ministry was reinstated, even though Lord Melbourne had previously told his secretary that being prime minister was "a damned bore."[38] And throughout this troubled political period, as the *Chronicle*'s leading "skirmisher and sharpshooter," Dickens was on the road.[39] Sent to report on the January elections in one of the most corrupt areas of the country, he ended up filing accounts from five different towns in the space of a week:

> January 10: Colchester
> January 12: Braintree
> January 13: Chelmsford
> January 14: Sudbury
> January 17: Bury St. Edmonds

If Dickens's schedule resembled a provincial theater tour, he was just as alert to the theatricality of hustings as he had been earlier to the lofty speeches and choruses of Parliament. Later he drew on this experience in "Doctor Marigold's Prescriptions" (1865), a story he adapted as one of his public readings, which features a "Cheap Jack," or traveling salesman, who points out that he and the politicians speak "in the same market-place" and use their patter to make equally unreliable promises: "Will you take me as I stand? You won't? Well, then . . . I'll throw you in anything you ask for. There! Church-rates, abolition of church-rates, more malt tax, no malt tax . . ."

The rhythms of this speech show Dickens settling into his satirical stride, but in 1835 he was far less sure which genre was best suited to what was going on around him. While his account of the Tory victory at

Colchester decided upon light comedy, as the successful candidate and his supporters solemnly processed around the town with "a Crown elevated on a long pole, the general appearance of which forcibly reminded one of Mayday," during a by-election in Kettering later that year he found himself in the middle of a snarling melodrama, as supporters of the Whig candidate William Hanbury were subjected to a cavalry charge by their Tory opponents wielding bludgeons and lead-weighted whips.[40] Both reports open in the same way—Colchester has "an unusually lively and bustling appearance," while Kettering presents "an unusual scene of life and bustle"—but thereafter the stories fork in different directions. All that joins them is Dickens's sense of being surrounded by instability and flux.[41]

Newspapers not only reported these changes, but were actively involved in them. Whether bolstering the status quo, fanning dissent, or offering models of satirical detachment, they were a crucial part of the political atmosphere they were attempting to chart. Improved distribution networks meant that in different parts of the country more readers than ever before could peruse the same words at the same time, usually a day or so after the newspaper had been printed in London, thus giving a significant boost to what Benedict Anderson has described as "the secular, historically clocked, imagined community" that was developing alongside slowly increasing levels of political representation.[42]

Not that newspapers like the *Times* and the *Chronicle* offered a model of harmony. Often their characters and stories, though crammed together on the same page, had nothing in common other than the historical coincidence of the date on the masthead. "Reading a newspaper," Anderson observes, "is like reading a novel whose author has abandoned any thought of a coherent plot," but this would not have prevented Dickens's readers from conjuring up meaningful private connections.[43] Compare the situation with that of modern newspapers. A political summit in Copenhagen, a murder in New York, a case of mistaken identity in Delhi: to see such events happening within a few inches of one another allows us to imagine hidden paths of communication even as we enjoy the pleasures of co-incidence. Newspapers encourage us to entertain fantasies in which the casual is magically transformed into the causal.

To put this another way, they encourage us to turn scrapbooks of people and events into novels like *Bleak House:*

> What connexion can there be, between the place in Lincolnshire, the house in town, the Mercury in powder, and the whereabout of Jo the outlaw with the broom, who had that distant ray of light upon him when he swept the churchyard-step? What connexion can there have been between many people in the innumerable histories of the world who, from opposite sides of great gulfs, have, nevertheless, been very curiously brought together?

The first question takes Dickens sixty-seven chapters and many hundreds of pages to answer. The second is less a question than a dilemma which he grappled with throughout his career. One way of summarizing his fiction would be to say that he attempted to show how many private worlds are contained in the public world we share—his writing is an unflagging celebration of the unique, the freakish, the stubbornly eccentric—while also reminding us of what we have in common. And whereas some writers might simply have instructed their readers to be more generous, or more sympathetic, Dickens's overwhelming popularity meant that he could put his ideas into practice. His writing bridged social divides. Whether his readers were scattered in space or brought together by one of his public performances, the same words transformed thousands of distinct individuals into a united audience. In this sense, one of the best answers to the question "What connexion can there have been between many people . . . very curiously brought together?" was Dickens himself. The curiosity of these people in one another was encouraged and rewarded by his curiosity in them.

The idea that people were connected by lines of writing was starting to emerge as an especially powerful argument in favor of newspapers in the years that Dickens was traveling round the country. Newspapers were always in circulation, always changing; they were the perfect vehicle for "the moving age." Dickens was especially drawn to the idea that, as he argued in a later public address, newspapers were "those engines which, working night by night, and all night long, were felt in their faintest throb throughout the civilised world."[44] By the time he made this speech to the Newsvendors' Benevolent Association in 1849, "throbbing engines" could have been an allusion to the mechanics of distribution as well as steam-powered presses, but even in the 1830s newspapers were associated with movement in a way that was guaranteed to appeal to Dickens. "The public press is now a stream of light and information flowing through the United Kingdom," an anonymous writer urged in 1832, "and should any Government be weak enough to arrest its progress, the obstruction must produce consequences fatal indeed to the public peace and tranquillity."[45] The link here between newspapers and a "United Kingdom" is made to seem as natural as a stream feeding irrigation channels, although the warning about obstructions suggests that the model the writer actually has in mind is a heart pumping blood around the body, as information flowed into London and was then redistributed to the furthest parts of the nation. Dickens would later draw on the same idea in a *Household Words* article that described how letters circulated around the country, pointing out that "the stoppage of Monday's Post Delivery in London would stop, for many precious hours, the natural flow of the blood from every vein and artery in the world, and its return from the heart through all those tributary channels."[46]

Dickens revisited the same metaphor of healthy circulation throughout his career. It is the focus of some of his most powerful writing, from his irritation at signs that read "NO THOROUGHFARE," to the elaborately interconnected structure of *Bleak House,* where Dickens's reference to "the moving age" comes in the context of a whole rogues' gallery of characters keen to bring things shuddering to a halt.[47] From the red tape of Chancery, to churchyards that are choked with corpses, to that inveterate hoarder Krook, whose death by spontaneous combustion leaves behind nothing but a few fatty deposits, the whole novel turns out to be a warning about the need to keep things moving if they are not to atrophy or explode. (The fact that Jo is forever being "moved on" serves as a warning not to confuse simple physical movement with moral progress.) And while it would be wrong to trace these concerns exclusively to the 1830s, Dickens would certainly not have been alone in thinking that, at a time of unprecedented change, news was being sent back to London and pumped out again like blood carrying oxygen around the country. This is what makes B. R. Haydon's 1831 painting *Waiting for the "Times," the Morning after the Debate on Reform, 8 October 1831* (Figure 13) into something more thoughtful than a joke about clubland etiquette. It is not just that the gentleman reading the paper is making someone else wait, but that, lolling in his chair, he is preventing the news from circulating freely. He spreads out across the canvas like a huge blood clot.

Looking back in 1865, Dickens was as astonished as anyone at what had been expected of him: "I have often transcribed for the printer from my shorthand notes . . . writing on the palm of my hand, by the light of a dark lantern, in a post chaise and four, galloping through a wild country, all through the dead of night, at the then surprising rate of fifteen miles an hour."[48] He never lost the excitement of writing on the move, even when it had largely been superseded by a form of writing that moved by itself and without producing any blots or smudges: the electric telegraph. In 1862, one of his notebook entries outlined a possible narrative situation: "Open a story by bringing two strongly contrasted places and strongly contrasted sets of people, into the connexion necessary for the story, by means of an electric message. Describe the message—*be* the message—flashing along through space—over the earth, and under the sea."[49] The tale was never written, probably because *Bleak House* had already staged a less technologically advanced version of the same idea, although Dickens gives a tantalizing glimpse of how he might have carried it off, employing a set of dashes that visually mimic the code invented by Samuel Morse in the 1840s. But nothing, not even the power of steam and electricity, could compete with what Dickens referred to as "the fascination of that old pursuit."[50]

Supplying newspaper copy was a pursuit in more than one sense, as journalists working for rival papers vied with one another to supply the fullest and most up-to-date reports before the presses rolled. They may have hunted as a pack—Dickens recalled writing down a hustings speech in Exeter while "two good-natured colleagues" held a handkerchief over his notebook to protect it from the pelting rain "in the manner of a state canopy in an ecclesiastical procession"—but when it came to the final rush back to London, it was every newshound for himself.[51] For a young writer like Dickens, it offered an exhilarating blend of novelty and tradition. Stepping inside an early morning coach, he could pride himself on moving with the times, but also enjoy feeling like a refugee from one of Tobias Smollett's novels. His breathless letters from these years show how hard he found it to shake off the thrill of the chase. Even writing several hours after his arrival at the next town, his prose continues to ring with the rhythms of a coach rattling through the mud: "On our first stage we have very poor horses. At the termination of the second, The Times and I changed Horses together; they had the start two or three minutes: I bribed the post boys tremendously & we came in literally neck and neck—the most beautiful sight I ever saw."[52]

By the 1840s, such stories inevitably sounded dated, although Dickens remained nostalgic for the old coaching-inns long after they had been replaced by glossy iron-and-glass railway stations, the secular cathedrals of the Victorian age. Many of his novels sought to recapture the old excitement, even if this put an uncomfortable strain on his powers of invention or his readers' patience. One paragraph in *Martin Chuzzlewit* describes a coach spinning on towards London:

> Yoho, past hedges, gates, and trees; past cottages and barns, and people going home from work. . . . Yoho, by churches, dropped down by themselves in quiet nooks, with rustic burial-grounds about them, where the graves are green, and daisies sleep—for it is evening—in

the bosoms of the dead. Yoho, past streams, in which the cattle cool their feet, and where the rushes grow; past paddock-fences, farms, and rick-yards; past last year's stacks, cut, slice by slice, away, and showing, in the waning light, like ruined gables, old and brown. Yoho, down the pebbly dip, and through the merry water-splash, and up at a canter to the level road again. Yoho! Yoho!

The harder Dickens works to bring this scene to life, the more he sounds like somebody drumming his fingers on the table.

There were also times when his body fell back far less self-consciously into the rhythms of his youth. In 1865, he explained that right up "to the present year of my life," whenever he listened to a dull speech, he found his hand tracing out shorthand symbols on the tablecloth, "taking an imaginary note of it all."[53] Even after all these years, he was still taking everything down, still on the move.

CHAPTER EIGHT

"Pickwick, Triumphant"

Two-thirds of the way through the *Pickwick Papers,* Mr. Pickwick looks at
his friends with "a good-humoured smile" and observes: "The only question is, Where shall we go to next?" While this gives him the perfect opportunity to display his trademark twinkle—"a sparkle in the eye which no
spectacles could dim or conceal"—it is also a knowing wink from Dickens
to the reader. "Where shall we go to next?" is a question at the heart of
all picaresque fiction, a form of writing that gives the pleasure of wandering a narrative shape; and few novels revel in their own waywardness as
gleefully as *Pickwick,* an ever-expanding route map of narrative digres-
sions, shortcuts, and dead ends in which the pleasure of the journey is far
more important than its final destination. Nor is Mr. Pickwick's question
exhausted by Dickens's novel. *Pickwick* ends with a cozy vignette of the
hero settled in Dulwich with his servant Sam Weller, "between whom and
his master there exists a steady and reciprocal attachment, which nothing but death will sever." It is a happy ending, insofar as any ending of a
novel we would prefer to continue can be considered happy, but this has
not prevented many readers from seeing the words that follow—"THE
END"—as a challenge or an affront. For anyone who has reached this
point, and has learned to think of himself or herself as an honorary member of the Pickwick Club, Dickens's words read strangely like a betrayal
of characters who are far too full of imaginative energy to be satisfied with
the thin plot he has provided for them. Perhaps this is why, in the years
since the final monthly number of *Pickwick* was published, the full stop
that follows "nothing but death will sever" has come to look less like a last
nail being hammered into place than a jack-in-the-box clicking shut, a
way of preparing the novel to burst back into life.

It did not take long for Dickens's characters to reveal their restlessness. In September 1837, a month before the final number was published, a weekly journal entitled *Pickwick in Boulogne* started to appear; alongside large pirated chunks of Dickens's novel, it included helpful information on local organizations such as the "Wesleyan Missionary Society at Calais." Within a few years the armchair traveler could also choose from G. M. W. Reynolds's *Pickwick Abroad; or, The Tour in France,* serialized in the *Monthly Magazine* from December 1837; the same writer's *Pickwick in America! Edited by "Bos,"* published in forty-four weekly parts in 1838–1839; and *Pickwick in India* (1839–1840), which abruptly ceased publication after seven chapters when the author—Reynolds again—wrote himself into a corner with a gloating description of Mr. Pickwick being devoured by a shark. Even the most ambitious Victorian explorer would have found it hard to keep up with the globetrotting antics of the Pickwickians once they broke out of Dickens's novel. But then, real people could never hope to compete with Dickens's characters, who remained members of a very different order of beings long after they had entered the world of their readers.

Here Dickens's imitators took their cue from the novel itself. When the first sentence of *Pickwick* referred to its hero as "the immortal Pickwick," this was largely a scoffing joke, part of a description that deliberately over-pitched its vocabulary to highlight the disparity between the blandness of the Pickwick Club's activities and its preening self-importance. Over the course of the next 700-odd pages, however, Dickens's mock-heroic tone gradually lost its purchase on his characters. Little by little, month by month, they started to live up to his rhetoric, and what was originally intended as a teasing satire slowly modulated into genuine admiration. Indeed, for many later readers a phrase like "the immortal Pickwick" came to seem less like a joke than an annunciation. For G. K. Chesterton, just as *Pickwick* was something more than a novel ("Even as a boy I believed there were some more pages that were torn out of my copy, and I am looking for them still"), so its characters were something more than human beings: fairies, or angels, or gods wandering the earth.[1] W. H. Auden agreed, arguing that we can imagine new adventures for Mr. Pickwick, just as we can for Sherlock Holmes or Falstaff, because such figures have drifted away from their original historical context into the ageless world of myth.[2] Nor are the novel's various offshoots and overspills limited to writing. From New York to Khartoum, the thousands of guesthouses, restaurants, bars, and clubs that have chosen "Pickwick" as their name stretch out across the world in a vast network of hospitality, at once shrines to Dickens's wandering gods and staging-posts in their genially relentless advance.

If *Pickwick*'s characters have entered the realm of myth, much the same is true of the story of how the novel was written. From the start, contemporaries of Dickens enjoyed relating how he "awoke one morning and found himself famous," and more than one recent critic has settled on the phrase "overnight success" to explain how the *Pickwick* craze changed Dickens's life for good.[3] Such stories appeal powerfully to our pleasure in quick-change transformations, as if *Pickwick* were the literary equivalent of a comic-book telephone booth, which Dickens entered as a modestly well-known sketch writer and exited as the most famous novelist in the world. They also match Dickens's own ambitions at the time, as can be seen in a letter he sent in mid-April 1836 which concluded with a postscript in boastfully ornate capitals: "PICKWICK, TRIUMPHANT."[4] The phrase is often quoted as evidence that the *Pickwick* craze was taking hold of the country; but at this stage in the novel's publication history, only a few weeks after the first number had appeared, it was largely a triumph of hope over experience. It would be several more months before Dickens could be sure that *Pickwick* wasn't a flop, and even then the novel's gradual emergence into public consciousness came about as much through accident as through design. The story of how this happened has been told so often, it has acquired a patina that obscures just how unlikely it was. With its tangled plot, reliance on coincidence, and rapid switches between comedy and melodrama, it rivals anything to be found in Dickens's fiction.

In his preface to the 1867 edition of *Pickwick,* Dickens explained how he was commissioned to write the novel. Edward Chapman and William Hall, two young publishers who had started to branch out into fiction, had noticed the publication of *Sketches by Boz* on February 8, 1836, and two days later Hall called upon Dickens in his lodgings. "When I opened my door in Furnival's Inn to the partner who represented the firm," Dickens wrote, "I recognised in him the person from whose hands I had bought, two or three years previously, and whom I had never seen before or since, my first copy of the Magazine in which my first effusion—a paper in the 'Sketches,' called MR. MINNS AND HIS COUSIN . . . appeared in all the glory of print."

Rarely has the opening of a door taken on such life-changing significance. The echoes of *Cinderella* make it sound as if Dickens were merely the latest beneficiary of a narrative pattern in which Prince Charming always tracks down the one who got away, just as the internal echoes of his description ("Furnival's . . . firm . . . first . . . first") hint at a scarlet thread of fate he could now detect running through his life. Of course, transforming ordinary subsequence (A then B then C) into meaningful consequence (A therefore B therefore C) is a common way of making sense of the past, but Dickens would have had to work hard to convince himself that the meeting with Hall was anything more than a chance reencounter. While it was undoubtedly a piece of good timing (Dickens does not speculate on what would have happened if he had been out when the publisher called), it was also the last link in a chain of events that could easily have veered in a different direction.

When Hall knocked on Dickens's door, he was not looking for a novelist. In November 1835 his firm had been approached by the popular illustrator and political caricaturist Robert Seymour with plans for a series of comic plates showing cockney (i.e., city-dwelling) sportsmen engaged in traditional country pursuits. These would be linked by prose descriptions, the whole package to be sold in paper-covered monthly numbers for a shilling. It was not an original idea: in 1829 Cruikshank had illustrated Thomas Hood's humorous poem "Epping Hunt," which described the misadventures of a city grocer on a stag hunt, and in 1831–1834 several stories by R. S. Surtees in the *New Sporting Magazine* had sniggered at the vulgarity and mistaken dignity of the fox-hunting grocer Jorrocks and other "smoke-dried cits."[5] Seymour himself had published a successful series of *Sketches* in 1833–1836 which depicted suburban Londoners "pursuing cats, birds, and stray pigs on foot or on horseback."[6] For the writer who agreed to work alongside him, however, this new project would be little more than hack work, and several had reportedly turned it down, including William Clarke, author of the popular *Three Courses and a Dessert* (1834), and the novelist and editor Charles Whitehead. It is likely that Whitehead had then recommended Dickens.[7] If so, presumably it was for the same reason that he had recently agreed to publish two of Dickens's pieces in Chapman and Hall's periodical the *Library of Fiction*—namely, Dickens's proven track record as a writer of short comic sketches—though as a fellow inhabitant of London's hand-to-mouth literary scene, Whitehead may also have recognized how attractive an extra £14 a month would be to a young reporter still making his way in the world.[8] If so, it was a generous and perceptive move.

"The Work will be no joke," Dickens wrote, conscious that comic works are rarely as much fun to write as they are to read, "but the emolument is too tempting to resist."[9] He responded equally positively to what were potentially far less welcome aspects of the project. The idea of cockney sportsmen attempting activities previously restricted to a rural elite chimed strongly with his interest in social mobility, and in particular with his recent efforts in *Sketches by Boz* to depict the lower middle class grappling with a world they were keen to explore but ill-equipped to understand. Even the prospect of serialization may have appealed—despite its usually being restricted to racy popular fiction such as Pierce Egan's *Life in London* or cheap reprints of older works—thanks to Dickens's nostalgia for novels published in parts "which used to be carried about the country by pedlars, and over some of which I remember to have shed innumerable tears before I had served my apprenticeship to Life."[10] Yet although he was warned that this was "a low, cheap form of publication, by which I should ruin all my rising hopes," the name he chose for his hero suggests that he also saw the work as an opportunity to move forwards in his career. "Pickwick" had been taken from a coach operator based in Bath (there is a moment in the novel when Mr. Pickwick is astonished to see his name blazoned across the side of a coach—a joke that is also an early form of product placement), and the full name of the company, "Moses Pickwick & Co.," brought together the origin of Dickens's pen name, "Boz," with his sense of the sort of narrative suitable for linking together a series of static plates: one in which the story would rattle along like a coach moving from stop to stop, picking up new characters and gathering new adventures along the way.

Dickens's matter-of-fact description of what happened next—"I thought of Mr. Pickwick, and wrote the first number"—accurately indicates how quickly things progressed. On February 16 he agreed to supply twenty-four pages of printed text, or around twelve thousand words, to accompany Seymour's four illustrations each month. A waggish prospectus duly appeared in the *Athenaeum* and the *Library of Fiction,* promising imminent publication of the adventures of "the ardent Pickwick, and his enthusiastic followers," together with smaller advertisements in the *Times* and several weekly newspapers.[11] Finally, on March 31, the first installment was published. It promptly hit a wall of indifference.

The reasons were not hard to find. With no time to plan anything new, Dickens had given his readers little more than a selection of highlights from his back catalogue. The first installment featured a labored spoof of parliamentary proceedings, followed by a sketch describing an altercation between Mr. Pickwick and a London cab driver that picked up where "Hackney Coach Stands" (*Evening Chronicle,* January 31, 1835) had left off, and then changed gear again by developing a comedy of mistaken identities that borrowed heavily from "The Great Winglebury Duel" (*Sketches by Boz*). In effect, Dickens had justified the title-page announcement "Edited by 'Boz'" by assembling a loose bundle of the literary forms for which he had become best known. Familiarity bred content. This was not an inherently bad idea; in such a competitive literary marketplace, the advice André Gide would later offer to young writers had long been understood as a principle of literary success: "The 'great public' only likes what it knows already; bring it something new . . . and it will be uneasy."[12] A much larger problem lay in the seemingly irresolvable mismatch between his and Seymour's conceptions of the work on which they were supposed to be collaborating.

Surprisingly, it appears that Dickens and Seymour had not yet met, and this was reflected in *Pickwick*'s pages, where two alternative versions of the work circled warily around each other and sometimes collided head-on. While the full title was intended to be generously accommodating for both writer and illustrator—*The Posthumous Papers of the Pickwick Club, Containing a Faithful Record of the Perambulations, Perils, Travels, Adventures and Sporting Transactions of the Corresponding Members*—Seymour's title page made it clear where his priorities lay. "Sporting Transactions" was satirically highlighted in a traditional Gothic font, Mr. Pickwick was depicted nodding off in a punt while his fishing rod strained invitingly in the water, and the words of the title were surrounded by enough quivers, oars, nets, guns, and other sporting paraphernalia to stock a small shop.[13] In contrast, Dickens's first installment—while it dutifully mimicked the facetious tone employed in *Jorrock's Jaunts and Jollities,* and gamely introduced a character, Mr. Winkle, who was keen on sporting pursuits, thereby allowing Seymour's illustration to feature another gun, more fishing tackle, a bulldog, a billiards triangle, and the antlers of a stag—was clearly the work of an urban writer. A publication billed as "illustrative of manners and life in the Country" was being irresistibly drawn back to Dickens's natural home-key.

This should hardly have come as a surprise to Seymour, who had previously illustrated an extract from Dickens's tale "The Bloomsbury Christening" when reprinting it in *Seymour's Comic Annual* (1834); but reading through the first number, he might have wondered whether even on its own terms Dickens's writing was capable of sustaining such a major project. The main comic character was Jingle, who turns out later to be a strolling actor, and who initially gave a good impression of having wandered into *Pickwick* by mistake. His dislocated style of speech was undoubtedly funny, but it also embodied the bumpy and discontinuous form of the work as a whole; even the dashes that punctuated his stories looked suspiciously like stitches inserted to keep them from falling apart. His potted summary of the death of his father-in-law, told to the Pickwick Club as they rattle towards Rochester, is typical of the nervous strain of comedy that opens the work: "Sudden disappearance—talk of the whole city—search made everywhere—without success—public fountain in the great square suddenly ceased playing—weeks elapsed—still a stoppage—workmen employed to clean it—water drawn off—father-in-law discovered sticking head first in the main pipe, with a full confession in his right boot." Mr. Snodgrass's "deeply affected" response to this "little romance" is to ask if he can write it down, to which Jingle replies "Certainly, Sir, certainly,—fifty more if you like to hear 'em." By the time the coach reaches Rochester, we are told, "the note-books, both of Mr. Pickwick and Mr. Snodgrass, were completely filled with selections from his adventures."

Given that we are supposed to be reading the papers of the Pickwick Club, the strong implication was that Jingle was being prepared as *Pickwick*'s star turn, to be brought on whenever Dickens wanted to interrupt the narrative with a comic set-piece. The only flaw in this plan was that Charles Mathews had already made the role his own. One of his most popular characters in the "At Home" series was Major Longbow, a figure in the Baron Münchhausen mold, whose tall tales on subjects such as ballooning are blurted out in the same staccato style: "Went up myself with Rosiere and Romaine from Boulogne, forty years ago—Montgolfier balloon—fire as large as the kitchen fire at the Thatched House tavern—three miles high took fire—there was a blaze—all Paris saw us—down we came slap-bang—like a cannon ball, 2840 yards high, French measure—down we came like a thunderbolt—Rosiere and Romaine, they both killed on the spot, I not hurt a bit—forty years ago—not a bit older now . . ."[14] Jingle was funny, but only in the way that a joke told a second time is funny, with a sense of punchlines being pulled.

The theatrical echoes may have been deliberate: a comic plot in which Jingle coolly borrows Winkle's clothes and then insults the fiery Dr. Slammer involved many of the stock ingredients of farce, and Dickens seems to have enjoyed treating his page as a type of stage that was too small for his characters to avoid bumping into each other. Unfortunately, all the indications from this first number were that the other main character was more like a refugee from the world of pantomime. As the sun rises at the start of Chapter 2, so Mr. Pickwick "burst[s] like another sun from his slumbers"—but for all his corklike buoyancy there is little at this point to suggest anything of substance behind his tights and spectacles. Even his shortness and stoutness, no doubt chosen by Dickens with an eye to developing a comic double-act with the tall and thin Jingle, made him look like less like a modern Falstaff than a clown padded up for some slapstick.

Meanwhile, the alternative double-act of Dickens and Seymour that was developing off-page showed that mistaken identities were not necessarily limited to comedy. In a spiteful pamphlet published many years later, Seymour's widow claimed that everything about *Pickwick*—plot, characters, the whole work—had come from her husband, and Dickens was merely a "struggling author" hired out of pity: "Had we been so callous to his sufferings the probability is that he would have been where a poor author is, or was, for he was said to be dying, and who was supposed to have been the author of some of the books which bore Mr. Dickens's name." The rumor that someone other than Dickens was responsible for his works ("I think a Mr. Morris") finds no support elsewhere; and perhaps fearing a libel action, even she was forced into the grudging concession "whether true or false I can neither affirm or deny."[15] Yet for all her niggling resentment, she was putting her finger on something crucial to *Pickwick*'s development: the author who had contributed the novel's opening chapters was significantly different from the one Seymour was expecting. The usual relationship between comic plates and letterpress was one in which text was strictly subordinate to image. In March 1836, while preparing his first independent publication, a collection of lithographed caricatures, Thackeray wrote to ask his publisher if there would be any text to accompany them, and, if so, "will you allow me to see it, before its appearance." That hardly suggested a relationship of equals.[16] But while Dickens was happy to collaborate with Seymour ("What a study for an artist did that exciting scene present!" he wrote hopefully, in a first chapter whose "Sporting Transactions" were limited to Mr. Pickwick's paper on tittlebats), a letter to Hall in which he concluded that, rather than following Seymour's lead, "I would like to take my own way," revealed that he was not prepared to play a secondary role.[17]

The firmness of this letter may have surprised his publishers, especially coming from such a young writer, but it was wholly characteristic of Dickens's self-belief. Though in 1836 John Forster noted his "spirited" expression, with eyes that were "wonderfully beaming with intellect and running over with humour and cheerfulness," others who met Dickens recognized that his commitment to hard work could produce a certain hardness of manner—according to Jane Carlyle, he had a face that looked "as if made of steel."[18] His "eager, restless, energetic outlook" found compromise indistinguishable from defeat; everything he wrote was a matter of all or nothing.[19] To an artist like Seymour—sensitive, overworked, easily humiliated—he must have seemed like a cuckoo in the nest. Matters came to a head with *Pickwick*'s second number, which opened with "dismal Jemmy" telling "The Stroller's Tale," a melodramatic story about a pantomime clown who drinks himself to death and suffers terrible hallucinations in his final moments: "There were insects too, hideous crawling things, with eyes that stared upon him . . . glistening horribly amidst the thick darkness of the place. The walls and ceiling were alive with reptiles."

In taking his own way, Dickens had decided to push the narrative in a wholly new direction. The story would create "a considerable sensation," he urged Seymour in a letter sent on April 14, but to nervous eyes it might have looked more like a snub: the clubbable drinking of the first number had been replaced by a solitary figure who hears a mocking voice saying

"Fill up his glass," and the "Sporting Transactions" had been reduced to a few imaginary creepy-crawlies. Worse still, when Seymour tried to illustrate the scene, the far less experienced Dickens rejected his drawing with some woundingly precise criticisms. There was something wrong with every figure, he pointed out, even if "the furniture of the room, you have depicted, *admirably.*" That may not have been intended maliciously. Dickens often happily confused items of furniture and their owners: a later story he inserted into *Pickwick* centers on an old mahogany chair in the bedroom of an inn that creaks into life and holds a detailed conversation with the guest. But it was scarcely diplomatic, any more than it was to follow up his story about a dying alcoholic by inviting Seymour to join him and their publishers for "a glass of grog" the following Sunday.[20]

Two days later, Seymour was discovered lying behind the summer-house at the bottom of his garden in Islington with his clothes on fire. He had shot himself: according to the coroner's report, the bullet had smashed his ribs and his heart was "torn in pieces." The penciled suicide note found beside him instructed his wife to "Blame . . . no one,"[21] but it was hard to avoid the suspicion that Dickens was partially responsible, even if he was not to blame, especially when Seymour's studio was searched for *Pickwick*'s missing illustrations and the plates "were found unfinished, with their faces turned to the wall."[22] One story that circulated was that the final "Clown" drawing was stained with Seymour's blood, and while this had no basis in fact, it grew around the unanswered question of Seymour's death as naturally as a pearl around a piece of grit.[23] Would this "melancholy-looking man," who had confessed to "such horrid thoughts," have been tempted into this final suicide attempt (his fourth) if he had not identified so strongly with Dickens's broken-down clown?[24] Was it merely a coincidence that the figure Dickens had originally rejected as "too repulsive" was even more horrifyingly emaciated and decrepit in Seymour's revised drawing? Whether or not there was a direct causal link between Dickens's behavior and Seymour's suicide—and a blank in the historical record between the Sunday of the letter and the Tuesday of the death has tempted many critics to turn a vague relationship of "and then" into a much tighter "and therefore"—it was the most violent of resignations imaginable on the part of an artist who had wanted to poke fun at suburban huntsmen, but instead ended up lying in a pool of blood with a string tied around the trigger of his "fowling-piece."[25]

Dickens wasted no time mourning. Inevitably, the death of an artist whose final work had been for a set of "Posthumous Papers" provoked some ghoulish curiosity, one response to which was a nineteen-line "Address" published in the May number of *Pickwick,* which wavered between apologizing for the missing plates and seeking to exploit the situation for commercial gain. "When we state that they comprise Mr. Seymour's last efforts," Dickens or his publishers wrote, "and that on one of them in particular (the embellishment to *The Stroller's Tale*) he was engaged up to a late hour of the night preceding his death, we feel that the excuse will be deemed a sufficient one." To Seymour's widow, publishing the drawings that had killed him must have seemed about as sensitive an action as a hangman's selling off sections of the noose after an execution. An "improved plan" was promised, which in the June number was revealed to be an extra eight pages of text, the number of illustrations being reduced from four to two. For this extra work, Dickens negotiated an increase in his monthly stipend from £14 to £21. The new illustrator was R. W. Buss, but his initial attempts at steel engraving suffered from his lack of experience, and these two "thin and scratchy" efforts were both his first and last contributions.[26] In the next number, he discovered that he had been replaced by Hablot Knight Browne, a young artist so compliant he even took on a new pen name, "Phiz," to fit more neatly with "Boz." (Like jigsaw-puzzle pieces, their names slotted together while remaining distinct, thus avoiding the confusion that the *Metropolitan Magazine*'s reviewer fell into with his announcement of *Pickwick* No. III "With illustrations by R. W. Boz.")[27] Without the requirement to devise a comic climax every six pages, and with an illustrator happily willing to follow his lead, there was now nothing to stop Dickens from going entirely his own way.

Years later, Buss wrote a plaintive account of how "ill-used" he had been by the "inconsiderate and ungentlemanly" Chapman and Hall, cast off with scant compensation and absolutely no explanation, and pointed out that if only he had been as well supported as Browne was, "I should have satisfied the public craving, as he has in time succeeded in doing."[28] Back in 1836, however, like many journals that circulated only briefly before finding their way to the rag shops, *Pickwick*'s time seemed to be nearly up. The print run of the third number was reduced to one thousand copies, too few to support production costs; and when extra copies were sent out to provincial booksellers on a sale-or-return basis, only around fifty per month were sold. Critically, too, *Pickwick* appeared close to collapse: the first review in the *Atlas* had summed it up briskly as "a strange publication" characterized by "exhausted comicality," and as *Pickwick* continued, the number of characters who fell asleep started to look worryingly like reviewers who had managed to infiltrate its pages.[29] Having started out as a demonstration of the creative process Edward Bulwer would later describe as the author "groping his way," working out his meaning as he went along, *Pickwick* was in severe danger of losing its way.[30]

The novel's fortunes turned on a single scene. Appropriately, it was set in a place dedicated to transitions: a coaching-inn. The introduction of Sam Weller in the fourth number of *Pickwick* has often been seen as the tipping point of Dickens's career, and with good reason, because in the course of a few pages he took a role usually seen as a comic walk-on part—like the anonymous Boots who makes a fleeting appearance in the first number—and turned him into the star of the show. Dickens also succeeded in creating the finest avatar of his career. Pictured standing pertly next to a row of boots and shoes, cleaning them "with a polish which would have struck envy to the soul of the amiable Mr. Warren," Sam Weller proceeds by offering a viciously accurate parody of the proceedings of Doctors' Commons, and then busies himself producing smart one-liners such as "What the devil do you want with me, as the man said ven he seed the ghost."[31] From Warren's blacking, to legal pursuits, to little spasms of storytelling: it was a rapid biographical sketch of the life Dickens had led so far, as if he had decided that the best way of saving his novel were to enter it in disguise and rearrange it from within.

Like Jingle, the character that Sam Weller was effectively to displace as the novel's resident comedian, Weller was not an entirely new creation. Privately, Dickens may have been remembering his childhood nurse Mary Weller, who used to announce her grim bedtime stories "by clawing the air with both hands, and uttering a long low hollow groan," which suggests that she took just as much pleasure in hamming up her material as Sam Weller does in his anecdotes of inventors turning themselves into sausages.[32] Dickens's readers would have been more familiar with the character Simon Spatterdash in Samuel Beazley's hit musical farce *The Boarding-House* (1811), whose best lines—such as "'I'm all over in a perspiration,' as the mutton-chop said to the gridiron"—had become known as "Sam Valerisms" after the comic actor Samuel Vale, who played the role in London during the early 1830s. "From Samuel Vale . . . to 'Samivel Veller,'" as F. G. Kitton noted, was "not a very abrupt transition."[33] Some might even have detected echoes of the Fool in *King Lear,* another follower of a foolish, fond old man who encourages him to look at disasters with a comic squint: "Cry to it, nuncle, as the cockney did to the eels when she put 'em i' th' paste alive."[34] (It is either one of the many coincidences of Dickens's life, or a sign of his astonishingly retentive memory, that the volume of Shakespeare he had consulted in the British Museum six years earlier was edited by "Samuel Weller Singer, F.S.A.")[35]

But Sam Weller was far more than a traditional comic foil. Whether poring over the newspaper "in real earnest," or making references to "patent double million magnifyin' gas microscopes of hextra power," he was a recognizably up-to-date figure. As such, he was the perfect guide for Pickwick, who ventures into the strange new world of the mid-1830s like an amateur anthropologist, and rapidly discovers that no country feels as foreign as one that can no longer be taken for granted. Indeed, although much of the novel's comedy comes from Pickwick's genius for being in the wrong place at the wrong time, in terms of his cultural significance

the blinking emergence into public life of this genial, curious, easily surprised figure could not have been more timely. As the effects of the 1832
Reform Bill continued to make themselves felt, Dickens's new double-act
of Samuel and Samivel struck a chord not because it was nostalgic for
a time when the working classes knew their place, or because it looked
forward to such relationships being established on an equal footing, but
because it evoked fears of social unpredictability (a servant fully abreast of
current affairs; an employer as plump and innocent as a baby), and then
calmed them through the democracy of laughter. Like Mr. Weller Senior's
approaches to his wife, their relationship became a way for the country as
a whole to contemplate the best way of "adjestin' our little differences."

Dickens's own attitudes towards class were rarely straightforward,
but then *Pickwick* contained plenty of clues that class was an inherently
complex matter. Although Weller refers ironically to Pickwick as "The
Governor" and "the hemperor," the symmetries of their relationship—
such as the way they take their positions on a coach, "the one inside and
the other out"—rarely confuse mutual dependence with questioning who
is in charge. Indeed, once their exchanges settle into a standard pattern,
they start to sound suspiciously like a model of stable class relations:

"Sam," said Mr. Pickwick.
"Sir," said Mr. Weller.

At the same time, such mirrored exchanges also recognize the vulnerability of social categories, and the ease with which "Sam" and "Sir" can
be transformed into each other. It is only a small step from this scene to
the moment near the end of the novel when Weller "doggedly" refuses to
abide by Pickwick's order to leave him in the Fleet:

"Sam," said Mr. Pickwick, calling after him, "Sam. Here."
But the long gallery ceased to re-echo the sound of footsteps. Sam
Weller was gone.

Calling Weller to heel shows how badly Pickwick has misunderstood the
nature of his doggedness, and it is through such moments that Dickens

succeeded in doing something far more subtle than merely announcing his allegiance to traditional social structures or more radical alternatives. Instead he balanced them inquiringly against each other, healing potential divisions by offering his writing as a literary go-between, "a sort o' connectin' link," that opened itself up to complex and sometimes contradictory ideas without taking sides.

The result was that sales of *Pickwick* soared: from 400 copies of the first monthly number, the print run eventually grew to nearly 40,000 copies every month. The availability of cheap paper and new printing technology such as steam-powered presses contributed to this success, as did increasingly efficient distribution networks, which came close to eliminating the usual time lag between city and country. Even more significantly, the relatively low cover price of a shilling meant that Dickens's readership was as diverse socially as it was geographically: it spanned the full range of rich and poor, the educated and the barely literate. Whether Dickens discovered this reading public or created it, a publication that had originally been advertised as a spoof of "life and manners in the Country" (i.e., the countryside) quickly expanded its reach until "the Country" included the whole nation. In effect, Dickens had invented a new literary form, which rapidly became an affordable alternative to novels published in three volumes, the standard model for new fiction since the eighteenth century. (Chapman and Hall's decision to issue *Pickwick* in flimsy green covers also gives them some claim to having invented the modern paperback.) Over the course of the century, serialization would attract other novelists, including Thackeray, Trollope, Thomas Hardy, and George Eliot, all of whom recognized that one of the key principles of a developing industrial economy applied to books just as much as any other product: large sales at a low price would always produce bigger profits than smaller sales at a higher price. Dickens's boast "PICKWICK, TRIUMPHANT" would turn out to be prophetic not only of his own work's success, but also of the Victorian novel as a whole.

The sense of public acclaim traditionally associated with a "triumph" is significant, because this was something that Dickens deliberately courted. The early reviewers had noticed how easily his work could be excerpted, and responded by filleting it into a series of set-pieces to be reprinted in their journals or magazines. While it was standard practice to provide readers with generous extracts of a work being discussed, allowing the reviewer to take a back seat and let the work more or less speak for itself, the miscellaneous nature of *Pickwick*'s early numbers meant that Dickens was especially open to this sort of piecemeal appropriation. The closer that reviewers looked at the construction of *Pickwick,* the more the cracks started to show. For a writer who was attempting to move away from short sketches to a more continuous form of narrative, this was potentially damaging. It is notable, for example, that when the *Sun* reviewed the second number, on May 2, 1836, it was as "an entertaining, miscellaneous collections [*sic*] of tales, anecdotes, &c., collected and arranged by Boz," and that the piece appeared not under the heading "Literature," but as part of a roundup of the contents of monthly magazines such as *Blackwood's* and *Fraser's.* In July and September, the *Sun* continued to describe *Pickwick* as "tales and sketches of character" and "amusing periodical sketches," while the first appearance of Sam Weller was singled out as "an ably sustained sketch" (September 2, 1836). A month later, however, while *Pickwick* was still being characterized as "sketches of low life," Weller had become "as well sustained a character as is to be met with in any of the novels of the present day" (October 1, 1836).[36] Dickens's characters were starting to give *Pickwick* a backbone of continuity. He responded by moving them away from a world of farce, in which characters simply bounced from incident to incident like balls on a pinball machine, and into a literary environment where breadth of experience also produced depth of understanding. Turning the pages of *Pickwick* would involve peeling away thin layers of personality until each character's heart was fully exposed to view.

At the same time, Dickens recognized that embedding a book in the public consciousness would mean writing in a style that encouraged borrowings and echoes. Two generous notices of the fourth and fifth numbers in the *Literary Gazette* had both quoted scenes involving Sam Weller, and

Dickens's response was to give readers more of what they wanted. Writing to Thomas Fraser, a subeditor at the *Morning Chronicle,* in August 1836, Dickens urged him to "give an occasional Extract from Pickwick" in his newspaper, and Fraser complied by inserting Sam Weller's explanation of "The Twopenny Rope" into the issue of September 9.[37] For an editor in search of reasonably self-contained pieces of entertainment, scenes involving Weller were the perfect choice. He was the king of the catchphrase: "Reg'lar rotation, as Jack Ketch said, ven he tied the men up"; "Out vith it, as the father said to the child, ven he swallowed a farden"; "Business first, pleasure arterwards, as King Richard the Third said ven he stabbed the t'other king in the Tower, afore he smothered the babbies." Collections of "Wellerisms" were quickly brought out by other publishers, alert to the fact that Weller's epigrams and aphorisms were both central to *Pickwick* and conveniently detachable from it.[38] Each one gave him an extra twist of uniqueness while making him even easier to imitate. Of course, comedians have long known the importance of catchphrases, those little verbal hooks that snag in an audience's mind; they are the triggers to shared memories, a form of social glue. And while the development of *Pickwick* meant that Dickens was having to learn how to work on several narrative scales at once, from the controlled explosions of one-liners to buried plot fuses smoldering away under the surface of his writing, much of his success can be attributed to the same principle: inserting material that became more rather than less funny with each repetition. Consider Fanny Kemble, writing to an American friend: "Consekens is, as Mr. Sam Weller says . . ." Or Harry Coverdale, accepting an invitation to a country home: "Then, as Sam Weller says, you may take down the bill, for I'm let to a single gentleman." Or Francis Burnard, picking up the cue of a single word: "My wisdom and remarks are limited, as Sam Weller has it."[39] By taking advantage of the simplest and most powerful marketing technique of all, "the power of word of mouth," Dickens had arrived at a blueprint for how to write a modern bestseller.[40]

"Boz has the town by the ear," the *Athenaeum* reported at the end of 1836, employing a clump of singular nouns that accurately indicated how quickly Dickens's readers found themselves being drawn together into a unified audience.[41] "I did not think there had been a place where English was spoken to which 'Boz' had not penetrated," Mary Russell Mitford wrote to an Irish friend on June 30, 1837; "All the boys and girls talk his fun."[42] Henry Vizetelly recalled that "no sooner was a new number published than needy admirers flattened their noses against the booksellers' windows . . . frequently reading it aloud to applauding bystanders."[43] A novel that was already crammed with stories started to generate even more, this time centered on its readers' responses. These ranged from the heartwarming anecdote of a father whose family could overhear him attempting to attain a "decent gravity" before reading them the latest number, his "apoplectic struggles" being punctuated by "occasional shouts" of laughter, to others that sounded like rival Wellerisms: the man who remembered an especially good scene during a church service, and rocked with silent laughter while his tears "dropped like rain upon the footstool" until he was evicted with a handkerchief crammed down his throat, or Captain Brown in Elizabeth Gaskell's *Cranford*, who is "deeply engaged in the perusal of a number of *Pickwick*, which he had just received," shortly before he is squashed by a passing train.[44] One of Fanny Burney's relations recalled "a ridiculous anecdote" of a young English nobleman traveling in Egypt who saw some characters on a pyramid and was delighted to think that he had found some hieroglyphics: "Imagine his disgust to find upon a nearer view 'Pickwick and Weller' cut upon the stone."[45] Disgust? The story practically shivers with pleasure. It also sounds like an appropriately warped homage to the episode in which Mr. Pickwick excitedly stumbles upon an ancient-looking inscription, which we later discover reads "BIL STUMPS HIS MARK." These fake graffiti signatures were no less revealing than the number of readers who were starting to claim that they were the originals of Dickens's characters.[46] The line between the real world and its fictional double was continuing to blur.

One sign of *Pickwick*'s growing commercial importance was the "Pickwick Advertiser," which was bound up with the main narrative from the fourth number onwards, alongside a note reminding potential advertisers that "the extensive and increasing circulation of this popular Work" made it "a desirable medium" for companies wishing to tap into its market. In time, this swelled from four to twenty-four pages, packed with advertisements pitched at everyone from the image-conscious (Agid Hassan's Circassian Hair Dye, "which will in a few hours change light, red, or grey Hair to a rich auburn or jet black . . . without injuring the roots") to the more down-at-heel (Woodhouse's Patent Corn Plaster, "for affording instant relief"). *Pickwick* was solidly embedded in the world of its readers. Someone who came across a reference to "a glass bottle that might hold about a quarter of a pint of smelling-salts" in Chapter 34 of the work could flick to the front of the number and discover advertisements for products such as "HANNAY's HIGHLY CONCENTRATED SMELLING-SALTS . . . a most useful appendage to the apartments of Invalids." Even those who disliked *Pickwick* could hardly avoid its material impact. There were Pickwick pastries and Fat Boy sweets, Pickwick chintzes and Weller corduroys; "Boz cabs might be seen rattling through the streets, and the portrait of the author of 'Pelham' or 'Crichton' was scraped down or pasted over to make room for that of the new popular favourite in the omnibuses."[47] The association with different forms of transport was especially appropriate for a work that was at once nostalgic for the days of coaching-inns and thoroughly up-to-date. It was a transitional work for a self-consciously transitional age.

Although much of this "Boz-mania" or "Boz-i-ana" was out of Dickens's control, there were other ways in which he deliberately cultivated his readers. The main narrative was spiced with topical allusions, like scraps of journalism that had accidentally fluttered into its pages, and Dickens adjusted the main sequence of events to ensure that they fell into step with the rhythms of real time, from a cricket match in the June number to a joke in March that looked back to Sam Weller's valentine the previous month. Like the viewers of a modern television soap opera, his readers enjoyed dropping in on the lives of his characters, and Dickens responded by giving regular updates on what the Pickwickians had been up to.[48] Staggering the narrative over a relatively long period of time had several other practical advantages: reviews were spread out over many months rather than coming all at once, while Chapman and Hall could reinvest their income from each number into the next month's publication costs, which meant that publicity, sales, and profits were inextricably connected. Most important, serialization encouraged the development of a far greater intimacy with Dickens himself. Not content with enjoying *Pickwick* from a distance, many of his readers wanted to join in. A "Notice to Correspondents" in the fifteenth number, squeezed into the bottom of a page like a little sigh, thanked them for the "immense number of communications" they had sent in as "suggestions," but pointed out that although they were doubtless "forwarded with the kindest intentions," it was "wholly out of our power to make use of any such hints."

If Dickens was sometimes exasperated by this growing intimacy with his readers, he also used it to his advantage. Accused of changing his mind about Mr. Pickwick by transforming him from a fool into a hero, Dickens responded by pointing out that people often seem to alter as we get to know them better: "In real life, the peculiarities and oddities of a man who has anything whimsical about him, generally impress us first, and . . . it is not until we are better acquainted with him that we usually begin to look below those superficial traits, and to know the better part of him."[49] The most important word here is also one of the smallest: "we." At the start of *Pickwick* it had been used in a purely editorial capacity, as when Dickens explained in the second number that "whatever ambition we might have felt under other circumstances, to lay claim to the authorship of these adventures, a regard for truth forbids us to do more, than claim the merit of their judicious arrangement, and impartial narration." By the end, when he could write about leaving "our old friend" in one of those happy moments "of which, if we seek them, there are ever some to cheer our transitory existence here," it had become a celebration of the happy complicity between the author and his ever-expanding readership: "we" was a party to which everyone was invited. For anyone who had accompanied *Pickwick* from its facetious start to its genuinely touching conclusion, Dickens's comments had another application besides. In pointing out that we often misjudge character until we get to know the person better, he might have been talking about himself.

❧❧❧

"With *Pickwick*," write John Butt and Kathleen Tillotson, "Dickens embarked upon his lifelong love-affair with his reading public; which, when all is said, is by far the most interesting love-affair of his life."[50] The wit of this is given a particular sting by the fact that two days after the first number of *Pickwick* was published, in a quiet ceremony at St. Luke's Church, Chelsea, Dickens was married to Catherine Hogarth. It is an intriguing juxtaposition. One of Dickens's main reasons for taking on *Pickwick* was that it would provide the regular income he needed to support a family, and on February 17, less than a week after accepting Chapman and Hall's offer, he continued his marriage preparations by moving into the solidly respectable address of 15 Furnival's Inn: a bedroom, dining room, and drawing room on the third floor, plus a basement kitchen and cellar room, leased for £50 per year in the same anonymous slab of a building he had lived in when he first left home.[51] Six weeks later, he and his "young girlish wife" were trundling away on the Rochester coach, to spend their honeymoon in the picturesque village of Chalk in Kent.[52] It was a curious echo of *Pickwick*'s first number, in which we are told that the Pickwick Club "resolved to make Rochester their first halting-place," although one wonders what Catherine made of the choice of target in Jingle's next story about the dangers of coach travel: "other day—five children—mother—tall lady, eating sandwiches—forgot the arch—crash—knock—children look round—mother's head off—sandwich in her hand—no mouth to put it in—head of a family off—shocking, shocking." One wonders still more how she responded to the rest of *Pickwick*, which either celebrated the joys of perpetual bachelordom, or followed a standard comic model by cheering lovers on towards marriage while seeing nothing but trouble and strife in the state of being married:

·[208]·

"Mr. Vinkle stops at home now," rejoined Sam. "He's married."

"Married!" exclaimed Pott, with frightful vehemence. He stopped, smiled darkly, and added, in a low, vindictive tone, "It serves him right!"

Some years after their acrimonious separation in 1858, Catherine gave the letters she had received from Dickens to her daughter Kate, asking her to pass them on to the British Museum, "that the world may know he loved me once."[53] Perhaps he did, but their surviving courtship correspondence gives only patchy grounds for thinking that theirs was ever a marriage of true minds, rather than something that occurred principally because Dickens wrote himself into the belief that it should.

Dickens had met Catherine through her father, George Hogarth, a former Edinburgh lawyer who had moved to London in August 1834 to join the staff of the *Morning Chronicle* as its music and drama critic, and was subsequently responsible for commissioning extra sketches from Dickens once he started editing the *Evening Chronicle* in January 1835. Dickens became a frequent visitor to the family home at 18 York Place, Brompton, and he moved fast to secure the affections of his colleague's plump, pretty, sleepy-eyed daughter. In February 1835, she reported in a letter that "Mr. Dickens improves very much on acquaintance"; by May, the month she celebrated her twentieth birthday, they were engaged.[54] The connection placed Dickens only a few degrees of separation away from literary fame. George Hogarth had formerly been a trusted adviser of Sir Walter Scott, by far the most popular novelist of the previous generation, whose career offered a model of how to rise from humble beginnings as a lawyer's clerk, and whose works were full of tempting launch pads for later writers.[55] (Mr. Pickwick's discovery of the "Bill Stumps" stone, for example, is only a thinly disguised version of a similar joke in Scott's 1816 novel *The Antiquary*.) Once again, Dickens set about turning himself into the hero of a romance—although having learned from his previous flirtation with Maria Beadnell, this time he did everything in his power to ensure that the story would have a different ending.

Other people's love letters are always hard to read, because they assume a form of intimacy that later readers can never reciprocate, but Dickens's letters to Catherine were an especially awkward mixture of endearing baby talk (she is often characterized as "coss"—i.e., cross) and stiff reserve. Many of them crossed the invisible line separating protectiveness from possessiveness, just as Dickens's desire to put things right when they quarreled was not always easy to distinguish from a conviction that "whatever I do must be right."[56] If he improved on acquaintance, he left Catherine in no doubt that she should seek to improve herself too. Any hint of petulance was swiftly crushed—"I *must* see you, and *will not be prevented*"—and although part of this may have been a private game, in which Dickens played the Petruchio to his "Kate," and she giggled coquettishly as he sought to tame her, there are also many letters entirely devoid of humor, in which he writes to his "dear Girl" less like a wife-in-training than a child needing to be kept in line: "Mind you are punctual my dear"; "I perceive you have not yet subdued one part of your disposition."[57]

In Dickens's defense, it should be noted that such attitudes were by no means unusual, and nothing he wrote approached the bluntness of Carlyle's letter to Jane before their marriage in 1826, which warned her that "the man should bear the rule in the house and not the woman," adding helpfully that this was "the Law of Nature herself which no mortal departs from unpunished."[58] There was also a more immediate context. Writing against the clock to meet newspaper deadlines, alongside his developing career as a sketch writer, meant that Dickens was usually exhausted and often ill, and many of his letters disintegrate into a plaintive list of symptoms: "I have a slight touch of rheumatism & am *perfectly deaf* . . . my aching head, and side . . . the dizziness affected my sight so much that I could scarcely see at all . . . a state of exquisite torture from the spasm in my side far exceeding anything I ever felt."[59] Yet none of that explains why he was so keen to invent nicknames for her, including "Tatie," "Mouse," "Titmouse," "Wig," and "my darling Pig," when he was content to sign off every letter to her with a plain "Charles Dickens." Was this the signature of a loving suitor or a professional writer? It was the first rumbling of a theme that would gain unstoppable momentum in the years after his marriage: his frustration that real people were so much harder to control than his characters; his anxiety that life seemed so unwilling to follow the "happy ever after" pattern of fiction.

The same anxiety is given a different shape in the pages of *Pickwick*, where Dickens's comedy is repeatedly interrupted by awkward questions about what kind of story he was—or should be—writing. "The Stroller's Tale," which would provoke the crisis with Seymour, had been inserted into the second number only a few days before Dickens left for his honeymoon on April 2. The assumption has usually been that the "dirty roll of paper" from which Dismal Jemmy reads this tale reflects Dickens's own methods of composition, and that, pressed for time before his wedding, he retrieved an unpublished fragment from his bottom drawer and unceremoniously wedged it into place. But this ignores the fact that "The Stroller's Tale" is only the first of many such stories inserted into the main narrative, creating unpredictable "shiftings and changings of the discourse" that come close to transforming the Pickwick Club's rambles into a style. Their subjects include a transported convict whose father responds to his return home by rupturing a blood vessel and dying in a "thick, sluggish pool" as the gore spurts out of his mouth and nose; and the legendary Prince Bladud, who is disappointed in love, swallowed up by the earth, and has his hot tears transformed into a gushing spring. Critics have usually responded to these tales either with suspicion or with downright hostility.[60] They have variously been read as little pilot balloons sent up to gauge the drift of public opinion, "pockets of darkness" that Dickens could neither repress nor properly incorporate into his novel, or evidence that he remained stubbornly intent on preserving the structure of a miscellany long after it had given birth to a novel.[61] The only thing most of his critics agree on is that these interpolated stories are unnecessary to the main narrative: they are fictional cul-de-sacs disguised as detours.

Viewed in another light, however, they are central to the development both of *Pickwick* and of Dickens. *Pickwick*'s plot hinges on the *Bardell v. Pickwick* court case, which brings together two rival versions of the same scene: Mr. Pickwick, conversing with his landlady, makes a few ambiguous remarks which he intends as a warning that he has employed a manservant and which she interprets as a marriage proposal. It is the situational equivalent of a pun, in which two different ideas occupy a single word or phrase, and it creates shockwaves that ripple out into the rest of the novel, even seeming to affect the printers of the tenth number, who misread Dickens's manuscript and printed it with two Chapter 28's in a row.

The ability of lawyers to draw salacious innuendo from the most matter-of-fact evidence, such as a note about dinner that reads "Dear Mrs. B.—Chops and Tomata sauce. Yours, PICKWICK," was a spoof of contemporary events. In the previous month, as a reporter for the *Morning Chronicle,* Dickens had covered the Norton-Melbourne case, where he had witnessed equally silly inferences being drawn from equally ordinary texts. The action brought against the prime minister, Lord Melbourne, by George Norton for engaging in "criminal conversation" (i.e., adultery) with his wife, Caroline Norton, had relied upon supposedly incriminating letters which the lawyers polished up like jewels: "'I will call about half past 4. Yours, Melbourne.' . . . The style and form of these notes, Gentlemen, seems to import much more than they contain. Cautiously, I admit, they are worded; there are no professions of love . . . but still they are not the letters of an ordinary acquaintance."[62]

Dickens also had a fictional model of scandalous accusations in mind. When Serjeant Buzfuz tries to wring the hearts of the jury by observing that "my client's hopes and prospects are ruined, and it is no figure of speech to say that her occupation is gone indeed," the allusion is to Othello's lament that Desdemona has, from his green-eyed point of view, proven herself unfaithful: "Othello's occupation's gone."[63] It is not surprising that Dickens's ear should have been caught by a play that takes the plot of a farce—a dropped handkerchief, overheard conversations, mistaken identities—and turns it into a brooding tragedy. *Pickwick* pushes the same strategy in the opposite direction. Repeatedly, Dickens puts the comic trajectory of his novel at risk by imagining more disturbing outcomes to its events, and then carefully avoids them; windows into alternative futures are opened a crack and then slammed shut. Even Mr. Pickwick's character finds itself coming under threat, displaying occasional flashes of temper before the narrative reasserts his smiling benevolence, like the sun coming out from behind a cloud. *Pickwick*'s interpolated stories follow the same logic. Spurting blood and gushing tears are not normally the stuff of comedy, but Dickens seems to have decided that any happy ending worthy of the name would have to be earned, and that, as Thomas Hardy would later put it, "if way to the Better there be, it exacts a full look at the Worst."[64] Just as Dickens had confronted Seymour's death by turning it to his own advantage, so his novel prevented the main narrative from succumbing to gloomy thoughts by introducing them in short controlled bursts. They are like a set of literary inoculations.

The parallels with Dickens's life are subtle but insistent. It is noticeable that the nearer we get to the end of the novel, the more Mr. Pickwick starts to behave like a novelist, by dissolving the Pickwick Club, distributing rewards to the most deserving characters, and, with a choice of words that sounds distinctly like Dickens speaking to his readers, announcing that "I shall never regret having devoted the greater part of two years to mixing with different varieties and shades of human character, frivolous as my pursuit of novelty may have appeared to many." But nowhere is he more like a novelist than in a slightly earlier scene in the Fleet Prison. Confronting Jingle and his miserable sidekick Job, he at first appears "undecided how to act."

> "Come here, Sir," said Mr. Pickwick, trying to look stern, with four large tears running down his waistcoat. "Take that, Sir."
>
> Take what? In the ordinary acceptation of such language, it should have been a blow. As the world runs, it ought to have been a sound, hearty cuff; for Mr. Pickwick had been duped, deceived, and wronged by the destitute outcast who was now wholly in his power. Must we tell the truth? It was something from Mr. Pickwick's waistcoat pocket, which chinked as it was given into Job's hand: and the giving of

which, somehow or other imparted a sparkle to the eye, and a swelling to the heart of our excellent old friend, as he hurried away.

The blank space following "Take that, Sir" is one that we are invited to fill
with a satisfying thwack, or perhaps a more protracted form of revenge:
the paragraph break could easily signal a swerve towards the sort of events
we have already encountered in the story of the "queer client," who is
thrown into a debtors' prison and responds by devoting the rest of his life
to crushing his former enemy. Instead, Mr. Pickwick chooses a different
narrative path, one that follows in the footsteps of Goldsmith's Vicar of
Wakefield, who is similarly tricked by a con man and then helps him when
they meet again in prison.[65] For Dickens's readers the scene is cheering
and chastening in roughly equal measures. By repaying his enemies with
kindness, Mr. Pickwick shows how easy it is to choose love over violence;
by asking us to look again at "Take that, Sir," Dickens reminds us that
this more generous option was available all along, even if it needed Mr.
Pickwick to show us the way.

Yet while *Pickwick* ends by triumphantly seeing off these rival narrative outcomes, Dickens remained haunted by the fear that his life might
fall into a far less happy groove. In October 1835 he sent his fiancée a copy
of Johnson's *Lives of the English Poets,* drawing particular attention to
the life of Richard Savage by turning down the page on which it began,
and urging her, "Now *do* read it attentively."[66] Why should he have been
so keen for Catherine to read the life of a poet he would later dismiss as a
"Vagabond" who "never could have obtained an honest living in any station of existence or at any period of time"?[67] According to Michael Slater,
the reasons are to be found in Dickens's past: Savage's miserable childhood, feelings of being rejected by his mother, and experience of debtors'
prisons, all of which Johnson sympathetically described, found powerful
echoes in Dickens's own life, so that "in pitying Savage she would be pitying her lover without knowing it."[68]

It is just as likely that Dickens was thinking about his future. While
Johnson remained the most famous example of a writer who had over-

come hardship to become a literary giant, Savage offered a disturbing alternative: a writer who drank away his talent, spent nights fretfully pacing the streets of London, and ended up as little more than a resentful magnet for charity. Johnson's original conclusion, before he added a sententious extra paragraph in revision, had implied that Savage's faults were chiefly a product of his circumstances: "Nor will any wise man easily presume to say, 'Had I been in Savage's condition, I should have lived or written better than Savage.'"[69] Perhaps Dickens agreed, and was sending the story to Catherine as a veiled explanation of why he needed to work so hard, however "coss" it made her, if he was to avoid Savage's fate. Or perhaps he was using the example of Johnson to show that what really mattered in the struggle for success was force of character, which is why this was Johnson's life of Savage and not the other way round. If that was what he had in mind, then signing his letters to her "Charles Dickens" indicated rather more than a suitor too nervous to relax into first-name terms. It was the seductive dangling of a carrot. By marrying such an ambitious writer, she too might end up "famous and caressed and happy."[70]

CHAPTER NINE

~~Novelist~~ Writer

Soon after Sam Weller is taken on by Mr. Pickwick, he is "transformed" by a new set of clothes: "a grey coat with the 'P.C.' button, a black hat with a cockade to it, a pink striped waistcoat, light breeches and gaiters, and a variety of other necessaries." He is far less sure what he has been transformed into: "I vonder whether I'm meant to be a footman, or a groom, or a game-keeper, or a seedsman," he ponders as he takes his seat on the coach. "I looks like a sort of compo of every one on 'em." The rest of *Pickwick* does not so much clarify this uncertainty as lovingly confirm it, as Sam enters into his various roles—traveling companion, stand-up comedian, personal bodyguard, master of ceremonies, cockney Jeeves ("Wery good, Sir")—with all the enthusiasm of a child rummaging around in a dressing-up box. Even his name alters its shape—"Sam," "Samuel," "Sammy," "Samivel," "Sammle"—according to the pressure of circumstances.

Yet it was not only in the pages of fiction that Dickens was contemplating the diverse futures that could be spawned by the same historical moment. June 29, 1836, the date of Sam Weller's first appearance, also marked the publication of Dickens's pamphlet "Sunday under Three Heads." Attributed to the pseudonymous "Timothy Sparks," it was a caustic attack on Sir Andrew Agnew's Sunday Observance Bill, which had been rejected at its second reading on May 18 but which still had considerable support among churchmen and moralists.[1] In seeking to ban everything from postal deliveries to concerts on the only day that many people were released from the regular grind of work, the Sunday Observance Bill struck at much that Dickens held dear, including the importance of individual freedom and what he saw as a healthy link in working-class culture between leisure and pleasure.[2] These were common enough views among radical politicians and journalists, although the history of his father's various financial embarrassments suggests that Dickens's criticism may have been colored by a private grudge: Sunday was also the one day of the week on which debtors might venture out of doors without fear of arrest.[3]

"Sunday under Three Heads" was especially stinging about the sabbatarians' hypocrisy, as seen in their enthusiasm for banning the coach services used principally by the poor to escape the grime of city life for a few hours, while venturing "not a word of a penalty on liveried coachmen and footmen"; and as seen, too, in the bill's requirement that "no person, upon the Lord's day, shall do, or hire, or employ any person to do any manner of labour"—the sizable exception to this rule being servants, on the tacit understanding that "the Baronet's dinner must be cooked on a Sunday, the Bishop's horses must be groomed, and the Peer's carriage must be driven." The same point is made more wryly in *Nicholas Nickleby,* when Mr. Gallanbile MP advertises for a cook with the warning that "no victuals whatever, cooked on the Lord's Day, with the exception of dinner for Mr. and Mrs. Gallanbile, which, being a work of piety and necessity, is exempted." The slippage between good works ("piety") and ordinary work ("necessity") is viewed by Dickens with particular scorn. This spoof advertisement is not dwelt on—within the context of the novel, it is merely a satirical hit and run—but Dickens's irritation lasted far longer. Eleven articles hostile to sabbatarianism were published in *Household Words* between June 1850 and October 1858, while G. J. Holyoake reported that Dickens deliberately spent his Sundays smoking a pipe and drinking beer in "protest against the doleful way of keeping Sunday then thought becoming."[4]

Dickens's finest fictional protest can be found in *Little Dorrit,* which includes among its many invisible prisons the Sundays endured by Arthur Clennam, each one a padlock clicking shut on the rest of the week:

> There was the dreary Sunday of his childhood, when he sat with his hands before him, scared out of his senses by a horrible tract. . . .

There was the sleepy Sunday of his boyhood, when, like a military de-
serter, he was marched to chapel by a picquet of teachers three times
a day. . . . There was the interminable Sunday of his nonage; when
his mother, stern and unrelenting of heart, would sit all day behind
a Bible. . . . There was a legion of Sundays, all days of unserviceable
bitterness and mortification, slowly passing before him.

Dickens's objections in this passage are as much imaginative as ideologi-
cal: the repetition of "There was" dramatizes not just the remorseless return of this tedium, week after week, but also his fear that a day in which
all activity was banned would produce a form of unnatural arrest, just
as "Sunday under Three Heads" points out that suspending postal deliveries "would stop, for many precious hours, the natural flow of blood
from every vein and artery in the world to the heart of the world." By
contrast, the pamphlet's description of how Londoners currently spend
their Sundays ("As It Is") is soon busy with verbs, as it pictures couples
venturing out on excursions "joking and laughing, and eating and drinking, and admiring everything they see" in ways that "know no bounds"—
a form of bursting enthusiasm that for Dickens is closely connected to
their freedom to travel.

The next two sections of Dickens's argument offer alternative visions
of how this happy scene might change. "As Sabbath Bills Would Make
It" projects a future in which Arthur Clennam's experience is the norm
rather than an unhappy exception, as Sunday becomes "a day of general
gloom and austerity" punctuated by dreary church services and the occasional drunken brawl. Finally, "As It Might Be Made" offers a different
model of the future, based on a village Dickens claims to have visited "a
summer or two back," in which a cheerful congregation streams out of
the church to play a game of cricket, watched by the clergyman "with
evident satisfaction." "It is such scenes as this," Dickens concludes, "I
would see near London on a Sunday evening." What is strange about this
description is not just that, in a period of unprecedented urban growth,
Dickens's vision of city workers "hurrying along . . . to the fresh and airy
fields" risks looking like a reversal of history, but also that in the previ-

ous month he had published an account of a cricket match (Dingley Dell versus All-Muggleton) that showed the Pickwickians enjoying just such an idyllic retreat. Yet even here there is no escape from evangelical fervor: of the 1,420 petitions presented to Parliament by the "ancient and loyal" borough of Muggleton, we are told, there are no fewer than 86 "for abolishing Sunday trading in the streets." *Et in Arcadia ego:* if Muggleton is a vision of the future, rather than a magically preserved bubble of the past, it is one that sabbatarianism hangs over like a curse.

❦⋯❦⋯❦

What of Dickens's own future? In 1840 he met Thomas Carlyle, whose forthcoming book *On Heroes, Hero-Worship and the Heroic in History* (1841) would include a chapter that championed authors as the heroes of an emerging age of print, and who described Dickens with genial condescension as "a quiet shrewd-looking little fellow, who seems to guess pretty well what he is, and what others are."[5] Dickens never lacked confidence, or at least was good at faking it in company, but as an author he remained far less sure of himself even after *Pickwick*'s success. The preface he wrote in October 1837 included a somewhat prickly defense of his compositional methods: "If it be objected to the Pickwick Papers that they are a mere series of adventures, in which the scenes are ever changing . . . [the author] can only content himself with the reflection, that . . . the same objection has been made to the works of some of the greatest novelists in the English language." The marked-up proofs of this preface for the 1847 Cheap Edition show that he contemplated changing "novelists" to "writers," although in the end he stuck with "novelists."[6] It was a little hover of uncertainty that indicated much larger doubts over where to place himself in the history of fiction.

To some extent, these doubts reflected the emergence of the novel during the 1830s as an unusually generous—in some eyes promiscuous—literary category. Not quite a genre, and not quite a form, it embraced everything from Ainsworth's seedy dramas of the London underworld to the drawling romances of the "silver-fork" school parodied by Dickens in *Nicholas Nickleby:*

> "Cherizette," said the Lady Flabella, inserting her mouse-like feet into the blue satin slippers, which had unwittingly occasioned the half-playful, half-angry altercation between herself and the youthful Colonel Befillaire, in the Duke of Mincefenille's *salon de danse* on the previous night. *"Cherizette, ma chère, donnez-moi de l'eau-de-Cologne, s'il vous plaît, mon enfant."*
>
> *"Merci*—thank you," said the Lady Flabella, as the lively but devoted Cherizette plentifully besprinkled with the fragrant compound the Lady Flabella's *mouchoir* of finest cambric, edged with richest lace, and emblazoned at the four corners with the Flabella crest, and gorgeous heraldic bearings of that noble family; *"Merci*—that will do."

"That will do" also neatly sums up Dickens's attitude towards this sort of snobbish nonsense, although not the attitude of the circulation libraries, which bought equally clunking three-decker romances by the hundreds, often attracted less by their literary merits than by the fact that they could be lent out one volume at a time, thus allowing a single novel to satisfy three readers at once. In unadventurous hands, the need to appeal to a broad readership was a particular discouragement to creative risk taking—hence the number of scenes in silver-fork novels that were as gorgeously detailed and empty as a Fabergé egg. Stale literary conventions shored up equally stale social conventions. The serial publication of *Pickwick* offered a rollicking alternative; yet Dickens's readers were often unsure how to respond to a "series of adventures" that had one foot planted in the world of the novel, another in the world of sketches and short stories, and hopped back and forth with impudent glee.

On June 2, 1836, under the title "Magazine Day," the *Sun* reviewed *Pickwick* alongside a notice of the first issue of Chapman and Hall's *Library of Fiction*—published on March 31, the same day as the first number of *Pickwick*—to which Dickens had contributed a comic skit entitled

"The Tuggs's at Ramsgate." The underlying premise of the story was familiar from Dickens's earlier sketches: an ambitious grocer unexpectedly comes into £20,000, and celebrates by taking his family off to the seaside, where they attempt to enter fashionable society and are conned out of a large slice of their inheritance. Of more particular interest is the fact that the reviewer saw this story and the latest number of *Pickwick* as twins: "They bear the same general resemblance to each other that Dromio of Ephesus bore to Dromio of Syracuse. Both are lively, smart, and versatile in manner, and our friend 'Boz' is leading contributor to both."[7] Perhaps the reviewer envisaged a future in which Dickens would continue to produce independent sketches alongside larger miscellanies, like Shakespeare's pair of Dromios walking off together at the end of *The Comedy of Errors:* "We came into the world like brother and brother,/ And now let's go hand in hand, not one before another."[8] There is no suggestion that one might turn out to be the dominant twin.

Dickens was equally uncertain about what he had produced, or how best to capitalize on its success. On November 1, 1836, he offered Chapman and Hall any "future periodicals" he might produce, and appointed them his official "periodical publishers."[9] The precision of this distinction can partly be accounted for by the fact that on August 22 he had signed an official agreement with a rival publisher, Richard Bentley, to write an as yet unnamed novel "to form three Volumes of 320 pages each," with an option on a second novel "of similar extent," with the further promise "that no other literary production shall be undertaken by the said Charles Dickens Esqre until the completion of the above mentioned novel."[10] Dickens had previously offered "a Work of Fiction" to John Macrone "in Three Volumes of the usual size"; but as he seems conveniently to have forgotten that agreement in his negotiations with Bentley, this was the first serious indication that he was contemplating a novel in the standard form.[11] Presumably only by thinking of it as a *literary* production, one that carried enough prestige to distinguish it from more ephemeral forms of fiction, could he abide by the terms of his contract while touting the idea of another periodical as a possible sequel to *Pickwick.*

Yet even this might have raised a few eyebrows in Chapman and Hall's Strand offices if they had known that on November 2, the day after Dickens wrote to them, he had sent another letter to Bentley pointing out "the assistance of 'Boz's' name" in any future publishing venture, and agreeing to edit and contribute to a new monthly magazine to be known as the *Wits' Miscellany*.[12] (When it was subsequently renamed *Bentley's Miscellany*, R. H. Barham was reported to have quipped, "But why go to the other extreme?") Usually writers play publishers off against each other in order to secure the best deal for themselves. Dickens's more ambitious strategy seems to have been to hope that he could write enough to keep everyone happy. This is why, only a handful of days before he signed the agreement with Bentley, he could tell Chapman and Hall that "I should be the most insensible, and at the same time the most jolter-headed scribe alive, if I had ever entertained the most remote idea of dissolving our most pleasant and friendly connection."[13] He did not want to dissolve that connection: he wanted to add to it, putting himself at the center of a web of literary alliances and obligations that only a writer of his "versatile" talents could satisfy.[14]

A summary of the other writings he published up to the end of 1836 shows that his confidence was not misplaced. Whether or not *Pickwick* was a "miscellany," that was certainly how Dickens was treating his career. He continued to file regular reports for the *Morning Chronicle,* and a month after the first number of *Pickwick* was published he was in Ipswich to report on a rowdy political meeting led by Daniel O'Connell ("the Liberator"), who was visiting the town as part of his "Justice for Ireland" campaign. Between June and October, further sketches appeared in the *Carlton Chronicle* ("The Hospital Patient" and "Hackney Cabs, and Their Drivers"), the *Library of Fiction* ("A Little Talk about Spring, and the Sweeps"), and *Morning Chronicle* ("Meditations in Monmouth-street," "Scotland Yard," "Doctors' Commons," and "Vauxhall Gardens by Day"), all of which were revised and republished in December as *Sketches by Boz: Second Series.* And still he had energy, only a week after agreeing on terms with Bentley, to haggle with another publisher, Thomas

Tegg, for a fee of £100 to write a children's book (never completed) to be called *Solomon Bell the Raree Showman*, "unless we should hit upon some other title, which we should consider a more catching one."[15]

Mary Hogarth, Dickens's sister-in-law, caught the mood of excitement when she wrote proudly that Dickens was being "courted and made up to by all the literary Gentlemen, and has more to do in that way than he can well manage," and more seasoned observers of the literary scene were under no illusion about why he was taking on so much.[16] As the reviewer Abraham Howard pointed out, he was "making hay while the sun shines." Viewed in the context of Howard's conclusion, in which he complained that "Mr. Dickens writes too often and too fast," presenting his thoughts in a "crude, unfinished, undigested state," this was chiefly a criticism.[17] Viewed in the context of *Pickwick*, though, it was also a grudging compliment. It is Mr. Pickwick, after all, whose "beaming face" is regularly associated with the sun, as if he were less an ordinary human being than an unstoppable force of nature, and who had managed to bring out a reciprocal warmth in his readers—a connection Dickens would underline in the final double number, published in the same month as Howard's review, by observing that he had chosen to bid his characters farewell "when the brief sunshine of the world is blazing full upon them."

Yet while Dickens's busy professional life made perfect sense in relation to his fledgling career, it also hinted at a more troubling aspect of his personality: the need to work ever harder, to drive himself to a point beyond exhaustion. Always there was the fear of opportunities passing by, always the urgency of "more irons in the fire: more grist to the Mill."[18] Even by the standards of contemporaries like Carlyle, whose cry "Produce! Produce!" at the climax of Book II of *Sartor Resartus* (1833–1834) would ring out across the rest of the century, Dickens was something of a fundamentalist when it came to the gospel of work.[19] Throughout his career, he used his pen like someone scratching an incurable itch. "I made it a rule to take as much out of myself as I possibly could, in my way of doing everything to which I applied my energies," David Copperfield recalls, shortly after deciding to pursue a career as a reporter; in short, he concludes, with a touch of masochistic pride, "I made a perfect victim of myself." Some of Dickens's complaints about being overworked while writing *Pickwick* are similarly hard to distinguish from covert boasts, as when he explained to the *Morning Chronicle*'s J. P. Collier in September 1836 that he was "over head and ears in work," or reached for a mournful pun to tell Cruikshank how "hard pressed" he was.[20] While his punishing schedule had some immediate costs—*Pickwick* deadlines were stretched, and he suffered a painful attack of "rheumatism in the face"—there were also the first stirrings of a longer-term worry that he might work himself into an early grave.[21] In June 1836, after reporting on the *Melbourne v. Norton* adultery trial, he told Macrone that he felt "tired to death."[22] It was only a figure of speech, but he knew from George Hogarth's connection with Walter Scott how easily it could end up as miserable reality. Many years later he could not forget the sight of Scott's old white hat at Abbotsford House, which had been "tumbled and bent and broken by the uneasy, purposeless wandering hither and thither of his heavy head," and he continued to be haunted by the "pathetic description" in John Gibson Lockhart's 1838 biography of Scott in his last illness, still trying to write his way out of debt, the pen falling from his hand as the tears coursed silently down his cheeks.[23]

The only sign that Dickens was prepared to take this warning seriously came on November 5, 1836, the day after he entered into his agreement with Bentley, when he resigned from the *Morning Chronicle*, explaining that it was in "exchange for a less burdensome and more profitable employment." No doubt his former employers were disappointed to lose their young star reporter, but Dickens's breezy assurance that "my time will not be very much occupied immediately" might have caused some surprise.[24] This was true of the *Miscellany*, the first issue of which would not appear until January 1837, but it was hardly true of Dickens's life as a whole. Anyone glancing at the posters for St. James's Theatre in 1836 would have seen that transforming himself from sketch writer to novelist, and from reporter to editor, were only two of the possible futures he was contemplating for himself. A third was as a playwright.

In May 1836, Dickens wrote to the composer J. P. Hullah—who had studied at the Royal Academy of Music alongside his sister Fanny—crowing that the popular English tenor John Braham had been heard "speaking highly of my Works and 'fame' (!) and expressing an earnest desire to be the first to introduce me to the Public, as a dramatic Writer."[25] In some ways, Braham was too late: for two years Dickens had been contributing sharp little theater reviews to the *Morning Chronicle,* and in the opening numbers of *Pickwick* he had continued to develop the self-conscious staginess of the *Sketches.* In an "Address" to the reader published on December 31, the same day the first number of *Bentley's Miscellany* appeared, he went even further by presenting himself as "Mr. Pickwick's Stage-Manager," a self-effacing joke that accurately registered how far his hero had taken on a life of his own. Like most jokes, it contained a kernel of genuine fear. "I have often and often heard him complain," his son Charles recalled, "that he could *not* get the people of his imagination to do what he wanted, and that they would insist on working out their histories in *their* way and not *his.*"[26] At the time of Dickens's letter to Hullah, only two numbers into *Pickwick*'s serialization, it was far from clear whether his characters would be interested in carrying out his plans for them, and even less clear what those plans were: his narrative was invitingly and disturbingly open-ended. But having recently married, and with the prospect of a family to support, Dickens was anxious to make more hay than fiction alone could provide. Life as a professional writer was not only "the most precarious of all pursuits," as he later described it in the dedication to *Pickwick,* because it was risky and prone to collapse; it was also "precarious" in the original sense of the word, meaning that it depended on the approval of other people.[27]

So far, Dickens had limited himself to print publication, where each story or installment functioned like a question to which an answer in the form of sales figures would be returned within a few days or weeks. The theater produced even faster returns. Playwrights may not have enjoyed much social prestige—comparing them with actors in 1833, Edward Bulwer sighed that "in the great game of honours" they were ranked somewhere beneath "those who amuse us"—but the audience's cheers or boos compressed the time-lag of publication into a matter of seconds.[28] And however high the odds against writing a theatrical hit (then, as now, it was far easier to write a spectacular miss), the potential rewards of a long run made the gamble of a script worthwhile for established and new writers alike. For Dickens, eager for applause and still dazzled by the footlights, the prospect was irresistible. In 1843, when the proprietor of the Haymarket Theatre was offering a prize of £500 for the best new comedy, Dickens told Douglas Jerrold how he would behave if he won: "I walk up and down the street at the back of the Theatre every night, and peep in at the Green Room Window—thinking of the time when 'Dick-Ins' will be called for, by excited hundreds, and won't come. . . . Then I shall come forward and bow—once—twice—thrice—Roars of approbation—Brayvo—Brarvo—Hooray—Hoorar—Hooroar."[29] If this anticipates the public reaction to his later reading tours, it also comes close to being a spoof of his emotions in 1836–1837, when the "Hooroar" of the crowd acted on him like a Siren's call.

Dickens's opportunity came about because the mercurial John Braham had recently taken over the lease of St. James's Theatre. Though Braham had spent a rumored £26,000 on refurbishments, the first season had been a financial disaster, and he was now looking for new plays that would fill the theater's coffers. Securing the services of "Boz" would have seemed like a smart business decision, given that he combined an established reputation as a storyteller with a certain novelty value as a playwright. Dickens had been introduced to Braham by J. P. Harley, the theater's leading comedian and stage manager, whom he had in turn met via Hullah, and within a few months he had firmed up this somewhat tenuous connection into two solid commissions. *The Strange Gentleman,* billed as "A Comic Burletta in Two Acts," opened on September 29, and after a more protracted gestation and a false start (Dickens had originally planned to write a comic opera about gondoliers, thus anticipating Gilbert and Sullivan by more than fifty years), it was followed by an operetta, *The Village Coquettes,* on December 6.

In later years, Dickens viewed these productions with a mixture of embarrassment and contempt: he told Frederick Lodder that if he possessed a copy of *The Strange Gentleman* in his house he would be happy to ensure its destruction by setting fire to the building, while a letter sent to R. H. Horne in 1843 declared that "both these things were done without the least consideration or regard for reputation. I wouldn't repeat them for a thousand pounds apiece, and devoutly wish them to be forgotten."[30] But for all his claims that the first play was "a sort of practical joke," and that the second was "done in a fit of d—ble good nature," his letters to Hullah at the time tell a rather different story.[31] They boast about the "literary and musical" friends who have heard a rehearsal of *The Village Coquettes* and are "enthusiastic in praise of the whole affair"; they buzz with satisfaction when relaying Braham's judgment on *The Strange Gentleman:* "Bet you ten pound it runs fifty nights."[32] In fact it ran for some seventy nights, propelled a good deal further than it deserved by Boz's name and an energetic cast; and if its success disturbed Dickens, he hid his feelings well. Nor did he show any great reluctance to tempt Bentley with the prospect of "a considerable sale" from print publication of *The Village Coquettes,* this time enlisting the "good authority" of George Hogarth, who "prognosticates wonders."[33] For a writer who had claimed only a few months earlier that "I really *cannot* do the tremendous in puffing myself," Dickens had remarkably few qualms about finding new ways of putting himself before the public.

Even so, his refusal to reprint these plays in later years is worth pausing over, because both were already repetitions-with-variations of previously published work. *The Village Coquettes* adapted a plot that can be traced back via several different versions to Charles Dufresny's 1715 comedy *La Coquette du village*—a literary genealogy that drew particular attention to the moment in Dickens's version when the central character of Squire Norton suddenly switches from cackling villain to unlikely hero, as if he had belatedly realized that he was in the wrong play. *The*

Strange Gentleman was similarly unoriginal; indeed, for anyone who had read "The Great Winglebury Duel" in the first series of *Sketches by Boz,* the "gentleman" in question would have been strangely familiar, because Dickens's farce was merely the same story translated into stage action and padded out with extra dialogue.

Recycling old material was hardly unusual in a literary economy where good ideas were always worth having more than once, and Dickens was by no means the only writer who treated form like a costume that could be altered to suit different contexts. Dramatizing a previously published piece had the additional benefit of consolidating the reputation of "Boz" as a writer of light comic sketches. Several reviews made this connection, including the *Courier*'s, which noted that the play was "from the pen of Mr. Charles Dickens, whose sketches under the title of 'Boz' have afforded a great deal of amusement to the town," and the *Spectator*'s, which applauded *The Strange Gentleman* as a "very clever and lively" comedy "by Mr. Charles Dickens, whose writings as 'Boz' are at present so popular."

The true identity of "Boz" had first been revealed in a publisher's advertisement printed in the *Athenaeum* on July 30, and it was soon a sufficiently open secret for other writers to make it the subject of playful allusions. *John Bull*'s reviewer observed that the play's author was "a gentleman who . . . had adopted the cognomen of 'Boz' in preference to playing the Dickens in his own name," and as late as March 1837 there was enough mileage in the pun for *Bentley's* to publish an "Impromptu" that ran: "Who the dickens 'Boz' could be / Puzzled many a learned elf; / Till time unveil'd the mystery, / And Boz appear'd as DICKENS' self!" At the same time, Dickens's name was still new enough for occasional mistakes to slip the attention of copyeditors: the *Champion* reported that *The Strange Gentleman* was "from the pen of Mr. Dicken."[34]

Dickens seems to have been in two minds about how best to present himself to the public: on December 3 he sent one press copy to the *Examiner* with a note beginning "'Boz' presents his compliments," and another to the music critic William Ayrton: "Mr. Dickens presents his compts."[35] The management of St. James's Theatre had no such qualms.

It was "Boz" whose *Pickwick* was on everyone's lips, and "Boz" whose name dominated the playbills, gradually expanding in size until, by the time of a benefit performance for Harley on March 13, 1837, it had become the typographic equivalent of a yell:

Mr. HARLEY

will In the Character of

MR. PICKWICK

Make his First Visit

TO THE ST. JAMES'S THEATRE,

And relate, to a Scotch Air, his

EXPERIENCES

OF

"A White Bait Dinner at Blackwall."

EDITED EXPRESSLY FOR HIM BY HIS BIOGRAPHER

"BOZ!" [36]

Such publicity presented Dickens with both an opportunity and a problem. The opportunity lay in exploiting what marketing professionals might now call "brand recognition," by adding the luster of *Pickwick* to anything new he wrote. The problem lay in the ease with which this persona could become a mask that would be impossible to remove. Already "Boz" was taking on a separate life in the public imagination: not only were the first barnacles of rumor starting to attach themselves to him, but in *Sketches* and *Pickwick* Dickens had encouraged his readers to construct a model of the writer that no single person could possibly live up to. Wise, witty, and bubbling over with invention, "Boz" reflected a distinctly flattering image of Dickens's readers back at themselves, so it should have come as no surprise that there were different expectations of what he looked like. Inevitably, most people discovered that the three dimensions of real life were no substitute for the endlessly shifting dimensions of the imagination. After the first night of *The Village Coquettes*, the *Examiner* reported, the audience "screamed for Boz," and he obliged with a curtain call. The curtains of St. James's Theatre were green, as were the covers of *Pickwick,* so in coming onstage Dickens would have looked strangely like the author himself emerging from his writing. Unfortunately, as the *Examiner*'s reviewer noted, the audience was left in "perfect consternation" at the failure of this dandyish young man to look like any of *Pickwick*'s characters: "he neither resembled the portraits of Pickwick, Snodgrass, Winkle, nor Tupman. Some critics in the gallery were said to have expected Samuel Weller."

Drawings made of Dickens at the time suggest that he was learning to play the role of Boz more successfully offstage. Thackeray depicts him as a sharply dressed man-about-town (Figure 14), nonchalantly puffing on a thin cigar, with an expression caught somewhere between the confident and the cocky. He is the very image of a successful young writer. Yet as he had learned from his curtain call, the gap between image and person was one in which misunderstanding could flourish. Even more worryingly, any writer who was content merely to please the public could find himself building a career on nothing more solid than the shifting sands of fashion. It was a dilemma his reviewers were not slow to recognize. The *Spectator*'s observation that Dickens's sketches were "popular" carried a potential sting in its tail; likewise the reviews of *The Strange Gentleman* in the *Champion* and the *Literary Gazette,* both of which noted that the play was based on one of Dickens's "popular sketches."[37] In all three articles, "popular" stops just short of turning a form of acclaim into something more like a sneer.

It would be only a slight exaggeration to say that the rest of Dickens's career was played out in the uncertain space between these two interpretations of "popular" writing. The word recurs in contemporary reviews as a question that is all the more powerful for being largely a matter of hints rather than explicit argument: Should popular writers be celebrated for entertaining the general public, or criticized for failing to rise above its demands? The phrase "popular culture" was first used in the modern sense in 1854, a year after the circus-master Sleary in *Hard Times* had explained that "people mutht be amuthed," but Dickens's critics remained uneasy about how far novels should position themselves at the heart of popular culture. Were they anything more than a way of amusing ordinary people? "If a man writes a popular work, he is sure to be snarled at," Thackeray pointed out in 1840, with the uncertain tone of a writer who was desperate to write precisely such works.[38] Margaret Oliphant did not snarl, though in 1855 she did delicately curl her lip at the reasons for Dickens's success: "It is to the fact that he represents a class that he owes his speedy elevation to the top of the wave of popular favour"—a rise that rewarded him for his willingness not to stray too far from "the air and breath of middle-class respectability."[39] Yet the same word that discriminated one class from another could also blur the distinctions between them: in 1870, Anthony Trollope noted that Dickens's novels were "popular from the highest to the lowest,—among all classes that read."[40]

Dickens's popularity cheered and irked his critics in roughly equal measure, but only one sought to get involved in the writing process itself: John Forster. The opening sentence in his *Life of Charles Dickens* (published 1872–1874) declared Dickens to be "the most popular novelist of the century," and few other writers at the time worried so productively about the relationship between popular fiction and its audience.[41] None was as influential in helping Dickens decide what sort of writer he should be, once it was clear that his popularity was more than a fad.

On paper, at least, their relationship got off to an awkward start. As the *Examiner*'s main theater critic, it was Forster who had reviewed *The Village Coquettes,* and although he poked fun at the production's "inefficient" orchestra and "disfiguring" costumes, his smile was eventually twisted into a genuine grimace of annoyance by the curtain call: a "disgusting farce" between leading actor and audience, in which Harley asked "if it were all right?" in a "whining, half-apologetic, all-familiar strain," and the spectators answered with "a great din" of applause. The appearance of Boz was even more irritating, and Forster responded by presenting him with a bouquet of compliments that included a quiet rebuke: "Now we have a great respect and liking for Boz; the *Pickwick Papers* have made him, as our readers are very well aware, an especial favourite with us; and we have no idea of his being exhibited gratis. Bad as the opera is, however, we feel assured that if Mr. Braham will make arrangements to parade the real living Boz every night . . . he will insure for [it] a certain attraction."[42] The ambiguity of "a certain attraction" was especially well-judged, as Forster acknowledged Dickens's box-office appeal, while observing that this didn't greatly distinguish him from the star of a menagerie or freak show. And Forster expected much more from writers than that.

The bookish and bullish son of a Newcastle butcher, Forster had rejected a university education in favor of the literary hurly-burly of London, and in his first published review he had offered a powerful defense of the public reputation of writers.[43] It was a manifesto he spent the rest of his life trying to uphold. Convinced that literature was as important to a developing nation as "services done by professors of arms, law, divinity, and diplomacy," but conscious of how easily a phrase like "the dignity of literature" could become an empty slogan, Forster committed himself to upholding it through his own example.[44] His bookplate included the motto "Follow Me," and nobody could have worked harder to put it into practice. Whether by encouraging ailing talents such as Charles Lamb—sad, lonely, often drunk—who came to treat his "dear boy" as a flattering hybrid of fan and apprentice, or by helping contemporaries such as Bulwer and Thackeray ("Whenever anybody is in a scrape we all fly to him [Forster] for critical refuge"), during the 1830s he turned himself from an ambitious journalist into something more like a one-man literary agency.[45] Like Naddo in Browning's long narrative poem *Sordello,* one of the many literary characters in which we catch fleeting echoes of his voice and manner, he was "busiest of the tribe / Of genius-haunters," although anyone who experienced the full force of his personality might have wondered whether Browning's lines contained a creative misprint.[46] Was Forster a haunter or a hunter?

No doubt Forster took a degree of vicarious pleasure in seeing his friends succeed, and his efforts on their behalf satisfied his overwhelm-

ing need to be needed, but his true loyalties were to a far more impersonal cause. However good a friend he was to individual writers, he was
a far greater friend to literature. Every deal he brokered was another step
towards making writers the moral compass of a potentially directionless
age. (As late as 1850, in an argument with Thackeray, he pointed out that
on the government pension list writers were grouped together with royal
coachmen.)[47] Of particular relevance to Dickens was Forster's stress on
the idea that good writing and popular writing should not be thought of
as mutually exclusive categories. Milton's hope that *Paradise Lost* would
"fit audience find, though few" had often been skewed into the assumption that the fit *were* the few, and that only writers who themselves lacked
discrimination could have a genuinely broad appeal.[48] It took a writer like
Dickens to prove that the same novel could please servants and cabmen
as well as readers of *Paradise Lost,* but it took a tireless campaigner like
Forster to persuade them that reading about Oliver Twist or Little Nell
might be more than a guilty private pleasure.

Forster's obsession with dignity was firmly rooted in personal experience. Scorned by some of his colleagues as a "low scribbler . . . totally
unused to the Society of Gentlemen," he had a talent for friendship, but
an absolute genius for making enemies, particularly when anxiety about
his social origins led him to take offense at real or imagined slights.[49] At
such moments, when he started hurling insults—and on one occasion a
water jug—his prickly defensiveness was hard to distinguish from the behavior of a bully. (It was reported that his butler was so cowed by him that,
after hearing that his own house was on fire, he finished serving dinner
in nervous silence before asking for permission to leave.) Yet although
at times he displayed the hide of a rhinoceros, battering his friends with
pomposity and condescension, at other times he seemed to have been
born without a skin at all. His perceptive description of Dickens as "often
uneasy, shrinking, and over-sensitive" underneath his "hard and aggressive" demeanor reads oddly like a confession he could neither bring himself to make nor altogether repress.[50]

For London's gossips, Forster was a particular gift. Stories about him trying to dance in shoes that were too big for him, or losing his temper with a hapless servant—a muttered "Biscuits," followed by a louder "BIScuits," and finally a roar of "*BIS*cuits!"—swiftly passed from anecdote into legend. According to one friend, Dickens "revelled" in these stories, and he could not resist laughing at the man he called "the Mogul"; his clumsy jokes, his foghorn attempts at whispering (a noise which, Dickens recalled, "seems to go in at your ear and come out at the sole of your boot"), his unwitting speech tics: "Monstrous!" "Incredible!" "*In-tol*-erable!"[51] Dickens could be savage in his glee, confessing during one of their theatrical productions that "I have always a vicious desire to electrify Mr. Forster (when he is acting) violently, in some sensitive part of his anatomy," but their relationship was far more complex than literary hero worship on one side and mocking tolerance on the other.[52] In many ways, Boz and "Fuz" needed each other.[53]

Just as Forster recognized his barely contained aggression in Dickens, so Dickens saw distorted reflections of himself in his friend. Not only had their lives followed a similar trajectory, from social obscurity to radical journalism via an interrupted career in the law (Forster had trained as a barrister), but Dickens was equally keen to stress the respectability of creative artists, which is why his dedication to *The Village Coquettes* had praised Harley for contributing to "the amusement of the public," but also for shedding a "lustre" over the theatrical profession by "the honour and integrity of your private life." Even Dickens's most famous fictional version of Forster reflected their shared tendency to push things to extremes. Forster's first review, written as an unusually prudish teenager, in which he had warned that certain passages in the 1828 edition of *The Keepsake* "would be apt to raise a blush on the cheek of a young English female," did not need more than a delicate nudge to become the catchphrase of *Our Mutual Friend*'s Podsnap, whose "question about everything was, would it bring a blush into the cheek of the young person?"[54] Yet like most of Dickens's most aggressive pieces of satire, this also trembled on the verge of self-parody. It was Dickens, after all, whose preface to *Pickwick* had expressed the earnest hope that "no incident or expression occurs which could call a blush into the most delicate cheek," and in this context Podsnap embodied a rather different kind of "cheek": an opportunity for Dickens to twit Forster with a horrifying vision of where their early moral concerns might have led them.

Forster's relationship with Dickens has usually been seen as more uneven than this. "As I look back," wrote the author and *Household Words* contributor Percy Fitzgerald, "I can never call up the image of Dickens without seeing Forster beside him; Forster seems always to interpose his bulky form. He was ever bustling about his friend, interpreting him and explaining him."[55] Such busy ministrations continued long after Dickens's death, as Forster set about writing a biography in which his own figure would also blot out any potential rivals. One reviewer complained that the book "should not be called the Life of Dickens but the History of Dickens' Relations to Mr. Forster," and admittedly it sometimes reads like an autobiography that has accidentally got tangled up with Dickens's life.[56] Yet however easily one could mock Forster for attempting to hitch a ride on Dickens's fame, overall it was Dickens who was the chief beneficiary of their friendship, and not only because the version of him loyally promoted in *The Life of Charles Dickens*—generous, pure-minded, faithful—was one he might have chosen for himself. (There is more than one sense in which Forster's biography is the life of a friend.) In 1851 Forster played the role of Hardman in a production of Bulwer's play *Not So Bad As We Seem,* a figure who has "a hard life of it," like all "men who live for others."[57] It was an affectionate piece of casting, not least because of Bulwer's stress on the generosity that Hardman's tough shell seeks to protect. Forster's generosity was one of the chief reasons Dickens stuck with him over the years, despite the rumors that in reality it was Forster who was sticking to him like a human burr. Forster was a hard man with a soft center. No less important was the fact that, throughout the years in which he acted as Dickens's unofficial editor, he refused to suspend his critical judgment. He was that terrifying figure all writers must keep in mind if their writing is to remain trim and alert: a reader who is hard to please. In many respects he was Dickens's critical conscience.

Sending Forster the proofs of his story *The Battle of Life* (the fourth of his five "Christmas books"), Dickens encouraged him to "knock out a word's brains here and there" if the writing started to drift into blank verse, as it often did when he was straining for sentimental effect, but Forster's editorial duties went far beyond the occasional verbal cull.[58] They included cutting installments to length, regularizing punctuation, and, crucially, offering suggestions designed to tighten Dickens's grip on his readers. "Don't fail to erase anything that seems to you too strong," Dickens urged when forwarding some chapters of *Barnaby Rudge,* and Forster obliged by filing away at a number of places where the writing bulged melodramatically. Reading the manuscript of *Dombey and Son,* Forster asked him to cut a passage describing Miss Tox's attempts to control pests by poking around in "sundry chinks and crevices of the wainscoat with the wrong end of a pen dipped in spirits of turpentine," probably because it showed too detailed a knowledge of dirty household chores, thus increasing its vulnerability to critics who were suspicious of what Dickens was doing with the other end of his pen. Dickens agreed. Going through *Bleak House,* Forster worried that the spikily satirical representation of Skimpole was too obviously based on the poet and essayist Leigh Hunt. Dickens smoothed it down. Even when he said things Dickens would have preferred not to hear, such as that Little Nell needed to die if *The Old Curiosity Shop* was to be completed satisfactorily, a sacrifice both to the marketplace and to the demands of the plot, Dickens listened carefully and did as Forster urged. What these revisions shared was a concern for correctness that was as much moral as aesthetic. They reflected Forster's conviction that what his period needed was improving literature: writing that was better not just because it was funnier or more moving than anything published before, but because it was designed to make its readers feel better, act better. And if Dickens was to be literature's champion, then Forster was happy to act as his squire: a guide, goad, and collaborator all in one.

Their first encounter took place over Christmas 1836, at Ainsworth's house. Dickens had read Forster's *Examiner* review of *The Village*

Coquettes, noting that it was "*rather* depreciatory" but "so well done that I cannot help laughing at it"; and although they were not to meet again for several weeks, Forster "remember[ed] vividly the impression then made upon me" by Dickens's cheerful eyes, waves of glossy chestnut hair, and alert expression "that seemed to tell so little of a student or writer of books, and so much of a man of action and business in the world."[59] He could not have chosen a better time of year to establish the foundations for a lasting friendship. Beginning with "A Christmas Dinner" in *Sketches by Boz,* Christmas was sunk deeply into Dickens's imagination. Year after year, his mind struck off in different directions; year after year, he returned to the same imaginative center, as Christmas exerted its gravitational pull. "Christmas was always a time which in our home was looked forward to with eagerness and delight," his daughter Mamie recalled, while his son Henry agreed that Christmas in the Dickens household "was a great time, a really jovial time, and my father was always at his best, a splendid host, bright and jolly as a boy and throwing his heart and soul into everything that was going on."[60]

Yet however cheerful these recollections, others observed that Dickens's enjoyment of Christmas seemed more determined, even ruth-less, than one might expect from someone with a genuinely boyish sense of fun. Whether Dickens was learning a new conjuring trick or mastering the steps to a dance, his son Charles nervously noted, there was always the same "alarming thoroughness with which he always threw himself into everything he had occasion to take up."[61] Perhaps his memories of Warren's Blacking were to blame. His family's accounts certainly suggest an attempt on Dickens's part to re-create his childhood as it should have been, rather than as it was. His fiction, too, reveals surprisingly mixed feelings over Christmas as a time of peace and joy. For all its visions of plum puddings and mistletoe, and all the readers who have come to think of Dickens as literature's answer to Santa Claus, he rarely describes a fam-ily Christmas without showing how vulnerable it is to being broken apart by a more miserable alternative. In *Great Expectations* it is the soldiers who burst into Pip's home on Christmas Day, saving him from a dinner in which the only highlight is Joe slopping extra spoonfuls of gravy onto his plate. In *The Mystery of Edwin Drood,* the young hero goes missing on Christmas Eve, leaving behind several clues that he had been murdered by his uncle. Saddest of all, in *A Christmas Carol* Scrooge is forced by the Ghost of Christmas Past to observe his boyhood self left behind at school, and weeps "to see his poor forgotten self as he used to be."

A Christmas Carol ends with Scrooge's rejection of a future in which he degenerates from a sour misanthrope into a corpse, avoiding it by latching onto a ready-made family in the shape of the Cratchits and showering them with gifts. In many ways he is another of Dickens's surrogate novelists, who begins by observing characters from a distance, but ends up meddling in their lives once they prove how much they deserve to be rewarded. But in describing a sharp-tongued individual being flooded by the Christmas spirit, Dickens may also have had someone else in mind: John Forster. As their friendship developed after that first meeting at Ainsworth's, in effect Forster became a member of Dickens's extended family, "a part, and an essential part, of our home," and for many years he and Dickens spent Christmas Day together, celebrating the anniversary of a relationship that was no less meaningful than Dickens's marriage and that lasted considerably longer.[62] In the development of his "love-affair" with the reading public, it was Forster who would act as the essential go-between, ensuring that after *Pickwick* Dickens consolidated his place in the nation's heart and at its hearth. And in this sense, Forster was not the only one who used their friendship to gain access to a growing family. So did Dickens.

CHAPTER TEN

Dickens at Home

On May 15, 1836, Dickens's sister-in-law Mary Hogarth sent an upbeat letter to her cousin reporting on a "most delightfully happy month" spent with the newly married couple at their lodgings in Furnival's Inn. Catherine was "as happy as the day is long," she observed; "they are more devoted than ever since their Marriage if that be possible," and Dickens is "such a nice creature and so clever."[1] The picture is reassuringly optimistic, even when we make allowances for the distortions created by such a wide-eyed view. The more pessimistic alternative was dramatized a few months later in Dickens's one-act farce *Is She His Wife? Or, Something Singular,* completed while he and Catherine were revisiting the scene of their honeymoon at Chalk. This time the distortions were generated by comic exaggeration, as Dickens poked fun at a recently married couple who devote themselves to scheming against each other and delivering quarrelsome one-liners such as "How little did I think when I married you, six short months since, that I should be exposed to such wretchedness!" Given the complexity of any marriage, it would be unfair to treat either of these pictures, romantic idealization or cynical debunking, as a true reflection of life at Furnival's Inn. Even putting them together only balances things out by playing different kinds of lopsidedness off against each other, like someone with a limp in both legs.

A few years later, Dickens's *Sketches of Young Couples,* dashed off for Chapman and Hall to exploit the market created by Queen Victoria's marriage in 1840, introduced a much broader set of models to choose from. Beginning with a narrative portrait of "The Young Couple" on their wedding day, a relationship full of untarnished potential, Dickens continues by describing several other couples as examples of how their life together might unfold or unravel. These include "The Loving Couple," who are "well-nigh intolerable" to anyone forced to witness their gooey baby talk, and "The Cool Couple," who sit together in chilly silence punctuated by "ironical or recriminatory" bickering. (It is hard to know how much weight should be attached to the fact that the husband's name is Charles; it could be anything from a private joke to a public snub.) None of the other couples is much more attractive, and for the most part Dickens's writing is governed by the sort of facetious tone he adopted whenever he wanted to sound witty but lacked any good jokes. His ironic mask slips only once, in a concluding address to anyone still contemplating marriage, where the light banter gives way to an unexpected burst of sincerity:

> Before marriage and afterwards, let them learn to centre all their hopes of real and lasting happiness in their own fireside; let them cherish the faith that in home, and all the English virtues which the love of home engenders, lies the only true source of domestic felicity; let them believe that round the household gods contentment and tranquillity cluster in their gentlest and most graceful forms; and that many weary hunters of happiness through the noisy world have learnt this truth too late, and found a cheerful spirit and a quiet mind only at home at last.

The sentence strides forward from clause to clause before alighting on "home at last" like a traveler giving a sigh of relief as he reaches his front door. It is like a miniature of Dickens's literary career to date.

Having published *Pickwick Papers* and *Oliver Twist,* both of which end with cozy domestic scenes, Dickens had also recently completed *Nicholas Nickleby,* which compounds the pleasure of returning home by having the hero move back into his father's old house, where he ensures that "nothing with which there was any association of bygone times was ever removed or changed." In all three novels, "home" is where the narrative "finds refuge, rest, or satisfaction," like a piece of music playing out a set of variations before finally resolving into its original key.[2] For Dickens, this pattern was a happy alliance of heart and head. There was a growing readership at the time for celebrations of home life, reflected in the 1836 publication of *Home; or, The Iron Rule,* the novel which inaugurated the influential career of Sarah Ellis as an author of conduct books and fiction, and the growing success of Felicia Hemans's 1827 poem "The Homes of England" ("The stately Homes of England,/How beautiful they stand!"), which not only became a popular anthology piece, but brought a new term, "stately home," into the language.[3] A cult of domesticity was starting to settle itself in the national psyche, and at the same time that Dickens was trying to establish a secure home life with Catherine, he was positioning himself to be the cult's high priest.

This is an aspect of Dickens that makes modern readers especially uneasy. We can gloss over his occasional eruptions of racism and sexism, reassured by the idea that he was shaped by his context just as much as he helped to shape it; we can even enjoy his sentimentality, by flattering ourselves with the thought that we are made of sterner and more discriminating stuff than his original readers, with their hair-trigger emotions and chiaroscuro morality. It is much harder to explain away the loving attention he gives to chirping crickets and humming hobs. The same elements that made a reviewer of *The Battle of Life* applaud Dickens as "a writer of home life, a delineator of household gods, and a painter of domestic scenes" are also those most likely to make us feel like uninvited guests.[4]

Writing from America as his first tour drew to a close in 1842, Dickens confessed that he was "FEVERED with anxiety for home," and his letter responded with an urgent crescendo of homesickness: "Oh home— home—home—home—home—home—HOME!!!!!!!!!!!"[5] It reads like a severely concertinaed vision of his fiction, in which "home" and the words associated with it in Dickens's private lexicon ("neat," "pleasant," "comfortable," and so on) are repeated so often they sound like someone trying to cast a spell. His writing often suffered as a result. The line between snugness and smugness in Dickens's fiction can be blurry, and with each repetition the concept of "home" itself became more unwieldy, like those pieces of cutlery displayed at the 1851 Great Exhibition that were too heavy and elaborately decorated to be of any practical use. Indeed, when Dickens sighs in *The Battle of Life,* "O Home, our comforter and friend," as if every house were really a church in disguise, or writes in *The Old Curiosity Shop* about "that love of home from which all domestic virtues spring," an idealized vision that comes close to crystallizing into a line of blank verse, it is tempting to conclude that he removed his brain along with his hat whenever he crossed the threshold. Yet the foundations of these ideas lay deep in his imagination, and it was the period of practical homemaking after his marriage that allowed him to put them to the test.

For Dickens, home is not only a physical shelter but an extension of the self, like an additional skin or an exoskeleton. At its simplest, this involves fictional scenes in which he jerks buildings momentarily into life, producing doorknockers that leer or windows that stare emptily down the street. More elaborately worked examples include the large number of houses that have grown to resemble their owners. In *Nicholas Nickleby,* Arthur Gride lives in a house that is as "yellow and shrivelled" as himself, greedily keeping him from daylight just as he hoards his money, while in *Bleak House* Jarndyce recalls how the family home was once as "shattered and ruined" as the uncle whose tenancy coincided with his suicide; with its "cracked walls" and "broken roof," it looked as if the brains had been "blown out of the house too." (The biblical sense of a "home" as a grave, like the "long home" that Ecclesiastes tells us we are traveling towards, is one that often haunts Dickens's fiction, reflected not only in domestic scenes that are offered as the nearest thing to paradise on earth, but also strange passages like the slow collapse of Mr. Dombey's house after his son dies—a decline in which the furniture shrinks, mold covers the walls, and mysterious piles of dust appear, as if sympathetically echoing what is happening to Paul's corpse.)[6] Other characters are more complicated, because for them "home" signifies a sense of self that cannot simply be repaired like a leaky roof. When Lady Dedlock in *Bleak House* writes to her husband explaining that "I have no home left," she means not just that she must leave Chesney Wold, but that her carefully constructed history lies in ruins. Similarly, when Silas Wegg asks the taxidermist Mr. Venus in *Our Mutual Friend,* "Am I still at home?," he is making a discreet inquiry about whether or not his amputated leg has been sold, but also rehearsing for the day when he will be able to "collect myself together like a genteel person"—a person like Mrs. Tapkins, in other words, who leaves the Boffins a card promising "Mrs. Tapkins at Home" rather than a stray limb.

Dickens himself was an inveterate home improver. Tavistock House was thoroughly remodeled over the years in which he lived there, and at Gad's Hill Place he continued to alter and add to the house's solid Georgian core—extending the drawing room, sticking on a conservatory, and creating several attic bedrooms—until its "pleasantly irregular" features reflected more than a decade of his changing moods.[7] He was equally charmed by homes that did not alter in themselves but could move from place to place, like the "perfect abode" of Peggotty's converted boat in *David Copperfield,* or Mrs. Jarley's caravan in *The Old Curiosity Shop,* which is decked out with neat white curtains and a "bright brass knocker" that beats out a cheerful tattoo as this "little house on wheels" jolts heavily along. Both are the human equivalent of a tortoise's shell. A variation on the idea can be seen in *Our Mutual Friend,* when Jenny Wren lets down her long, golden hair to create a "bower," which she does for the same reason that Wemmick pulls up his drawbridge in *Great Expectations:* it allows her to retreat into a world of her own making. Dickens also enjoyed playing with the idea in his private life. In 1864 the actor Charles Fechner sent him a two-story wooden chalet, which came in ninety-seven pieces and was assembled like a huge jigsaw puzzle on some land opposite Gad's Hill Place. Decked out with mirrors, and reached via a tunnel dug underneath the Dover Road, it quickly became Dickens's favorite place to work. As a building that could always be taken apart and reassembled elsewhere, like the "wooden pavilion" that houses Sleary's traveling circus in *Hard Times,* it was the next-best thing to writing in a mobile home.

Dickens's novels do not merely describe homes; in some ways, they *are* homes. *Bleak House* is the star example here, because Dickens deliberately encourages the idea that his twisting and turning narrative reflects the titular house's higgledy-piggledy architecture, "where you go up and down steps out of one room into another, and where you come upon more rooms when you think you have seen all there are, and where there is a bountiful provision of little halls and passages." Even when Dickens is not describing homes, he is creating them, as he did in his public readings, by encouraging his audience to think of themselves as an extended family gathered around his hearth. On the page, similarly, Dickens worked hard to present himself as the ideal host, handing out jokes like someone reaching into a bottomless bag of gifts. His hospitality could be suffocating; as G. K. Chesterton wryly observed, in some of his stories he continued to "pile up the cushions until none of the characters could move."[8] On the other hand, a week before she described *Oliver Twist* as "excessively interesting," Queen Victoria confessed to her diary that she never felt "quite at ease or at home when reading a Novel"; and although that may have reflected her private sense of duty, it is also a perceptive piece of literary criticism.[9] The same novels of the period that celebrate home as a precious ideal also draw attention to how precarious it is, and no writer was better than Dickens at plumping up his readers' cushions while whipping away the chair from underneath them. Despite occasional fantasies in which he transformed himself into "a cheerful creature that chirrups on the Hearth," nobody was more suspicious of his attempts to work a "vein of glowing, hearty, generous, mirthful, beaming reference in everything to Home and Fireside" than Dickens himself.[10]

Narrative snapshots like the Cratchits' happy family Christmas may linger in the memory, but in Dickens's fictional world they are set against a background where the domestic ideal is far more likely to be flaking around the edges. In the worst cases, even the talismanic word "home," described in *Martin Chuzzlewit* as "a name . . . stronger than magician ever spoke," finds its powers evaporating. In *David Copperfield,* when Emily writes to tell Mr. Peggotty she has eloped with Steerforth, she repeats "home" like a moth beating its wings against the window—"When

I leave my dear home—my dear home—oh, my dear home!—in the morning . . . it will be never to come back, unless he brings me back a lady"— but the writing snags only briefly before, like Emily herself, it moves on. There is a sad parallel later in the novel when Mr. Peggotty explains how he pursued his niece across Europe—"Ever so fur as I went . . . Ever so fur she run . . . ever so fur in the night"—where even the echoes of Dickens's favorite song, "Home, Sweet Home" ("Be it ever so humble, there's no place like home"), seem powerless to tempt her back.[11]

Nor is Emily an isolated case. Dickens's suspicion of his own rhetoric often makes itself felt in a gap between theories of domestic felicity and the grubby truth of how his characters actually live. His later works, in particular, are far more likely to depict ideal homes as unrealized blueprints than as real places. In *The Cricket on the Hearth*, Caleb Plummer weaves stories about his "enchanted home" to fool his blind daughter into thinking that their creaky wooden shack is actually as trim and spruce as the dollhouses he makes, while in *Great Expectations* Mr. Pocket compensates for his chaotic home life by writing tracts on "the management of children and servants" which are "considered the very best text-books on those themes." In seeing through the fictions his characters have created, Dickens casts skeptical glances at everything he enthusiastically celebrates elsewhere.

The usual biographical explanation for this disenchantment has been the collapse of Dickens's marriage, which he marked by having his dressing room converted into a single bedroom and, in a neat compromise between the practical and imaginative sides of his personality, sealing the door between his and Catherine's rooms with bookcases. Yet similar doubts make themselves felt much earlier in his career, with Mr. Bumble in *Oliver Twist* rhapsodizing "Oh, Mrs. Corney, what a angel you are!," only to discover when they are married that she cannot be handled as easily as her teaspoons. The same potential for disillusionment is built into even Dickens's blandest domestic ideals. In 1850, after rejecting several possible titles for his new journal, including *The Household Voice*, *The Household Guest*, and *The Household Face*, he chose *Household Words*, adapting a phrase from a suitably well-known line in *Henry V:* "Familiar in his mouth as household words."[12] When he launched the journal's successor, *All the Year Round,* after Forster mildly suggested that Dickens's first choice of title, *Household Harmony,* might not be a happy one in light of the very public failure of his marriage, Dickens once again turned to Shakespeare, and each issue duly appeared with "The Story of Our Lives from Year to Year" printed on the masthead. Presumably he was hoping that his readers would not pay too much attention to the line's original context, because it is adapted from *Othello,* which begins with the hero explaining how he wooed Desdemona by telling her "the story of my life / From year to year" but ends with him smothering her.[13] So much for piling up the cushions.

In subtler ways, too, Dickens saw the home as a place full of potential danger. "A Dinner at Poplar Walk" establishes an imaginative pattern in which unwelcome relatives are only some of the troublesome individuals who break into or break up the happy home. Dickens's female characters are especially vulnerable to having their private space invaded and pawed over. In *The Old Curiosity Shop,* Quilp settles himself in Little Nell's room and gleefully discovers that her little bed is "much about my size," while in *Bleak House* Inspector Bucket's first step in tracking down Lady Dedlock is to secure himself in her "spicy boudoir" and rummage around in her private belongings, "opening and shutting table-drawers, and looking into caskets and jewel-cases." In both examples, the hint of displaced sexual energy makes the narrative function of these characters clear. They are Dickens's licensed home-wreckers, who dedicate themselves to smashing up everything he held most dear. John Carey has written well about these figures, claiming that they represent anarchic tendencies Dickens could neither repress nor allow himself openly to express. Instead, they leak out in events like Silas Wegg's evening routine in *Our Mutual Friend,* during which he walks to the Boffin house so that he can gloat over his power "to strip the roof off the inhabiting family like the roof of a house of cards," or, in *Barnaby Rudge,* the behavior of Gabriel Varden, who throws his wife's house-shaped collecting box onto the floor and crushes it to pieces under his heel.[14] Of limited relevance to Dickens's plots, but crucial to his imagination, both incidents show that the side of him who once exclaimed "Blow [i.e., Damn] Domestic Hearth!" was present in his fiction all along.[15]

Such events are also a narrative necessity. Passages like the description of Bella's housework in *Our Mutual Friend* clearly thrill Dickens ("Such weighing and mixing and chopping and grating," he gushes, "such dusting and washing and polishing, such snipping and weeding and trowelling . . ."), but it is hard to imagine them being turned into a plot. *The Cricket on the Hearth,* similarly, opens with a scene in which the kettle "hum-hum-hums" and the cricket "chirp-chirp-chirps," but their antics have about as much narrative interest as a lump of coal until Tackleton enters, dismissing home as "Four walls and a ceiling" and threatening to scrunch the cheery cricket underfoot. He is the real center of the story. Without him, none of the alternative narrative outcomes glimpsed in the pages that follow, such as infidelity and murder, would be available, and the reappearance of the kettle and cricket on the final page would be merely another performance of the same domestic ritual, rather than a noisy celebration of his failure to destroy their home. Like all of Dickens's finest home-wreckers, he makes the happy ending possible by putting everything it represents at risk.

Different versions of the same idea can be found throughout Dickens's fiction. Often they are hidden away in the corners of his writing, where they have a clear view of what the main plot is up to. Take Esther's efforts in *Bleak House* to "establish some order" in the Jellybys' slovenly home. Mr. Jellyby makes a start on the family's storage problems:

> But such wonderful things came tumbling out of the closets when they were opened—bits of mouldy pie, sour bottles, Mrs. Jellyby's caps, letters, tea, forks, odd boots and shoes of children, firewood, wafers, saucepan-lids, damp sugar in odds and ends of paper bags, foot-stools, blacklead brushes, bread, Mrs. Jellyby's bonnets, books with butter sticking to the binding, guttered candle-ends put out by being turned upside down in broken candlesticks, nutshells, heads

and tails of shrimps, dinner-mats, gloves, coffee-grounds, umbrel-las—that he looked frightened, and left off again.

The slightly labored joke is that Mrs. Jellyby is too busy worrying about overseas missions to put her own house in order, just as Esther's attempt to tackle the family's clutter reflects her desire to establish harmony wherever she goes. Dickens's narrative technique is like a hybrid of both characters, as he amasses details into joyfully indiscriminate piles before rearranging them into meaningful patterns. He told one correspondent in 1839 that he kept his ideas "on different shelves of my brain, ready tick-eted and labelled, to be brought out when I want them," and his skill in *Bleak House* lies in his ability to mess up these shelves before, like the bus-tling Esther, he puts them "a little to rights."[16] Yet throughout the novel, there is the fear that writing may not be able to keep chaos at bay, any more than Jo can keep his crossing clean. Words on the page may look like objects sitting on neat rows of shelves, but in a world where they struggle to remain distinct from each other, so that "M'lud" is only one further contraction away from becoming "mud," they are always in danger of col-lapsing back into a shapeless pool of ink. Dickens's scenes of domestic happiness are equally fragile. No matter how loudly Esther jingles her housekeeping keys, she cannot drown out the sound of the ballad that Skimpole sings about Jo after he has effectively encouraged him to go and die in the streets: "Thrown on the wide world, doomed to wander and roam,/Bereft of his parents, bereft of a home."

Similarly, no matter how often Dickens ended his novels with scenes like Cruikshank's rejected illustration to *Oliver Twist* (Figure 15), show-ing a beaming Oliver comfortably settled in the bosom of his family, he could not rid his imagination of the less happy alternatives. Cruikshank's final illustrations (Figures 16 and 17) show how closely he understood what would eventually become a dominant theme in Dickens's novel. The penultimate image shows Fagin in prison, mad with fear on the eve of his execution, while the bars on his cell window cast lengthening shadows; the final image shows Oliver in church, alongside the saintly Rose Maylie,

staring at a memorial tablet illuminated by a small lead-paned window set
in the same position on the wall. The visual echo creates a little diptych of
rival narrative outcomes. It is the novel's final warning that a cozy fireside
is not the only place a figure like Oliver might have ended up if he proved
to be as wicked as Fagin or as "weak and erring" as his mother.

❦

Such anxieties were especially keen in the months following Mary
Hogarth's stay in 1836. By the end of the year, Catherine was expecting her first child, and no matter how "tastefully and elegantly" Dickens
had furnished what Mary grandly described as their "suite of rooms," or
how nostalgically Dickens later looked back on his time there (the "snug
chambers" of Furnival's Inn are praised in *Martin Chuzzlewit* as "the perfection of neatness and convenience"), nothing could disguise the fact
that his lodgings were far too small for a growing family.[17] Even if they had
been prepared to squash themselves in a little longer, it would have been
legally tricky to do so: a clause in the lease of Dickens's previous chambers at No. 13 had specified that "the said Charles Dickens shall not and
will not at any time during the continuance of the Tenancy permit or suffer any Children to reside or live in the said Chambers," and the lease for
No. 15 probably included a similar refusal to suffer any little children.[18]

"He is wandering again," remarks Fanny of a character named Charles
in *The Strange Gentleman;* and even for a writer who had spent much
of his adult life on the move, Dickens was forced into an unusually no-
madic existence in the opening months of 1837, as he instructed house
agents while shuttling between addresses in London and Chalk, where
Catherine had gone to convalesce after giving birth to a son on January 6.[19]
Dickens's restlessness was echoed in the jerky development of *Pickwick*.
In January Mr. Pickwick leaves Dingley Dell and visits a tatty London
street where there are "always a good many houses to let"; in February
the attention switches to Sam Weller, who prior to the trial is "perpetually
engaged in travelling from the George and Vulture to Mr. Perker's chambers and back again"; finally, in March they travel together to Bath, where

Mr. Pickwick decides on a stay of "at least two months" and rents half a house in the Royal Crescent that is "larger than they required." Both the settling-down of the narrative and the detail about finding new lodgings reflect developments in Dickens's life, because in March he agreed to take over the lease of 48 Doughty Street at an annual rent of £80. A handsome, flat-fronted Georgian townhouse built in 1801, it stretched five floors from basement to attic (Figure 18), and had enough space not only for his wife and baby, but also for his sixteen-year-old brother Fred, now working as an accounts clerk in John Macrone's office, and for his sister-in-law Mary—all of whom moved in at the start of April. It was his first proper family home.

These days, Doughty Street is a decidedly upmarket address, shared by a mixture of well-heeled residents and businesses advertised by discreet brass plaques, but in 1837 it occupied a far more uncertain position in London's imaginative geography. Situated on the ragged edges of Bloomsbury, and part of an expansion of the Doughty estate from the 1790s onwards that was intended to create elegant squares and leafy avenues to rival those of the West End, the street had grown in unpredictable spurts, and by the 1830s found itself in a location with a reputation caught somewhere between respectability and raffishness. Like many areas trumpeted by estate agents as "up-and-coming," it seemed far happier remaining in a state of arrested development, and attitudes towards it were mixed. Theodore Hook's novel *Maxwell* (1830) has some snobbish fun describing a seasoned traveler in search of a Bloomsbury dinner party getting lost in the nearby "deserts of Gray's Inn Road and the wilds of Brunswick Square."[20] On the other hand, the journalist Edmund Yates, who in 1860 lived at No. 43, boasted that Doughty Street was "none of your common thoroughfares to be rattled through by vulgar cabs," but had a gate at each end graced by "a porter in a gold-laced hat, with the Doughty arms on the buttons of his coat" preventing trespassers from "intruding on the exclusive territory."[21] The relationship between exclusivity and a fear of intruders was a complex one. Although Doughty Street's proximity to Gray's Inn made it popular with lawyers, it was also uncomfortably close to Saffron Hill, one of London's most notorious rooker-ies, so the gold braid and buttons were probably there to deter thieves and beggars, as well as to reassure the residents.[22] At once aspirational and edgy, a little pocket of middle-class gentility that was keen to expand its influence but nervous about being swallowed up by poverty, Doughty Street was the perfect address for Dickens at a time when, despite the continuing success of *Pickwick*, his reputation was far from assured. That much is clear from the fact that his house agent Thomas Handisyde, in writing to the owner of No. 48, felt the need to explain that Dickens was "known by the name of Boz" only a few sentences after referring to him as "Mr. Wickens."[23]

Today the house is preserved as a museum, and while the visitors who push open its green front door may enjoy the illusion of entering a por-tal into the nineteenth century, in fact it more closely resembles a corri-dor between the past and the present. While the floorboards may creak with age, and authentic slivers of Dickens's life are preserved under glass, the air is filled with the sound of actors' voices caught on loops of tape and with the clinking of teacups. The drawing room on the first floor, last restored in 1983, offers an especially uncanny overlap of the old and the new (Figure 19). Three sash windows swaddled in net curtains cast their gloomy light onto a flowery carpet woven from an 1829 design, lilac woodwork based on "microscopically examined" paint scrapings, and a selection of furniture in Dickens's favorite rosewood, all of it set off by flickering electric bulbs and a vase of artificial flowers. In an interior so busy with look-alikes, it is something of a shock to come across a sturdy plum-colored armchair and realize that it is the same one Dickens sat in to be sketched by Cruikshank in 1837 (Figure 20). When it was donated to the museum in 1949, it came with a family tradition that Dickens had brought it with him from Furnival's Inn, which, if true, reveals a good deal about his tastes. So do the checkbook stubs that show how much of the furniture he purchased for Doughty Street was secondhand.[24]

This was more than a matter of thrift. For Dickens, history quietly ticked away in old pieces of furniture, giving them an added narrative significance, which is why he rarely describes a clock without adding that it is "old," and makes the narrator of *Master Humphrey's Clock* choose his beloved grandfather clock as the place where he stores the "piles of dusty papers" on which he and his human friends have written their stories.[25] When Master Humphrey confesses that he has become "attached to the inanimate objects that people my chamber," it is tempting to wonder whether he shouldn't perhaps get out more often to meet some real people; but his sense that they are "old and constant friends" rather than "mere chairs and tables which a little money could replace" is fully in line with Dickens's own views. (By contrast, characters who choose new furniture, such as *Our Mutual Friend*'s sticky-fingered Veneerings, or who follow the flighty Skimpole's example in *Bleak House* by being "bound to no particular chairs and tables," are all roundly condemned.) An old chair might change its appearance over the years, gently molding itself to the contours of its owner, as in the domestic scene described in Philip Larkin's poem "Home Is So Sad," where the chair is "Shaped to the comfort of the last to go / As if to win them back," but it also acquired a patina of memory that could not be passed on to a later owner.[26] However long visitors to Doughty Street look at Dickens's chair, they will never be able to see it through his eyes.

Other items in the house give a more accurate impression of Dickens's life there. Tucked away in his bedroom on the second floor, for example, are some scenes from a toy-theater version of *Oliver Twist*, originally sold in printed sheets containing a selection of wobbly cardboard figures ready to be cut out and fixed into place.[27] Like the characters in Dickens's boyhood version of *The Miller and His Men*, they were entirely at the mercy of the owner's fingers. Dickens may not have approved of the choice of play, given his sensitivity to unauthorized adaptations of his work, but the same fantasy of control can be seen in his enthusiasm for other miniature domestic worlds. He was especially drawn to dollhouses, which not only make regular appearances in his fiction, but also provided a model for the various holiday homes he sought out, like the rose-covered "doll's house of many rooms" he found in Boulogne in 1853, or the "perfect doll's house" he rented in Lausanne during 1846, enthusiastically telling Douglas Jerrold that it was small enough to fit into the hall of his previous Italian palazzo.[28] It is difficult to take such fantasies altogether seriously now, particularly after Henrik Ibsen's clear-eyed analysis of their failings in his play *A Doll's House;* yet while Dickens was fully aware of the dangers of treating women like dolls (in *David Copperfield,* Emily is provided with a "little house" that is "as neat and complete as a doll's parlour," and she cannot escape quickly enough), when he describes Esther's move into a "rustic cottage of dolls' rooms" at the end of *Bleak House,* or Ruth Pinch's establishment of a new household in *Martin Chuzzlewit* ("No doll's house ever yielded greater delight to its young mistress"), the tone is unashamedly one of cooing pleasure. The combination of littleness and neatness seems to have been especially irresistible to Dickens, in architecture as in women, because it offered a concentrated version of something that was potentially far less manageable. It was the very essence of domesticity.

With its high ceilings and large windows, Doughty Street was far too generously proportioned to be thought of in this way, but that did not prevent Dickens from adopting much the same attitude towards it that he had towards the miniature "stone-fronted mansion with real glass windows, and door-steps, and a real balcony" he recalled playing with as a boy ("A Christmas Tree"). Just as he carefully stored a "little set of blue crockery" and "diminutive utensils" in his toy mansion, bringing them out of the kitchen for imaginary tea parties, so in a grown-up house everything had its place. "There never existed, I think, in all the world, a more thoroughly tidy or methodical creature than was my father," reported his daughter Mamie; and in Dickens's later homes, the routine was organized along tightly directed lines.[29] "To each boy was appropriated a particular peg for his hats and coats," Henry Dickens recalled; "a parade was held once a week for overhauling the inevitable fresh stains on our garments; and one of us was deputed in turn to be the general custodian of the implements of the games, whose duty it was to collect them at the end of the day and put them in their appointed places."[30] In life, as in fiction, the pleasure of creating a mess was modest compared to that of tidying it up afterwards, and the quasi-biblical phrase "appointed places" leaves one in no doubt about how seriously Dickens took the process. A home was a theater that required a stage manager to drill the actors in their parts, or— to adopt an engineering rather than a theatrical definition of "parts"—a "machine" that needed to be kept in good working order.[31]

At times, Dickens acknowledged, his "love of order" seemed "almost a *dis*order," and this was especially true of the routines he developed on his travels, when he would rearrange the furniture in hotel rooms to create a reassuringly familiar environment before he could go to sleep.[32] On longer trips he was even more precise, carefully unpacking his inkstand and little bronze desk ornaments like a ship dropping anchor, and spreading out his pens "in the usual form" before he could start writing.[33] Meanwhile, even during extended absences, he hated the thought of anything being moved at home. "Keep things in their places," he warned Catherine in 1844; "I can't bear to picture them otherwise."[34] In *David Copperfield,* similarly, when Agnes visits David's lodgings she rearranges the furniture to re-create the layout of Aunt Betsey's cottage, and puts his books back into "the old order of [his] schooldays." One aim of housekeeping, it seems, was simply to keep things as they were. Yet while Dickens's narrator is clearly charmed by this idea, Agnes finds herself in a novel that makes some determined efforts to break its spell. Although we are supposed to take her homemaking skills as a clue that David will eventually choose her to replace sweet but silly Dora, Dickens invests far more energy into his depiction of Miss Murdstone, who cannot resist meddling in the smooth running of the Copperfield home. She is one of Dickens's most gloriously unrepentant home-wreckers. Having revealed her true colors soon after her arrival by "making havoc in the old arrangements," she becomes so convinced that the servants have secreted a man somewhere on the premises that she repeatedly dives into the coal cellar in search of him, and "scarcely ever opened the door of a dark cupboard without clapping it to again, in the belief that she had got him."[35] The angel in the house jostles on the page with her demonic double, and although the novel ends with

David and Agnes "sitting by the fire, in our house in London," their levels of domestic commitment are hardly a match for the man-hunting Miss Murdstone.

Dickens was far less adapt at seeing through domestic ideals in his own life. In February 1839, he published the installment of *Nicholas Nickleby* that described Kate and Mrs. Nickleby's move to a new cottage owned by the Cheeryble brothers, inaugurating a period of "hope, bustle, and light-heartedness." By March, after learning that his father was once again in financial trouble, despite cadging several "loans" from Chapman and Hall behind his back, Dickens decided that the only solution was to move his parents to a new cottage as well, preferably far enough away from London to prevent them from racking up more debts. Accordingly he traveled to Devonshire, and within a day of his arrival had rented Mile End Cottage, situated in the village of Alphington on the road between Exeter and Plymouth. Dickens's letters make it clear why this "jewel of a place" appealed to him. With its rambling architecture ("cellars and safes and coalholes everywhere") and "exquisitely clean" appearance, it was like one of his fictional houses brought to life, the ultimate pop-up illustration. Soon he was hugging himself over its "neat little passage," "beautiful little drawing-room," and "little bedrooms," and a year later he told Forster that "I don't believe there is anywhere such a perfect little doll's house"—the ultimate accolade.[36] At no stage did he appear to consider that his parents might be reluctant to move to an unseen house in an unknown part of the country, or that what tickled him as "little" might be considered cramped or poky by anyone obliged to live there. Within days he had received an "unsatisfactory epistle from mother," and by July both parents were sending him letters full of "sneezing" (i.e., strongly worded) passages from a house they not unreasonably viewed as a place of banishment.[37] Not much hope, bustle, or lightheartedness there.

For Dickens, their unwillingness to be granted the sort of happy ending he reserved for his virtuous characters was perplexing, although in September he comforted himself by giving exactly the same reward to the Nickleby family, who end the novel back in Devonshire and are gratifyingly content with their lot. (Three months later, Dickens gave himself a slightly different version of the same reward, because the success of *Nicholas Nickleby* meant that he could afford to move to a larger house, and the grand residence he chose next to Regent's Park, 1 Devonshire Terrace, offered a perfect compromise between his dreams of pastoral retirement and the practical need to stay in London.) While Dickens's fictional characters were at liberty to resist his idealizing tendencies, as when *Our Mutual Friend*'s Bella Wilfer tells her husband that she wants to be "something so much worthier than the doll in the doll's house," it seems the same was not true of his relatives.

The glimpses we have of Dickens's life in Doughty Street indicate that, when it came to his own domestic arrangements, he was quite prepared to cut across the grain of social expectations at an angle of his own. For example, noting Dickens's "intense love for, and enjoyment of, everything connected with his home," Richard Renton (one of Forster's early biographers) pointed out that "his work and his home" were "kept perfectly distinct."[38] That may have been a comforting idea to anyone still convinced of the merits of "separate spheres," the Victorian social model which viewed the workplace as a thrusting masculine environment and the home as a soft feminine retreat; but it is hard to square with the life of a professional writer who spent most working days in his study, which in Doughty Street opened directly onto the drawing room.[39] In fact, there is evidence that Dickens deliberately enjoyed smudging the boundary between traditionally masculine and feminine roles. The strangely disembodied women in his fiction who jangle their housekeeping keys like charms may reflect his private feminine ideal, a figure conflating the roles of mother, sister, and housekeeper that was later taken on in his home by Georgina Hogarth after he decided his own wife was not up to the task; but they also cast an intriguing light on Dickens's views of himself.

When he finally met Queen Victoria in 1870, they discussed the servant problem and "the cost of butcher's meat, and bread," and in Doughty Street the cash book listing payments to tradesmen and servants (their numbers eventually swelling to include a cook, housemaid, nurse, and manservant) was in his writing, not Catherine's, indicating how strong his hand was in running the household.[40] The same pattern continued throughout their marriage. In 1857, Dickens wrote to W. H. Wills, the subeditor of *Household Words,* that he was "going to Newgate-Market with Mrs. Dickens after breakfast to shew her where to buy fowls," which hardly suggests she had been a keen shopper in the previous twenty years.[41] A few months earlier, Nathaniel Hawthorne had recorded in his diary how "careful" Dickens was of his wife, "taking on himself all pos-sible trouble as regards his domestic affairs, making bargains at butchers and bakers, and doing, as far as he could, whatever duty pertains to an English wife"—a description that manages to sound both admiring and slightly appalled.[42] Forster was equally wary, pointing out that Dickens's love of home was so strong that "even the kind of interest in a housewife which is commonly confined to women, he was full of," before gruffly going on to explain that this meant "there was not an additional hook put up wherever he inhabited, without his knowledge," thereby relieving anyone worried about Dickens's masculinity by making it clear that his "home concerns" were centered on ironmongery rather than soft furnish-ings.[43] Forster does not quote a letter in which Dickens crows about buy-ing glassware and "two *magnificent* china Jars" for Furnival's Inn, "all, I flatter myself, slight bargains"; nor does he mention a note from Dickens's agent to the owner of 48 Doughty Street which sounds suspiciously as if it were being dictated by someone hovering at his elbow: "Mr. Dickens mentions also that the ceiling requires to be cleaned."[44]

Probably he did not feel any need to, given that the side of Dickens he saw most of during this period was not the writer confined to his study, but the active man capable of walking fifteen miles a day, or riding out to Hampstead and back before dinner. At Doughty Street, Dickens's working days quickly settled into a steady rhythm: writing in the morn-ing, energetic exercise in the afternoon, and socializing with friends in the evening. Home, sweat, home. The harder he worked to create settled domestic scenes in his novels, the more he needed to escape from them in his own life. Or perhaps it was simply the process of writing that made him so restless, as if the movement of his hand across the page were like the winding-up of a spring that needed to be released. Dickens never came closer to a portrait of the writer at work than the scene in *Nicholas Nickleby* where Nicholas arrives in London and tries to work out what to do next. Possibilities come and go in his mind, like fragments of plot that refuse to settle; but it is not until he walks out into the street "in the hope of leaving his thoughts behind" that he creates the next important link in the novel by overhearing Sir Mulberry Hawk's smutty talk about his sister. Dickens's writing life seems to have worked along similar lines: only by trying to lose his train of thought could he find it, just as only by leaving his home could he enjoy returning to it.

On December 9, 1837, Charles Dickens's first child was christened Charles Dickens—or, more specifically, Charles Culliford Boz Dickens, "Culliford" being the name of Dickens's maternal great-uncle, and "Boz" being a late addition shouted out by his father during the service.[45] It was standard practice to name your first son after yourself, and over the rest of the century it chimed with a growing sense that children were not so much miniature versions of their parents as opportunities to put right the mistakes of the past.[46] It is an idea Dickens plays with skeptically in *Dombey and Son,* where little Paul Dombey is far too frail to survive the burden of hope his father places upon him, but then advances more optimistically in *Great Expectations,* when Pip returns to the old forge and discovers "I again!"—that is, Joe and Biddy's son, whom they have named Pip in the hope that he will "grow a little bit like you." The first thing the narrator does is take his young namesake down to the churchyard and "set him on a certain tombstone," as Magwitch did to himself as a child, although he manages to resist the temptation to topple little Pip backwards or threaten to rip out his heart and liver, thereby transforming what could have been a simple repetition into a touching scene of redemption. By the time Charles (later known as Charley) was christened, nearly a year after his birth, Dickens was in a confident mood, making jokes about his "infant phaenomonon" *(sic)* that glanced proudly at his latest literary offspring, *Nicholas Nickleby,* as well as at his son.[47] His mind was far less easy during the month of Charley's birth, however; and for all his mock-pompous celebrations at being "presented . . . with a son and heir," it seems to have started a serious train of reflection about how he had come to be the man he was.[48]

The clearest sign of this came in the opening week of January 1837, when only a few days before Charley's arrival he celebrated another literary birth in the shape of the first number of *Bentley's Miscellany.* This contained Dickens's sketch "The Public Life of Mr. Tulrumble," a satire on political ambition set in the fictitious provincial town of Mudfog, and by January 18 he had "hit upon a capital notion" for the second number, which he thought would be "an exceedingly good one."[49] It turned out to be another story set in Mudfog, the first installment of *Oliver Twist,* which appeared in February alongside Cruikshank's illustration of "Oliver asking for more." It was not yet certain how the work would develop, and at this stage Dickens may have intended his "Mudfog Papers" to be a loose collection like *Sketches by Boz,* rather than a coherent narrative: Kathryn Chittick has noted that the title first appeared in *Bentley's Miscellany* as "Oliver Twist" rather than *Oliver Twist.*[50] The success of the February number was decisive: a thousand extra copies had to be printed, and as the months went on, the title of Cruikshank's illustration became increasingly self-referential. The more appallingly Oliver was treated, the more people wanted to read about him, and once again Dickens responded by meeting his readers' expectations and then outstripping them.

With no fear of having to abandon his story until it reached a natural conclusion, Dickens could draw out *Oliver Twist* until the gaps between installments became places to pause for breath rather than potential escape routes. In this way, it repeated the pattern of *Pickwick;* but whereas Dickens's previous work—which at the start of January was exactly half-way through its twenty-month serialization—revolved around a series of comic figures he had grown more attached to as they revealed more of themselves, the hero of *Oliver Twist* was close to Dickens's heart from the start. He was the first and most melodramatic product of Dickens's conviction that, given the neglect he had suffered as a child, "I might easily have been, for any care that was taken of me, a little robber or a little vagabond," and the result was a haunting collision of rival pasts and presents. Not only does Oliver's life replay the events of Dickens's childhood in a different key—born in a fictitious town that is modeled on Chatham, he too is a "little gentleman" who finds himself among common men and boys, and is terrified that someone called Fagin will drag him down to the same level—but after arriving in London, Oliver seems curiously drawn towards the world of his adult creator.

His benevolent protector Mr. Brownlow, for example, has the same name as the secretary of the Foundling Hospital (effectively an orphanage) that was situated in Russell Square, a few hundred yards from Dickens's home. Dickens rented a pew in its chapel, and owned a copy of Brownlow's *Charities of London* (1836), so he could hardly have been unaware of the symmetry involved in having Oliver saved by a neighbor who had himself been an orphan. More curious still is that, of all the places in London he could have chosen as Fagin's lair, he selected "a house near Field-lane," right at the heart of the stinking slum that was practically on his doorstep. In fact, the chapter that describes how the Artful Dodger leads Oliver there, through a "very narrow and muddy" street where the air is "impregnated with filthy odours," was written in the first days after Dickens moved to Doughty Street, and was published in *Bentley's* at the end of April. Just as Oliver's being introduced to Fagin was less a piece of invention than a memory that had been shaken loose from its moorings, so Oliver's ascending "the dark and broken stairs" was like a distorted echo of Dickens's climbing up to his new first-floor study, where he could look out over the rooftops and catch the occasional whiff of a world he had managed to escape.

Dickens's brother-in-law Henry Burnett recalled an evening spent at Doughty Street, during which he, his wife, and Catherine were "sitting round the fire cosily enjoying a chat," when Dickens entered the room:

"What, you here!" he exclaimed; "I'll bring down my work." It was his monthly portion of *Oliver Twist* for *Bentley's.* In a few minutes he returned, manuscript in hand, and while he was pleasantly discoursing he employed himself in carrying to a corner of the room a little table, at which he seated himself and re-commenced his writing. We, at his bidding, went on talking our little nothings,—he every now and then (the feather of his pen still moving rapidly from side to side), put in a cheerful interlude. It was interesting to watch, upon the sly, the mind and the muscles working (or, if you please, *playing*) in company as new thoughts were being dropped upon the paper. And to note the working brow, the set mouth, with the tongue slightly pressed against the closed lips, as was his habit.[51]

The story might be read in any number of ways: as a triumph of Dickens's powers of concentration, perhaps, or an illustration of his methods of composition, as he drew his characters out of himself and then channeled these physical tics and grimaces into the rhythmic movements of his hand traveling across the page. It also carries another submerged warning about the fragility of such cozy domestic scenes.

This is made clearer by a parallel from later in Dickens's career. "Like writing a book in company" was how he chose to describe the rehearsals for his amateur dramatic production of *The Frozen Deep,* a play co-authored with Wilkie Collins, which he staged in the schoolroom of Tavistock House, his final London home, in January 1857.[52] Typically, he took great pains over the authenticity of costumes and props, boasting that there was scarcely anyone in the cast "who might not have gone straight to the North Pole itself, completely furnished for the winter"; but the greatest *coup de théâtre* involved his polar explorers opening a door at the rear of the stage (a space created by removing the schoolroom's bay window) to reveal the howling Arctic outside—actually a piece of his garden, enclosed in a specially constructed shed, where the illusion was completed by a white backdrop and flurries of paper snow that the stagehands scattered from above.[53] Creating a space that was at once familiar and foreign, home and abroad, Dickens's staging generated a particular emotional charge in the final scene, when Wardour, played by Dickens himself in a wild gray wig, staggered onstage in search of Clara, the woman for whom he has saved his rival and sacrificed himself. "I must wander, wander, wander," he explains, "restless, sleepless, homeless—till I find her!" His success ("Found!") represents both a triumph of domestic values and their deadly cost, as he wins a kiss from his "sister" Clara before nobly expiring center-stage. The curtain falls, the audience rises, and Tavistock House returns to normal, but only after revealing its potential to be a strange and savage place, where the strains of "Home, Sweet Home" drifting across the stage turn out to be a Siren call driving Wardour on to his death.

A similar tension is at work in Burnett's story about the writing of *Oliver Twist,* because at the same time that Dickens was attempting to create a settled domestic life in Doughty Street, he was busy terrifying himself with far nastier alternatives on the page: houses that are broken into, or—in the case of Mr. Bumble, sitting in the chilly workhouse parlor and gloomily contemplating a paper fly-cage dangling from the ceiling—houses that turn out to be the sort of traps from which there is no escape; characters like Nancy, whose reward for insisting that "I must go home" is to be bludgeoned to death; most crucially, Oliver himself, who leaves his "wretched home" in the workhouse and walks to London because it is "the very place for a homeless boy, who must die in the streets unless some one helped him." Sentence by sentence, Dickens was building towards the final image of a happy home and then knocking it down again. No wonder his pen was "moving rapidly": it was having to switch back and forth between being a trowel and a sledgehammer.

CHAPTER ELEVEN

Is She His Wife?

In the early hours of June 20, 1837, the great bell at Windsor began to toll, and the next day the *Times* reported that "shortly thereafter the streets were filled with groups of persons discussing the merits and lamenting the loss of the good old king."[1] As the affectionate tone of this account indicates, "good old" William IV, who had died "like an old lion" after failing to shake off his annual attack of asthma, was mourned far more sincerely than the fat and dissolute recluse he had succeeded.[2] Assessing William's prospects in 1830, Charles Greville had briskly summed him up as "a kind-hearted, well-meaning, not stupid, burlesque, bustling old fellow," and concluded that "if he doesn't go mad [he] may make a very decent King"—madness being a genuine fear in the context of William's recent family history and the rumors that already he exhibited "oddities."[3] These included a deep distrust of foreigners (especially the French) and an irrepressible streak of tactlessness, both of which endeared him to his subjects, although neither prevented the final verdict on his reign from being a decidedly muted one after the initial shock of his death had passed. The *Times* struck a popular note in an article that repeatedly found itself clutching at negatives—"He met with no adventures on a wide scale. He displayed no gross, nor great, nor memorable attributes. . . . He was not a man of genius nor of superior talent, nor of much refinement"—as if secretly mourning a nonexistent king alongside the less talented alternative who had taken his place.[4] Few commentators seemed able to resist this ghostly twin. Even Greville's analysis of the king as "not stupid" unavoidably conjured up a picture of someone stupid while simultaneously drawing a line through it. (One modern biographer goes further still by referring to William as "the reverse of brilliant," like a photographic negative of the bright figure he might have been.)[5] In an atmosphere where grief mingled awkwardly with disappointment, some of the kindest words came from his eighteen-year-old niece Victoria, who wrote simply, "Poor old man! I feel sorry for him."[6]

Celebrating her accession to the throne, the *Times* dropped any pretense at objectivity, trumpeting "our young Queen VICTORIA—may her name be an augury of triumphant fortune!"[7] This nimbly sidestepped the proclamation of succession, which had correctly announced her as "our only lawful and rightful liege Lady Alexandrina Victoria I, Queen of Great Britain and Ireland." It also tactfully ignored the king's attempt in 1831 "to change my favourite and dear name Victoria to that of Charlotte," a suggestion one MP countered by offering "Elizabeth" as a name likely to make her even more popular with her future subjects.[8] Fortunately, one of the benefits of being queen is that one takes advice rather than orders; so after meeting the Privy Council for the first time, she simply signed the register as "Victoria," and Queen Victoria is how she remained, thus averting a future in which critics could ponder the rise of the Alexandrinian novel, or in which history could skip several beats by witnessing the coronation of Elizabeth II in 1838.

The old king died, a new queen took the throne, and at the time Dickens was silent about both. This was unusual for a writer who had already revealed how sensitive his finger was to the country's pulse, but in June 1837 he was mourning a death that was far closer to home. In fact, it had occurred in his home. On the evening of Saturday, May 6, a month after moving into 48 Doughty Street, he had accompanied Catherine and Mary to St. James's Theatre. It had been a good month for Dickens. On April 8, Chapman and Hall had celebrated the first anniversary of *Pickwick* by holding a special dinner at which they presented Dickens with an additional check for £500. On May 3, at a Literary Fund event held in the Freemasons' Tavern in the company of "a host of persons associated with the literature of the country," Dickens had made his first public speech. He replied to a toast to "the health of Mr. Dickens and the rising Authors of the Age," thanking those present for the "flattering encouragement" that had "smoothed his path to the station he had gained," and sat down to "[*Cheers*]."[9] Finally, the April number of the *Court Magazine and Monthly Critic* had included a substantial essay offering "Some Thoughts on Arch-Waggery, and, in Especial, on the Genius of 'Boz.'" The author of this piece concluded that Dickens was personally responsible for a "sudden taste for crowding upon the sunny side of the road" in the work of his contemporaries, and reproduced a full-page engraving (Figure 21) of Dickens "taken in a mood of inward contemplation."[10] (Actually the engraving depicts Dickens glancing sideways at some blobbily drawn spectators enjoying a Punch and Judy show outside his window—a scene that much more accurately reflects the kind of source from which he drew his early inspiration.)[11] And so to St. James's Theatre, where the bill on May 6 included Dickens's farce *Is She His Wife?*

After the family party returned home, Mary retired at about 1:00 A.M. "in the best health and spirits."[12] Within moments Dickens heard a strangled cry, and on rushing into her room he discovered that she had collapsed. Although she swallowed a little brandy from his hand, at about 3:00 P.M. the following afternoon she died in his arms—so calmly and gently, Dickens wrote, that he "continued to support her lifeless form" long after she had stopped breathing. The precise cause of death was never established, although the doctors summoned to Doughty Street concluded that "her heart had been diseased for a great length of time." There was no debate over the state of Dickens's heart: broken.[13]

"You cannot conceive the misery in which this dreadful event has plunged us," he wrote shakily the next day. "Since our marriage she has been the grace and life of our home—the admired of all, for her beauty and excellence—I could have better spared a much nearer relation or an older friend, for she has been to us what we can never replace, and has left a blank which no one who ever know her can have the faintest hope of seeing supplied."[14] His touching uncertainty over which tense to use in talking of Mary was repeated in the days that followed, as he struggled to come to terms with the idea that she had slid irrevocably into the past. "She has been our constant companion since our marriage," he told

Ainsworth; to George Cox he explained that she was "a young and lovely girl, who has been the grace and ornament of our home."[15] His letters returned in dazed fashion to the same words—"grace," "love," "blank," "constant"—until, ten days after Mary's death, he summed up his feelings "calmly and dispassionately" in a letter to his oldest friend, Thomas Beard: "I solemnly believe that so perfect a creature never breathed. . . . She had not a fault."[16]

The impact on Dickens's writing was equally devastating. Emptying his calendar to grieve and to deal with the funeral arrangements, he canceled the next number of *Pickwick,* due to appear at the end of May, and replaced the June installment of *Oliver Twist* in *Bentley's* with a short note to his readers: "Since the appearance of the last Number of this Work the Editor has to mourn the sudden death of a very dear young relative to whom he was most affectionately attached, and whose society had been, for a long time, the chief solace of his labours." Dickens's explanation that he had been "obliged to seek a short interval of rest and quiet" did nothing to stop idle tongues wagging, however, and at the end of June he was obliged to open the sixteenth number of *Pickwick* with an "Address" attacking the "various idle speculations and absurdities" that had been swirling around in the previous weeks. "By one set of intimate acquaintances, especially well informed, he has been killed outright," he wrote; "by another, driven mad; by a third, imprisoned for debt; by a fourth, sent per steamer to the United States; by a fifth, rendered incapable of any mental exertion for evermore . . ." The strained humor did nothing to disguise his sense of annoyance and hurt; the gossips and fact-manglers, he wrote, had "pained him exceedingly."

The hiatus in Dickens's fiction did not prevent him from trying to work through his feelings in print. The August number of *Bentley's* included an anonymous three-stanza elegy in the series "Songs of the Month":

> I stood by a young girl's grave last night,
> Beautiful, innocent, pure, and bright,

Who, in the bloom of her summer's pride,
And all its loveliness, drooped and died.[17]

Something more than slack grammar seems to be at work in that swerve of attention between the first and second lines. Does "Beautiful, innocent, pure, and bright" refer to the "young girl" or to the "I" standing beside her grave? The third line largely resolves this hovering ambiguity, but it does not explain whether the speaker's adjectives are intended to capture his memory of the living girl or her appearance now as an angel. Such uncertainty is fully in keeping with the private mythology Dickens was developing over these weeks. So is the overlap in phrasing with the epitaph he composed for Mary's tombstone:

Mary Scott Hogarth
Died 7th May 1837
Young Beautiful and Good
God in His Mercy
Numbered Her With His Angels
At the Early Age Of
Seventeen

The key adjectives—"young," "beautiful," "good"—were a standard choice in contemporary works that sought to elevate real women into aesthetic and ethical ideals. The same trio had recently appeared in everything from a grammar book, where "She was young, and beautiful, and good" is used to demonstrate the use of ellipsis (it is a shortened version of "She was young, she was beautiful, and she was good"), to James Hogg's popular *Winter Evening Tales,* where the poem "Halbert of Lyne" includes a loving description of some ewes "as young, as beautiful, and good,/As any bred on Lyne."[18] In choosing such a familiar verbal pattern, Dickens was starting to think of Mary as "one of a kind" in the sense of a type, or model, in place of the competing sense of a unique and irreplaceable individual; and the same drift of thought was carried through into *Oliver Twist* some months after he picked up the thread of his narrative.

In the April 1838 number of *Bentley's,* Rose Maylie is introduced as a girl who is "at that age, when, if angels be for God's good purposes enthroned in mortal forms, they may be without impiety supposed to abide in such as hers." The next sentence reveals who she is based on, as Dickens informs his readers that "she was not past seventeen," and what follows tries hard to reconcile her physical appearance ("her deep blue eye," "her noble head," and so on) with the suspicion that as an angel she does not have a mortal body at all—or, as Dickens more evasively puts it, "Cast in so slight and exquisite a mould . . . earth seemed not her element." Final confirmation that she is a fictional version of Mary comes later in the novel, as Harry Maylie nervously observes that "when the young, the beautiful, and good, are visited with sickness, their pure spirits insensibly turn towards their bright home of lasting rest."[19] His concern is more than theoretical: one of the novel's key scenes, published shortly after the anniversary of Mary's death, describes how Rose is struck down by a mysterious illness, during which she appears to be "trembling between earth and heaven," just as Mary was in the hours she lay in Dickens's arms. This time, however, Dickens was determined to give the story a different ending. Fiction would be a way of putting death in its place.

⁂

By the time of Mary's death in May 1837, three months after Dickens started to write *Oliver Twist,* the main shape of his narrative was starting to emerge. It was to be his most sophisticated piece of counterfactual storytelling yet. The final version of the story is now so well known, we tend to ignore how often it is crossed by false trails and studded with dead ends, but at its heart lay Dickens's sense of how many different outcomes could be produced by the same set of events. Take the fulcrum of the plot on which Oliver's fortunes turn, as, "desperate with hunger and reckless with misery," he approaches the workhouse official in charge of dealing out rations of gruel and utters the famous words, "Please, sir, I want some more." Few lines resonate more powerfully in the popular imagination. Since its original publication in the February 1837 number of *Bentley's,* it has been used in so many different settings that it has acquired near-proverbial force; what started off as a small boy asking for an extra helping, Juliet John points out, has become "symbolic of rebellion, aspiration, entrepreneurship, democracy, capitalism, the quest for identity, appetite. . . . Oliver asks for more and he eventually gets more—he presages the American dream."[20]

Perhaps that explains why, when the line is referred to in advertisements or cartoons, and even in some books, it is routinely misquoted as "Please, sir, can I have some more?" In turning a bald statement of fact into a polite question, the misremembered version opens itself up to any number of answers, not all of which concern themselves with a starving child who "wants" (both desires and lacks) enough to eat. Yet the picture of Oliver nicely asking for more is a perfectly good response to the novel as a whole. Like many novels with happy endings, what happens in the closing pages of *Oliver Twist* cannot avoid setting up shockwaves that ripple back to the start of the story, dislodging anything that gets in their way. Not only does Oliver end up with far more than he might have expected, with his rescuer Mr. Brownlow growing "attached to him more and more as his nature developed itself," but as a child with impeccable middle-class origins he is revealed to have been worthy of this reward all along. In misquoting his words, giving them an extra polish of good manners, we are merely collaborating in the illusion that a child brought up in the workhouse will behave like a little gentleman—the sort of child who deserves much (food, safety, love) but demands nothing.

Yet although the trajectory of Oliver's life may appear inevitable to modern readers, it was far less certain at the time this scene was originally published. The first installment in *Bentley's* shied away from a firm narrative resolution, and instead tailed off with a paragraph in which Dickens explained that he might spoil the rest of his work "if I ventured to hint just yet, whether the life of Oliver Twist will be a long or a short piece of biography." That was both a playful nod to the conventions of eighteenth-century fiction and a frank acknowledgment that he didn't yet know himself. Having agreed to supply Richard Bentley with an "original article of my own writing" every month, initially he may have thought of "Oliver Twist" as a short tale that would allow him to hit out at the Poor Law and then move on. By the seventh installment the story had gained enough momentum for Dickens to joke about it as "my prose epic," claiming that its "scope and bearing" were part of "long-considered intentions and plans," and on September 28 he signed a new contract with Bentley to republish *Oliver Twist* in three volumes. But even at this stage, it seems more likely that his "long-considered intentions and plans" had been to write *a* novel rather than specifically *this* novel, and in any case *Oliver Twist*'s narrative lurched from incident to incident in a way that was far more unpredictable than the smoothly planned progress of Dickens's later serialized works. Hence the number of narrative options he left open, such as the "minute inscription" on a trinket that Fagin pores over "long and earnestly" (it never appears again), and his attempts in the final chapters to unravel what had become a bewilderingly snarled plot.

Dickens's doubts over what would happen next are reflected in several references to the power of chance—or, for those who prefer a clearer plot to their lives, destiny—as he and his characters felt their way forward together. The first installment points out that at birth Oliver lay gasping for a time, "poised between this world and the next," and much of what follows involves him in similar either/or dilemmas. Even his decision to travel to London comes after he escapes into the open street and looks "to the right and to the left, uncertain whither to fly," before taking the same route as the wagons he has seen "toiling up the hill" away from Mudfog.

Set against this uncertainty is the conviction of many characters that they have the gift of second sight. The most common version of this is the assumption that Oliver, who is named "Twist" by Bumble, as if gloomily anticipating his later greed ("twist" was nineteenth-century slang for a "capacity for eating, appetite"), will end up dying in accordance with another popular meaning of "twist": to be hanged.[21] The gentleman in the white waistcoat is convinced "that boy will be hung," and hardly anyone who spends time in Oliver's company during the opening chapters comes to a different conclusion. To the policeman who first locks him

up, he is "young gallows," and the long shadow of the scaffold repeatedly falls across Dickens's writing, as it prepares us for Oliver's seemingly
inevitable drop. Rarely is a stolen handkerchief described without a grim
pun about where it might lead the thief, as when the silk handkerchiefs in
Fagin's den are left "hanging" over a clothes-horse and those drying in
Field Lane "hang dangling from pegs outside the windows."[22] Charley
Bates makes the connection even clearer, by explaining the meaning of
"scragging" via a pantomime that involves tugging his neckerchief into
the air, dropping his head on one shoulder, and jerking out "a curious
sound through his teeth." Further reminders include a broadside ballad
depicting three tiny hanged figures that Fagin has pinned up over the fire-
place in his den—a display that Cruikshank shows him gesturing towards
with a satanic-looking fork. This is more than just a prod to the reader's
memory. It is also a way of drawing Oliver's attention to the narrative
genre into which the Artful Dodger has diverted him: that loose collection
of stories recounting the lives of criminals—many of them legendary figures like Dick Turpin who already occupied an uncertain middle ground
between fact and fiction—that formed a popular literary fad throughout
the 1830s, and that were collectively known, after one of London's most
notoriously grim prisons, as the "Newgate novel."

Although warnings about the criminal's fate had long been popular in
fictional lives (in *Tom Jones* we are told, with reference to the foundling
hero, "It was the universal Opinion of all *Mr. Allworthy's* Family, that he
was certainly born to be hanged"), recent works such as Edward Bulwer's
Paul Clifford (1830) had made this narrative trajectory as familiar as the
route of a London omnibus.[23] Today *Paul Clifford* is chiefly remembered
for the purple prose of its opening ("It was a dark and stormy night . . ."),
but it was the ending that would have struck a louder chord with its original readership, as the highwayman hero makes an impassioned speech in
court pointing out that he became a criminal only after being forced to
associate with hardened felons as a boy: "when the dark side of things is
our only choice, it is useless to regard the bright."

Fagin's approval of such sentiments is clear from the reading matter he leaves Oliver the night before his first housebreaking expedition: "a history of the lives and trials of great criminals." Modeled on the bestselling *Newgate Calendar,* with pages that are "soiled and thumbed with use," it features "dreadful crimes that made the blood run cold" in descriptions so vivid "the sallow pages seemed to turn red with gore, and the words upon them to be sounded in his ears as if they were whispered in hollow murmurs by the spirits of the dead." The ambiguity of this makes it uncertain whether the voices belong to victims who are begging for vengeance, or executed criminals whose whispers are luring Oliver to follow their example. Either way, Fagin's motives for leaving the book are plain: it is a crash course in criminality and a script for the kind of story Oliver has fallen into. Presumably Fagin is hoping he will be seduced by the glamour of crime, in the same way that some readers of Ainsworth's *Jack Sheppard* were said to have been after it replaced *Oliver Twist* in *Bentley's.* Lord William Russell's valet Courvoisier claimed in 1840 that the story had inspired him to cut his sleeping master's throat, while one of the young thieves interviewed for Henry Mayhew's *London Labour and the London Poor* confessed that he had joined a group of purse snatchers after being "much impressed" by a theatrical adaptation; seeing it a second time with a friend, both were "remarkably pleased" with its depiction of criminal life, "and soon after determined to try our hand at housebreaking."[24]

Yet far from slackening Oliver's moral fiber, the book about great criminals actually firms it up, as he falls on his knees and prays to die at once rather than be reserved for such "fearful and appalling" crimes. What follows has more than a touch of self-pity, as Oliver continues "in a low and broken voice" to lament his plight, "a poor outcast boy . . . desolate and deserted . . . in the midst of wickedness and guilt." The tone of this sounds much closer to Dickens's voice than Oliver's, like a spar of private reminiscence jutting through the surface of the text; and here it may be significant that the job of Bob Fagin, Dickens's protector in the warehouse where he'd had to cover pots of blacking with pieces of oiled paper, was to show him "the trick of using the string and tying the knot"—a homely detail that the novel grotesquely transforms into a fear of being strung up on the gallows.[25] Crucially, however, Oliver turns away from this ending, just as *Oliver Twist* turns away from becoming a Newgate novel. Indeed, if Dickens's hero lives up to his surname, it is not by getting himself executed, but by repeatedly wriggling out of the stories in which other characters try to place him. Rejecting the chance to become a "twister" (a slang term for thief), as he slips between one story and another, one narrative outcome and another, he proves himself to be a "twist" in two other senses of the word: "A turning aside, a deviation," and "The part of anything at which it divides or branches."[26] He is like a living embodiment of a twist in the tale.

This process of rejecting alternative narrative strands begins early in the novel, with a scene in which Oliver is sized up by a villainous chimney-sweep looking for an apprentice, and the local magistrate looks for an inkstand so that he can sign the legal papers:

> It was the critical moment of Oliver's fate. If the inkstand had been where the old gentleman thought it was, he would have dipped his pen into it and signed the indentures, and Oliver would have been straightway hurried off. But, as it chanced to be immediately under his nose, it followed as a matter of course that he looked all over his desk for it, without finding it; and happening in the course of his search to look straight before him, his gaze encountered the pale and terrified face of Oliver Twist.

In rejecting the chimney-sweep's application, the magistrate does more than prevent Oliver from facing the prospect of a different sort of suffocating death, this time by being stuffed up a chimney. He also halts the development of a plot like the one Dickens had previously outlined in "A Little Talk about Spring, and the Sweeps," a short sketch published in the *Library of Fiction* the previous year and recently reprinted in the second series of *Sketches by Boz*. Here Dickens relates various popular legends of boy sweeps who turn out to be the children of gentlemen, and mentions one curly-headed apprentice in particular, encountered when they were both children, who explained that "he believed he'd been born in the

vurkis [workhouse], but he'd never know'd his father"—information the
young Dickens takes as firm evidence that the boy's long-lost parent will
soon turn up in a coach "to take him home to Grosvenor Square." That
never happens, and Dickens sadly reports that the sweep is now an adult,
still stuck in the same profession, possessed of "a decided antipathy to
washing himself" and a pair of legs that are "very inadequate to the support of his somewhat unwieldy and corpulent body." The nicely spoken
Oliver might seem a much better candidate for a modern reworking of
such legends, but the villainous sweep never appears again, and while
his introduction raises some fleeting doubts about the nature of Oliver's
birth, for the moment this piece of the plot is kept firmly in the background. "Tossing aside the piece of parchment" on which Oliver's in-
dentures are written, the magistrate resembles a novelist throwing his first
draft in the wastebin.

Dickens's second aborted plot involves Oliver being engaged as an
apprentice by Sowerberry the undertaker. This is initially more promising, because the subtitle Dickens chose for his novel, *The Parish Boy's
Progress,* carried strong echoes of the cautionary tales made famous by
William Hogarth in his series of engravings *A Harlot's Progress* (1731)
and *A Rake's Progress* (1735). Oliver's discovery that there is a second apprentice, in the form of Noah Claypole—a "big charity-boy" first introduced eating great hunks of bread and butter—is even more significant,
because it pushes him into an updated version of *Industry and Idleness*
(1747), Hogarth's sequence of twelve engravings depicting a hardworking
apprentice who becomes Lord Mayor of London, and his lazy workmate
who is hanged as a thief at Tyburn.[27] Given Hogarth's fondness for populating his prints with little narrative clues—the first plate of *Industry and
Idleness* shows the idle apprentice asleep at his post in close proximity
to decorative images of a whip, fetters, and a noose—the fact that Oliver
sleeps among the coffins in Sowerberry's workshop again plays on the
expectation that he is being prepared for his fate, this time by practicing
at being dead. Yet once more Oliver rejects this future, not only by running away from the undertaker's, but also by responding to Noah's taunts

about what would have happened to his mother if she had lived ("she'd have been hard labouring in Bridewell, or transported, or hung") by seizing him by the throat and shaking him until his teeth chatter. It is a sly warning that, of Mudfog's two runaway apprentices, Noah is the more likely candidate for hanging, whereas Oliver will turn out to be the hero of a very different type of "progress"—a moral fable like *The Pilgrim's Progress* (1678) in which, like John Bunyan's Christian, he must risk succumbing to evil in order to triumph over it at last.[28]

This change in the narrative's direction is signaled in the running heads Dickens added to the 1867 edition of his novel, where "The Young Pilgrim's Progress" appears above the chapter in which Oliver escapes to London. The interruption of one kind of story by another is typical of the novel as a whole, in which Oliver rarely goes on a journey without its being detoured or hijacked, and plot lines are repeatedly dangled before being withdrawn.[29] It is a world in which every action is surrounded by a cluster of ghostly alternatives, signaled by an insistent counterfactual grammar of "could have," "would have," and "might have." Dickens cannot even describe a boy pickpocket's oversized clothes without wondering how—or whether—he will grow up to fill them: there is a special pathos in the first appearance of the Artful Dodger, who has "all the airs and manners of a man," but betrays his youth by wearing a "man's coat, which reached nearly to his heels." Even Fagin, that jagged caricature of wickedness, seems to have caused some hesitation when Dickens was trying to work out how best to finish the novel; "I don't know what to make of him," Dickens told Forster.[30] There is no evidence that Dickens ever contemplated a scene like the one in Lionel Bart's musical *Oliver!* where Fagin's song "Reviewing the Situation" imagines a set of comic alternatives to his current way of life (marrying a grasping wife, or dazzling duchesses with his wealth), before resolving "I'm a bad 'un and a bad 'un I shall stay"; but Dickens's doubts accurately reflected how far the novel's early mood of uncertainty had spread.

Fagin's character is often seen through two pairs of eyes at once, as the innocent gaze of Oliver meets the much more knowing gaze of Dickens's narrator. Repeated epithets such as "the merry old gentleman" show Dickens playing these perspectives off against each other, because they show Fagin from the viewpoint of a small boy who assumes that someone who says "Ha! ha! ha!," as the wily Fagin frequently does, must have made a joke, and also from that of an adult who is aware that "the old gentleman" is slang for the devil. Curiously, only one adjective separates this thumbnail description from that of the other major character who is regularly characterized as an "old gentleman": Mr. Brownlow. To some extent the echo reveals how close divergent paths can appear to the person trying to decide which to follow, as the coach taking Oliver to Mr. Brownlow's home rattles away "over nearly the same ground as that which Oliver had traversed when he first entered London in company with the Dodger," and only turns "a different way when it reached the Angel at Islington." (That detail of "the Angel" is wonderfully placed, transforming a genuine London landmark into a crossroads where two possible fates diverge, and two kinds of storytelling—urban realism and moral fable—collide head-on.) At the same time, the references to Fagin as a "merry old gentleman" include a note of regret. As so often happens when Dickens applies a thick layer of irony to his writing, he cannot quite extinguish the thought of a parallel world in which irony's invisible quotation marks would be erased by sincerity and trust. In this case it is the world of *Pickwick*, which Dickens was still writing alongside *Oliver Twist*, and which had featured another "merry old gentleman" in the "Good-Humoured Christmas Chapter" published a few months earlier:

> "Come," said Wardle, "a song—a Christmas song. I'll give you one, in default of a better."
>
> "Bravo," said Mr. Pickwick.
>
> "Fill up," cried Wardle. "It will be two hours good, before you see the bottom of the bowl through the deep rich colour of the wassail; fill up all round, and now for the song."
>
> Thus saying, the merry old gentleman, in a good, round, sturdy voice, commenced without more ado—

But just as Fagin's den is at best a poor impersonation of Dingley Dell, so his "merry" demeanor is only a snarling parody of Wardle's genuine good humor. Each time Fagin bursts out with "Ha! ha! ha!" it sounds like someone knocking on a door that has long been shut and bolted.

The surviving portion of the *Oliver Twist* manuscript shows that this way of thinking was also built into Dickens's methods of composition.[31] Compared to his later manuscripts, which forced the typesetters to pick their way around little crevasses of deletion and ballooning second thoughts, this one is remarkably clean. Written in a fluent hand, each chapter drives purposefully towards a conclusion that is marked with an inky flourish; and where there are corrections, they usually involve no more than a word or two. Take the opening sentence of Chapter 12:

> The coach rattled away down Mount Pleasant and up Exmouth Street—over nearly the same ground as that which Oliver had traversed when he first entered London in ~~the~~ company with the Dodger—and turning a different way ~~at Islington~~ when it reached the angel at Islington stopped at length ~~in a qui~~ before a neat house in a quiet shady street near Pentonville.

While Oliver ends up traveling in a new direction, Dickens's pen does not, pausing only to inject some extra narrative detail before the sentence smoothly rolls on to Pentonville. It is a form of "revision" in which he looked again at the picture in his mind and encouraged the two sides of his writing personality—the confident improviser and the more cautious perfectionist—to collaborate until they had come up with a sentence that satisfied them both. Dickens's revisions are the little pauses for thought he introduces to prevent him from getting ahead of himself. To this extent they fit closely with some of his ongoing narrative experiments in *Pickwick*, where looking again at what had previously been taken for granted is central both to the developing plot of *Bardell v. Pickwick* and to a style that switches unpredictably between melodrama and farce. Yet

Oliver Twist pushes the technique in a new direction, and it does so by adapting a technique that is much more familiar from poetry.

One of the obvious advantages of poetry over prose is that the writer can control where each line ends. The word "verse" comes from the Latin *vertere,* meaning "to turn," and this provides a helpful way of thinking about some of the possible uses of line-endings, because although a poet can apply them as mechanically as the carriage return on a typewriter, they can also be used to think about other kinds of "turning." The end of a line of poetry can depict a moment of genuine transformation; equally, it can represent a flicker of hesitation that does nothing to alter the direction of the sentence as it wraps around the line-break. This uncertainty can itself be a helpful imaginative resource. Milton, for example, often works the ethical drama of *Paradise Lost* into the hesitations and self-qualifications of his syntax, as when Eve promises to return from her gardening by noon and the narrator interrupts with a sudden note of doom:

> O much deceiv'd, much failing, hapless Eve,
> Of thy presum'd return! event perverse!
> Thou never from that hour in Paradise
> Found'st either sweet repast, or sound repose . . .[32]

While this appears to start off as an absolute condemnation, "Of thy presum'd return" pulls us up short by revealing that we, too, were deceived in assuming that Eve is guilty of anything just yet. As the poem continues, of course, and Eve is tempted to eat the apple, we learn that her mistake about when she will return is a warning of the much larger error to come; but at this stage, Milton's syntactic delay breathes into the outcome an air of curiosity and speculation that the narrative itself has lost. His poem makes the past surprising again.

Writing in prose, Dickens did not have this particular resource to draw on, but his revisions show that he was similarly keen to entertain possible futures before committing to them. The largest deletions in the *Oliver Twist* manuscript tend to occur at the beginnings of pages, as he takes a fresh sheet of paper and then, after writing anything from a single orphan phrase to a dozen or more lines, crosses it out, turns the sheet over, and starts again. Frequently he tests out a line of thought, reaches a dead end, and then uses the rough draft to jumpstart an improved version. Once safely beyond those tricky opening lines, he usually picked up enough momentum to carry him safely through to the end of the page. But there is one occasion when this process of revision sent him backtracking much further.

Chapter 33 describes how one night Rose Maylie is struck down by an illness so sudden and serious that, "in the very short time since their return home, the hue of her countenance had changed to a marble white-ness." As her life hangs in the balance, Oliver creeps away to the local churchyard and weeps quietly among the gravestones, where he is inter-rupted by a funeral service. Here Dickens's manuscript shows that he took a new sheet of paper and continued his description of the mourners:

> and there was a mother—a mother once—among the weeping train. But the sun shone brightly and the birds sang on.
> And now what a host of ~~thoughts and recollections~~ reflections crowded upon Oliver's mind and busied themselves at his heart. We need be careful how we deal with those about us, for every death brings with it to some small circle of survivors bitter thoughts of so much omitted and so little done, so many things forgotten and so many more that might have been repaired

Composed shortly after the first anniversary of Mary Hogarth's death, this is in every sense a raw piece of writing. Reaching the word "repaired," Dickens crossed out the whole passage, picked up another sheet of paper, and wrote out a new version with a couple of additional sentences:

> and there was a mother—a mother once—among the weeping train. But the sun shone brightly, and the birds sang on.
> Oliver turned homewards, thinking on the many kindnesses he had received from the young lady, and wishing that the time could come over again, that he might never cease showing her how grateful and attached he was. He had no cause for self-reproach on the score

of neglect, or want of thought, for he had been devoted to her service, and yet a hundred little occasions rose up before him on which he fancied he might have been more zealous, and more earnest, and wished he had been. We need to be careful how we deal with those about us, when every death carries to some small circle of survivors, thoughts of so much omitted, and so little done, so many things forgotten, and so many more which might have been repaired

The revised version performs a nervous balancing act of self-reproach and self-justification that might be true to any mourner's feelings, but for Dickens it had an additional function that was much more personal. The chapter climaxes with Oliver's return to the Maylie house, where Rose continues to flutter on the brink of death, and her family sits waiting in fearful silence as the sun slowly sets. Unlike Mary Hogarth, though, she recovers, in a scene of prayers and fainting joy that represents yet another kinking or stymieing of the outcome we might expect, especially given the clues provided by her name. *Nomen non est omen:* compared to the image of fragile beauty so beloved of poets, this Rose is remarkably resilient. It was Dickens's most deeply felt rewriting of history, as he returned to the traumatic scene in Doughty Street on May 7, 1837, and pushed events in the direction they should have followed rather than the one they did.

The scene's imaginative power also stretched far into the future. In making Oliver pray for history to be repeated so that "he might never cease showing her how grateful and attached he was," Dickens was reminding himself of another of the powers he enjoyed as a novelist. Fiction could give him any number of second chances, any number of opportunities to put his loyalty to the test. Mary would live on not only in his memory—already given a physical shape with the birth of his second child, Mary (Mamie) Dickens, on March 6, 1838—but also in his writing. Finally he would be able to answer the call of that old joke business card: "Charles Dickens, Resurrectionist" had found the perfect subject.

Rose Maylie's brush with death climaxes with her mother crying out "My dear child! She is dead! She is dying!" and being reassured by the doctor that "she will live to bless us all for years to come." Dickens took a very similar attitude to his young relative. For years after he laid her body in the ground of Kensal Green Cemetery, he continued to grieve for her in a way that came close to denying the fact of death altogether. The more he thought about her, the more alive she seemed, as if her death were not a single event but a process that could be halted or reversed at his own discretion.

From the start, Dickens's mourning went well beyond the dutiful attentions of a brother-in-law. Often it seemed more like that of a bereaved husband, as when he thanked Mrs. Hogarth for a lock of Mary's hair and told her that "I have never had her ring off my finger by day or by night, except for an instant at a time to wash my hands, since she died."[33] He also kept her clothes, imagining how they would "moulder away in their secret places, as her earthly form will in the ground," and occasionally taking them out to meditate on them as fragile *memento mori*.[34] For years he harbored a desire to be buried beside her, telling Forster that "I cannot bear the thought of being excluded from her dust"; and when Mary's grandmother and young brother anticipated him by dying within a few days of each other, he was almost inconsolable at the thought that they would usurp his place, complaining that "it seems like losing her a second time." Grudgingly he accepted that he would have to "give it up," and comforted himself by arriving early at the cemetery so that he could gaze on her coffin when the grave was opened.[35]

Nor was Mary merely a passive vessel of his love. For months she visited him every night in his dreams, "sometimes as a spirit, sometimes as a living creature"; and although, interestingly, these dreams stopped as soon as he told Catherine about them, by then he had successfully bypassed the unconscious by incorporating them into his everyday thoughts. "The recollection of her is an essential part of my being," he later explained to Mrs. Hogarth, "and is as inseparable from my existence as the beating of my heart is."[36] Like a personalized form of pantheism, he sensed Mary's presence everywhere. In America, where he was rapturously received in 1842, he felt, "in the best aspects of this welcome, something of the presence and influence of that spirit which directs my life"; and when staying in a hotel perched over the roaring Niagara Falls, he was convinced that she must have been there "many times, I doubt not, since her sweet face faded from my earthly sight."[37] Two years later, during a trip to Genoa, fretful and unable to work, he dreamed of Mary again; this time, she was draped in blue like a Renaissance Madonna. Stretching out his arms, he called the spirit "Dear," at which it recoiled slightly ("I ought not to have addressed it so familiarly"), and he then entreated it to tell him which was "the True religion." Was it Roman Catholicism? "For *you* it is the best," the spirit replied tenderly, and he woke up with tears running down his face.[38] Why Mary Hogarth would be encouraging him to join a faith he was about to depict in *Pictures from Italy* as an ugly sham he does not say. Perhaps she was simply taking on the coloring of her surroundings.

Something similar occurs in Dickens's fiction after *Oliver Twist*, where the pressure of events frequently causes the features of his heroines to rearrange themselves into those of his dead sister-in-law. Having saved Rose Maylie, he would later be far more ruthless with heroines such as *David Copperfield*'s Dora, whose nickname is "Little Blossom"; David sits at his desk and weeps to think "Oh what a fatal name it was, and how the blossom withered in its bloom upon the tree." Fortunately, Dora is later revealed to have been merely a temporary refuge for his affections, unlike her replacement, Agnes, whose status as "the better angel of my life" is secured not only by the fact that her name is a near-anagram of "angel," but also by her evocation of Mary Hogarth's epitaph. "She was so true," David concludes, "she was so beautiful, she was so good"—a little prose hymn that contains a sad private joke in the replacement of "young" with "true," reflecting the number of years Agnes has spent dutifully waiting for him to make his move. Like all of Dickens's most virtuous female characters, she is stamped with Mary's impression like a seal in wax.

In *The Old Curiosity Shop,* similarly, Little Nell is carried to her grave while the funeral bell rings its "remorseless toll" for her, "so young, so beautiful, so good," an episode which caused Dickens to roam the streets lost in grief. "Old wounds bleed afresh when I only think of the way of doing it," he told John Forster when nerving himself to write the scene. "Dear Mary died yesterday, when I think of this sad story."[39] Variations on the pattern are possible—when Paul Dombey decides that his sister Florence is "so young, and good, and beautiful!" this is yet another clue that the finger of fate is pointing towards him rather than her—but its basic shape remained unaltered for the rest of Dickens's career. Fiction provided Mary with a series of alternative lives, and Dickens with a series of opportunities to gloss the world with her presence.

How closely these fictional characters were modeled on the real Mary Hogarth is hard to say, and not only because in other respects she left such a light footprint on the historical record. In the letters written soon after her funeral, composed on mourning stationery marked with a thick black border, already Dickens can be seen reshaping potentially unruly memories into a more compliant image. "I have lost the dearest friend I ever had," he wrote to one correspondent, before going on to repeat what was to become his standard conclusion, one that made her death sound both unfair and somehow inevitable: "she had not a single fault."[40] She exhausted superlatives. More usefully, she became a center around which his scattered feelings of "an old unhappy loss or want of something" could crystallize.[41] In life the "chief solace of his labours," in death she became a powerful combination of leading lady and muse.

Some years later, after Dickens had concluded that his married life was "blighted and wasted," he was quick to enlist Mary as a retrospective witness to the fact that he and Catherine had been "miserable" from the start. At one stage he even hinted darkly that Catherine may have been indirectly responsible for her sister's death, given that "it is her misery to live in some fatal atmosphere which slays every one to whom she should be dearest."[42] That was a startling revision of his attempts to make sense of events at the time, and may even have been a way of displacing his own obscure feelings of guilt. It was Dickens, after all, who on May 6 had given his wife and sister-in-law a note in lieu of tickets to be presented to the manager of St. James's Theatre, "Admit two Angels to Paradise," which with hindsight could have seemed like tempting fate.[43] It was also Dickens who chose Hampstead, where he and Catherine spent a fortnight recovering from Mary's death, as the place where Bill Sikes stops to rest after he has murdered the teenage prostitute Nancy, a figure who haunts Sikes like a malign version of Mary's benevolent presence.

It would be closer to the truth to say that Dickens's growing unhappiness with Catherine was a mirror reflection of his growing obsession with her sister, because if the atmosphere in Doughty Street did produce a fatality, it was Dickens's marriage to a woman who was too large, too clumsy, and altogether too alive to be a satisfactory angel. (The contrast adds a special poignancy to a letter written at the time in which Catherine sympathetically echoed her husband, drawing on the same consolatory language and even the same seesawing tenses: "Oh Mary is it not dreadful to think she has left us for ever," she told her cousin, "although it is a blessed change for her, for if ever there was an angel she is one.")[44] Immediately after Mary's death, Catherine suffered a miscarriage; and while Dickens was briskly sympathetic in praising her as "a fine-hearted noble-minded girl," he does not seem to have considered the possibility that her grief might have been every bit as deep and lasting as his own.[45] The day before Mary's funeral, he wrote to his publisher Edward Chapman that "it will be no harder time to anyone than myself"—this despite his convalescing wife and a mother-in-law who had arrived in time to witness her first daughter's death "and remained here in a state of total insensibility for a week afterwards."[46] Nor could he avoid the suspicion that Catherine's bodily weakness, already reflected in a bout of postpartum depression after Charley's birth, somehow reflected a weak will or a weak mind. Her very presence drew attention to her angelic sister's absence.

The situation was hard to put into words, which is perhaps why Dickens needed the feint of fiction to make sense of it, but it was sharply outlined in pictorial form by Daniel Maclise. In 1837, he produced a pencil sketch (Figure 22) of Dickens, Mary (eyes cast demurely downwards), and Catherine all seen in profile. At the time, when Mary was Dickens's companion and Catherine's sister, her place in the center would have seemed fitting: she was at the heart of the household, the bridge between husband and wife. But like those trick pictures from later in the century that showed two images in one, such as a group of playing children whose features also make up the outline of a skull, there is another way of looking at it. Viewed from a longer historical perspective, Mary comes between husband and wife more like a barrier than a bridge. A similar effect is created by the letters Dickens wrote immediately after Mary's death. Seen from one angle, they breathe nothing but love and loyalty towards his wife; seen from another, their contents start to rearrange themselves into a confession that already he preferred the dead sister to the living one. To Ainsworth he explained that Mary was "the dear girl whom I loved, after my wife, more fervently and deeply than anyone on earth"; and while that parenthesis "after my wife" might be read as nothing more than an expression of propriety, it also contained a latent power that would only be revealed once Dickens realized that he would continue to love Mary long after he stopped loving his wife.[47]

Inevitably, this has led some critics to wonder whether Dickens chose the wrong Hogarth.[48] Should he have waited until the dazzling but under-age Mary was old enough to marry, rather than settle for her dull-witted but available sister? A *grand guignol* version of the idea lies at the center of *Jack Maggs,* Peter Carey's 1997 novel, which reshapes Dickens's early life by colliding fact against fiction until it produces the hybrid form that James Joyce, in *Finnegans Wake,* wittily characterized as "fict." In Carey's plot, the ambitious young novelist Tobias Oates makes his sister-in-law Lizzie pregnant after a secret romance, and when his wife, Mary (this is a fictional game of many levels), finds out, Lizzie's bedroom is the setting for a tragic farce in which, after unwittingly taking two doses of miscarriage pills, she dies thrashing around in blood-soaked sheets. It is an intriguing counterfactual alternative to Dickens's real situation in 1836–1837; but although Carey superbly evokes the whispered conversations and muffled footsteps of an affair and a marriage going along side-by-side in the same house, there is no evidence that Mary was a serious rival to Catherine until she was dead. Then she was in every sense untouchable.

Catherine's response to all this is hard to gauge. Most of what we know about her in this period comes from Dickens's letters; and although in these we learn a good deal about how he coped with his grief, her cameo appearances rarely extend to more than a line or two. Her inner life is largely a blank to us, as perhaps it was to him. The partial exception came some years later, when she published a slim, sixty-page cookbook entitled *What Shall We Have for Dinner?* under the pseudonym Lady Maria Clutterbuck.[49] If that choice of name had Dickens's fingerprints all over it, they were applied even more generously to the spoof preface in which Lady Clutterbuck boasted of her husband's "great gastronomical experience." The rest of the book is mostly taken up with "Bills of Fare for from two to eighteen persons," plus a short appendix of recipes for dishes "the preparation of which may not be generally understood": "Potato Balls," "Italian Cream," "To Boil Cauliflower with Parmesan," "Salmon Curry," and so on. While some of the dishes may be unfamiliar to modern eyes—Lark Pie, Lamb's Head, Pig's Jaw—most of the suggested meals involve fancy variations on a standard trio of meat, potatoes, and pudding, and a surprising number include favorites such as "Water Cresses" (forty appearances), "Macaroni" (fifty-six), and "Toasted Cheese" (forty-two) without any disguise at all. The book's critical reception was as modest as its size: "more meals than one would have thought possible with bloaters," was Margaret Lane's double-edged comment, while another reviewer observed that "no man could possibly survive the consumption of such frequent toasted cheese."[50]

The key question, however, for a book dropped into such a busy marketplace—ten years later it would be joined by the larger and infinitely more useful *Mrs. Beeton's Book of Household Management*—was why it had been published at all. While its menus were probably an accurate reflection of how the Dickens household entertained—"such an overloaded dessert!" Jane Carlyle wrote with disgusted relish after one of their dinner parties in 1849, "pyramids of figs raisins oranges—ach!"—they over-shot everyday life by some distance.[51] (When Dickens invited friends to Doughty Street, he never offered anything more ambitious than "a chop" or "some cold lamb and a bit of fish.")[52] They are as much a fiction as those scenes in *Pickwick* where Dickens's narrative keeps threatening to turn into a menu, such as Sam Weller's summary of the Saracen's Head: "Wery good little dinner, Sir, they can get ready in half an hour—pair of fowls, Sir, and a weal cutlet; French beans, 'taturs, tart, and tidiness." Perhaps Dickens encouraged Catherine to compile the book because he wanted to give her a taste of authorship, or even to involve her more close-ly in his imaginative world, the generous provision of foodstuffs being one of his own literary trademarks. If so, it is odd that the preface specifically points out that Lady Clutterbuck's husband is dead, even if she piously expresses the belief that "my attention to the requirements of his appetite secured me the possession of his esteem until the last." Odder still is the fact that the character in *David Copperfield* to whom David gives a cook-book, "prettily bound . . . to make it look less dry and more inviting," is the charming but doomed Dora, whose answer to the question of how to make Irish stew (a dish that appears four times in *What Shall We Have for Dinner?*) is "Tell the servant to make it." After this unpromising start, her main use for the book is to train her little dog Jip to stand on it, which, David reports, makes her "so pleased . . . that I was very glad I had bought it." Catherine's response is not recorded.

❦⁓❦⁓

In one respect, Mary Hogarth's premature death was well timed. A week before her ill-fated trip to the theater, Dickens had published a short es-say in *Bentley's* that perfectly re-created the sort of gossipy environment in which his own next steps would be scrutinized. "Some Particulars Concerning a Lion" begins by noting that although lions in the wild may look fierce and noble, those seen "under the influence of captivity, and the pressure of misfortune," such as the mangy specimens kept in London's Zoological Gardens, are far less impressive. Much the same is true, Dickens concludes, of literary "lions," the celebrities of the publishing circuit.

The term "lions" was much in vogue at the time. It encompassed both genuinely important writers and those lucky enough to have been caught up in their slipstream; and as an accolade that could be bestowed by others but not claimed for oneself, other than with the addition of a fig leaf of irony, it neatly encapsulated the steady drift towards a literary market in which the power to make or break reputations lay in the hands of ordinary readers. Even those who hated the practice of "lionism" could see what it revealed about changing literary fashions. "Literary 'lions' have become a class," Harriet Martineau tartly observed in 1839, which "testifies to the vast spread of literature among our people," and she was in no doubt that anyone who had this sort of widespread appeal had proved only that they were good at attracting "the number of minds from which a superficial and transient sympathy may be anticipated." Quality of writing and quantity of sales, according to Martineau, are always likely to exist in creative tension. While this was a relatively new problem, she conceded, the sight of "lionisers" attempting to lure star names to their parties was just a modern variation on the old theme of "social vanity." Literary lions were being flattered and cajoled into playing the same sort of role that used to be taken by "my lord's fool, and my lady's monkey."[53]

Dickens had a more ambivalent attitude towards literary "lionism," as one might expect from a writer who was already starting to garner a good deal of money and fame from what Martineau sneered at as the "worship of popular authors." Already in *Pickwick* he had taken the sort of scene that caused her particular irritation—a coterie of small-town snobs "gathered together to make the most of a literary foreigner who may be passing through"—and turned it into gleeful comedy, as he described the tireless efforts of Mrs. Leo Hunter to talk up Count Smorltork, setting off a polite ripple of approval that starts with herself ("Wonderful man, Count Smorltork"), passes through Pott ("Sound philosopher") and Snodgrass ("Clear-headed, strong-minded person"), and ends with a "chorus of bystanders," who "took up the shout of Count Smorltork's praise, shook their heads sagely, and unanimously cried 'Very!'" A few years later, when Dickens himself was a literary foreigner passing through America, he was greeted in a style that was like a greatly extended version of Count Smorltork's reception, albeit by hosts who were far more aggressive in making him jump through hoops and roar on demand.[54] He still managed to see the funny side, telling Forster that at his hotel in Niagara Falls there were rumors of an artist painting a full-length portrait of him, and although one of the chambermaids thought that the canvas in question, "which has a great deal of hair," was actually someone else, "I am pretty sure that the Lion is myself."[55]

Just as he enjoyed spotting likenesses of himself, and from the 1840s onwards was far from shy about releasing publicity photographs, so he was pleased when other people realized they were in the presence of the inimitable original. His son Henry recalled how Dickens was once walking through the Zoological Gardens when a little girl, "catching sight of my father, ran back to her mother crying out delightedly, 'Oh, mummy! mummy! it is Charles Dickens,'" and "my father, who had heard and seen it all, was strangely embarrassed; but oh, so pleased, so truly delighted."[56] The chime of "delightedly" and "delighted" nicely captures the pleasure Dickens and his readers took in each other, but the setting also warns of how potentially imprisoning this sort of attention could be. Indeed, it is likely that Dickens's regular visits to the same zoo, where one friend reported that "He chaffed with the monkeys, coaxed the tigers and bamboozled the snakes, with a dexterity unapproachable," were partly an expression of fellow-feeling.[57] He too sometimes felt as if he had been trapped and put on display for public entertainment.

In "Some Particulars Concerning a Lion," this emerges in Dickens's description of a painfully awkward social gathering during which a writer is brought into the drawing room by his "keeper," and obliged to stand there being petted by strangers, while his admirers are free to disappear into private corners to whisper about "whether he was shorter than they had expected to see him, or taller, or thinner, or fatter, or younger, or older; whether he was like his portrait, or unlike it; and whether the particular shade of his eyes was black, or blue, or hazel, or green, or yellow, or a mixture." It is a curious piece of writing, not because it stresses the lionized writer's lack of freedom, as he is carefully shepherded from drawing room to cab, but because it sets these constraints against Dickens's own playfully rambling style. Both might be interpreted as a form of complaint. The essay was added at the last minute, after it became clear that the May number of *Oliver Twist* would not be long enough to meet Dickens's contractual requirement to supply Richard Bentley with sixteen pages of printed matter every month.[58] Only in terms of its page count could this installment be thought to fall short—its highlights included Oliver's escape to London, his first meeting with the Artful Dodger, and his arrival in Fagin's den—but Bentley had already proven himself to be a stickler for contractual fine print, recalculating Dickens's stipend according to the last fraction of every page, while allowing himself a generously free hand when it came to editorial policy. Viewed in this context, Dickens's description of the literary lion looks less like empty social chatter than the prolixity of someone grimly eking out an idea until he reaches his allotted number of words.

For the next three years, Dickens's relationship with Bentley settled into a regular routine: a period of mutual suspicion would eventually break out into flurries of angry letters, to be followed by further negotiations, the drawing up of revised publishing agreements, and the restoration of an uneasy peace. Neither side emerged particularly well from these disputes. By digging in his heels over the idea that he should offer Dickens more generous terms to reflect his growing reputation, Bentley revealed himself to be stubborn as well as a stickler. Dickens, on the other hand, treated legally binding contracts like drafts he could rewrite depending on his mood: from August 22, 1836, to July 2, 1840, he successfully renegotiated the terms of his original contract with Bentley on no fewer than eight separate occasions—and in so doing, he revealed once again how difficult he found it to distinguish between feeling self-righteous and being in the right. There is a peculiar aptness in the fact that a novel he originally promised to Macrone as *Gabriel Vardon* (Dickens later altered the spelling of his character's name to "Varden," thereby releasing a pun on the cockney pronunciation of "warden"), then transferred to Bentley, and finally published in 1841 with Chapman and Hall as *Barnaby Rudge*, featured a locksmith as its main character.

But Dickens's contract with Bentley was only one of the factors that was making him feel unsettled and nettled in the months after Mary's death. Even when he wasn't being cornered in drawing rooms, he was starting to think of writing as an imprisoning set of routines. Towards the end of June 1837, while completing the latest installment of *Pickwick*, he told Forster, "I can't get out," ruefully comparing himself to the star-ling in Laurence Sterne's novel *A Sentimental Journey* who sings "I can't get out—I can't get out"; and when he finally managed to escape from Doughty Street a few days later, he chose to take a sightseeing trip with Forster and the actor William Charles Macready to Coldbath Fields and Newgate prisons.[59] A similar chafing at restraints can be seen in his fic-tion. This is the period in which both *Pickwick* and *Oliver Twist* gravi-tate towards prisons, and personal liberty is threatened by powerfully impersonal external forces, while in his next novel, *Nicholas Nickleby*, Dickens provided Tim Linkinwater with a blind blackbird who has lost his voice and spends his days dreaming and dozing in his cage. His name is Dick.

It would be tempting to conclude from this that, in the general gloom of bereavement, Dickens again found himself being drawn back to Warren's Blacking warehouse and the Marshalsea, with all the associated anxiet-ies about being trapped and stared at. That is certainly possible. But it is equally possible that he was starting to face up to the reality of life as a professional writer, in which the free exercise of his imagination would be offset by decades of deadlines and word counts, and the feeling that his pen was attached to him like a ball and chain. There is genuine alarm in one of *Pickwick*'s scenes, published the previous September, which de-scribes Mr. Pickwick being trundled away fast asleep in a wheelbarrow to the local pound, and waking up to find himself being gawped at by a group of strangers:

"Let me out," cried Mr. Pickwick. "Where's my servant? Where are my friends?"

"You an't got no friends. Hurrah!" And then there came a turnip, and then a potato, and then an egg; with a few other little tokens of the playful disposition of the many-headed.

A sociable picnic is transformed into its nightmarish double, in which Pickwick is pelted with food rather than offered it to eat, and a select group of friends is replaced by a nameless and faceless mob. It is an equally terrifying double of the life Dickens might have to face as a novelist, wholly at the mercy of a "many-headed" public, who might respond to his overtures by jeering, "You an't got no friends. Hurrah!"[60]

Hemmed in by responsibilities on all sides, Dickens's response was to escape through travel. In July 1837 he was with Catherine and Phiz in France and then Belgium; in August he took Catherine and Charley to Broadstairs in Kent for a seaside holiday, where Forster joined them; by November the Dickens family was in Brighton, although here he complained that lacking a male companion "my notions of the place are consequently somewhat confined, being limited to the Pavilion, the chain Pier, and the Sea."[61] But however much he moved around, one thing remained constant: his sense that no experience would feel complete without Mary being there to share it. "I can solemnly say," he told Mrs. Hogarth on October 26, "that waking or sleeping I have never once lost the recollection of our hard trial and sorrow, and I feel that I never shall."[62] Even worse than the prospect of jeers was the certainty of a silence at the heart of any future applause.

CHAPTER TWELVE

Being Dickens

More evidence that a career as a novelist was starting to emerge from the chrysalis of *Pickwick* came in July 1837, when Dickens was the subject of a long and thoughtful article in John Stuart Mill's *London and Westminster Review*. Like other prestigious quarterly journals, the *Westminster* carefully guarded its reputation as a publication written chiefly by and for intellectuals, so it rarely wasted its book reviews on what most people were actually reading. Charles Buller's article broke from this pattern, by assembling generous extracts from *Sketches by Boz* (first and second series), *Pickwick* Nos. 1–15, and *Bentley's* Nos. 1–6, and analyzing "the foundation of a popularity extraordinary on account of its sudden growth, its vast extent, and the recognition which it has received from persons of the most refined taste, as well as from the great mass of the reading public." Buller's explanation for this popularity, which he attributed chiefly to Dickens's skill at portraying "the comic peculiarities of the lower orders of Englishmen," was far less interesting than the unanswered question that bubbled away under the surface of his analysis—namely, how a single writer, no matter how "prolific and fertile," could be responsible for so many different kinds of writing. As with Homer, Buller pointed out, "the various excellencies of the style of 'Boz' have been by many considered too numerous to be combined in one individual"; but however tempting it was to view them as the product of a committee or clique, "the world may now feel at rest as to the personality and the unity of 'Boz.' Mr. Charles Dickens is the acknowledged author of these works."[1]

In attempting to reassure his readers, Buller could hardly have done a better job at stimulating their curiosity. How was it possible to "feel at rest" when reading an author who was so hard to pin down? Dickens's writing retained its capacity to surprise long after his plots had disclosed their secrets. Indeed, the real secret was how he had managed to create a style that was at once instantly recognizable and impossible to categorize. For all the attempts of humorists to sum him up, such as the "recipe" for "A Startling Romance" that appeared in the first issue of *Punch* ("Take a small boy . . . stew him well down in vice . . .—boil him in a cauldron of vice and improbabilities. . . . Serve up with a couple of murders—and season with a hanging-match. N. B. Alter the ingredients to a beadle and a workhouse—the scenes may be the same, but the whole flavour of vice will be lost. . . . Strongly recommended for weak stomachs"), what Dickens's readers were discovering was that he was a literary escape artist who specialized in establishing expectations and then wriggling free.[2]

Throughout his career, Dickens found a particular kind of imaginative release in adopting restraints—from his readers' potentially narrow tastes to the limitations on space imposed by serial publication—and then giving them the slip. He was equally good at shrugging off his critics. In January 1838 he published a "Poetical Epistle from Father Prout to Boz" in *Bentley's*. It started off as a standard publicity puff ("Immense applause you've gained, oh, Boz! through continental Europe"), moved into an awkward middle section on "some poor nearer home" who should not be ignored ("I mean the starving Irish"), and blithely concluded that such gloomy thoughts "o'ercometh not the glow of England's humour":

> Write on, young sage! still o'er the page pour forth the flood of fancy;
> Wax still more droll, wave o'er the soul Wit's wand of necromancy.
> Behold! e'en now around your brow th'immortal laurel thickens;
> Yea, SWIFT or STERNE might gladly learn a thing or two from
> Dickens.[3]

While hardly a distinguished piece of writing (the thudding collisions of Prout's rhymes show that he still had a thing or two to learn from Byron), this tries hard to capture the building momentum of Dickens's career, through its energetic clusters of verbs, internal rhymes that spill over from word to word, and lines that rhythmically topple past their expected endings. The only really jarring note is struck by that final chime of "thickens" and "Dickens." What should be a triumphant climax to the poem, summing up a literary phenomenon in a single word, turns into something far more open-ended. At the last moment, the form buckles and Dickens slips away.

Something similar was happening in the diary Dickens had just started. Written in a copy of *The Law and Commercial Daily Remembrancer* for 1838, with one page given over to each day, it is by far the most detailed of the four fragmentary diaries he wrote in the years 1838–1841, although he seems to have been in two minds about whether to treat it chiefly as a record of his life or an engagement planner.[4] From the start, he sought a balance between looking back and looking forward:

Monday, January 1, 1838

A sad new Year's Day in one respect, for at the opening of the last year poor Mary was with us. Very many things to be grateful for, since then, however. Increased reputation and means—good health and prospects. We never know the full value of blessings 'till we lose them (we were not ignorant of this one when we had it, I hope) but if she were with us now, the same winning, happy, amiable companion— sympathising with all my thoughts and feelings more than any one I knew ever did or will—I think I should have nothing to wish for, but a continuance of such happiness. But she is gone, and pray God I may one day through his mercy rejoin her.

This shifts awkwardly between private and public forms of speech: does "we" refer to Dickens and his wife, or is it an editorial "we" that has one eye fixed on the mirror and another on the general public? The next entries, from January 2 through January 14, were written in a single burst of retrospection, suggesting that Dickens's initial resolution was wavering; but hidden away among the rapid summaries of his day-to-day activities—walking in Regent's Park, attending a quadrille party, or visiting the smoky ruins of the Royal Exchange after it had burned down—there are further clues that he was thinking ahead. These include tentative plans to collaborate with Harrison Ainsworth on the *Lions of London,* a one-shilling monthly periodical to feature old and new stories of city life; as well as a failed attempt to obtain life insurance ("the 'Board' seem disposed to think I work too much," he grumbled).[5]

Whether recording the past or projecting possible futures, most of these entries showed a distinct lack of sustained self-analysis. This isn't altogether surprising. Dickens often donned a performance mask when asked to reflect upon himself. An 1856 autobiographical sketch he wrote for Wilkie Collins, for example, concluded with "Here I am"—a studiedly nonchalant version of the catchphrase ("Here we are!") made famous by the clown Joseph Grimaldi—before he switched to a different branch of popular entertainment, telling Collins that "I feel like a Wild Beast in a Caravan, describing himself in the keeper's absence."[6] Dickens was similarly wary of portraits of himself, which he tended to regard with a kind of amused detachment, as when he wrote to W. P. Frith in 1859 about his painting of "the gifted Individual whom you will transmit to posterity," almost as if it depicted someone else.[7] (The only clue he is referring to himself comes with the "I" he quietly smuggles into "Individual.") Nor were diaries exempt from his suspicion. In *The Mystery of Edwin Drood,* the likelihood that John Jasper has murdered his nephew is intensified when he confesses that he keeps a diary in which he has recorded "a morbid dread . . . of some horrible consequences resulting to my dear boy," while in *Nicholas Nickleby* Dickens sharply observes that some of the "craftiest scoundrels" who ever lived "will gravely jot down in diaries the events of every day, and keep a regular debtor and creditor account with Heaven, which shall always show a floating balance in their own favour."

Writing novels was a more honorable kind of fiction, because it did not try to disguise the fact that the author was pretending to be someone else. That is why a cartoon like the one inspired by his second American reading tour, in 1867–1868 (Figure 23), is insightful as well as funny, because whether he is depicted as a paunchy Pickwick or a plaintively bearded Little Nell, every character is identifiably Dickens. It shows how successfully he had translated into his writing the paradox John Forster identified in his social life: whether Dickens was telling a joke or taking part in a game, Forster wrote, "he seemed to be always the more himself, for being somebody else, for continually putting off his personality."[8] The same is true of his fiction, where time and again he demonstrated that he was never more himself than when escaping into other lives.

Dickens's diary put a rather different gloss on Forster's pen-portrait, because whenever he got too close to himself in these scrappy pages, he was quick to deflect his attention elsewhere. Self-confrontation alternated with self-avoidance, as if the writer were playing a game of hide and seek with himself. The longest entry, written on January 14, provides a textbook example. Starting with a paragraph in which he made "a stedfast resolution" not to neglect his diary or dress up the facts, he promised to write down "what rises to my lips—my mental lips at least—without reserve," admitting that "although I dare say I shall be ashamed of a good deal in it, I should like to look over it, at the year's end." After a paragraph break, he continued: "In Scott's Diary which I have been looking at this morning, there are thoughts which have been mine by day and by night, in good spirits and bad, since Mary died." There followed two extracts on dealing with grief which he carefully copied out from Sir Walter Scott, as he recognized in an earlier writer feelings that were his own, even if he could not have put them into precisely these words without Scott's help. The next day he gave up writing his diary ("I grow sad over this checking off of days, and can't do it"), and a fortnight later he traveled to Yorkshire with Hablot Browne to investigate the brutal boarding schools he was about to depict in *Nicholas Nickleby,* where children were imprisoned in a way that put his own sad checking-off of days firmly into perspective. Self-analysis gave way to public scrutiny.

But although Dickens officially stopped writing his diary on January 15, returning to it only sporadically in later months to note important events and tot up his traveling expenses, in another way he continued it in disguise, by "putting off his personality" into two more works he was writing in January alongside *Oliver Twist.* They are no less revealing of his state of mind.

The first started off as a piece of hackwork. In 1836, Joseph Grimaldi had written about four hundred pages of autobiographical notes; and realizing that his bulky manuscript needed some editorial refining, he turned it over to the journeyman journalist Thomas Egerton Wilks to "rewrite, revise and correct." By the time Wilks's version of the *Memoirs of Joseph Grimaldi* reached Richard Bentley in September 1837, a few months after Grimaldi's death, the book was nearly unrecognizable and wholly unpublishable. It had been crudely cut, was interspersed with anecdotes "gleaned" from conversations with the author, and had been inexplicably translated into reported speech.[9] Bentley turned to Dickens. At first Dickens was reluctant to take over a "very badly done" project that was "so redolent of twaddle," but in November he agreed to deliver a new version within two months for an advance of £300.[10] By January 5, 1838, he had completed the central portion of the text, much of it dictated to his father, leaving only the introduction and conclusion to write. Part of the agreement with Bentley was that Dickens should appear as the editor rather than author of the work; but after it went to press in February, he admitted that he had enjoyed "telling some of the stories in my own way," and it is not hard to find places where the events are given an unmistakably Dickensian character.[11] His imagination imbues every page like a watermark.

The main narrative arc of the life, in which Grimaldi won fame and fortune through a combination of talent and hard work, was especially appealing to Dickens, and many of the traits he stresses in Grimaldi's character, such as his obsessive punctuality and punishing work schedule ("Idleness wearied him more than labour"), are treated with a sympathy born of self-knowledge. Dickens's introduction stretches this sympathy until it borders on self-identification. Praising Grimaldi's "energy and perseverance," he concludes that his subject's life proves how "a very young person may overcome all the disadvantages and temptations incidental to . . . a most precarious pursuit, and become a useful and respectable member of society." (There are quiet echoes here of Dickens's reference to authorship as the "most precarious of all pursuits," in his 1837 preface to *Pickwick*.) The loss of the original manuscript makes it impossible to know how much of what follows was tidied up by Dickens or wholly invented by him, but telling Grimaldi's story in his own way produced several overlaps with his other writings. At its simplest, this involved him viewing the events of Grimaldi's life as plot fragments that could be pieced together in different forms, such as the scuffle during which a thief is severely wounded while breaking into Grimaldi's house— a narrative climax Dickens later adapted for the April number of *Oliver Twist*, in which Oliver is shot during a failed burglary attempt.

More subtle are the connections between Grimaldi's life and Dickens's enduring fascination with the secret misery of performers. Rarely did Grimaldi take the stage, in Dickens's version of events, without some disaster befalling him; throughout his life, laughter and agony accompanied each other like a remorseless double-act. While playing a robber at Sadler's Wells he accidentally shot himself in the foot, so that the boot "puffed out to a great size, presenting a very laughter-moving appearance to everybody but the individual in it, who was suffering the most excruciating agony." During a pantomime appearance in Liverpool he fell through a trapdoor onstage, and played the rest of the scene "as though nothing had happened to discompose him" even though he was "in agony" throughout. His life was an extended comedy of errors. It is another version of the idea Dickens had already explored in *Pickwick*'s story of the starving clown: "The jest on the lip and the tear in the eye, the merriment on the mouth and the aching of the heart, have called down the same shouts of laughter and peals of applause a hundred times."

Perhaps this is why he made Grimaldi part of a performance tradition that harked back to the realms of myth. Although never explicitly named in the book, Grimaldi's great predecessor in Dickens's eyes was a clown who existed only in the alembic of memory: *Hamlet*'s Yorick. Dickens reports that Grimaldi, after the death of his wife, was summoned to the theater "to set the audience in a roar" after "chalking over the seams which mental agony had worn in his face." He followed a similar route after the death of his friend Richard Hughes, when in order to attend the funeral he was forced to run from a pantomime rehearsal to the graveyard, returning just in time "to set the audience in a roar." Both events recall the graveyard scene in which Hamlet contemplates the skull of the clown he knew as a child: "Here hung those lips that I have kissed I know not how oft. Where be your gibes now? Your gambols? Your songs? Your flashes of merriment that were wont to set the tables on a roar?"[12] The allusion also reaches back into Dickens's past. When a reviewer in the *Athenaeum* complained that the whole book was written in trademark "Pickwick style," and voiced the suspicion that the author had "never seen Grimaldi on the stage," Dickens wrote a sharply worded rebuke in which he claimed that he had been brought to London in 1819 or 1820 for a performance by Grimaldi, "in whose honour I am informed I clapped my hands with great preciosity."[13] While the elegiac tone of the *Memoirs* was appropriate for a book published posthumously, it was also a response to another loss—that of Dickens's childhood—which could only be restored through writing.

As Dickens's narrative edged closer towards the present, however, it started to resemble a continuation of his diary by other means. The final chapter, written during January 1838, opened with a stark warning to "all those who now, reaping large gains from the exercise of a glittering and dazzling profession, forget that youth and strength will not last for ever, and that the more intoxicating their triumphs now, the more probable is the advent of a time of adversity and decay." It reads less like someone else's memoirs than a private *aide mémoire,* albeit one that Dickens was to prove remarkably good at ignoring. His descriptions of Grimaldi's success as a touring actor indicate why. Although he is frank about the toll these performances took on Grimaldi's creaking body, there is an unmistakable glint in his calculations of the "immense sums" Grimaldi earned; on several occasions he gives up analysis altogether, and simply lists the raw numbers in a series of long, admiring whistles. Seen from the perspective of Dickens's later reading tours, and the letters in which he boasts of his own box-office receipts, such passages are like the blueprint for a get-rich-quick scheme. They are also a dreadful warning.[14] "It was only by a most careful observation that anyone could form an idea of the extent of his sufferings, for . . . he held it as a maxim that 'No man had a right to break an engagement with the public if he were able to be out of bed.'"[15] That was how George Dolby remembered the final reading tour, when Dickens insisted on performing "Sikes and Nancy" night after night, taking on the roles of both the murderer and his victim—before collapsing offstage, mute with exhaustion and drenched with sweat. It might just as easily be a passage from Grimaldi's *Memoirs*.

The second book Dickens was busy compiling in January was entitled *Sketches of Young Gentlemen,* shortly to be published by Chapman and Hall. This offered far more scattered autobiographical reflections. A slim volume of fewer than a hundred pages, it had been commissioned to sit alongside the same publisher's recent *Sketches of Young Ladies* by "Quiz" (Edward Caswall), as a companion volume and a riposte. Caswall's gimmick had been to write a pseudo-scientific guide, like a parody of a bird-watcher's manual, intended to distinguish the various "classes" of "the female species" (his subtitle was *In Which These Interesting Members of the Animal Kingdom Are Classified*), including "The Busy Young Lady," "The Romantic Young Lady," and "The Manly Young Lady." While the comedy of this premise was somewhat strained, and Caswall too often mistook condescension for wit (no cliché goes unturned in sketches like "The Stupid Young Lady," in which the main character turns out to be fat as well as stupid, and sighs "like the plaintive grunt of a sleeping pig"), his tone of bustling facetiousness, allied with the promise of "Sketches" and a selection of illustrations by Hablot Browne, strongly indicated the audience he had in his sights.[16] Quiz and Phiz were intended to be supplements, or possibly rivals, to Boz and Phiz. Caswall even explicitly twits

Dickens by making "The Literary Young Lady" chatter vacuously about the latest number of *Pickwick:* "Have you seen it, Mr. P—? Dear delightful Mr. Pickwick, how I love him!"[17]

Happy to rise to the challenge, or perhaps to the bait, Dickens responded with a set of short sketches—"The Bashful Young Gentleman," "The Military Young Gentleman," "The Political Young Gentleman," and nine others—intended to put this interloper in his place. Following a tongue-in-cheek dedication "To the Young Ladies" that promised to avenge Caswall's calumnies, his volume largely followed the same narrative pattern; but whereas Caswall had remained professionally detached from his subjects, peering at them through the literary equivalent of a pair of binoculars, Dickens was far more involved. Occasionally he sank little boreholes of memory into his writing. In "The Funny Young Gentleman," the climax of the titular wag's singularly unfunny antics shows him hiding underneath a table "and suddenly reappearing with a mask on," which frightens one little boy so much he goes into convulsions. It is a strange episode that makes sense only in the context of Dickens's own childhood, during which he was so terrified by a "dreadful Mask" (the capital letter elevating it to the status of a fetish or bogeyman), that the "mere recollection" of it, he wrote in "A Christmas Tree," "the mere knowledge of its existence anywhere, was sufficient to awake me in the night all perspiration and horror, with, 'O I know it's coming! O the mask!'"

But Dickens's sense of sympathy extended much further than this. Even when coolly appraising his characters from the outside, he cannot stop himself from imagining what the world might look like through their eyes. "The Out-And-Out Young Gentleman," for example, a clerk who "does as little as he can," is fond of taking up multiple seats in public, where "he lies with his knees up, and the soles of his boots planted firmly on the cushion, so that if any low fellow should ask him to make room for a lady, he takes ample revenge upon her dress"—and Dickens's description captures not only his attitudes but also his vocabulary ("low fellow"), anticipating how the incident might be relayed as a swaggering anecdote by the young gentleman himself. With each sketch taking up roughly six generously printed pages, there is no space for piercing psychological insight; these characters are deliberately made as flat as playing cards, and much of the pleasure in reading the book comes from seeing Dickens shuffle so quickly between them. In effect, *Sketches of Young Gentlemen* was another admiring tribute to Charles Mathews: a quick-change routine in which the writer could switch faces as well as voices, while ensuring that the outline of his own features remained visible beneath all these different masks.

The idea held a particular appeal for Dickens. In 1851 he co-authored a one-act farce with Mark Lemon entitled *Mr. Nightingale's Diary,* which gave him the opportunity to play Mr. Gabblewig, a lawyer who plans to win Mr. Nightingale's daughter by disguising himself as five characters in swift succession, including a servant named Charley who has amateur dramatic ambitions, and a comic old woman based on *Martin Chuzzlewit's* word-mangling Mrs. Gamp. (The play was written as an afterpiece to Bulwer-Lytton's *Not So Bad As We Seem; or, Many Sides to a Character,* in which Dickens played the role of Flexible.) Mr. Nightingale's character as a self-absorbed hypochondriac is indicated by the fact that he keeps a diary, "my only comfort," in which he records his daily symptoms; and the route to his redemption is marked out by Gabblewig, who advises him to "burn that book, and be happy!" The conclusion Dickens expects his audience to draw is that diaries promote a brooding concentration on the self, narrowing the writer's sympathies to an audience of one, whereas real life provides opportunities for a more generous expansion of the self, as when two people fall in love.

The same is true of that vicarious form of living known as fiction. Dickens may have decided to give up his diary at the end of January because it sat so oddly with the range and public nature of his other literary activities. *Oliver Twist, Bentley's, Sketches of Young Gentlemen,* Grimaldi's *Memoirs,* book reviews for the *Examiner,* the first glimmerings of *Nicholas Nickleby:* he was putting off his personality in far more directions than could comfortably be distilled into a single page each day. It was, he told Ainsworth, a "dreadful" workload.[18] It was also as near as he had yet come to making life in his Doughty Street study resemble one of Mathews's "At Home" performances.

If Dickens's diary struggled to represent the sheer busyness of his life, artists were at an even greater disadvantage. According to Leigh Hunt, Dickens's face contained "the life and soul . . . of fifty human beings," and capturing such quicksilver energy in a single image was practically impossible.[19] Samuel Laurence's answer to this challenge was simply to ignore it, producing a portrait in 1837 that depicted Dickens as a dreamy young Romantic, the literary heir of Shelley and Keats, viewed through the soft focus created by working in chalk (Figure 24). Far more accurate was George Cruikshank's attempt, drawn in the same year, which went to the opposite extreme by refusing to settle on a definitive image (Figure 25). Instead, Cruikshank sketched a series of heads and outlines clustered around a hazily drawn Dickens sitting with his legs nonchalantly crossed. These sketches were not intended to be put on display: they are studies for something still emerging, a work in progress. But then, one might say much the same about Dickens at the time they were drawn, which is why they are by far the best pictorial representation of his early life to have survived. Cruikshank labeled the main drawing *Sketch of Charles Dickens,* where both "sketch" and "Dickens" are firmly singular, but the other six images tell a different story. They swirl with movement, bursting from one another into new expressions, new attitudes. They are like six characters in search of an author.

❧ ❦ ❧ ❦

Cruikshank's sketch was a sign of the times. Dickens was establishing his reputation at the start of a period in which the "individual" would come to be viewed as an increasingly complex entity—far more fragmented and mutable than that term (from the Latin *individuus,* meaning "indivisible" or "inseparable") might suggest. Writers such as Thomas Carlyle had expressed firm confidence in the self's inalienable coherence, as demonstrated in the "ME" that allows Teufelsdröckh to withstand the "Everlasting No" at the crucial moment of *Sartor Resartus* (1833–1834). But as the century developed, the work of new disciplines such as psychology would show that the self behaved much more like a verb than a noun; it was an unfolding process, rather than a static object. Trying to define it was like putting one's finger on a blob of mercury; applying extra pressure only made it scatter in more directions. Both during Dickens's lifetime and afterwards, writers would adopt in various ways the notion that, as Arthur Rimbaud famously claimed, "JE est un autre" ("I is an other"), but few would ignore it altogether.[20] It extended from monstrous double-acts like Dr. Jekyll and Mr. Hyde, to Walt Whitman's self-answering question in *Leaves of Grass:* "Do I contradict myself? / Very well, then, I contradict myself, / I am large—I contain multitudes," a claim that demonstrated how subtly an idea can turn around the axis of a line of verse, given that "Very well, then" could represent either a shrug of acceptance or a defiant tilt of the chin.[21] Nor was the capacious Whitman an isolated case when it came to promoting the idea that writers contained many different people within the same skin. As Oscar Wilde pointed out in *The Picture of Dorian Gray,* one of the great attractions of literature—for readers as well as writers—is that it provides "a method by which we can multiply our personalities"; and few periods were as attuned to the creative possibilities of this idea as the Victorian age, with its development of the multiplot novel, the dramatic monologue, and other literary forms that allowed writers to splinter into many alternative selves.[22] Dickens was merely extending the same principle into his own life.

Some of these selves never made it past the earliest embryonic stage. In February 1838, Dickens agreed to write a new comic work for Chapman and Hall, to be titled "Boz's Annual Register and Obituary of the Blue Devils," and in mid-March he contemplated a stage adaptation of *Oliver Twist.* Neither ever appeared; but of these two nonworks, the second was the more significant, because it revealed his growing anxiety about the many unauthorized theatrical versions of his work that had started to compete against one another without any advantage to himself. (His mind had probably been concentrated by the fate of *Pickwick,* which had been so scuffed and dented by plagiarists that its original outline was now scarcely recognizable.) He was too late: by the end of the month an adaptation by Gilbert à Beckett was already playing at St. James's Theatre, despite the fact that *Oliver Twist* was only halfway through its serialization in *Bentley's* and, as Dickens pointed out, "nobody can have heard what I mean to do with the different characters in the end, inasmuch as at present I don't quite know, myself."[23]

Though this version was swiftly hooted off the stage, within a year five others had been attempted, the most successful of which, George Almar's *Oliver Twist: A Serio-Comic Burletta* at the Surrey Theatre, concluded with Sikes's jumping off a roof and being accidentally strangled—a scene that had been published only days before the opening night in November. According to Forster, Dickens attended this production, and "in the middle of the first scene he laid himself down upon the floor in a corner of the box and never rose from it until the drop-scene fell."[24] It was an understandable reaction, not only to the slapstick melodrama being played out in front of him (Bumble's response to being stripped of his office is "I am galvanised with horror! I shall faint!"), but also to the more general problem that was dogging his success.[25] Having long battled a fear of his career "going astray," these unauthorized literary add-ons and knock-offs meant that his identity as a writer was now in serious danger of drifting away from his control. Popularity and anonymity, it turned out, were not mutually exclusive categories.

Later that year, Dickens would describe in *Nicholas Nickleby* how Mr. Lillyvick visits his poor relations the Kenwigs, and declares that he is "not particular" about where he sits. "If he had been an author, who knew his place," Dickens writes, "he couldn't have been more humble." Looking at the number of separate works generated by *Oliver Twist*, in addition to excerpts that were reprinted elsewhere, including several passages that appeared in the *Times* next to stories about the misery of workhouse life, Dickens would have been forgiven for wondering exactly what his own place in the world was. Published under the pen name "Bos," the weekly parts of Edward Lloyd's *Oliver Twiss* (1838–1839) eventually ran to more than twice the length of Dickens's novel, and in its sympathetic portrayal of characters such as Polly (Nancy) and the Knowing Cove (the Artful Dodger) it went even further than its original in telling the story from a ground-level point of view. Still more reformist in tone was a rival *Oliver Twiss,* by "Poz," featuring a familiar-yet-strange cast that included "Fumble" the beadle and "Merryberry" the undertaker, but that also depicted Oliver's father starving to death in a workhouse and his socially ostracized mother committing suicide; the title page cheekily declared "Copyright secured by Act of Parliament." In theory, copyright law should have protected Dickens's work in Britain for twenty-eight years from the date of first publication—a term that was extended to forty-two years by the Copyright Act of 1842—but such legal niceties were of little help when it came to dealing with publishers whose output trod such a fine line between paraphrase and plagiarism.[26] "The vagabonds have stuck placards on the walls," Dickens noted wearily, "each saying that *theirs* is the only true Edition."[27]

Confronted by such impudence, he was sometimes capable of seeing the funny side, and even of joining in the joke. When John Macrone died in 1837, for instance, Dickens put aside their earlier differences and set about editing a three-volume anthology to raise money for his destitute family; when the work eventually appeared, in 1841, he chose to title it *The Pic Nic Papers*—a literary soundalike that came close to beating the imitators at their own game.[28] More often, though, the number of authors hanging onto his coattails pushed Dickens's sense of humor to its limits and beyond. In March 1838, a "Proclamation" appeared in newspapers and on handbills, advertising the imminent start of *Nicholas Nickleby,* and attacking "some dishonest dullards resident in the by-streets and cellars of this town" who "impose upon the unwary and credulous, by producing cheap and wretched imitations of our delectable Works." The rest of the proclamation struggled to maintain this balance between ire and irony, as Dickens explained that his imitators were too poor for him to sue, like vermin who are "not worth the killing for the sake of their carcases"; the piece concluded with a notice "To Pirates" warning that if they attempted to steal any part of his new novel, "we will hang them on gibbets so lofty and enduring, that their remains shall be a monument of our just vengeance to all succeeding ages." In *Cleave's London Satirist,* this was pointedly printed next to Edward Lloyd's advertisement for *Oliver Twiss.* Lloyd decided to fight fire with fire. On March 31, when Dickens published the first number of *Nicholas Nickleby,* the same journal carried a proclamation from "Bos," set up in identical type, complaining of those who were "ambitious to rob us of a share of that fame and patronage which we hope and trust for these our humble exertions . . . to merit and receive," and declaring that such "offenders, delinquents, aggressors and criminals" were "contemptible insects, whom it would be the height of barbarity to tread upon." The same day he published the first number of *Nickelas Nickelbery.*[29]

Compared to such displays of comic brio, the scene Dickens shoe-horned into a later installment of the novel, in which Nicholas attacks writers who "hastily and crudely vamp up ideas not yet worked up by their original projector," and concludes that there is no difference between this sort of "pilfering" and "picking a man's pocket in the street," was little more than a piece of private grumbling. It also deliberately missed a much larger target. "Boz" had become such a marketable commodity that his name was enough to guarantee substantial sales, yet his publishers, far from protecting this commodity, seemed keen to work it as hard as they could. As early as June 1837, not content with splashing references to Boz across advertisements for his firm, Macrone had attempted to reissue *Sketches by Boz* in a monthly format identical to that of *Pickwick,* ignoring Dickens's plea that only a few months into the serialization of *Oliver Twist,* "the fact of my name being before the town, attached to three different publications at the same time, must prove seriously prejudicial to my reputation."[30] In the end, Macrone sold the copyright to Chapman and Hall, who reissued *Sketches* in twenty monthly parts from November 1837, and addressed—superficially—Dickens's fear of saturating the market by publishing it in pink paper covers rather than in *Pickwick*'s distinctive green. What neither publisher appeared willing to consider was that simply increasing the number of Dickens's publications might divide rather than multiply his impact; neither, it seemed, had learned the lesson offered by Sir Walter Scott's patchy sales towards the end of his life—a decline in popularity Dickens attributed to the simple fact that *"he never left off."*[31]

Some of the other problems generated by Dickens's fame were even harder to fix. Writing in the *Examiner* on September 2, 1838, Dickens tackled a controversial pamphlet that had been published by the son of James Ballantyne, Scott's former printer and business partner. The younger Ballantyne felt that his father had been unfairly marginalized by John Gibson Lockhart in Lockhart's seven-volume biography of the novelist. The detailed attention this pamphlet gave to relatively minor matters, Dickens wrote, such as Scott's disparaging nicknames for his printer, was proof that its author saw James Ballantyne as the key figure, forgetting that to most readers "he is only interesting as a second- or third-rate actor in the sad drama of Scott's life and death." Every life is a center to some people and at best a peripheral presence to others, but when it came to an author like Scott, Dickens concluded, "the magic of his name" was enough to make otherwise unremarkable individuals feel that they had been transformed by contact with him. At this point, a review that had started off as a defense of Lockhart came perilously close to turning into an exercise in self-justification, because while Dickens was now in a position to joke about his status as a writer "of universal popularity," he had also become increasingly conscious of the extent to which widespread fame denied him the opportunity to know his readers personally.[32] During 1838, his correspondents started to include several strangers, to whom he wrote declining an invitation to attend a dinner of "the Pickwick Club" in London (April 21); "expressing his pleasure at acquiring popularity in Germany" (July 9); and telling a firm of New York publishers that he would have to postpone writing something for them "until I visit America, which I hope to do before very long" (August 31).[33] Demands on his time were not yet at the level they would reach later in his career, when he would be the target of endless begging-letter writers, whose more inventive requests included a donkey and a Gloucester cheese. Nor was he yet forced to endure the attentions of genteel stalkers like Percy Fitzgerald, whose diary in 1858 listed the excitements ("saw him in street on Tuesday, and spent a feverish day tracking him about the town") and disappointments ("Dickens came not after all, but good-naturedly sent his card by post") of a life spent patiently following in his idol's footsteps.[34] In the eyes of the autograph hunters and lionizers, however, Dickens had already made the transition from popular literary figure to "public character."

This term, much in vogue during the 1830s, was routinely applied to anyone in the public eye, including the sort of individuals who might now be referred to as "celebrities" or "personalities," although usually with the expectation that there was some substance to ballast their fame. Dickens was not convinced; and in his early writing, the phrase is usually tweezered with invisible quotation marks to indicate his distaste. In *Sketches by Boz,* he applies it to actors who are paid to swell crowd scenes in professional theaters, as when a star-struck youth chats to "some mouldy-looking man in a fancy neckerchief, whose partially corked eyebrows, and half-rouged face, testify to the fact of his having just left the stage or the circle"; the "mingled air of envy and admiration" evinced by the youth's companions, Dickens reports, "sufficiently shows in what high admiration these public characters are held." By 1838, his tone had grown even sharper: the brief summary at the head of Chapter 42 of *Oliver Twist,* published in November, describes how Noah Claypole "becomes a public Character in the Metropolis," demonstrating the hunger for fame that could affect sneak thieves as well as theatrically inclined clerks, even if the strong implication is that in his case it will be achieved only through one of the broadsheets sold at the foot of the gallows.

The assumption that public characters willingly put themselves on display was satisfied by Dickens's election to the Athenaeum Club in May 1838, where he was one of an impressive cohort of new members including William Charles Macready and Charles Darwin, and his public profile was raised still further by two invitations that summer to Lady Holland's legendary parties at Holland House. (Caroline Fox, the sister-in-law of his notoriously autocratic hostess, met him there in 1839 and "liked everything but the intolerable dandyism of his dress.")[35] There were even suggestions that fame had turned his head, or at least had made him turn his back on his earlier life. On November 17, 1837, Edward Blackmore, one of Dickens's previous employers at the solicitors Ellis and Blackmore, spotted him at Covent Garden Theatre after a performance of *Fra Diavolo:* "He passed me two or three times," Blackmore reported, "without taking any notice and it appeared to me that he had no wish to recognize me."[36]

Yet if part of being a public character involved cultivating a certain image, the other part was wholly beyond the individual's control, depending as it did on the unpredictable forces of gossip and rumor. Earlier writers had sometimes used this to their advantage. In 1812, the year of Dickens's birth, Byron "awoke one morning and found [him]self famous" following the publication of the first two cantos of *Childe Harold's Pilgrimage,* a poem that deliberately encouraged readers to guess how far Byron's romantically gloomy hero, named "Childe Burun" in the original version, was based on himself. Subsequently he was swamped with letters, containing everything from locks of hair to marriage proposals, sent by excited female readers each of whom had filled in the teasing blanks of his poem and come to the conclusion that the only logical solution to his unhappiness was herself. The six elegies addressed to Thyrza, added to the first and second editions of the poem, were especially alluring, given that they seemed to open a window onto the innermost recesses of Byron's heart, inviting readers to imagine themselves as potential Thyrza substitutes. Not until 1974 was the gap between this fantasy and the reality of Byron's heartbreak revealed, when an extra elegy was discovered in the archives of his publisher John Murray; it was addressed to a beautiful boy ("Te, te, care puer"), and "Edleston, Edleston, Edleston," the name of the choirboy Byron had fallen in love with at Cambridge, was written across the top like a sad refrain.[37] This might have come as an unpleasant shock to some of his admirers in 1812, but most would have expected it to have been brought to their attention, even if it was bundled up in paraphrase and innuendo. Indeed, it was widely assumed that, as a public character,

Byron should expect to find his private life being pored over; as one reviewer explained in 1830, with reference to Thomas Moore's biography of the poet, "The phrase, 'intrusion into private life,' appears to us mere cant, as applied to a public character. Those who come openly forward to place the great stake of their lives on opinion, must expect its exercise . . . and it is unfair to repine, that the curiosity he himself has excited, he himself must gratify."[38]

Whereas Byron had enjoyed being the author of his own legend, creating a public image and then standing mockingly to one side, Dickens was more cautious. In *Pickwick* he had already satirized "Public Men" like Eatonswill's rival journalists Slurk and Pott (Pott is another figure who is described as a "public character"), and by the time he started *Oliver Twist* he had decided that fiction worked best not when the author spoke to his audience from a distance, like someone with a megaphone addressing a crowd, but when he presented himself as their friend.[39] This is why his original prospectus for *Bentley's* noted that its "management" had been "entrusted to 'Boz'—a gentleman with whom the public are already on pretty familiar terms."[40] It was a claim that was supported by its own "pretty familiar" tone, designed to make his readers feel that in opening his new journal they were also being taken into his confidence.

One should not sentimentalize Dickens's "friendship" with his readers. After reading *The Chimes* in 1844 to his inner social circle, he wrote to Catherine with evident satisfaction, "If you could have seen Macready last night—undisguisedly sobbing, and crying on the sofa, as I read—you would have felt (as I did) what a thing it is to have Power."[41] Audience reaction to his public appearances was sometimes even more extreme. During one reading he gleefully observed "a contagion of fainting," and estimated that "we had from a dozen to twenty ladies borne out, stiff and rigid," while an amateur production of *The Frozen Deep* staged in Manchester made him realize what "a good thing" it was "to have a couple of thousand people all rigid and frozen together, in the palm of one's hand."[42] His relationship with the reading public was sometimes less like an exercise of sympathy than a battle of wills. But from *Oliver Twist* onwards, as he slowly moved away from representing himself as "Boz," he tried to put the more generous lessons of *Pickwick* into practice. His writing would deliberately tangle together Dickens the private individual and Dickens the public figure. He would become the sort of novelist who could expand horizons, with a narrative voice that moved freely in time and space, while making his readers feel that he was at their side throughout as "guide, philosopher and friend." This was a phrase borrowed from Alexander Pope's *Essay on Man* that he rarely employed without applying irony in varying thicknesses: William Dorrit's only flaw as a "fraternal guide, philosopher and friend" in *Little Dorrit* is that he brings ruin on his brother, while Dickens's preface to the 1848 Cheap Edition of *Nicholas Nickleby* recalled that he was inspired to write about Dotheboys Hall after reading of a boy who came home from school with a suppurated abscess "in consequence of his Yorkshire guide, philosopher, and friend, having ripped it open with an inky penknife." But Dickens tended to reserve his greatest mockery for the ideas to which he was most strongly attracted, and these barbs did not prevent him from attempting to embody the ideal with perfect seriousness in his own writing.

It was not always a straightforward process, particularly when Dickens proved himself to be so willing to blur the line between his real and fictional selves. For all his insistence on biographical accuracy (in February 1838 he sent a detailed list of corrections to the editor of the *Durham Advertiser* when one of its journalists misreported some facts about his life), even after publishing *David Copperfield* he was tempted to treat his life story as just another narrative that needed to be edited or rewritten.[43] His different accounts of the origin of *Pickwick* provide a case in point. In the original 1837 preface, Dickens recalled how "deferring to the judgment of others in the outset of the undertaking, [the author] adopted the machinery of the club, which was suggested as that best adapted to his purpose." By the time of the Charles Dickens Edition in 1867, his memory having been sharpened by three decades of success, he had changed his mind: "My views being deferred to, I thought of Mr. Pickwick, and wrote the first number." The question of which version is true is less significant than Dickens's assumption that the facts were as easy to alter as his adjectives and commas. It is a revision of which Mr. Bounderby, the supposedly self-made man in *Hard Times* who turns out to have invented a whole alternative past for himself, would be proud.

In April 1838, Dickens celebrated his second wedding anniversary, which he spent not only with Catherine, as one might expect, but also with Forster, whose appearances on such occasions were starting to make him seem less like a friend than a permanent best man. (It is unlikely that their relationship went further than intimate friendship, but Dickens was not embarrassed about employing the most tenderly romantic language when reminding Forster that "it was your feeling for me and mine for you that first brought us together, and I hope will keep us so, till death do us part"—an echo of the marriage service that would turn out to be far more appropriate for Forster than for Catherine.)[44] The same social mix of family and friends was carried through into the summer. Most of June and July was spent in Twickenham, where the guests visiting his rented Regency villa included Ainsworth, Thackeray, Maclise, Hullah, and Beard, in addition to Forster, who enjoyed strenuous sessions of bar-leaping, bowling, and quoits, together with gentler amusements such as the "Gammon Aeronautical Balloon Association for the Encouragement of Science and the Consumption of Spirits," all conducted by a host who evidently relished his role as master of the revels. It was a pastoral interlude every bit as idyllic as the one he had fashioned for his hero in February's number of *Oliver Twist,* although in some ways it harked back to a more distant past, reviving the kind of entertainments that had been popular in rural communities before they were overtaken by more commercially driven leisure pursuits.[45]

Dickens also kept up to date with events happening in the outside world. The most spectacular of these was Queen Victoria's coronation, which brought London to a standstill on June 28 with a day of public festivities that included free entry to the theaters, fireworks displays, and an enormous fair in Hyde Park.[46] No fewer than 400,000 tourists were said to have come to the city just to catch a glimpse of Victoria's carriage rolling over the specially graveled roads to Westminster Abbey; and among the crush of revelers was Dickens, who had been asked to write an account for the *Examiner*. In the end, his contribution amounted to just four paragraphs on "the amusements of the people" in Hyde Park, in which he described the numerous refreshment booths and entertainment tents offering everything "from tragedy to tumbling"—a sight that gave "a strong and additional proof that the many are at least as capable of decent enjoyment as the few."

Unremarkable in itself, Dickens's brief sketch takes on a very different complexion when viewed in its original context, because it was stitched onto the end of an unusually skeptical article entitled "The Queen's Coronation" that was almost certainly written by the *Examiner*'s radical editor, Albany Fonblanque. Having started by confessing that "we do not profess ourselves admirers of a Coronation," Fonblanque continued by criticizing such lavish displays of pomp as altogether "a thing opposed to the growing sense of the times," which he characterized as "the ascendancy of the Many as distinguished from the Few." This is why, he argued, it is necessary to consider the kind of entertainment that appeals to the social majority, and "by what means such a taste as this is best to be cultivated in its noblest and most intelligent shapes." Read against this background, Dickens's contribution assumes a double significance. First, in describing Hyde Park's "eager, busy crowd," he answers Fonblanque's question by pointing out that the "happy, hearty" nature of their fun entirely refuted the "crude and narrow" criticisms of those who assumed that the behavior of "the very worst members of society" was an accurate guide to "the whole mass of the people." Second, and more subtly, by choosing Dickens to conclude a piece on how to entertain "the Many," Fonblanque quietly answered his own question.[47] An editorial that began by complaining about the coronation of a new monarch ended by offering an alternative: someone who was prepared to earn popular acclaim. It was far more radical than the assumptions lying behind Thackeray's mock-coronation of Dickens in 1840: "Long mayest thou, O Boz! reign over thy comic kingdom. . . . Mighty prince! at thy imperial feet, Titmarsh, humblest of thy servants, offers his vows of loyalty and his humblest tribute of praise."[48] The *Examiner* was implicitly confirming Dickens as the champion of a new democracy of taste.

For several months before Victoria's coronation, the press had been filled with surveys of earlier reigns, particularly that of Elizabeth I, and although the ceremony was widely seen as a celebration of historical continuity, inevitably it also encouraged a good deal of peering into the future. What would a Victorian age look like? Or sound like? While most commentators were cautiously optimistic, they recognized that 1838 was a pivotal year that might turn the nation's fortunes in any one of a number of directions. "What the future may bring forth during the time that Victoria holds the stewardship of these realms, it is, of course, impossible to conjecture," wrote William Cox in an article on the contemporary literary scene, before going on to do precisely that. For most readers, his list of the "many excellent and charming writers" active at the time now reads less like a literary *Who's Who* than a simple *Who?* He names "Croly, Milman, Horace Smith, Theodore Hook, Banim . . . not forgetting Allan Cunningham, Professor Wilson . . ." ("Not forgetting" carries a particular sting in its tail, given that most of these authors are now only marginally better known than "Anon.") Cox's principal tip for future success was Edward Bulwer, who "remains, without dispute, the leading *active* great man." It was a sensible choice: an MP since 1831, who had spoken in favor of the Reform Bill, Bulwer had a much longer track record of success than Dickens, dating back to the publication of *Pelham* in 1828, and his later works such as *The Last Days of Pompeii* (1834) had sold in the tens of thousands. Moreover, he was unmistakably a novelist, who published weighty three-volume works under his own name, rather than miscellanies and paper-covered pamphlets under a chirpy pseudonym.

Yet the popularity of Bulwer's elegant but orotund fiction was waning; and although Cox may not have realized it at the time, his hopes for the future of the novel were much more likely to be answered by the young writer he singled out as being "in the hey-day of his vigour." "Something fresh and vigorous is wanting," he urged, "and any great original mind manifesting itself . . . at the present time, would be sure of the attention and admiration of millions." "Fresh," "vigorous," and "original" were hardly appropriate adjectives for Edward "It-was-a-dark-and-stormy-night" Bulwer, but they were an excellent fit for "the graphick and eccentrick 'Boz.'"[49] Even Bulwer might have agreed. "In life as it is, lies the true empire of modern fiction," he wrote in July; "in the stir and ferment, the luxuriant ideas and conflicting hopes, the working reason, the excited imagination that belongs to this era of rapid and visible transition."[50] It seems appropriate that the phrase he chose as the climax of this list—"excited imagination"—had been employed by Dickens four months earlier in the March installment of *Oliver Twist*.[51] It is even more appropriate that Dickens returned to the same phrase in many of his future works, including *Barnaby Rudge, Bleak House,* and *Dombey and Son,* as he set about developing his reputation as the creative fulcrum of the age.

Highlighting the role played by the imagination was an unusual approach to "this era of rapid and visible transition." Far more typical was Walter Besant, looking back in 1888 from the perspective of Queen Victoria's Golden Jubilee, celebrated the year before; his list of major achievements in the previous fifty years was driven principally by steam and statistics. While the decades prior to Victoria's accession had been little more than an overhang from the eighteenth century, he argued, "The nineteenth century actually began with steam communication by sea; with steam machinery; with railways; with telegraphs; with the development of the colonies; with the admission of the people to the government of the country; with the opening of the Universities; with the spread of science; with the revival of the democratic spirit."[52] The seeds of all these developments had been planted by the end of 1838. Highlights of that year included the installation of the nation's first commercial electric telegraph alongside a fifteen-mile stretch of railway track; the publication in May of the People's Charter and National Petition, with its demands for a range of political reforms including universal male suffrage; and the towing of the *Temeraire,* one of the most famous of Nelson's fighting ships, up the Thames to a wrecking dock on September 6, a scene depicted the following year in Turner's painting *The Fighting "Temeraire,"* in which a squat steam tug sits alongside the doomed ship, ghost-pale against a bloody sunset. By contrast, 1838 also saw the launch of the *Great Western,* the first Atlantic steamship, which on July 21 was puffing towards New York with 118 passengers on board, including the soprano Jane Shirreff, who had recently appeared lightly disguised in *Sketches of Young Gentlemen* as "that talented and lady-like girl Sheriff."[53]

When we view these events together, it is hard not to see them as cogs in a single machine moving inexorably towards what we now think of as the Victorian age, although at the time they lacked the satisfying congruence of hindsight. Nor were they all accepted without question. With so many possible futures opening up, the public mood was far more ambivalent—excited and wary, optimistic and skeptical—and Dickens, for all his commitment to progress, was quick to recognize how dangerous it would be to put the driving forces of science and technology into the wrong hands. His caution was expressed in two additional papers he published in *Bentley's,* a "Full Report of the First Meeting of the Mudfog Association for the Advancement of Everything" in October 1837, and a follow-up "Report of the Second Meeting . . ." in September 1838. Both were parodies of the work undertaken by the British Association for the Advancement of Science, which had been founded in 1831 "to give a stronger impulse and more systematic direction to scientific enquiry," reflecting contemporary attempts to professionalize the discipline—efforts that would also lead one of the period's greatest polymaths, William Whewell, to coin the term "scientist" in 1834.[54] (Paradoxically, the drive to professionalize science went hand-in-hand with attempts to popularize it: 1838 also marked the opening of the Polytechnic Institution at 309 Regent Street, where new inventions could be demonstrated to the public.) The British Association was already a soft target, mocked in the *Times* as the "British Ass," and criticized for confusing genuine research with humbug and quackery.[55] Dickens had previously poked fun at it in the opening chapter of *Pickwick*, where Mr. Pickwick's "Observations on the Theory of Tittlebats" are received as an immense contribution "to the advancement of knowledge, and the diffusion of learning," and in these new papers he was quick to remind readers of the shadowy alternative life the Association had been leading in the world of satire.

Some of the action is set in the "Pig and Tinder Box" public house, a detail Dickens had lifted from George Cruikshank's 1835 *Comic Almanack*, where a parody of the Association's "Proceedings" had also included a report sent from an investigator who "has discovered that there are exactly nine millions, one hundred and sixty-four thousand, five hundred and thirty-three hairs on a tom-cat's tail," as well as a paper read by Sawney Suck-Egg, Esq., "on the possibility of extending the realms of space, and adding to the duration of eternity."[56] Dickens went even further. Not only did he frame his account in the breathily excited style made familiar by real reports of the Association's activities in the *Athenaeum*, but he chose examples that brought together lofty abstraction and finicky precision in ever more absurd forms: the suggestion that "infant schools and houses of industry" should be established for performing fleas so that they could contribute to "the productive power of the country," for instance, or an "animated discussion" about the cranial development of a murderer, whose skull is produced for inspection before being reclaimed by a member of the public who declares it to be "a coker-nut as my brother-in-law has been a-carvin' to hornament his new baked tatur-stall."

By locating his version of the organization in Mudfog, Dickens was implicitly linking it to the satire on political economy he had already published in the opening chapters of *Oliver Twist;* the link became an explicit in-joke when a member asks "whether it would be possible to administer—say, the twentieth part of a grain of bread and cheese to all grown-up paupers, and the fortieth part to children," and is told that "Professor Muff was willing to stake his professional reputation on the perfect adequacy of such a quantity of food to the support of human life—in workhouses." A genuine fear that the world would become disenchanted by science, drained of all meaning other than tables of facts and figures, is sunk into

Dickens's account of the calculations made by Mr. Slug concerning the number of fairy-tale books in circulation around London: *Jack the Giant-killer*, 7,943; *Ditto and Beanstalk*, 8,621; *Ditto and Jill*, 1,998. Here, too, he was following Cruikshank's lead, because the *Comic Almanack* had included a description in which the "Horticultural Society of Seven Dials" is presented by the Society of Antiquaries "with the identical pumpkin converted by the fairy into Cinderella's chariot."[57]

Where Dickens departs from Cruikshank is in describing crackpot schemes so outlandish that the imaginative drive of his writing quickly outpaces its targets. One inventor removes a tiny railway engine from his waistcoat pocket, and explains how it can be attached to the feet when needed, allowing commuters to whiz into work "at the easy rate of sixty-five miles an hour." Another suggests that the "enormous number of twenty-one million nine hundred thousand skewers" purchased annually from pet food sellers could be used to construct "a first-rate vessel of war" for the navy, to be called the *Royal Skewer*. Best of all are the detailed plans published in the September 1838 Mudfog paper for "an entirely new police force, composed exclusively of automaton figures," to be kept within a walled theme park, where they could be beaten up by young noblemen wanting to let off steam, at which they "would utter divers groans, mingled with entreaties for mercy, thus rendering the illusion complete, and the enjoyment perfect." This boisterous fun would be followed by an appearance before two automaton magistrates, made with "wooden heads, of course"; whenever a small spring was pressed, one of them would burble "that he was sorry to see gentlemen in such a situation" and the other would "express a fear that the policeman was intoxicated." In Cruikshank's illustration (Figure 26), a clock-faced clerk takes notes while two policemen display a selection of detachable heads and limbs; just visible in the background are their colleagues, neatly stacked on shelves like library books.

Much of Dickens's satire is directed towards the sense of entitlement demonstrated by the sort of young noblemen who might have enjoyed some of the park's other attractions, including permission to drive their carriages onto pavements and knock down pedestrians "procured from the workhouse at a very small charge per head"; but the passage as a whole is far more than a topical swipe at the gentry. Dickens's policemen and magistrates are hybrid figures who resemble some of the celebrated real automata of the age, such as the Silver Lady, a foot-high figure bought by Charles Babbage in 1834, which "used an eye-glass occasionally, and bowed frequently, as if recognising her acquaintances," but also fairy-tale creatures like those found in the tales of E. T. A Hoffmann.[58] Part fact and part fiction, Dickens's figures reveal his suspicion of scientists like David Brewster, a founding member of the British Association, whose *Letters on Natural Magic* (1832), in setting out to expose how conjuring tricks and mechanical marvels worked, had dourly equated enchantment with fraud, and scoffed at automata as no more than "toys which once amused the vulgar" but "are now employed in extending the power and promoting the civilisation of our species."[59] Brewster congratulated himself on being hard-headed; but in Dickens's view, such efforts to unweave the rainbow were in fact as wooden-headed as one of his mechanical magistrates. A civilization that could be perfectly measured would be unworthy of the name, and in this context Dickens's fantasy does more than satirize genteel muggers and the impersonal machinery of the law. It also finds a place for the imagination in an age increasingly obsessed with scientific and technological progress.

❧ ❧ ❧

A few weeks after the publication of his second Mudfog paper, Dickens found himself witnessing a version of this progress firsthand. At the end of October, accompanied by Hablot Browne, he traveled through the Midlands and North Wales to visit the cotton mills, stopping off en route at Warwick Castle and the ruins of Kenilworth. Compared to these places, with their tranquillity and sense of history, the industrial north came as something of a shock, with its "miles of cinder-paths and blazing furnaces and roaring steam-engines" that loomed through the cold wet fog, creating "such a mass of dirt gloom misery as I never before witnessed."[60]

Three years later, this landscape would reappear as the terrifying waste-
land Little Nell wanders through in *The Old Curiosity Shop,* in which
tall brick chimneys point accusingly at the sky as they pour out their
"plague of smoke," and strange engines spin and writhe "like tortured
creatures; clanking their iron chains, shrieking in their rapid whirl from
time to time as though in torment unendurable, and making the ground
tremble with their agonies." It is a modernized version of Dante's Inferno,
a steam-powered hell, although what shocked Dickens in person brings
unmistakable energy to his writing. His choice of metaphor is especially
noteworthy. These engines are in torment because they are forever in mo-
tion but unable to escape; with their clanking chains and shrieks of agony,
they resemble patients in Bedlam or captured wild animals, close relations to the mechanical pistons that nod their heads up and down like
"melancholy mad elephants" in *Hard Times.*

In 1838, however, Dickens managed to escape this landscape by
means of a different kind of engine that produced a "rapid whirl": the
railway. Just two years earlier, in the last major journey of *Pickwick,* he
had sent his hero from Birmingham to London by stagecoach. Now there
was an alternative: the London-to-Birmingham route, one of the first
commercial lines in the country, had opened for business in September,
and on Thursday November 8 Dickens used it to return the 112 miles to
London, departing early in the morning with Forster, who had met him
at the Adelphi Hotel in Liverpool, and arriving at Euston Square Station
later the same day. It was a key moment in his career.

The London and Birmingham Railway was widely seen as one of the
wonders of the age. Thomas Roscoe's record of its construction, which
he published the following year alongside a handy checklist of the land-
marks that were visible from the carriage windows, opened with a paean
to "unquestionably the greatest public work ever executed, either in ancient or modern times"; in comparison, he announced, the Great Wall of
China "sinks totally into the shade." Warming to his theme, he offered
some impressively improbable statistics: the cost of construction laid out
in pennies would "form a continuous band round the earth at the equa-

tor," while the amount of earth moved would circle the globe more than three times "if spread in a band one foot high and one foot broad." Even the "Grand Entrance" to Euston Square acquires an edge of excitement in his writing: with its "majestic Doric portico" leading to an iron-columned railway shed "brilliantly lighted with gas," customers walking into it from the street could experience a form of architectural time travel. Frequently Roscoe abandons analysis altogether, and simply sits back to admire what amounted to a manmade form of the sublime:

> When it is considered that the mighty impulse which bears hundreds of human beings at the speed of from twenty to forty miles in an hour, is given without a breath of animated life—that not one effort is made except by blind inanimate matter . . . the effect of the whole is indescribably strange and impressive, and calculated to raise a new train of thought and reflection.[61]

Ironically, the joke of that last sentence was not an original one. Trains were revealing themselves to be the shuttles of power and trade that would weave the new fabric of the nation, and already it had become clear that this would be a disorienting process. The railway shrank space and time, but in doing so it removed from passengers any sense of personal contact with their surroundings. Traveling at a steady eight to ten miles per hour, the stagecoach passenger physically experienced every rut and pothole; the railway passenger merely gazed out the window at a series of identical cuttings and embankments. Worse still, traveling at up to forty miles per hour meant that the world became an unrecognizable blur: in a letter dated August 22, 1837, Victor Hugo described the view from a train window as one in which flowers "are no longer flowers but flecks, or rather streaks, of red or white," while towns and trees "perform a crazy mingling dance on the horizon."[62]

Spatial disorientation was often mixed with a sense of historical dislocation. The illustrations for Thomas Roscoe's book show groups of traditionally dressed farm laborers impassively looking on as railway lines slice their way through the countryside; every scene is as orderly as a toy locomotive chugging past wooden cows and sponge-topped trees. Dickens's attitude was far more ambivalent. In the editorial farewell to *Bentley's* he published in February 1839, he pointed out that "we have fallen upon strange times, and live in days of constant shiftings and changes," and he recalled a railway journey from Manchester to London during which "I suddenly fell into another train—a mixed train—of reflection" (the old joke again) on seeing the guard "looking mournfully about him as if in dismal recollection of the old roadside public-house—the blazing fire—the glass of foaming ale—the buxom handmaid and admiring hangers-on of tap-room and stable." The following year, in *Master Humphrey's Clock*, he gave Sam Weller's coachman father, Mr. Weller senior, a speech expressing his grave suspicions about the engine as "a nasty, wheezin,' creakin,' gaspin,' puffin,' bustin' monster," having experienced the competition firsthand after "a goin' down to Birmingham by the rail."

Railways could also give rise to more personal "trains of reflection." *Mugby Junction,* a Christmas story Dickens published in December 1866, opens with a solitary traveler passing through a make-believe Midlands railway station. A "shadowy train" goes by him in the gloom, and as the metaphor develops it is revealed to be a sad projection of his life. The survivor of an unhappy childhood, who is later "coupled to" a miserable career, the traveler drags his past behind him like a set of grimy freight wagons: "lumbering cares, dark meditations, huge dim disappointments, monotonous years, a long jarring line of the discords of a solitary and unhappy existence."[63] Typically, Dickens manages to find some wry comedy in the situation by making his own sentence mimic the "long jarring line" of the train, coupling his clanking clauses together and slowly grinding towards the buffers of a full stop. As the story continues, however, Dickens's hero comes to realize that even the longest and most heavily laden train is not doomed to follow the same path forever. Gazing down at the junction from above, he observes the "wonderful ways" in which different railway lines cross and curve among one another, veer off in unexpected directions, or suddenly double back upon themselves. And once the traveler accepts that his life, too, is "a Junction of many branches, invisible as well as visible, and joined . . . to an endless number of byways," he discovers that he is free to travel in any number of directions, and connect with any number of other people's lifelines. The "gentleman for Nowhere," as he is known around the station, becomes the gentleman for everywhere.

Dickens might have been writing about himself on the day he passed through Euston Square Station. He had returned to London with some urgency to see *Oliver Twist* through the press, because although it was to continue being serialized for several more months in *Bentley's,* he had persuaded (or cajoled, or bullied) Richard Bentley into agreeing that it should also be published as a book, in place of the work he had undertaken to write in 1836: "a Novel, the Title of which is not determined, to form three Volumes."[64] By November 8 the title had long been determined, and within a few days Dickens had tidied up the final details of publication, after checking the proofs of the final chapters and requesting a new illustration from Cruikshank to replace the rejected "Fireside Plate." All he still had to decide was which name should appear on the title page. The first few sheets off the press ascribed the novel to "Boz"—the name under which *Oliver Twist* had appeared in *Bentley's.* Then Dickens changed his mind. On November 12 he wrote to Bentley asking that his advertisements be revised: "The substitution of 'Charles Dickens' for 'Boz,' is the extent of the alteration I wish in them."[65] The title page was also to be altered. After *Sketches by Boz,* the *Pickwick Papers* ("Edited by Boz"), and the serialized version of *Oliver Twist* ("BY BOZ"), Dickens was ready to remove his disguise: *Oliver Twist. By Charles Dickens.*[66] What had started as a satirical sketch on workhouses was now being retrospectively claimed as a novel worthy of carrying his name. It was a literary romance every bit as satisfying as Oliver's discovery that he had been a gentleman all along.

The three volumes of *Oliver Twist* appeared in booksellers' windows just in time to take the place of October's issue of the *Edinburgh Review,* which had carried a long and appreciative article by T. H. Lister praising Dickens's "remarkable powers of observation . . . exuberant humour . . .

mastery in the pathetic . . . dramatic power . . . great truthfulness," and pointing out that the most popular author of the day was "well entitled to his popularity—and not likely to lose it."[67] Dickens was "delighted." "It is all even *I* could wish," he told Forster, "and what more can I say!"[68]

Postscript: Signing Off

"Which way?" asked Newman, wistfully.
"To Kingston first," replied Nicholas.
"And where afterwards?" asked Newman. "Why won't you tell me?"
"Because I scarcely know myself, good friend," rejoined Nicholas.
—*Nicholas Nickleby,* Chapter 22, September 1838

Dickens hated goodbyes. According to his daughter Mamie, he had "such an intense dislike for leave-taking that he always, when it was possible, shirked a farewell," and "knowing this dislike, [we] used only to wave our hands or give him a silent kiss when parting."[1] Only once did George Dolby, the manager of his final public reading tour, hear him say "good bye" rather than his "usual parting words" of "good day" or "good night," expressions which were "always followed quickly by an appointment for our next meeting."[2] It was as if he were trying to give his life the same serialized form as his fiction.

Nobody was more puzzled by this need than Dickens himself. "Why is it," he asked in *The Old Curiosity Shop,* that on the eve of a long voyage, "while we have the fortitude to act farewell have not the nerve to say it," so that even close friends "will separate with the usual look, the usual pressure of the hand, planning one final interview for the morrow, while each knows that it is but a poor feint to save the pain of uttering that one word?" Dickens's fiction is full of scenes in which this pain is either deferred as long as possible, or drawn out in a way that allowed him to play the roles of both torturer and victim. He was especially attracted to the long goodbye:

> "Good bye. Good bye. I can hardly believe you're going. It seems, now, but yesterday that you came. Good bye! my dear old fellow!"
>
> —*Martin Chuzzlewit*

"Good bye, Pip!—You will always keep the name of Pip, you know."
"Yes, Miss Havisham."
"Good bye, Pip!"

—*Great Expectations*

"So good bye," said Nicholas; "good bye, good bye."

—*Nicholas Nickleby*

Dickens was equally reluctant to part with his characters. The preface he wrote for *David Copperfield* soon after finishing the novel pointed out that an author "feels as if he were dismissing some portion of himself into the shadowy world, when a crowd of the creatures of his brain are going from him for ever."[3] But even as he reluctantly ushered his characters towards the exit, he found ever more ingenious ways of cheating his own conclusions. Never did Dickens prove his mastery of suspense better than when his stories had apparently finished.

Three years after the hero of the *Pickwick Papers* explained that "My rambles, Sam, are over," he came blinking into view again in *Master Humphrey's Clock,* when Dickens decided to boost flagging sales by bringing his most popular characters back to life. *Great Expectations* ended twice, as he changed his mind about his original downbeat conclusion and replaced it with a happier alternative, thereby allowing Pip and Estella to walk out of the novel hand-in-hand while also preserving the original idea of two stories going in separate directions. Pip and Estella are reconciled, but only at the cost of Dickens's narrative being forced down diverging paths instead. In other novels Dickens simply suspended the usual force of full stops, turning them into something more like buttons marked "pause" or wormholes into possible futures. In the case of *David Copperfield,* he answered his fears about his characters "going from him forever" by having the hero project himself forward to his deathbed: "realities are melting from me," says David as he expires, but the saintly Agnes is still beside him "pointing upward!" *Bleak House* went further still by breaking off with Esther's "even supposing—," where the dash did not so much draw a line under the story as open it out even further. For a character called Esther Summerson, it was the perfect ending: a dash that was like a distant horizon on which the sun was forever rising.

One of the lists in Dickens's memorandum book was "Available names," and among the possibilities he adopted (a neat tick appears next to "Sapsea," which went into *Edwin Drood*, and another next to "Silverman," the hero of *George Silverman's Explanation*), or ignored (Towndling, Mood, Guff, Treble, Chilby . . .) was a section on "Terminations":

> ———straw
> ridge
> bridge
> brook
> bring
> ring
> ing[4]

The final name-endings produced by Dickens's imaginative whittling (-bring, -ring, -ing) look suspiciously like present participles. That might not have surprised his critics, some of whom, such as G. H. Lewes, enjoyed comparing his characters to wooden toys that ran on wheels, or "brainless frogs" that repeatedly performed the same actions when tickled or pricked with a pin.[5] Yet Dickens was keenly aware of his characters as creatures who needed to be kept alive by the flow of ink from day to day, and whose identities were consequently no more fixed than his own. Even their signatures suggested the potential for future developments, as when *Little Dorrit*'s Rigaud adds his assumed name, Blandois, "in a small complicated hand" next to the name of the Dorrit family in the visitors' book of the Great St. Bernard monastery, a signature which ends "with a long lean flourish, not unlike a lasso, thrown at the rest of the names." It is a thinly veiled warning of the threat he will pose in the chapters to come.

Dickens's own signature was no less full of potential. On October 27, 1838, shortly before returning to London for the publication of *Oliver*

Twist, he signed the visitors' book at Shakespeare's birthplace in Stratford-upon-Avon: *"Charles Dickens Doughty Street London."*[6] It was a pilgrimage that would remain popular throughout the nineteenth century, as writers came to pay their respects or stake a claim. From Byron to Tennyson, the visitors' book was full of names jostling for position to take on Shakespeare's role as the nation's favorite writer. Dickens's signature was more settled now: the neat copperplate of the early letters had been replaced by a busy adult scrawl, and the confident flourish underpinned "Dickens" more strongly than "Charles." It was far closer to the signature that from 1867 onwards would be printed in gold on the covers of Chapman and Hall's twenty-one-volume "Charles Dickens Edition," a stamp of authority signifying Dickens's "watchfulness over his own edition."[7] But in 1838 his literary identity was still invitingly open-ended. A year later, on the second anniversary of the publication of the *Pickwick Papers* in volume form, he sent the publisher Edward Chapman a first edition inscribed with a passage he had added to *Oliver Twist* during one of his bitter disputes with Richard Bentley:

> "How should you like to grow up a clever man, and write books?" said the old gentleman.
>
> "I think I would rather read them Sir," replied Oliver.
>
> "What! Wouldn't you like to be a book-writer?" said the old gentleman.
>
> Oliver considered a little while, and at last said he should think it would be a much better thing to be a bookseller; upon which the old gentleman laughed heartily, and declared he had said a very good thing, which Oliver felt glad to have done, though he by no means knew what it was.

This inscription was signed "Charles Dickens" and witnessed by "Boz": two names given in two different styles of handwriting.[8]

Dickens's public image was equally divided. In 1838, Weld Taylor lithographed the 1837 chalk drawing by Samuel Laurence, and reproduced it as "the first authorised published portrait of the Novelist," together with a facsimile of Boz's signature, although Taylor later recalled that "he was half inclined to have his own name—but I think he was guided by my opinion that his name was at that time scarcely familiar enough for the public, whereas everybody was acquainted with the writings of 'Boz.'"[9] Other artists were much less sure of themselves, or of Dickens: in 1837, Horace Pym produced a drawing which he inscribed "Charles Dickens," although when Henry Burnett made a copy in 1838 the name reverted to "Boz." Meanwhile, an advertisement for *Bentley's* drawn by Browne in March 1837 (Figure 27), which showed Dickens leading a burly porter staggering under the weight of copies of the magazine, assumed he could be recognized without any name at all.

This confusion would last for another decade. Reviewing Daniel Maclise's portrait of Dickens in the 1840 Royal Academy exhibition, Thackeray seemed unsure whether he was looking at one writer or two: "Here we have the real identical man Dickens: the artist must have understood the inward 'Boz' as well as the outward before he made this admirable representation of him."[10] In fact, Dickens's twin identities coexisted on the page until the publication of *Dombey and Son* in monthly parts, "By CHARLES DICKENS," in 1847–1848. Before then, "Boz" was delegated to write the comic works and paper-covered installments, while "Dickens" devoted himself to serious journalism, adding his name to the novels only when they were reprinted in hardback form. That did not prevent many readers from being disappointed with the later works, or harking back nostalgically to their earlier, funnier predecessors.[11] Although the writer who had "risen like a rocket" had certainly not "come down like the stick," as had been prophesied, anyone reading *Bleak House* or *Our Mutual Friend* was bound to feel that something had been lost. Boz was less like a firework than the first stage of a space rocket that had been jettisoned so that Dickens's reputation could continue to rise.

For Dickens, on the other hand, the uncertainty over his name was far less significant than the other doubts and self-divisions that continued to haunt him. No author enjoyed greater success; no author was more terrified of failure. The two feelings were inextricably woven together. As late as 1842, during a trip to America in which a barber sold off locks of his hair and New Yorkers queued for hours merely to shake him by the hand, he decided that "I should have lived and died, poor, unnoticed," if he had been born in the country currently lionizing him.[12]

His name was now such a valuable property that Richard Bentley was using it in advertisements for other authors as a form of endorsement by association; in January 1839, when Dickens resigned as editor of *Bentley's Miscellany*, Bentley offered him an extra £40 per year just for the privilege of continuing to use it.[13] Yet this was the same name that was still being put at risk by the begging-letters and debts of his father, who had a rather different understanding of what it meant to write for money, and would continue to do so until Dickens instructed his solicitor Thomas Mitton to insert a notice in the newspapers disowning the unpaid bills of anyone "having or purporting to have the surname of our said client."[14]

A month after the publication of *Oliver Twist*, Dickens again tried his hand at drama, with a farce entitled *The Lamplighter*. This time his effort was rejected by Macready, who noted in his diary on December 5 that "the dialogue is very good . . . but I am not sure about the meagreness of the plot."[15] Dickens responded by converting it into a piece of madcap comic prose, "The Lamplighter's Story," which he subsequently published in *The Pic Nic Papers*. It signaled the end of his attempts to be a professional playwright, although that did not mean he abandoned the theater. Instead, he absorbed it even further into his fiction, as can be seen in *Nicholas Nickleby*, already halfway through its serialization, which revealed how successfully he could adopt the hammy dialogue and melodramatic posturing he openly satirized but secretly thrilled to.

That was only one of the alternative lives his novels would continue to probe, because in becoming a novelist Dickens had found a form that was capacious enough to accommodate all the other possible identities, all the abandoned stories and apocryphal selves, that would be squeezed out of his own future. And he is still changing. Not even death has stopped him, as generations of later readers have gone on enjoying his work, revising what it means, repeatedly returning to a writer who seems as reluctant as ever to say goodbye. He is still becoming Dickens. So perhaps the best way to leave him is not with a conclusion but with a moment frozen in time, like one of those Victorian theatrical tableaux in which the hero pauses center-stage before his story continues.

It is December 12, 1838, and Dickens is attending a dinner of the Literary Fund, established in 1790 to give financial aid to impoverished authors, and now one of several organizations aiming to enhance the standing of professional writers like himself.[16] There is still a long way to go. It is only four years since an article entitled "The Influence of the Press" super-ciliously tucked "novels" into a list of "those lighter productions which attract and are alone read by the multitude—newspapers, magazines, re-views, novels, superficial travels . . ."; but already Dickens's works have caused a startling revaluation of what the novel is and what it can do.[17] His presence here tonight rounds off a period of exactly five years since his first story was published, in December 1833—five years during which, as Thackeray will later note with mingled admiration and envy, "he calmly and modestly came and took his place at the head of English literature."[18]

As dessert is passed around and cigars are lit, Dickens stands to speak. He is not yet twenty-seven years old, and it is a shock to see how young he still looks; a few years from now, when he attends a banquet in his honor at Edinburgh, he will be described as "little, slender, pale-faced, boyish-looking."[19] During this later speech, despite the "tremendous" sight of hundreds of well-wishers crammed into the city's Waterloo Rooms, he will pride himself on remaining "as cool as a cucumber"; and he is equally self-possessed at the moment, standing before an audience of his peers.[20] He speaks confidently but not arrogantly; he cracks jokes but without softening the look of steely determination in his eyes. There is the trace of a lisp, a burr or slight thickening of his voice on certain words, but otherwise it is a perfectly pitched performance. (So crisp is his phrasing, so polished his timing, that some of his listeners suspect the speech may have been rehearsed.) He sits down to warm applause, and one of the other writers present—perhaps Ainsworth, though it is hard to tell in the creeping fog of cigar smoke—raises his glass to propose a toast.

It is the sort of snapshot that will shortly be available in a form other than words. Within less than a month, on January 7, 1839, the French Academy of Sciences will announce the invention of the daguerreotype, the first commercially viable form of photography; and after the French government purchases the patent from the inventor, Louis Daguerre, the world will start to fill up with images sliced out of time. Soon the drawing rooms of Dickens's readers will teem with miniature versions of themselves, flattened into albums or staring out glassily from the walls. No social gathering will be complete without a camera there to capture it for posterity, producing all those unsmiling scenes—solemnity being the only way, when exposure times are so long, of ensuring that one's features do not disappear in a blur of movement—that are so familiar, and so unfair, as images of the Victorian age.

But what if Dickens's life had been stopped in a different way that evening? What if he had died—from a rogue chicken bone, perhaps, or a massive stroke like the one that would eventually kill him in 1870—as suddenly and unexpectedly as Mary Hogarth? Suddenly the future would have as many holes in it as a sponge. Most of the characters depicted in Robert Buss's unfinished painting *Dickens's Dream* (Figure 28) would melt back into the shadows. The English language would quietly contract, losing more than two hundred words and phrases Dickens brought into fiction for the first time: *boredom, butter-fingers, cross-fire, devil-may-care, dustbin, fairy story, footlights, funky, melodramatically, messiness, narratable, old dear, paperchase, seediness, set piece, sharp practice, slow-coach, snobbish, spectacularly, unyielding, whoosh* . . . Above all, there would be a Dickens-shaped gap in literary history, which would be felt whenever someone opened the first half of *Nicholas Nickleby* and realized that the author had fallen through the page like a trapdoor.

But this doesn't happen. The other writers break out of their toast, and the dinner continues. Life goes on. Dickens looks around him, smiles broadly, and then, like Mr. Datchery sitting down to breakfast in the final words of *Edwin Drood,* "falls to with an appetite."

Notes
Acknowledgments
Index

Notes

Wherever possible I have quoted from Oxford University Press's Clarendon editions of the novels or from the paperback editions published by Oxford World's Classics, although in the case of works published in the early part of Dickens's career, the main focus of this book, I have quoted from the original newspapers, magazines, or monthly parts. Some of Dickens's sketches were published under generic titles; if the subject of a particular sketch is unclear, I have adopted the revised title used in *Sketches by Boz* (e.g., "Hackney Coach Stands" for "Sketches of London No. 1"). While no attempt has been made to regularize punctuation, obvious printing errors have been silently corrected. Given the number of quotations from Dickens's writings in this book, and the number of alternative editions available, I have supplied page numbers only where this information is relevant in some way. Other works referred to frequently in the Notes are abbreviated as follows:

Journalism	*The Dent Uniform Edition of Dickens' Journalism,* ed. Michael Slater and John Drew, 4 vols. (London: J. M. Dent, 1994–2000)
Letters	*The Letters of Charles Dickens,* ed. Madeline House, Graham Storey, et al., 12 vols. (Oxford: Clarendon, 1965–2002)
Life	John Forster, *The Life of Charles Dickens,* ed. A. J. Hoppé, 2 vols. (London: J. M. Dent, 1966; orig. pub. 1872–1874)
Memoranda	*Charles Dickens' Book of Memoranda,* ed. Fred Kaplan (New York: New York Public Library, 1981)
Speeches	*The Speeches of Charles Dickens,* ed. K. J. Fielding (Oxford: Clarendon, 1960)

Prologue

1. The relationship between computer and novel is assessed in Francis Spufford, "The Difference Engine and *The Difference Engine,*" in *Cultural Babbage: Technology, Time and Invention,* ed. Francis Spufford and Jenny Uglow (London: Faber and Faber, 1996), 266–290. Dickens's relationship with Babbage, who provided one of the models for Daniel Dyce in *Little Dorrit,* is discussed in Jay Clayton, *Charles Dickens in Cyberspace: The Afterlife of the Nineteenth Century in Postmodern Culture* (New York: Oxford: Oxford University Press, 2003), ch. 4. Clayton points out (p. 111) that the machine depicted by William Gibson and Bruce Sterling in their novel *The Difference Engine*

(London: Victor Gollancz, 1990) is actually the Analytical Engine, designed by Babbage as the Difference Engine's successor, although they use the name of the earlier machine.

2. Many of Gibson and Sterling's most outlandish details turn out to be fragments that have broken away from history and drifted into the world of fiction. In 1891, for example, *Scientific American* announced that "Dr. Varlot, a surgeon in a major hospital in Paris, has developed a method of covering the body of a deceased person with a layer of metal in order to preserve it for eternity," and accompanied its report with a drawing showing the glossy cadaver of a small child surrounded by a spaghetti of electrical cables. The report is reprinted in Leonard de Vries, ed., *Victorian Inventions* (London: John Murray, 1971), 100–101.

3. Niall Ferguson, Introduction, in Ferguson, ed., *Virtual History: Alternatives and Counterfactuals* (London: Picador, 1997), 2.

4. Edward Gibbon, *The Decline and Fall of the Roman Empire,* 6 vols. (London: Everyman, 1994), 6:341; Winston Churchill, *The Aftermath: Being a Sequel to "The World Crisis"* (London: Macmillan, 1941), 386. Niall Ferguson discusses these examples in *Virtual History,* 13.

5. Blaise Pascal, *Pensées,* trans. A. J. Krailsheimer (London: Penguin, 1995), 120.

6. William Gibson and Bruce Sterling, *The Difference Engine* (London: rpt. Vista, 1996), 47.

7. Ibid., 111, 229, 36, 72.

8. "The tutelary and controlling spirit . . . connected with a place, an institution, etc."; "With reference to a nation, age, etc.: Prevalent feeling, opinion, sentiment, or taste; distinctive character, or spirit" (*Oxford English Dictionary,* s.v. "genius," 1 and 3b).

9. R. H. Horne, *A New Spirit of the Age* (1844); Alfred Austin, "Charles Dickens," *Temple Bar* 29 (July 1870); both reprinted in Philip Collins, ed., *Dickens: The Critical Heritage* (London: Routledge and Kegan Paul, 1971), 201, 534.

10. Anne Thackeray Ritchie, *Records of Tennyson, Ruskin and Browning* (London: Macmillan, 1892), 310.

11. Samuel Smiles, *Self-Help* [1859], ed. Peter W. Sinnema (Oxford: Oxford University Press, 2002), 34, 113. I refer to Edward Bulwer, as this is the name by which he was known during the years covered by this book; under the terms of his mother's will, he changed his surname to Bulwer-Lytton in 1844.

12. Philip Larkin, *Collected Poems,* ed. Anthony Thwaite (London: Faber and Faber, 1988), 81–82.

13. Andrew Miller discusses some examples of Victorian novels that play on this idea in "Lives Unled in Realist Fiction," *Representations* 98 (Spring 2007), 118–134.

14. William James, "The Will to Believe," in *Writings, 1878–1899* (New York: Library of America, 1992), 626.

15. Sweeney Todd first appeared in a Victorian penny dreadful entitled *The String of Pearls* (1846–1847), though the story is set in 1785.

16. Philippians, 2:12.

17. "N.E.M.O." was also the first pseudonym adopted by Dickens's illustrator Hablot Knight Browne ("Phiz"). It was "indicative of his self-effacing nature," according to Jane R. Cohen, *Dickens and His Original Illustrators* (Columbus: Ohio State University Press, 1980), 61.

18. Dickens, "A Fly-Leaf in a Life," reprinted in *Journalism,* 4:388.

19. Walter Dexter, "The True Story of the Grave of Dick," *Dickensian* 31 (1935), 4.

20. John Bayley, "*Oliver Twist:* 'Things as They Really Are,'" reprinted in *Charles Dickens: A Critical Anthology,* ed. Stephen Wall (Harmondsworth: Penguin, 1970), 442. According to John Forster, Dickens was "much startled" when it was pointed out that David Copperfield's initials "were but his own reversed," and "protested it was just in keeping with the fates and chances which were always befalling him" (*Life,* 2:78).

21. *Memoranda,* 9, 17, 18, 20. Fred Kaplan, editor of the *Memoranda,* points out some of the places in Dickens's published works where he did make use of other notes.

22. Anonymous letter reprinted in Kathryn Chittick, *Dickens and the 1830s* (Cambridge: Cambridge University Press, 1990), 9.

23. *Letters,* 6:452; *The Centenary Edition of the Works of Thomas Carlyle,* ed. H. D. Traill, 30 vols. (London, 1896–1899), 3:181, 139.

24. "The Bride's Chamber," in Dickens, *The Lazy Tour of Two Idle Apprentices.*

25. Tennyson, *The Devil and the Lady,* I.iii.40–42.

26. Henry James, *Autobiography,* ed. Frederick W. Dupee (London: W. H. Allen, 1956), 389.

27. F. G. Kitton, *Charles Dickens by Pen and Pencil,* 2 vols. (London: Frank T. Sabin, John F. Dexter, 1890).

28. *Letters,* 1:xxiv.

29. Dickens's autobiographical fragment, reprinted in *Life,* 1:25.

1. Lost and Found

1. Angus Reach, Letter to *The Morning Chronicle,* reprinted in *Labour and the Poor in England and Wales, 1849–1851,* ed. Jules Ginswick, 5 vols. (London: Cass, 1983–1991), 1:48.

2. *The Times,* 29 November 1831, cited in Sarah Wise, *The Italian Boy: Murder and Grave-Robbery in 1830s London* (London: Jonathan Cape, 2004), 116.

3. Henry Mayhew, *London Labour and the London Poor,* 4 vols. (London: Griffin, Bohn, 1861–1862), 3:484 (hereafter cited as *LLLP*).

4. Henry Mayhew and John Binny, *The Criminal Prisons of London, and Scenes of Prison Life* (London: Griffin, Bohn, 1862), 45.

5. See Richard L. Stein, *Victoria's Year: English Literature and Culture, 1837–1838* (Oxford: Oxford University Press, 1987), 135–176.

6. *LLLP,* 4:281–282. In *Oliver Twist,* Noah Claypole is introduced to this line of work ("the kinchin lay") by Fagin, who explains that the aim is to grab the money of any child sent out on an errand "and then knock 'em into the kennel, and walk off very slow, as if there was nothing the matter but a child fallen down and hurt itself. Ha! ha! ha!" Stein notes that the public fear of kidnapping greatly outweighed the statistical risk: an appendix in *LLLP* (p. 147) showing "the number of persons committed for ABDUCTION in every 10,000,000 of the male population" came up with a total of twenty-three reported cases in a ten-year period across all of England and Wales.

7. See Wise, *The Italian Boy,* 73.

8. Edward Pelham Brenton, Open letter to the Bishop of London, published in 1832 as part of the collection *On Population, Agriculture, Poor Laws and Juvenile Vagrancy.*

9. See Wise, *The Italian Boy,* 224.

10. *Life,* 1:14.

11. *LLLP*, 2:144.

12. Jo's real-life counterparts included George Ruby, a boy crossing-sweeper whose testimony at a case heard at the Guildhall on 8 January 1850 had been described in *The Household Narrative of Current Events* (May 1850), Dickens's regular monthly supplement to *Household Words*, and a dying orphan boy observed by Dickens in a Ragged School dormitory for homeless men and boys, described in his article "A Sleep to Startle Us" (reprinted in *Journalism*, 3:49–57). During the serialization of *Bleak House*, Dickens published two more essays in *Household Words*, co-written with Henry Morley, that explicitly dealt with the problem of London's street children: "Boys to Mend" (11 September 1853) and "In and Out of Jail" (14 May 1853).

13. Dickens's number plans for the closing chapters are reprinted in the Oxford World's Classics edition of *The Old Curiosity Shop*, ed. Elizabeth M. Brennan (Oxford, 1998), 571.

14. Matthew, 18:12–14.

15. *Memoranda*, 18.

16. Henry F. Dickens, *The Recollections of Sir Henry Dickens* (London: Heinemann, 1934), 45.

17. *Life*, 1:19.

18. Anonymous, "The Natural History of Rats," *Chamber's Edinburgh Journal* 3 (1835), 10. Rodwell's book was published in 1858.

19. My account follows that given by John Forster in his *Life of Charles Dickens*, although Michael Allen has recently argued from legal records that James and George Lamert (or Lamerte) were in fact the same person, and that the real owner of Warren's Blacking at the time Dickens worked there was Lamerte's brother-in-law William Edward Woodd; see Michael Allen, "New Light on Dickens and the Blacking Factory," *Dickensian* 106 (2010).

20. G. C. Babington to T. Babington (23 December 1825), cited in Boyd Hilton, *A Mad, Bad, and Dangerous People? England, 1783–1846* (Oxford: Clarendon, 2006), 398.

21. Edmund Yates, *Kissing the Rod: A Novel* (1866), cited in Hilton, *A Mad, Bad, and Dangerous People?* 399.

22. See T. P. Cooper, "Dickens and His Heraldic Crest," *Dickensian* 18 (1922).

23. Cited in Christopher Hibbert, *The Making of Charles Dickens* (London: Longmans Green, 1967), 56.

24. See Liza Picard, *Victorian London: The Life of a City, 1840–1870* (London: Weidenfeld and Nicolson, 2005), 106.

25. G. K. Chesterton, *Charles Dickens* [1903], 20th ed. (London: Methuen, 1943), 24.

26. Charles Dickens, *Dickens' Working Notes for His Novels*, ed. Harry Stone (Chicago: University of Chicago Press, 1987), 235.

27. John Carey gives further examples in *The Violent Effigy* (London: Faber and Faber, 1973), 18–22, to which this paragraph is indebted.

28. John Milton, *Paradise Lost*, ix.1067.

29. Reported by John Payne Collier, *An Old Man's Diary, Forty Years Ago* (London, 1872), 4:13; an alternative version, originally published in the *True Sun* in 1832, is reprinted with an additional six verses in John Drew, *"The Pride of Mankind": Puff Verses for Warren's Blacking, with Contributions Attributed to Charles Dickens* (Oswestry, U.K.: Hedge Sparrow Press, 2005).

30. Dickens's broadsheet on the "Great International Walking Match" is reprinted in *Journalism,* 4:410–415, and discussed in Michael Slater, *Charles Dickens* (New Haven: Yale University Press, 2009), 581.

31. Michael Allen, *Charles Dickens' Childhood* (Basingstoke: Macmillan, 1988), 111.

32. Public Record Office, ADM 1 3659.

33. Death certificate held at the General Register Office, quoted in Angus Easson, "John Dickens and the Navy Pay Office," *Dickensian* 74 (1978), 41.

34. *Life,* 1:26.

2. The Clerk's Tale

1. *Speeches,* 240–241.

2. "Our School," *Journalism,* 3:36.

3. Ibid., 36–37; see Arthur Humphreys, *Charles Dickens and His First Schoolmaster* (Manchester: Percy Brothers, 1926).

4. Another school friend recalled that "at that time Dickens took to writing small tales, and we had a sort of club for lending and circulating them" (*Life,* 1:41), although it is not clear whether these were part of "Our Newspaper" or a literary sideline.

5. Reprinted in Robert Langton, *The Childhood and Youth of Dickens* (London: Hutchinson, 1912), 89.

6. The "Occasional Register" appeared in the first four issues of *All the Year Round:* 30 April, 7 May, 14 May, and 21 May 1859.

7. Willoughby Matchett, "Dickens at Wellington House Academy," *Dickensian* 7 (1911).

8. Gladys Storey, *Dickens and Daughter* (London: F. Muller, 1939), 56.

9. *Life,* 1:42.

10. Ibid., 1:40.

11. See James L. Smith, ed., *Victorian Melodramas* (London: J. M. Dent, 1976), xiii–xiv.

12. *Life,* 1:42.

13. Percy H. Fitzgerald, *Memories of Charles Dickens, with an Account of "Household Words" and "All the Year Round"* (Bristol, 1913), 42.

14. *Journalism,* 3:40.

15. *The Letters of Arthur Henry Hallam,* ed. Jack Kolb (Columbus: Ohio State University Press, 1981), 434.

16. *King Lear,* IV.i, in *The Oxford Shakespeare: The Complete Works,* ed. Stanley Wells et al., 2nd ed. (Oxford: Oxford University Press, 2005), 1174.

17. *Letters,* 5:659.

18. William J. Carlton, "Mr. Blackmore Engages an Office Boy," *Dickensian* 48 (1952), 163.

19. Ibid., 164.

20. Reproduced in F. G. Kitton, *Charles Dickens by Pen and Pencil,* 2 vols. (London: Frank T. Sabin, John F. Dexter, 1890), 1:129.

21. Ibid., 1:130.

22. George and Weedon Grossmith, *The Diary of a Nobody* [1892] (London: Penguin, 1965), 130.

23. G. M. Young, *Early Victorian England, 1830–1865,* 2 vols. [1934] (London: Oxford University Press, 1951), 1:179.

24. Kitton, *Charles Dickens by Pen and Pencil,* 1:131.

25. John Coleman, *Fifty Years of an Actor's Life,* 2 vols. (London: Hutchinson, 1904), 2:544.

26. Ibid., 2:23–24; Dickens's love of fancy clothes is also discussed in Christopher Hibbert, *The Making of Charles Dickens* (London: Longmans Green, 1967), 112–113.

27. John Carey, *The Violent Effigy* (London: Faber and Faber, 1973), 89–91.

28. Henry James, Review in *The Nation,* 21 December 1865, reprinted in Philip Collins, ed., *Dickens: The Critical Heritage* (London: Routledge and Kegan Paul, 1971), 481.

29. This example is taken from Hibbert, *The Making of Charles Dickens,* 113.

30. "An Old Stager," *The Actor's Handbook* (London: L. Dicks, 1878), 8.

31. Kitton, *Charles Dickens by Pen and Pencil,* 1:129.

32. See Garrett Stewart, *Dickens and the Trials of Imagination* (Cambridge, Mass.: Harvard University Press, 1974).

33. W. J. Carlton sketches out the history in *Charles Dickens: Shorthand Writer* (London: C. Palmer, 1926).

34. Thomas Gurney, *Brachygraphy: or, An Easy and Compendious System of Short-Hand, Adapted to the Various Arts, Sciences and Professions,* 15th ed. (London, 1825), 8.

35. Sir Joseph Archer Crowe, *Reminiscences of Thirty-Five Years of My Life* (London: J. Murray, 1895), 35.

36. William R. Hughes, *A Week's Tramp in Dickens-Land* (London, 1891), 21.

37. Abraham Hayward, Unsigned review of the *Pickwick Papers,* I–XVII, and *Sketches by Boz,* in the *Quarterly Review* (October 1837), reprinted in *Dickens: The Critical Heritage,* ed. Collins, 62. The metaphor of the skyrocket clearly rankled with Dickens, who wrote to John Forster on 3 November 1837 about his plans for *Oliver Twist:* "I hope to do great things with Nancy. If I can only work out the idea I have formed of her, and of the female who is to contrast with her, I think I may defy Mr. Hayward and all his works" (*Letters,* 1:328).

38. "Wills, wives, and wrecks" is A. P. Herbert's much-quoted phrase, referring to the jurisdiction of the indirect successor of Doctors' Commons—the Probate, Divorce, and Admiralty Division of the High Court; see Herbert, *Holy Deadlock* (London: Methuen, 1934), 109.

39. Carlton, *Charles Dickens: Shorthand Writer,* 48.

40. Ibid., 57–67.

41. "Doctors' Commons" (*Sketches by Boz*).

42. Anonymous, *The Book of Humour, Wit, and Wisdom* (London, 1874), 218.

43. "Doctors' Commons" *(Sketches by Boz).*

44. "Doctors' Commons," in *Knight's Cyclopaedia of London,* 6 vols. (London: Charles Knight, 1841–1844), vol. 3.

45. Dickens's petition formally withdrawing his name from the Middle Temple list of students is dated 17 March 1855; it is reproduced in William J. Carlton, "A Companion of the Copperfield Days," *Dickensian* 50 (1953), 16. Dickens contemplated becoming a magistrate at various points in the years 1843–1854; see *Letters* 3:570 and note, and 4:566.

46. See H. Montgomery Hyde, *The Trials of Oscar Wilde* (New York: Dover, 1973), 14.

47. "Doctors' Commons" *(Sketches by Boz).*

3. Up in the Gallery

1. J. H. Friswell, *Modern Men of Letters Honestly Criticised* (London, 1870), 12–13.
2. John Dickens's duties included sending to Members of Parliament the proofs of their speeches for correction; by 1833 he had entered the public gallery of the House of Commons as a reporter for the *Morning Herald*. See William J. Carlton, "John Dickens, Journalist," *Dickensian* 53 (1957), 5–11.
3. Charles Kent, "Charles Dickens as a Journalist," *Time: A Monthly Miscellany of Interesting and Amusing Literature* 5 (July 1881), 366.
4. Robert Stephen Rintoul, *Spectator*, 17 September 1831, cited in E. E. Kellett, "The Press," in G. M. Young, *Early Victorian England, 1830–1865*, 2 vols. [1934] (London: Oxford University Press, 1951), 2:13.
5. Ibid.
6. Thomas Babington Macaulay, "Hallam's Constitutional History," *Edinburgh Review* 48 (September 1828), 165.
7. Reported in Kathryn Chittick, *Dickens and the 1830s* (Cambridge: Cambridge University Press, 1990), 16.
8. In 1831, a journal article described them as "a class of hand-to-mouth gentlemen" who lived in shabby lodgings and "vegetate in unknown places," while "waging a perpetual war with tailors and a legion of duns." *Fraser's Magazine* 4 (October 1831), 319.
9. See Arthur Aspinall, "The Social Status of Journalists at the Beginning of the Nineteenth Century," *Review of English Studies* 21 (July 1945).
10. William Makepeace Thackeray, *The Adventures of Philip*, 1862 ed., 3:30–31; cited in Chittick, *Dickens and the 1830s*, 15.
11. Samuel Smiles, *Self-Help* [1859], ed. Peter W. Sinnema (Oxford: Oxford University Press, 2002), 28. James Grant, *The Great Metropolis* (London, 1836), lists the impeccable social credentials of some of those involved in parliamentary reporting. They included "the son of Mr. Hazlitt" on the staff of the *Morning Chronicle*, "Mr. Leigh Hunt's son" on the *True Sun* (the pun is carefully avoided), and "last and greatest of all, Mr. Byron, a cousin of Lord Byron," who was a reporter on the *Times*.
12. See *Letters*, 1:10n.
13. James Grant, *The Newspaper Press*, 3 vols. (London: Tinsley Brothers, 1871–1872), 1:296. John Barrow claimed that Dickens was quite simply "the best reporter in the gallery"; see Charles Knight, *Passages of a Working Life during Half a Century*, 3 vols. (London: Bradbury and Evans, 1865), 3:37.
14. R. Shelton Mackenzie, *Life of Charles Dickens* (Philadelphia: T. B. Peterson and Brothers, 1870), 46.
15. *Letters*, 1:2.
16. T. S. Eliot, "Whitman and Tennyson," *Nation and Athenaeum* 40 (18 December 1926), 426.
17. Cited in Asa Briggs, *The Age of Improvement, 1783–1867* (London: Longman, 1959), 261.
18. *Hansard's Parliamentary Debates*, cited in Boyd Hilton, *A Mad, Bad, and Dangerous People? England, 1783–1846* (Oxford: Clarendon, 2006), 418.
19. Charles Dickens, "The Devil's Walk," reprinted in Walter Dexter, *The Love Romance of Charles Dickens* (London: Argonaut, 1936), 46.

20. Cited in Hilton, *A Mad, Bad, and Dangerous People?* 430; Briggs, *The Age of Improvement,* 239; Hilton, 432.

21. *Parliamentary Papers* (1878), 17:20, 32; Matthew Bevis makes the connection in *The Art of Eloquence: Byron, Dickens, Tennyson, Joyce* (Oxford: Oxford University Press, 2007), 89–90.

22. See Bevis, *The Art of Eloquence,* 90.

23. [William Maginn], "Place-Men, Parliament-Men, Penny-a-Liners, and Parliamentary Reporters," *Fraser's Magazine* 2 (October 1830), 282–294 (293).

24. James T. Fields, *Yesterdays with Authors* (Boston, 1900), 231.

25. See John M. L. Drew, *Dickens the Journalist* (Basingstoke, U.K.: Palgrave Macmillan, 2003), 197n.

26. Mackenzie, *Life of Dickens,* 47.

27. *True Sun,* 22 June 1832, cited in Drew, *Dickens the Journalist,* 16.

28. *Letters,* 2:379.

29. See Hilton, *A Mad, Bad, and Dangerous People?* 432–433.

30. *Letters,* 6:123.

31. Ibid., 6:524–525.

32. Charles Kent, "Dickens as a Journalist," *Time: A Monthly Miscellany of Interesting and Amusing Literature* 5 (July 1881), 369; "Our Honourable Friend," *Household Words* (31 July 1853); Dickens reported by the Rev. Whitwell Elwin, in Warwick Elwin, ed., *Some XVIII Century Men of Letters,* 2 vols. (London, 1902), 1:249.

33. See Philip Collins, ed., *Dickens: Interviews and Recollections,* 2 vols. (London: Macmillan Press), 2:291.

34. Grant, *The Newspaper Press,* 1:296–297.

35. The story is told in Justin McCarthy, *A History of Our Own Times,* 4 vols. (London, 1880), 1:176; variations are discussed in W. J. Carlton, "Dickens and O'Connell," *Notes and Queries* 188 (April 1945), 147.

36. *The English Constitution* (1867), in *The Collected Works of Walter Bagehot,* ed. Norman St. John-Stevas, 15 vols. (London: The Economist, 1965–1986), 5:206–209.

37. *Report from the Select Committee on Dramatic Literature: With the Minutes of Evidence* (2 August 1832), 60.

38. Ibid., 60, 159.

39. Ibid., 27.

40. Smith, ed., *Victorian Melodramas,* vii.

41. *A Regency Visitor,* ed. E. M. Butler (London: Collins, 1957), 83.

42. Henry Mayhew, *London Labour and the London Poor,* 4 vols. (London: Griffin, Bohn, 1861–1862), 1:18–19.

43. Reprinted in Michael R. Booth, *Theatre in the Victorian Age* (Cambridge: Cambridge University Press, 1991), 8.

44. Extracts from playbills reprinted in James L. Smith, *Melodrama* (London: Methuen, 1973), 6.

45. The play is reprinted in Smith, ed., *Victorian Melodramas,* and is discussed in Harmut Ilsemann, "Radicalism in the Melodrama of the Early Nineteenth Century," in *Melodrama: The Cultural Emergence of a Genre,* ed. Michael Hays and Anastasia Nikolopoulou (Basingstoke, U.K.: Macmillan, 1996), 191–207.

46. See Julia Swindells, *Glorious Causes: The Grand Theatre of Political Change, 1789 to 1833* (Oxford: Oxford University Press, 2001), 32–35.

47. Henry Crabb Robinson, *The London Theatre, 1811–1866: Selections from the Diary of Henry Crabb Robinson*, ed. Eluned Brown (London: Society for Theatre Research, 1966), 129–134.

48. Review given in Mrs. Mathews, *Memoirs of Charles Mathews, Comedian*, 4 vols. (London, 1838–1839), 4:50–51.

49. The 1822 text of Charles Mathews, *Travels in Air, on Earth and on Water* is reprinted in Richard L. Klepac, *Mr. Mathews at Home* (London: Society for Theatre Research, 1979), 70–98 (71).

50. See F. G. Kitton, *Charles Dickens by Pen and Pencil*, 2 vols. (London: Frank T. Sabin, John F. Dexter, 1890).

51. *Life*, 1:14.

52. Arthur Murphy, *The Apprentice* (1760), reprinted in *The Plays of Arthur Murphy*, ed. Richard B. Schwartz, 4 vols. (New York: Garland, 1979), 2:115.

53. *Oxford Magazine* 6 (1771), 215. The spouting clubs are discussed in Gillian Russell, "Private Theatricals," in *The Cambridge Companion to British Theatre, 1730–1830*, ed. Jane Moody and Daniel O'Quinn (Cambridge: Cambridge University Press, 2007).

54. See the headnote by Michael Slater in *Journalism*, 1:120.

55. *Hamlet Travestie* was Poole's first play, and it was often revived; in 1823 the role of Hamlet was taken by Charles Mathews.

56. The plays are discussed in *Nineteenth-Century Shakespeare Burlesques*, ed. Stanley Wells, 5 vols. (London: Diploma Press, 1977), 2:x–xii.

57. They are reprinted in full in Charles Haywood, "Charles Dickens and Shakespeare; or, The Irish Moor of Venice, *O'Thello*, with Music," *Dickensian* 73 (1977), 67–88.

58. "Charles Dickens was extremely sensitive as to the possibility of any rubbish being given to the public in the form of 'early writings,' so much so that, when a young lady showed him with great pride a manuscript of some play written by him when he was very young, he made a bargain with her by making her a present of a Christmas-Book just completed, on condition that she gave up the boyish production to him—which he had the satisfaction of putting into the fire with his own hands." Georgina Hogarth, cited in Christine Alexander, "The Juvenilia of Charles Dickens: Romance and Reality," *Dickens Quarterly* (March 2008).

59. Haywood, "Charles Dickens and Shakespeare," 69.

4. Mr. Dickin

1. There are three surviving manuscript versions of the poem with minor variations; here I follow Robert Hanna in treating the Charles Dickens Museum copy, written in the hand of Maria's sister Margaret, as the most authoritative. See Robert C. Hanna, "Before Boz: The Juvenilia and Early Writings of Charles Dickens, 1820–1833," *Dickens Studies Annual* 40 (2009), 231–364.

2. *Life*, 1:8–9.

3. *Hamlet*, I.ii, *The Oxford Shakespeare: The Complete Works*, ed. Stanley Wells et al., 2nd ed. (Oxford: Oxford University Press, 2005), 686.

4. John Payne Collier, *An Old Man's Diary, Forty Years Ago,* 4 vols. (London: Printed by Thomas Richards, 1872), 4:15.

5. *Letters,* 7:544.

6. Ibid., 4:346; 7:557.

7. Maria Beadnell's album is preserved in the Charles Dickens Museum, 48 Doughty Street, London.

8. *Letters,* 7:534.

9. Letter from Dickens's cousin to Thomas Wright (21 January 1895), cited in Peter Ackroyd, *Dickens* (New York: HarperCollins, 1990), 146.

10. *Letters,* 1:5.

11. Ibid., 1:3–4.

12. *Sketches from Mr. Mathews at Home! An Excellent Collection of Recitations, Anecdotes, Songs, &c. &c.* (London, 1822), 2.

13. *Life,* 1:50.

14. Mamie Dickens, *My Father as I Recall Him* (London: Roxburghe, 1896), 49–50.

15. James Hamilton, in *The History, Principles, Practice and Results of the Hamiltonian System (*1829), advocated the teaching of languages "by observation, not by rules" (*Letters,* 4:245n).

16. *Letters,* 4:245.

17. George Henry Lewes, *On Actors and the Art of Acting* (London, 1875), 61.

18. Westland Marston, *Our Recent Actors: Recollections,* 2 vols. (London, 1888), 2:161.

19. William Charles Macready, *Macready's Reminiscences, and Selections from His Diaries and Letters,* ed. Sir Frederick Pollock, 2 vols. (London: Macmillan, 1875), 2:12.

20. Michael Baker, *The Rise of the Victorian Actor* (London: Croom Helm, 1978), 18.

21. *Letters,* 1:10–11.

22. *Life,* 1:49.

23. *Letters,* 1:30.

24. Collier, *An Old Man's Diary,* 4:13–15.

25. "Private Theatrical Regulations," written out by Henry Austin (secretary of Dickens's amateur acting company) and signed by Dickens; reprinted in Hanna, "Before Boz," 333–334.

26. The handbill is reproduced in Lola L. Szladits, ed., *Charles Dickens, 1812–1870: An Anthology* (New York: New York Public Library, 1970), 8.

27. *Letters,* 1:19.

28. T. S. Eliot, "The Love Song of J. Alfred Prufrock," reprinted in *The Complete Poems and Plays of T. S. Eliot* (London: Faber, 1969), 16.

29. *Letters,* 1:17, 23, 29.

30. *As You Like It,* II.vii, *The Oxford Shakespeare,* 666.

31. *Letters,* 4:346.

32. Dickens and George Sala, "First Fruits," *Household Words* (15 May 1852), reprinted in *Uncollected Writings from "Household Words," 1850–1859,* ed. Harry Stone (Bloomington: Indiana University Press, 1968), 417.

33. *Letters,* 7:523.

34. Ibid., 7:532.

35. Ibid., 7:544–545.

36. Georgina Hogarth, unpublished memorandum, cited in Michael Slater, *Dickens and Women* (London: J. M. Dent, 1983), 68.

37. *Letters,* 1:16-17.

38. The reminiscences of Maria's nursemaid, printed in the *Daily Chronicle* (18 March 1912), cited in Slater, *Dickens and Women,* 72.

39. *Letters,* 1:32.

40. Ibid., 7:557.

5. "Here We Are!"

1. Charles Dickens, ed., *Memoirs of Joseph Grimaldi* [1838] (London: Pushkin Press, 2008), 55.

2. The *OED*'s first citation is a letter from Harriet Martineau to G. J. Holyoake in 1852.

3. See Arlene Young, "Virtue Domesticated: Dickens and the Lower Middle Class," *Victorian Studies* 39 (Summer 1996), 483–511.

4. George Gissing, *Charles Dickens: A Critical Study* (London: Gresham, 1903), 42.

5. Mary Douglas, *Purity and Danger: An Analysis of the Concepts of Pollution and Taboo* (London: Routledge and Kegan Paul, 1966), 35.

6. I owe these examples to John Carey, *The Violent Effigy* (London: Faber and Faber, 1973), 128–129; other owners of comic umbrellas include Mrs. Sanders in the *Pickwick Papers,* who keeps her thumb pressed on the spring of her large umbrella "with an earnest countenance, as if she were fully prepared to put it up at a moment's notice," and the Cockney tourist Mr. Davis in *Pictures from Italy,* who has a "great green umbrella" he uses to trace out tomb inscriptions.

7. "Chit Chat," *Metropolitan* 8 (October 1833), 125.

8. Poole's story is collected in John Poole, *Sketches and Recollections,* 2 vols. (London, 1835); Pocock's theatrical adaptation is discussed in Edward Costigan, "Drama and Everyday Life in *Sketches by Boz,*" *Review of English Studies* 28 (November 1976), 403–421.

9. "My Aunt's Poodle," reprinted in Poole, *Sketches and Recollections,* 2:88, 101.

10. *Chambers's Edinburgh Journal* 1 (1832), 1.

11. Ibid., 3 (1834), 2; and 4 (1835), 1.

12. See Richard D. Altick, *The English Common Reader* [1957], 2nd ed. (Columbus: Ohio State University Press, 1998), 336.

13. Ibid., 338.

14. Ibid., 288.

15. *Monthly Magazine* 17 (December 1833), n.p.

16. Cited in F. J. Harvey Darton, *Dickens: Positively the First Appearance* (London: Argonaut, 1933), 47.

17. *Monthly Magazine* 17 (December 1833), 601, 609.

18. Ibid., 17 (January 1834), n.p.

19. Ian Hamilton, "Sohoitis," *Granta* 65 (Spring 1999), 296.

20. James Grant reported in 1836 that Captain Holland had edited the *Monthly* "with much good taste" until he sold it in 1835: "It was one of the most readable of the metropolitan periodicals; but as no money was spent on advertising it, and very little in the shape of paying for contributions, it slowly fell off in circulation." James Grant, *The Great Metropolis,* 2 vols. (London, 1836), 2:309.

21. An Old Printer, *A Few Personal Recollections* (London, 1896), 46–47.
22. *Life*, 1:50.
23. *Bell's New Weekly Messenger*, 28 December 1833, 98.
24. *London Weekly Magazine*, 66 (December 1833).
25. *Letters*, 1:33.
26. Ibid.
27. Lady Emily Lutyens, *A Blessed Girl: Memoirs of a Victorian Childhood* (London: R. Hart-Davis, 1953), 58–59.
28. Compare Samuel Smiles: "Riches and rank have no necessary connexion with genuine gentlemanly qualities. The poor man may be a true gentleman,—in spirit and in daily life. He may be honest, truthful, upright, polite, temperate, courageous, self-respecting, and self-helping,—that is, be a true gentleman." Samuel Smiles, *Self-Help* [1859], ed. Peter W. Sinnema (Oxford: Oxford University Press, 2002), 327–328.
29. "Sentiment" appeared in *Bell's Weekly Magazine*, 7 June 1834; it was Dickens's only contribution to this journal.
30. Boyd Hilton, *A Mad, Bad, and Dangerous People? England, 1783–1846* (Oxford: Clarendon, 2006), 37.
31. "The Side-Scenes of Society," *Punch* 4 (January–June 1843), republished as Albert Smith, *The Natural History of Stuck-Up People* (London, 1847), 53.
32. Grant, *The Great Metropolis*, 1:277–278.
33. G. K. Chesterton, *Charles Dickens* [1903], 20th ed. (London: Methuen, 1943), 11.
34. "Passage in the Life of Mr. Watkins Tottle," *Monthly Magazine* 19 (February 1835), 137.
35. The suggestion is made by Duane DeVries in *Dickens's Apprentice Years: The Making of a Novelist* (Brighton, U.K.: Harvester, 1976), 55n.
36. *Life*, 1:11.
37. Ibid., 1:55.
38. Thomas Carlyle, "Signs of the Times" (1829), reprinted in Carlyle, *Scottish and Other Miscellanies* (London: J. M. Dent, 1967), 245.
39. *Life*, 1:55.

6. Becoming Boz

1. Respectively, the *Sun* on "Mrs. Joseph Porter, 'Over the Way'" (1 January 1834); *Bell's New Weekly Messenger* on "A Dinner at Poplar Walk" (8 December 1833); and the *Sun* (1 April 1834); all cited in Kathryn Chittick, *Dickens and the 1830s* (Cambridge: Cambridge University Press, 1990), 47. The *Sun* had previously described "Horatio Sparkins" as "clever" (1 February 1834).
2. John Dickens's letter is cited in John M. L. Drew, *Dickens the Journalist* (Basingstoke, U.K.: Palgrave Macmillan, 2003), 22.
3. James Grant, *The Great Metropolis* (London, 1836), 2:47.
4. Idem, *The Newspaper Press*, 3 vols. (London: Tinsley Brothers, 1871–1872), 1:287.
5. R. Shelton Mackenzie, *Life of Charles Dickens* (Philadelphia: T. B. Peterson, 1870), 52. Mackenzie was less convinced that Black appreciated Dickens's literary efforts, arguing that this is why the sketches were switched to the *Evening Chronicle* after a few months.
6. See Talbot Penner, "Dickens: An Early Influence," *Dickensian* 63 (1967), 159.

7. F. G. Kitton, *Charles Dickens by Pen and Pencil,* 2 vols. (London: Frank T. Sabin, John F. Dexter, 1890), 1:133–135.

8. An advertisement which appeared in the *Morning Chronicle* on 10 and 17 January 1835.

9. Richard Maxwell argues that, whatever its stated intentions, the *Evening Chronicle* was primarily designed for a rural audience, which may be one reason Dickens decided to switch his sketches to *Bell's Life in London;* but the fact that all of the *Evening Chronicle* sketches were also eventually republished in the *Morning Chronicle* meant that Dickens never fully lost touch with the city's readers. See Richard Maxwell, "Dickens, the Two *Chronicles,* and the Publication of *Sketches by Boz,*" *Dickens Studies Annual* 9 (1981), 21–32.

10. *Letters,* 1:63–64, 72.

11. Ibid., 1:7.

12. Ibid., 1:50, 38.

13. *Speeches,* 371.

14. Malcolm Gladwell, *Outliers: The Story of Success* (London: Allen Lane, 2008), 67, 119.

15. Thomas Carlyle, "Characteristics" (1831), reprinted in Carlyle, *Scottish and Other Miscellanies* (London: J. M. Dent, 1967), 194.

16. Gibbons Merle, "Newspaper Press," *Westminster Review* 10 (1829), 216–237.

17. Raymond Williams estimates that by 1840 "getting on for twelve million" of mainland Britain's twenty million inhabitants were literate, and points out that a growing readership led to, and was fed by, a steady increase in the number of books being published: from an average of 580 per year in the period 1802–1827 to more than 2,600 by the middle of the century. See Raymond Williams, *Writing in Society* (London: Verso, 1983), 69–70.

18. Cited in Gordon N. Ray, *Thackeray: The Uses of Adversity, 1811–1846* (New York: McGraw-Hill, 1955), 194–195.

19. William Makepeace Thackeray, *The History of Pendennis* [1848–1850] (Newcastle upon Tyne: Cambridge Scholars Publishing, 2008), 1:329.

20. D. J. Taylor, *Thackeray* (London: Chatto and Windus, 1999), 101–104.

21. Raymond Williams, *The Long Revolution* (London: Chatto and Windus, 1961), 237.

22. Thackeray, *Pendennis,* 1:326.

23. Edgar Browne, *Phiz and Dickens as They Appeared to Edgar Browne* (London, 1913), 102.

24. Thomas Miller, *Godfrey Malvern; or, The Life of an Author,* 2nd ed. (London, 1844), 92, 152, 194. Such scenes were written with particular feeling: the *Dictionary of National Biography* points out that "Miller's life was a tragic example of aspirations crushed by Victorian Grub Street."

25. George Colman, the Younger, *Broad Grins,* 7th ed. (London, 1819), 1–2.

26. Diary entry for 13 December 1838, reprinted in *Letters,* 1:637. John Forster's papers included the memorandum of an earlier projected club, with himself and Dickens as the only members. The five rules, drawn up in Dickens's handwriting, are at once facetious and meticulous, beginning with "1st. That [Dickens's] personal Coffee and Muffins be, from and after the above-mentioned date provided at the sole cost and charge of the club./Upon which Mr. Forster gives notice of the following amendment/To insert after the word 'Muffins,' the words 'and steak,' and to insert after the word 'provided' the words 'for Mr. Forster.'" See *Letters,* 1:637.

27. Mayhew, who was born in the same year as Dickens, would continue to shadow his career via some clumsy exercises in cut-and-paste plagiarism. Mayhew's 1838 farce *But However* contained a character whose jerky manner of speaking was an attempt to cash in on the success of Alfred Jingle in *Pickwick Papers*, while his novel *Paved with Gold* (1858) was a deliberately realistic rewriting of *Oliver Twist*, featuring a runaway boy who comes to London and goes to the bad. Paul Schlicke notes how frequently Dickens's sketches were republished in other British and American publications during the 1830s, appearing "in their entirety, or virtually unabridged, in *at least 140 different locations* in newspapers and periodicals." Paul Schlicke, "'Risen Like a Rocket': The Impact of *Sketches by Boz*," *Dickens Quarterly* 22 (March 2005), 3–18 (5).

28. *Journalism*, 2:10; *Letters*, 1:42.

29. *Life*, 1:50; see Chapter 4 above.

30. Jerry White, *London in the Nineteenth Century* (London: Jonathan Cape, 2007), 193. The practice was widely condemned: in his article "Bill-Sticking" (*Household Words*, 22 March 1851), Dickens describes coming across an old warehouse "so thickly encrusted with fragments of bills" that it looked more like a richly barnacled ship's keel. He concluded that it could never be pulled down other than in "one adhesive heap of rottenness and poster" (*Journalism*, 2:341).

31. Parry's watercolor is analyzed in detail in Richard L. Stein, *Victoria's Year* (New York: Oxford University Press), 45–55; Stein notes how many of the posters are concerned with "apocalyptic scenes and historical catastrophes," and argues that they represent questions such as: "Is London, too, destined to sink into ruins? . . . Is 'modernization' of the City really only the prelude to its ultimate wreck?" (52).

32. G. K. Chesterton, Introduction to the Everyman edition of *Sketches by Boz* (London: J. M. Dent, 1907; repr. 1968), vii.

33. See White, *London in the Nineteenth Century*, 238.

34. *Annual Register, 1827*, Chronicle, 21.

35. This discussion draws on Rosemarie Bodenheimer, *Knowing Dickens* (Ithaca: Cornell University Press, 2007), 118–125.

36. *Letters*, 1:115.

37. William Harrison Ainsworth, *The Rivals: A Serio-Comic Tragedy*, printed in *Arliss's Pocket Magazine* (1821) under the pseudonym T. Hall.

38. S. M. Ellis, *William Harrison Ainsworth and His Friends*, 2 vols. (London: John Lane, 1911), 2:74.

39. John Sutherland, *Victorian Novelists and Publishers* (London: Athlone, 1976), 160.

40. Ellis, *William Harrison Ainsworth and His Friends*, 2:264.

41. *Letters*, 1:47n.

42. Ibid., 1:49, 47.

43. Ibid., 1:51.

44. Ibid., 1:7.

45. Ibid., 1:12.

46. All these details are taken from Richard Altick, *The Shows of London* (Cambridge, Mass.: Harvard University Press, 1978), 394, 360, 338, 177, 377–378.

47. Dickens was an admirer of both attractions, publishing an article that praised Madame Tussaud's as a "national institution" ("History in Wax," *Household Words*, 18 February 1854) and becoming a regular visitor to what would later become London Zoo.

48. Altick gives a full history of the Colosseum in *The Shows of London*, ch. 11, from which the following account is drawn.

49. *Morning Chronicle*, 10 July 1835, reprinted in *Journalism*, 2:14–17. Dickens wrote a follow-up report on 13 October, complaining that one of the advertised attractions— "the courses of the Enchanted Chariot, and round flights of the Mechanical Peacock" —kept breaking down (*Journalism*, 2:17–18).

50. [Charles Buller], "The Works of Dickens," *London and Westminster Review* (July 1837), reprinted in Philip Collins, ed., *Dickens: The Critical Heritage* (London: Routledge and Kegan Paul, 1971), 53.

51. *The Works of Thomas Hood*, 10 vols. (London: E. Moxon, 1869–1873), 1:354; Hook, *The Choice Humorous Works* (London, 1873), 345–346. The parallels are pointed out by Virgil Grillo, *Charles Dickens's "Sketches by Boz": End in the Beginning* (Boulder: Colorado Associated University Press, 1974), 60–62.

52. Pierce Egan, *Life in London; or, The Day and Night Scenes of Jerry Hawthorn, Esq. and His Elegant Friend Corinthian Tom* (London, 1822), 127. It is one of the quietest jokes of comic history that the names Tom and Jerry should have been used not only for a cartoon cat and mouse, but also for the husbands safely tucked away in suburbia in the 1970s BBC sitcom *The Good Life*.

53. Ibid., 191–192.

54. *The Letters and Private Papers of William Makepeace Thackeray*, ed. Gordon N. Ray, 4 vols. (London: Oxford University Press, 1945–1946), 1:187, 208.

55. William Wordsworth, *The Prelude* (1805), vii.118–120.

56. Harold Begbie, *Life of William Booth: The Founder of the Salvation Army*, 2 vols. (London: Macmillan, 1920), 1:99.

57. Grant, *The Great Metropolis*, 1:10.

58. Arthur Conan Doyle, *The Complete Sherlock Holmes*, 2 vols. (New York: Barnes and Noble, 2003), 2:232.

59. *Oxford English Dictionary*, s.v. "sketch" 4 (from 1789).

60. Ibid., s.v. "sketch" 1 (from 1668): "A rough drawing or delineation of something, giving the outlines or prominent features without the detail, esp. one intended to serve as the basis of a more finished picture, or to be used in its composition; a rough draft or design."

61. *Memoranda*, 14.

62. Cited in Philip Collins, "Dickens and London," in *The Victorian City: Images and Realities*, ed. H. J. Dyos and Michael Wolff (London: Routledge and Kegan Paul, 1973), 551.

63. J. C. Hotten, *Charles Dickens: The Story of His Life* (London, 1870), 36–37.

64. See Andrew Sanders, *Charles Dickens, Resurrectionist* (London: Macmillan, 1982), ix.

65. *Letters*, 1:97.

66. Ibid., 1:110.

67. Ibid., 5:414. Analyzing the failed business dealings that led to Macrone's early death in 1837, John Sutherland summarizes his life as "a great might-have-been of early Victorian publishing." John Sutherland, "John Macrone: Victorian Publisher," *Dickens Studies Annual* 13 (1984), 243–259 (258).

68. Paul Schlicke notes that from 1 February 1836 to 3 February 1837, Macrone placed no fewer than sixty-three advertisements for Dickens's publication in the *Sun* alone. Schlicke, "Risen Like a Rocket," 6.

69. The revisions are discussed in John Butt and Kathleen Tillotson, *Dickens at Work* [1957], rev. ed. (London: Methuen, 1968), ch. 2.

70. *Letters*, 1:115.

71. Ibid., 1:123.

72. Ibid., 1:124n.; see R. A. Gettmann, *A Victorian Publisher: A Study of the Bentley Papers* (Cambridge: Cambridge University Press, 1960), ch. 3.

73. Dickens is also pictured by Cruikshank among the theater spectators being distracted by Thomas Potter's drunken antics in Dickens's tale "Making a Night of It," *Sketches by Boz*, 2nd series (London: John Macrone, 1836).

7. The Moving Age

1. *Letters*, 1:82.

2. Editorial footnote, ibid.

3. Unsigned review (March 1836), reprinted in Philip Collins, ed., *Dickens: The Critical Heritage* (London: Routledge and Kegan Paul, 1971), 30.

4. Henry James, "London," reprinted in *English Hours* [1905], ed. Leon Edel (Oxford: Oxford University Press, 1981), 11.

5. See Jerry White, *London in the Nineteenth Century* (London: Jonathan Cape, 2007), 98.

6. These phrases were especially popular after the founding of the Society for the Diffusion of Useful Knowledge, in 1827, although one of Keats's letters had referred to "the grand march of intellect" as early as 7 May 1818.

7. *London Labour and the London Poor*, 4 vols. (London: Griffin, Bohn, 1861–1862), 3:44.

8. John Ruskin, Letter to Charles Eliot Norton (19 June 1870), reprinted in *Charles Dickens: A Critical Anthology*, ed. Stephen Wall (Harmondsworth: Penguin, 1970), 191.

9. *Letters*, 7:163, 695.

10. Dickens, "On Duty with Inspector Field" (1851), reprinted in *Journalism*, 2:363.

11. *Letters*, 7:193. Andrew Sanders places Dickens's views in context in *Dickens and the Spirit of the Age* (Oxford: Clarendon, 1999), 154–186.

12. George Augustus Sala, *Charles Dickens* (London: George Routledge, 1870), 12. John Forster similarly noted that Dickens's days were "divided for the most part between working and walking, the same wherever he was" (*Life*, 2:213).

13. *Letters*, 4:612.

14. Ibid., 1:52.

15. Reported in White, *London in the Nineteenth Century*, 14.

16. William Makepeace Thackeray, *Ballads* (1855), 217.

17. *Letters*, 1:97.

18. Ibid., 1:119.

19. Dickens, "The Late Calamitous Event at Hatfield House," reprinted in *Journalism*, 2:24–25.

20. David Cecil, *The Cecils of Hatfield House* (London: Constable, 1973), cited in *Journalism*, 2:23.

21. *Letters*, 1:100–101.

22. Ibid., 1:100.

23. Ibid., 1:40, 106.

24. Matches were a recent enough invention to have made "flare" into a knowingly up-to-

date piece of slang: matches that worked when struck against a rough surface were invented in 1827, and sold as "Lucifers" from 1829.

25. Many other originals for Miss Havisham have been suggested, including the "White Woman" Dickens recalled from his childhood. In the essay "Where We Stopped Growing" (1853), he describes how she used to haunt Berners Street in London: "She is dressed entirely in white, with a ghastly white plaiting round her head and face, inside her white bonnet. . . . She is a conceited old creature, cold and formal in manner, and evidently went simpering mad on personal grounds alone—no doubt because a wealthy Quaker wouldn't marry her. This is her bridal dress. She is always walking up here, on her way to church to marry the false Quaker" (*Household Words*, 1 January 1853). A letter of 6 September 1858 offers the sketch of a possible story: "Some disappointed person . . . prematurely disgusted with the world for some reason or no reason, . . . retires to an old lonely house . . . resolved to shut out the world and hold no communion with it." The plot was fully worked up as "Tom Tiddler's Ground" in the Christmas number of *All the Year Round* for 1861, written at the same time that Dickens was working on *Great Expectations*.

26. *Life*, 1:51.

27. E. A. Smith, *Lord Grey, 1764–1845* (Oxford: Clarendon, 1990), 307. I am drawing here on Michael Slater's headnote to the report in *Journalism*, 2:3.

28. Charles Mackay, reprinted in F. G. Kitton, *Charles Dickens by Pen and Pencil*, 2 vols. (London: Frank T. Sabin, John F. Dexter, 1890), 1:134.

29. Ibid.

30. *Journalism*, 2:7.

31. See D. G. Wright, *Democracy and Reform, 1815–1885* (London: Longman, 1970), 140.

32. Llewellyn Woodward, *The Age of Reform, 1815–1870*, 2nd ed. (Oxford: Clarendon, 1962), 95.

33. Ibid., 58.

34. *Hansard's Parliamentary Debates* 26 (1834), 3; the events are evocatively described in A. N. Wilson, *The Victorians* (London: Hutchinson, 2002), 9–14.

35. James Anthony Froude, *Thomas Carlyle; A History of the First Forty Years of His Life, 1795–1835*, 2 vols. (London: Longmans, Green, 1882), 2:292. The crowds are memorably recorded in two paintings by J. M. W. Turner (1835), which depict thousands of blurry faces lit up by the flames.

36. *Speeches*, 206.

37. Harry Stone explores this aspect of Dickens's writing in *Dickens and the Invisible World: Fairy Tales, Fantasy, and Novel-Making* (London: Macmillan, 1980).

38. Woodward, *The Age of Reform*, 100.

39. The phrase is Macaulay's, cited in John M. L. Drew, *Dickens the Journalist* (Basingstoke, U.K.: Palgrave Macmillan, 2003), 53.

40. *Journalism*, 2:14.

41. Ibid., 13, 26.

42. Benedict Anderson, *Imagined Communities*, rev. ed. (London: Verso, 2006), 35.

43. Ibid., 33.

44. *Speeches*, 102, 191.

45. Anonymous, "Short-Hand Writing and the Press," *The Schoolmaster, and Edinburgh Weekly Magazine* 1 (1832), 93.

46. Dickens, *Household Words* (22 June 1850); the passage is discussed in David Trotter, *Circulation: Defoe, Dickens and the Economies of the Novel* (Basingstoke, U.K.: Macmillan, 1988), 103.
47. Dickens, *Household Words* (7 January 1854).
48. *Speeches,* 347.
49. *Memoranda,* 19.
50. *Speeches,* 347.
51. Ibid. The rain was an occupational hazard: in 1833, a reporter accused of misreporting one of Daniel O'Connell's parliamentary speeches claimed that "during his walk from Westminster to Fleet Street, the rain, which was falling heavily at the time, had most unfortunately streamed into his pocket, and washed out the notes he had made." Michael MacDonagh, *Parliament: Its Romance, Its Comedy, Its Pathos* (Westminster: P. S. King, 1902), 376–377.
52. *Letters,* 1:58.
53. *Speeches,* 348.

8. "Pickwick, Triumphant"

1. G. K. Chesterton, *Charles Dickens,* [1903], 20th ed. (London: Methuen, 1943), 41.
2. W. H. Auden, "Dingley Dell and the Fleet," reprinted in Auden, *Selected Essays* (London: Faber, 1964).
3. Unsigned review of *Oliver Twist, Quarterly Review* 64 (1839), 84, echoing Byron's description of *Childe Harold*'s impact. Another unsigned review (probably by G. H. Lewes) of Dickens's work up to *Oliver Twist* had previously used the same phrase; see the *National Magazine and Monthly Critic* 1 (December 1837), 445. On Dickens as an overnight success, see, e.g., Jasper Fforde's "Afterword" to the Signet Classic edition of *Pickwick Papers,* 873; Jane Rabb Cohen, *Charles Dickens and His Original Illustrators* (Columbus: Ohio State University Press, 1980), 20; Robert M. Cooper, *The Literary Guide and Companion to Northern England* (Athens: Ohio University Press, 1995), 270.
4. *Letters,* 1:147.
5. Robert Smith Surtees, *Jorrock's Jaunts and Jollities; or, The Hunting, Shooting, Racing, Driving, Sailing, Eating, Eccentric, and Extravagant Exploits of that Renowned Sporting Citizen, Mr. John Jorrocks, of St. Botolph Lane and Great Coram Street* (London: W. Spiers, 1838), 7. Other similar works included John Poole's series *A Cockney's Rural Sports.*
6. Cohen, *Charles Dickens and His Original Illustrators,* 40.
7. The evidence is assessed in K. J. Fielding, "Charles Whitehead and Charles Dickens," *Review of English Studies,* n.s. 3 (1952), 141–154.
8. See *Letters* 1:121n. "The Tuggs's at Ramsgate" appeared in the first number of the *Library of Fiction* (April 1836), and "A Little Talk about Spring, and the Sweeps" in the third number (June 1836).
9. *Letters,* 1:129.
10. See Dickens's 1867 preface to the *Pickwick Papers.* The fullest account of this context is given in Robert L. Patten, "*Pickwick Papers* and the Development of Serial Fiction," *Rice University Studies* 61 (Winter 1975), 51–74.

11. Anonymous, "The *Pickwick* Advertisements and Other Addresses to the Public," *Dickensian* 32 (1936), 86–90.

12. André Gide, "Advice to a Young Writer," *London Magazine* 5 (May 1958), 11–17 (14); first published as "Conseils au jeune écrivain," *Nouvelle Revue Française*, 1 August 1956, 225–234.

13. The illustration of Mr. Pickwick leaned heavily on Seymour's earlier contributions to Richard Penn's *Maxims and Hints to an Angler and Miseries of Fishing*, published in 1833, which purported to be the minutes of the Houghton Fishing Club and featured a fat, bald figure wearing tights and spectacles.

14. Charles Mathews, *Travels in Air, on Earth and on Water*, reprinted in Richard L. Klepac, *Mr. Mathews at Home* (London: Society for Theatre Research, 1979), 116–117. Earle R. Davis notes some of the earlier literary characters who may have influenced Mathews, particularly Captain Crowe in Smollett's *Sir Launcelot Greaves* (1762), and contemporary parallels in the writings of Theodore Hook and Edward Bulwer, while the grocer Jorrocks had employed similar speech patterns in *Jorrock's Jaunts and Jollities*. See Earle R. Davis, "Dickens and the Evolution of Caricature," *PMLA* 55 (March 1940), 231–240.

15. Reprinted in Walter Dexter and J. W. T. Ley, *The Origin of Pickwick* (London: Chapman and Hall, 1936), 90.

16. *The Letters and Private Papers of William Makepeace Thackeray*, ed. Gordon N. Ray, 4 vols. (London: Oxford University Press, 1945–1946), 1:300.

17. Dickens, 1867 Preface to *Pickwick*.

18. *Life*, 1:65; Jane Carlyle, quoted in F. G. Kitton, *Charles Dickens: His Life, Writings, and Personality* (London: Blackwood, Le Bas, 1902), 437.

19. *Life*, 1:65.

20. *Letters*, 1:146.

21. Coroner's inquest, reported in the *Times*, 22 April 1836, 7.

22. *Letters*, 11:179.

23. See J. Grego, ed., *Pictorial Pickwickiana: Charles Dickens and His Illustrators*, 2 vols. (London, 1899), 1:71.

24. *The Times*, 22 April 1836, 7.

25. Robert L. Patten, for example, describes how "on 17 April Dickens met his *Pickwick* illustrator, Robert Seymour, for the first and only time: Seymour committed suicide three days thereafter." Robert L. Patten, *George Cruikshank's Life, Times, and Art*, 2 vols. (London: Lutterworth, 1992–1996), 2:26.

26. R. W. Buss, "My Connexion with *The Pickwick Papers*" (dated 2 March 1877), reprinted in Dexter and Ley, *The Origin of Pickwick*, 125.

27. Dexter and Ley, *The Origin of Pickwick*, 76; the error was repeated in the *Metropolitan Magazine*'s review of No. IV.

28. Dexter and Ley, *The Origin of Pickwick*, 126–129.

29. Ibid., 67; also see Elliot D. Engel and Margaret F. King, "*Pickwick*'s Progress: The Critical Reception of *The Pickwick Papers* from 1836 to 1986," *Dickens Quarterly* 3 (1986), 56–66.

30. Edward Bulwer, "On Art in Fiction" (1838), cited in Philip Davis, *The Victorians* (Oxford: Oxford University Press, 2004), 285.

31. Steven Marcus has argued that Weller Senior, who boasts of allowing his son to "run in the streets . . . and shift for himself," is a comic variant of John Dickens, just as Sam's occupation recalls a passage in the autobiographical fragment by Dickens in which he explains how "I degenerated into cleaning [my father's] boots of a morning." Steven Marcus, *Dickens: From Pickwick to Dombey* (London: Chatto and Windus, 1965), 32.

32. Dickens, "Nurse's Stories" *(The Uncommercial Traveller).*

33. F. G. Kitton, *Dickensiana: A Bibliography of the Literature Relating to C. Dickens and His Writings* (London: G. Redway, 1886), 451.

34. *King Lear,* II.iv, *The Oxford Shakespeare,* 922.

35. The call-slip is reproduced in F. G. Kitton, *A Supplement to Charles Dickens by Pen and Pencil* (London: Frank T. Sabin, John F. Dexter, 1890), facing p. 15.

36. See Kathryn Chittick, *"Pickwick Papers* and the *Sun, 1833–1836," Nineteenth-Century Fiction* 39 (1984), 328–335.

37. *Letters,* 1:166.

38. For example, *The Beauties of Pickwick,* "Collected and arranged by Sam Weller" (1838), *Sam Weller's Pickwick Jest Book* (1837), *The Sam Weller Scrap Sheet* (1837), and *Sam Weller's Budget of Recitations* (1838). The phenomenon of "Wellerisms" is discussed with great insight in John Bowen, *Other Dickens: Pickwick to Chuzzlewit* (Oxford: Oxford University Press, 2000), 64–66.

39. See Amy Cruse, *The Victorians and Their Books* (London: George Allen and Unwin, 1935), 160.

40. Malcolm Gladwell, *The Tipping Point: How Little Things Can Make a Big Difference* (London: Little, Brown, 2000), 170, attributing the success of Rebecca Wells's *Divine Secrets of the Ya-Ya Sisterhood* (1996) to the momentum built up by public readings and book group discussions.

41. *Athenaeum,* 31 December 1836, 916. The *Metropolitan Magazine* had earlier used very similar phrasing: "Boz . . . has completely taken possession of the ear, and of the heart too, of his countrymen" (September 1836, 13).

42. Quoted in George H. Ford, *Dickens and His Readers: Aspects of Novel Criticism since 1836* (New York: W. W. Norton, 1965), 7.

43. Henry Vizetelly, *Glances Back through Seventy Years: Reminiscences,* 2 vols. (London: K. Paul, Trench, Trübner, 1893), 1:123.

44. Herman Merivale, "About Two Great Novelists," *Temple Bar* 83 (1888), 201; Anonymous, "Remonstrance with Dickens," *Blackwood's* 81 (1857), 491. George Ford prints a number of similar stories in *Dickens and His Readers,* 6–10.

45. Cruse, *The Victorians and Their Books,* 161.

46. Even John Forster falls victim to this enthusiasm, moving swiftly from the suggestion that Pickwick was based on a man called John Foster, to the claim that "the original of the figure of Mr. Pickwick bore my name" (*Life,* 1:59). A grudging footnote admits that "whether Mr. Chapman spelt the name correctly, or has unconsciously deprived his fat beau of the letter "r," I cannot say; but experience tells me that the latter is probable" (*Life,* 1:147).

47. Unsigned review of *Pickwick* Nos. I–XVII and *Sketches by Boz, Quarterly Review* 59 (1837), 484.

48. See John Butt and Kathleen Tillotson, *Dickens at Work* (London: Methuen, 1957), 73–74;

and David M. Bevington, "Seasonal Relevance in *The Pickwick Papers*," *Nineteenth-Century Fiction* 16 (1961), 219–230.

49. Dickens, 1867 Preface to *Pickwick*. Reviewers had used similar language: "Sam Weller improves upon acquaintance" (*Metropolitan Magazine*, January 1837, 6). Dickens's growing indulgence towards his characters is clear from the way he interprets Mr. Pickwick's behavior; from "he gazed sternly" and "gazing with solemn sternness" early in the novel, we move towards a situation in which the hero is "trying to look stern," and finally a sentence that suggests some of his generosity has rubbed off on the narrator: "Mr. Pickwick . . . looked sternly—if Mr. Pickwick ever could look sternly."

50. Butt and Tillotson, *Dickens at Work*, 75.

51. See *Letters*, 1:131.

52. Henry Burnett (Dickens's brother-in-law, husband of Fanny Dickens), reported in Kitton, *Charles Dickens: His Life, Writings, and Personality*, 36.

53. Reported in Gladys Storey, *Dickens and Daughter* (London: F. Muller, 1939), 180.

54. Leslie Staples, "New Letters of Mary Hogarth and Her Sister Catherine," *Dickensian* 63 (1967), 76.

55. In *Self-Help*, Samuel Smiles singles out Scott for the "admirable working qualities" he'd acquired when "trained in a lawyer's office, where he pursued for many years a sort of drudgery scarcely above that of a copying clerk." Samuel Smiles, *Self-Help* [1859], ed. Peter W. Sinnema (Oxford: Oxford University Press, 2002), 99.

56. *Letters*, 1:63.

57. Ibid., 1:76, 73, 69, 110.

58. Quoted in Michael Slater, *Dickens and Women* (London: J. M. Dent, 1983), 105.

59. *Letters*, 1:60, 71, 86, 119.

60. The earlier critical history of the interpolated tales is summarized in Deborah A. Thomas, *Dickens and the Short Story* (Philadelphia: University of Pennsylvania Press, 1982).

61. See Marcus, *From Pickwick to Dombey*, 41; and Philip Hobsbaum, *A Reader's Guide to Charles Dickens* (London: Thames and Hudson, 1972), 33.

62. Trial transcript, quoted in Butt and Tillotson, *Dickens at Work*, 71.

63. *Othello*, III.iii, in *The Oxford Shakespeare*, 892.

64. Thomas Hardy, "In Tenebris—II," in *The Complete Poetical Works of Thomas Hardy*, ed. Samuel Hynes, 3 vols. (Oxford: Clarendon, 1982–1985), 1:207.

65. Oliver Goldsmith, *The Vicar of Wakefield* [1776], ed. Arthur Friedman (Oxford: Oxford University Press, 2006), 125–126.

66. *Letters*, 1:85.

67. Ibid., 6:560. Dickens was replying to a correspondent who had suggested that the Guild of Literature (of which he was a committee member) might subscribe to a memorial.

68. Michael Slater, "How Dickens 'Told' Catherine about His Past," *Dickensian* 75 (1979), 3–6.

69. Samuel Johnson, *Lives of the English Poets: A Selection*, ed. John Wain (London: J. M. Dent, 1975), 314.

70. *Life*, 1:23.

9. ~~Novelist~~ Writer

1. See Norris Pope, *Dickens and Charity* (London: Macmillan, 1978), 42–95. Agnew had been attempting to bring forward legislation since 1832, and was the main figure behind eight separate Sabbath bills introduced in the years 1833–1838, supported by organizations that included the Lord's Day Observance Society (founded in 1831) and the Christian Instruction Society, whose recent publications on the matter had included *A Statement on the Awful Profanation of the Lord's Day* (1829) and *The Law of the Sabbath* (1830).

2. Dickens's lifelong commitment to the "amusements of the people" is discussed in Paul Schlicke, *Dickens and Popular Entertainment* (London: Allen and Unwin, 1985).

3. Jerry White describes the nervous excursions of the "once-a-week men" or "Sunday-promenaders" in *London in the Nineteenth Century* (London: Jonathan Cape, 2007), 218–219.

4. G. J. Holyoake, *Sixty Years of an Agitator's Life,* 2 vols. (London: T. F. Unwin, 1892), 2:235.

5. Thomas Carlyle, "The Hero as a Man of Letters" (the chapter in question), was originally a lecture delivered on 19 May 1840, two months after Carlyle met Dickens. Quotation is from letter to John Carlyle (17 March 1840), reprinted in C. R. Sanders et al., eds., *The Collected Letters of Thomas and Jane Welsh Carlyle,* 36 vols. to date (1970–), 12:80–81.

6. Dickens's proofs are held at the Forster Collection of the Victoria and Albert Museum, London.

7. See Kathryn Chittick, "*Pickwick Papers* and the *Sun,* 1833–1836," *Nineteenth-Century Fiction* 39 (1984), 333.

8. *The Comedy of Errors,* V.i, in *The Oxford Shakespeare,* 305.

9. *Letters,* 1:189.

10. The agreement is reprinted in *Letters,* 1:648–649.

11. Ibid., 1:150. The title of this proposed work was *Gabriel Vardon, the Locksmith of London,* later renamed *Barnaby Rudge.* Dickens's failure to write it led to arguments first with John Macrone, and then with Richard Bentley. It was not published until 1841, by Chapman and Hall.

12. *Letters,* 1:190.

13. Ibid., 1:189.

14. The word "versatile," chosen by the *Sun* reviewer, echoed Dickens's puff for *Sketches by Boz* in the *Morning Chronicle:* "a variety of original papers by the same versatile author." *Letters,* 1:123.

15. Ibid., 1:163.

16. Letter to Mary Scott Hogarth (15 May 1836), reprinted ibid., 1:689.

17. [Abraham Hayward?], unsigned review of *Pickwick* Nos. I–XVII and *Sketches by Boz, Quarterly Review* 59 (October 1837), reprinted in Philip Collins, ed., *Dickens: The Critical Heritage* (London: Routledge and Kegan Paul, 1971), 62.

18. *Letters,* 1:137.

19. On Thomas Carlyle's place as the "major prophet" of the gospel of work, see Walter E. Houghton, *The Victorian Frame of Mind, 1830–1870* (New Haven: Yale University Press, 1957), 251–256.

20. *Letters,* 1:178, 200.

21. Ibid., 1:199.

22. Ibid., 1:153.

23. Ibid., 6:427. Dickens wrote three articles on the controversy surrounding Lockhart's biography of Walter Scott; they were published by the *Examiner* in 1838. See Chapter 12 below.

24. *Letters,* 1:190.

25. Ibid., 1:151.

26. Philip Collins, ed., *Dickens: Interviews and Recollections,* 2 vols. (London: Macmillan, 1981), 1:120.

27. From the Latin *precarius:* "given as a favour, depending on the favour of another, (of property) held by tenancy at will, uncertain, doubtful, suppliant" (*OED,* s.v. "precarious").

28. Edward Bulwer, *England and the English* (London: Richard Bentley, 1833), 81.

29. *Letters,* 3:510–511.

30. F. G. Kitton, *Charles Dickens by Pen and Pencil,* 2 vols. (London: Frank T. Sabin, John F. Dexter, 1890), 1:103.

31. *Letters,* 3:598.

32. Ibid., 1:156, 167.

33. Ibid., 1:173.

34. Early reviews of *The Strange Gentleman* are reprinted in Walter Dexter, "A Stage Aside: Dickens's Early Dramatic Productions," *Dickensian* 33 (1937), 81–85.

35. *Letters,* 1:203.

36. Reprinted in Kitton, *Dickens by Pen and Pencil,* 1:102.

37. Dexter, "A Stage Aside," 82–83.

38. William Makepeace Thackeray, "Fielding's Works," *The Times,* 2 September 1840, reprinted in Thackeray, *Critical Papers in Literature* (London, 1904), 207.

39. Margaret Oliphant, "Charles Dickens," *Blackwood's Magazine* 77 (April 1855), reprinted in Collins, ed., *Dickens: The Critical Heritage,* 327.

40. Anthony Trollope, "Charles Dickens," *St. Paul's Magazine* (July 1870), reprinted in Collins, ed., *Dickens: The Critical Heritage,* 342.

41. *Life,* 1:3.

42. [John Forster], unsigned review of *The Village Coquettes, Examiner,* 11 December 1836, 792.

43. John Forster, "Remarks on Two of the Annuals," *Newcastle Magazine* (1829), 27–38, cited in James A. Davies, *John Forster: A Literary Life* (Leicester: Leicester University Press, 1983). Much of the information in this section is drawn from Davies's fine and fair-minded book.

44. John Forster, "Encouragement of Literature by the State," *Examiner,* 5 January, 1850, 2. The context was Forster's dispute with Thackeray over the latter's representation of the literary profession in *Pendennis.*

45. *The Letters and Private Papers of William Makepeace Thackeray,* ed. Gordon R. Ray, 4 vols. (London: Oxford University Press, 1945–1946), 2:252.

46. *The Poems of Robert Browning: 1826–1840,* ed. John Woolford and Daniel Karlin (London: Longman, 1991), 514.

47. John Forster, "The Dignity of Literature," *Examiner,* 19 January 1850, 35.

48. John Milton, *Paradise Lost,* vii.37.

49. This was R. H. Barham's comment opposite Forster's name on the members' list of the Garrick Club; cited in Davies, *John Forster,* 82.
50. *Life,* 1:34.
51. See Peter Ackroyd, *Dickens* (New York: Harper Collins, 1990), 207; *Letters,* 8:119.
52. *Letters,* 6:450.
53. "Fuz" was Carlyle's nickname for Forster, adapted from Lady Lytton's bitchy 1839 novel *Cheveley; or, The Man of Honour,* where "Fuzboz" appears as a "remarkably plebeian looking" journalist who acts as "a sort of lick-dust" to anybody "of any celebrity to whom he could get access" (118).
54. Forster, "Remarks on Two of the Annuals," 33–34.
55. Percy Fitzgerald, cited in Ian Hamilton, *Keepers of the Flame: Literary Estates and the Rise of Biography* (London: Hutchinson, 1992), 153.
56. Ibid., 156.
57. Edward Bulwer Lytton, *Not So Bad As We Seem; or, Many Sides to a Character* (London: Chapman and Hall, 1851), 15.
58. On Forster's revisions, see Davies, *John Forster,* 158–183.
59. *Letters,* 1:210; *Life,* 1:65–66.
60. Mamie Dickens, *My Father as I Recall Him* (London: Roxburghe, 1896), 26; Henry Dickens, *My Father as I Knew Him* (London: William Heinemann, 1934), 44.
61. Collins, ed., *Dickens: Interviews and Recollections,* 1:133.
62. *Letters,* 3:211.

10. Dickens at Home

1. Mary Hogarth to Mary Scott Hogarth, reprinted in *Letters,* 1:689.
2. *Oxford English Dictionary,* s.v. "home," sense 5.
3. Felicia Hemans, "The Homes of England," *Blackwood's Magazine* (April 1827), 392; often reprinted.
4. Anonymous review of *The Battle of Life,* in *Morning Chronicle* (24 December 1846).
5. *Letters,* 3:248.
6. Ecclesiastes 12:5.
7. *Letters,* 3:31. On Dickens's alterations, see David Parker, "Dickens at Home," in Murray Baumgarten and H. M. Daleski, eds., *Homes and Homelessness in the Victorian Imagination* (New York: AMS Press, 1998), 65–75.
8. G. K. Chesterton, *Charles Dickens* [1903], 20th ed. (London: Methuen, 1943), 128.
9. Viscount Esher, ed., *The Girlhood of Queen Victoria: A Selection from Her Majesty's Diaries between the Years 1832 and 1840,* 2 vols. (London: John Murray, 1912), 2:83.
10. *Life,* 1:371.
11. The same line is echoed more craftily by Uriah Heep, whose ambition to wheedle his way into the Wickfield house is foreshadowed in sly references to his "umble dwelling" and "numble abode."
12. *Henry V,* IV.iii, in *The Oxford Shakespeare,* 616.
13. *Othello,* I.iii, ibid., 879.
14. See John Carey, *The Violent Effigy* (London: Faber and Faber, 1973), 16–17.
15. Reported in Charles and Mary Cowden Clarke, *Recollections of Writers,* 2nd ed. (London: Sampson Low, Marston, Searle and Rivington, 1878), 324.

16. *Letters,* 1:558.

17. Ibid., 1:689.

18. John Greaves, *Dickens at Doughty Street* (London: Elm Tree Books, 1975), 11.

19. Charles Dickens, *The Strange Gentleman, and Other Plays* (London: Heinemann Educational, 1972), 31.

20. Theodore Hook, *Maxwell* (London: H. Colburn and R. Bentley, 1830), 130.

21. Edmund Yates, quoted in David A. Hayes, *East of Bloomsbury* (London: Camden History Society, 1998), 38.

22. When the author and wit Sydney Smith moved into No. 14 in 1804, he discovered that he was "in the midst of a colony of lawyers." Anonymous review of *A Memoir of the Reverend Sydney by His Daughter, Lady Holland, Edinburgh Review* 102 (1855), 248.

23. Leslie Staples, "48 Doughty Street: Dickens Negotiates," *Dickensian* 55 (1959), 6.

24. See David Parker, "The Reconstruction of Dickens's Drawing-Room," *Dickensian* 78 (1982), 13.

25. Other examples can be found in *The Seven Poor Travellers* (a "queer old clock" appears in the first story), *Nicholas Nickleby* (in Chapter 22 Smike recalls the "old clock" that furnished one corner of the room where he slept as a child), and *Dombey and Son* (in Chapter 14, as the school holidays approach, the "grave old clock" at Dr. Blimber's adds a tone of "personal interest" to its ongoing "formal enquiry" of "how, is, my, lit, tle, friend").

26. Philip Larkin, *Collected Poems,* ed. Anthony Thwaite (London: Faber and Faber, 1988), 119.

27. The play was originally published by John Redington sometime in the period 1850–1876, and then by his son-in-law Benjamin Pollock, who took over the business following Redington's death. The museum's version contains some plates bearing Redington's name and others bearing Pollock's name, indicating that it was printed after 1876.

28. *Letters,* 7:99, 4:565. During 1855, following his stay in Boulogne, Dickens found apartments in another "doll's house, but really pretty within," in Paris (*Letters,* 7:723).

29. Reported in W. T. Shore, *Charles Dickens and His Friends* (London: Cassell, 1909), 24.

30. Henry F. Dickens, *Memories of My Father* (London: V. Gollancz, 1928), 25.

31. Gladys Storey, *Dickens and Daughter* (London: F. Muller, 1939), 101.

32. *Letters,* 6:635.

33. Ibid., 4:174.

34. Ibid., 4:216.

35. The comparison between Agnes and Miss Murdstone is made in Frances Armstrong, *Dickens and the Concept of Home* (Ann Arbor, Mich.: UMI Research Press, 1990), 35.

36. *Letters,* 1:517–522, 2:109.

37. Ibid., 1:528; 1:560.

38. Richard Renton, *John Forster and His Friendships* (London: Chapman and Hall, 1912), 88–89.

39. See John Tosh, *A Man's Place: Masculinity and the Middle-Class Home in Victorian England* (New Haven: Yale University Press, 1999), 18. Tosh explores the shift in attitudes that took place during the 1830s, from treating the home as a place of work to viewing it as a refuge from work.

40. George Dolby, *Charles Dickens as I Knew Him* (London: T. Fisher Unwin, 1885), 45–48. The checkbook payments that Dickens made after he opened a bank account at

Coutts & Co. in November 1837 are analyzed in Lillian Nayder, *The Other Dickens: A Life of Catherine Hogarth* (Ithaca, N.Y.: Cornell University Press, 2010), 65–66.

41. *Letters,* 8:253. Michael Slater offers a more generous interpretation in *Dickens and Women* (London: J. M. Dent, 1983), 128.

42. Nathaniel Hawthorne, *The English Notebooks,* ed. Randall Stewart (London: Oxford University Press, 1941), 379.

43. *Life,* 2:395.

44. *Letters,* 1:139; letter from Thomas Handisyde to Joseph Staines Banks (18 March 1837), reprinted in Leslie Staples, "48 Doughty Street: Dickens Negotiates," *Dickensian* 55 (1959), 6.

45. According to Lord Redesale's *Memories* (London: Hutchison, 1915), Charley Dickens told this story at Eton; see *Letters,* 1:339n.

46. See Andrew Miller, "Lives Unled in Realist Fiction," *Representations* 98 (Spring 2007), 124.

47. *Letters,* 1:338.

48. Ibid., 1:221.

49. Ibid., 1:224.

50. Kathryn Chittick, *Dickens and the 1830s* (Cambridge: Cambridge University Press, 1990), 74.

51. F. G. Kitton, *Charles Dickens by Pen and Pencil,* 2 vols. (London: Frank T. Sabin, John F. Dexter, 1890), 1:139.

52. *Letters,* 8:256

53. Ibid., 8:265. See Robert Louis Brannan, ed., *Under the Management of Mr. Charles Dickens: His Production of "The Frozen Deep"* (Ithaca, N.Y.: Cornell University Press, 1966).

11. Is She His Wife?

1. *The Times,* 21 June 1837, 4.

2. The description of William IV is by Benjamin Disraeli, in *Lord Beaconsfield's Letters, 1830–1852,* ed. R. Disraeli, new ed. (London, 1887), 113. When it came to William's predecessor, George IV, *The Times* did not pull its punches in declaring that "there never was an individual less regretted by his fellow-creatures than this deceased King" (29 June 1830).

3. Charles Greville, *The Greville Memoirs, 1814–1860,* ed. L. Strachey and R. Fulford, 8 vols. (London: Macmillan, 1938), 2:6.

4. *The Times,* 20 June 1837, 4.

5. Philip Ziegler, *King William IV* (London: Collins, 1971), 227.

6. Monica Charlot, *Victoria: The Young Queen* (Oxford: Blackwell, 1991), 80.

7. *The Times,* 21 June 1837, 4.

8. Charlot, *Victoria: The Young Queen,* 85.

9. *Speeches,* 1.

10. Anonymous, "Some Thoughts on Arch-Waggery, and, in Especial, on the Genius of 'Boz,'" *Court Magazine and Monthly Critic* 10, no. 4 (April 1837), 185–187.

11. See Paul Schlicke, *Dickens and Popular Entertainment* (London: Allen and Unwin, 1985).

12. *Letters,* 1:257.
13. Ibid.
14. Ibid.
15. Ibid., 1:257–258.
16. Ibid., 1:259.
17. Anonymous, "Song of the Month, No. VIII," *Bentley's Miscellany* 2 (1837), 109.
18. Roswell Chamberlain Smith, *English Grammar on the Productive System* (London: J. Steen, 1834), 182; James Hogg, ed., *Winter Evening Tales, Collected among the Cottagers* [1820], 2 vols. (Philadelphia: Walker, 1836), 1:146. Possibly influenced by Dickens, Robert Browning later found his pen falling into the same groove when summing up Pompilia, the doomed heroine of *The Ring and the Book* (1868–1869), as "young, / Good, beautiful" (1:774–775).
19. The fact that Nancy later uses exactly the same words in her conversation with Rose— "When ladies as young, and good, and beautiful as you are . . . give away your hearts, love will carry you all lengths"—is supposed to demonstrate that these qualities are innate rather than Harry's silver-tongued invention.
20. Juliet John, ed., *Charles Dickens's Oliver Twist: A Sourcebook* (London: Routledge, 2006), 1.
21. John Camden Hotten, *The Slang Dictionary* (London: J. C. Hotten, 1864), 264; *Oxford English Dictionary,* s.v. "twist," sense 9c, playing on the idea of wringing someone's neck, or the image of a dangling body slowly turning at the end of a rope. John Bowen explores some of the other implications of "twist" in *Other Dickens: Pickwick to Chuzzlewit* (Oxford: Oxford University Press, 2000), 97.
22. See John O. Jordan, "The Purloined Handkerchief," *Dickens Studies Annual* 18 (1989), 1–17.
23. Henry Fielding, *Tom Jones,* Book III, ch. 2.
24. Henry Mayhew, *London Labour and the London Poor,* 4 vols. (London: Griffin, Bohn, 1861–1862), 4:347.
25. *Life,* 1:22.
26. *OED,* "twist," senses 20 and 3a.
27. Concerning the influence of William Hogarth's *Industry and Idleness* on both Dickens's novel and *Jack Sheppard* (which Ainsworth described as "simply a prose version" of Hogarth's sequence), see Paul Davis, "Imaging *Oliver Twist:* Hogarth, Illustration, and the Part of Darkness," *Dickensian* 82 (1986), 158–176.
28. On Oliver's final destination as a secular version of John Bunyan's Paradise—"a little society, whose condition approached as nearly to one of perfect happiness as can ever be known in this changing world"—see Anny Sadrin, *Parentage and Inheritance in the Novels of Charles Dickens* (Cambridge: Cambridge University Press, 1994), 32.
29. John Bowen makes this point in *Other Dickens,* 94.
30. *Letters,* 1:441.
31. The manuscript is preserved in the Forster Collection at the Victoria and Albert Museum in London.
32. Milton, *Paradise Lost,* ix.404–407. This aspect of Milton's poetic technique is discussed in Christopher Ricks, *Milton's Grand Style* (Oxford: Clarendon, 1963).
33. *Letters,* 1:323.
34. Ibid., 1:516.

35. Ibid., 2:410.
36. Ibid., 3:483–484.
37. Ibid., 3:35, 211.
38. Ibid., 4:197.
39. Ibid., 2:181–182.
40. Ibid., 1:263.
41. *David Copperfield*, ch. 44.
42. *Letters*, 8:558–560.
43. "Paradise" was a slang term for the gallery of a theater, also referred to as "the gods." The information is given in a letter written by Mary Howitt on 3 March 1839, reprinted in *Dickensian* 17 (1921), 152.
44. See Michael Slater, *Dickens and Women* (London: J. M. Dent, 1983), 111.
45. *Letters*, 1:263–264, 260.
46. Ibid., 1:259, 263.
47. Ibid., 1:260.
48. See J. W. T. Ley, "The Double Tragedy of Mary Hogarth," *Dickensian* 33 (1937), 205–210.
49. Lady Maria Clutterbuck [Catherine Hogarth Dickens], *What Shall We Have for Dinner?* (London, 1851; 2nd ed., 1852). Catherine had played the part of Lady Maria Clutterbuck in Dickens's production of *Used Up* at Rockingham Castle in 1851.
50. Margaret Lane quoted in Slater, *Dickens and Women*, 133. "No man could possibly survive": Catalogue to the Victoria and Albert Museum's centenary exhibition *Charles Dickens* (London: Victoria and Albert Museum, 1970), 8.
51. Quoted in Slater, *Dickens and Women*, 132.
52. See, e.g., *Letters*, 1:287, 344, 364, 427, 440.
53. Harriet Martineau, "Literary Lionism" (1839), reprinted in *Harriet Martineau's Autobiography*, 3 vols. (London: Smith, Elder, 1877), 1:205–225.
54. Dickens's visit to America was marked by a "Quizzical and Satirical Extravaganza" entitled *Boz* that opened at the Olympic Theatre in New York on 11 April 1842, with scenes that included "What Befell the Lion When He Landed" and "The Lion Besieged." See *Letters*, 3:224n.
55. Ibid., 3:233.
56. Henry F. Dickens, *Memories of My Father* (London: V. Gollancz, 1928), 17.
57. See Peter Ackroyd, *Dickens* (London: Sinclair-Stevenson, 1990), 280.
58. Dickens's essay was published as one of the "Stray Chapters by 'Boz'" in *Bentley's Miscellany* during 1837; the first had been "The Pantomime of Life," in March.
59. *Letters*, 1:274. The same allusion is made in October 1838 (1:440). Compare 1:346, "I am a prisoner for the day and evening"; and 1:415, "here I am chained."
60. I owe this idea to Bradley Deane, *The Making of the Victorian Novelist: Anxieties of Authorship in the Mass Market* (London: Routledge, 2003), 49.
61. *Letters*, 1:328.
62. Ibid., 1:323.

12. Being Dickens

1. Charles Buller, "The Works of Dickens," *London and Westminster Review* 5 (July 1837), 194–215 (195).

2. Anonymous, "Literary Recipes," *Punch* 1 (7 August 1841), 39.

3. Dickens, "Poetical Epistle from Father Prout to Boz," *Bentley's Miscellany* 3 (January 1838), 71. "Father Prout" was the literary pseudonym of the Irish humorist Francis Sylvester Mahony.

4. The diary is part of the Forster Collection in the Victoria and Albert Museum, and is reproduced in *Letters,* 1:629–638.

5. Compare Dickens's entry on 2 January 1838 ("With Ainsworth all day, at Macrone's place on business") with his letter to Ainsworth later that month (*Letters,* 1:358). The *Lions of London* reached the stage of advertisements and an illustration by Cruikshank for the first issue, before Ainsworth canceled the project.

6. *Letters,* 8:131–132.

7. Ibid., 9:9. Jean Ferguson Carr discusses this aspect of Dickens in "Dickens and Autobiography: A Wild Beast and His Keeper," *ELH: English Literary History* 52 (Summer 1985), 447–469.

8. *Life,* 2:399–400.

9. Grimaldi's biographer Richard Findlater outlines the publication history in his edition of the *Memoirs of Joseph Grimaldi* (London: MacGibbon and Kee, 1968), 353–357.

10. *Letters,* 1:326.

11. Ibid., 1:373.

12. *Hamlet,* V.i.

13. *Letters,* 1:382.

14. On the possibility that in revising Grimaldi's *Memoirs* Dickens was also constructing a script for his own life, see Leigh Woods, "The Curse of Performance: Inscripting the *Memoirs of Joseph Grimaldi* into the Life of Charles Dickens," *Biography* 14 (1991), 138–152.

15. George Dolby, *Charles Dickens as I Knew Him* (London: T. Fisher Unwin, 1885), 227.

16. "Quiz" (Edward Caswall), *Sketches of Young Ladies* (London: Chapman and Hall, 1837), 38.

17. Ibid., 22.

18. *Letters,* 1:359.

19. *Life,* 1:66.

20. Jacob Korg offers a helpful overview in "The Rage of Caliban," *University of Toronto Quarterly* 37 (October 1967), 75–89.

21. Walt Whitman, *Leaves of Grass* (1860 edition), ed. Jason Stacy (Iowa City: University of Iowa Press, 2009), 103.

22. Oscar Wilde, *The Picture of Dorian Gray,* ed. Isobel Murray (Oxford: Oxford University Press, 1974), 143.

23. *Letters,* 1:388.

24. *Life,* 1:100.

25. George Almar, *Oliver Twist: A Serio-Comic Burletta* (London: Samuel French, ca. 1885), 60.

26. The state of British copyright law in the 1830s is discussed by Catherine Seville, *Literary*

Copyright Reform in Early Victorian England (Cambridge: Cambridge University Press, 1999). British writers enjoyed no copyright protection in America until the end of the century, although an 1854 Act of Parliament enabled American authors to secure British copyright for their work if they were present in Britain or any of its dependencies at the time of publication.

27. *Letters*, 1:350.

28. Dickens's title may have been inspired by Pierce Egan, *The Pilgrims of the Thames: In Search of the National!* (serialized 1836–1837; one-volume edition, 1838), a genial romp in which the echoes of *Pickwick* include the first subhead in Chapter 10: "The Pilgrims Turn Pic-nic-ians" (188).

29. See Louis James, *Fiction for the Working Man, 1830–1850* (Oxford: Oxford University Press, 1963), 63.

30. *Letters*, 1:269–270.

31. Ibid., 2:365.

32. Ibid., 1:380.

33. Ibid., 1:398, 411, 431.

34. Percy H. Fitzgerald, *Memories of Charles Dickens* (Bristol: J. W. Arrowsmith, 1913), 7.

35. Lord Ilchester, *Chronicles of Holland House, 1820–1900* (London: Murray, 1937), 241.

36. Philip Collins, ed., *Dickens: Interviews and Recollections,* 2 vols. (London: Macmillan, 1981), 1:10.

37. See Fiona MacCarthy, *Byron: Life and Legend* (London: John Murray, 2002), 146.

38. Unsigned review of John Galt, *The Life of Lord Byron,* in *The Literary Gazette; and Journal of Belles Lettres, Arts, Sciences, &c.* (1830), 572.

39. I am drawing here on Bradley Deane's excellent discussion of authorial friendship in *The Making of the Victorian Novelist* (New York: Routledge, 2003), 27–57.

40. Reprinted in *Letters*, 1:683.

41. Ibid., 4:235.

42. Ibid., 12:283, 8:488.

43. Ibid., 1:367–368.

44. Ibid., 1:281. Compare the spoof letter sent to Forster on 27 July in which Dickens pretends to be "Louisa," who confesses that "I have loved you, and I could have wished, and have wished with all a woman's ardour that you were mine" (*Letters*, 1:422).

45. Paul Schlicke discusses this shift in *Dickens and Popular Entertainment* (London: Allen and Unwin, 1985), 4–5.

46. *Annual Register . . . of the Year 1838* (1839), 108.

47. Albany Fonblanque and Charles Dickens, "The Queen's Coronation," *The Examiner,* 1 July 1838, 402–403.

48. William Makepeace Thackeray, "A Pictorial Rhapsody," *Fraser's Magazine* 22 (July 1840), 113.

49. William Cox, "Facts and Fancies," *New-York Mirror* 16 (1838), 100. Cox was an English journalist who wrote frequently for the *New-York Mirror* from 1829 onwards.

50. Edward Bulwer, "Lady Blessington's Novels," *Edinburgh Review* 47 (July 1838), 356–357.

51. At the end of Chapter 26 of *Oliver Twist*, Monks is convinced that he has seen the shadow of a woman, but after giving "several very grim laughs" eventually confesses that "it could only have been his excited imagination."

52. Walter Besant, *Fifty Years Ago* (London: Chatto and Windus, 1888), vii. Besant's tone of "amused curiosity" mixed with "open condescension" is discussed in Richard L. Stein, *Victoria's Year* (Oxford: Oxford University Press, 1987), 11.

53. See *Letters*, 1:417.

54. *Report of the British Association for the Advancement of Science* (London, 1832), 41. The history of the Association is discussed in Jay Clayton, *Charles Dickens in Cyberspace* (Oxford: Oxford University Press, 2003), 81–104.

55. See G. A. Chaudry, "The Mudfog Papers," *Dickensian* 70 (1974), 104–112 (106).

56. "Rigdum Funnidos" (pseud.) and George Cruikshank, *The Comic Almanack for 1836: An Ephemeris in Jest and Earnest* (London: Charles Tilt, 1835), 36–37.

57. Ibid., 37.

58. Charles Babbage, *Passages from the Life of a Philosopher* (London: Longman, Green, Longman, Roberts, and Green, 1864), 17.

59. David Brewster, *Letters on Natural Magic* (London: John Murray, 1832), 286.

60. *Letters*, 1:447.

61. Thomas Roscoe, *The London and Birmingham Railway; With the Home and County Scenes on Each Side of the Line* (London, 1839), 1–3, 39, 42–43.

62. Victor Hugo, quoted in Wolfgang Schivelbusch, *The Railway Journey: The Industrialization of Time and Space in the Nineteenth Century*, rev. ed. (Berkeley: University of California Press, 1986), 55–56.

63. The ideas had been brewing for some time: in 1864 Dickens complained that he was forced to "carry through life as long and heavy a train of dependents as ever was borne by one working man" (*Letters*, 10:338).

64. Dickens's agreement with Richard Bentley is dated 22 August 1836 and reprinted in *Letters*, 1:648.

65. Ibid., 1:453.

66. Dickens had previously experimented with his own name on the title page of the one-volume edition of *Pickwick*, before reverting to "Boz" for the serialization of *Oliver Twist* and *Nicholas Nickleby*.

67. [T. H. Lister], review of *Sketches by Boz* (first and second series), *Pickwick Papers*, *Oliver Twist*, and *Nicholas Nickleby*, in *Edinburgh Review* 68 (1838–1839), 76–77.

68. *Letters*, 1:438.

Postscript

1. Mamie Dickens, *My Father as I Recall Him* (London: William Heinemann, 1934), 118.

2. George Dolby, quoted in F. G. Kitton, *Charles Dickens by Pen and Pencil*, 2 vols. (London: Frank T. Sabin, John F. Dexter, 1890), 2:27.

3. Dickens's phrasing was almost identical to that of a letter he had sent to Forster when "within three pages of the shore" (*Letters*, 6:195).

4. *Memoranda*, 22.

5. G. H. Lewes, "Dickens in Relation to Criticism," *Fortnightly Review* 17 (February 1872).

6. *Letters*, 1:447. Dickens's signature is on page 173 of the visitors' book; he signed it again during another visit on 6 April 1840 (p. 270).

7. Advertisement in the *Athenaeum* (4 May 1867), 600.

8. The inscription is reproduced in Arthur Waugh, *A Hundred Years of Publishing* (London: Chapman and Hall, 1930), opposite p. 44.
9. Weld Taylor, quoted in Kitton, *Charles Dickens by Pen and Pencil*, 2:5.
10. William Makepeace Thackeray, quoted ibid., 2:24–27.
11. See Anonymous, "Boz versus Dickens," *Parker's London Magazine* 2 (February 1845), 122–128.
12. *Letters*, 3:158. Dickens's anxieties were strengthened by the lack of copyright protection in America.
13. See Robert L. Patten, *Charles Dickens and His Publishers* (Oxford: Clarendon, 1978), 83–85.
14. Ralph Straus, *Dickens: A Portrait in Pencil* (London: Gollancz, 1928), 110; the notice appeared in 1841. Dickens's brother Alfred had also started writing clandestine begging-letters to Chapman and Hall. In one of them, he requests "with the greatest reluctance possible" the loan of a £5 note to "relieve him from the most awkward dilemma." See Waugh, *A Hundred Years of Publishing*, 42.
15. See *Letters*, 1:465n.
16. In November 1836 Dickens had attended a dinner of the Literary Fund Club, a monthly dining society presided over by John Cam Hobhouse. This was his introduction to the organization that would later become the Royal Literary Fund. In May 1837 he accepted an invitation to be a steward at the anniversary dinner; in March 1839 he was elected to the main committee. The organization's changing fortunes, including Dickens's later disillusionment and resignation, are discussed in Nigel Cross, *The Common Writer: Life in Nineteenth-Century Grub Street* (Cambridge: Cambridge University Press, 1985), 8–37.
17. [Archibald Alison], "The Influence of the Press," *Blackwood's Edinburgh Magazine* 36 (September 1834), 373–391 (373).
18. Reported in George Augustus Sala, *Charles Dickens* (London: G. Routledge and Sons, 1870), 15–16.
19. Michael Slater, *Charles Dickens* (New Haven: Yale University Press, 2009), 166.
20. *Letters*, 2:311.

Acknowledgments

My greatest debts are to Peter Straus, my agent at Rogers, Coleridge and White, for his great loyalty and kindness during the years in which this book took shape; and to John Kulka, my editor at Harvard University Press, who has been a model of helpfulness and tact from our first exploratory discussions to the time when a chunkier-than-expected manuscript thudded onto his desk.

In addition to the readers appointed by Harvard University Press, for whose advice I was and remain grateful, I would also like to thank the following for reading earlier versions of this book, answering queries, or being otherwise generous and encouraging: Jacqueline Baker, Edith Bouvier, Laurence Brockliss, Susan Burton, Mac Castro, Toby Garfitt, Will Hammond, Philip Horne, Matthew Ingleby, Tabitha Jones, Judith Luna, Robert Macfarlane, Laurie Maguire, Dan Mallory, Tom Marks, Jeff Miller, David Paroissien, Seamus Perry, Adrian Poole, Corinna Russell, Florian Schweizer, Anne Toner, Carolyn Tucker, and my colleagues and students at Magdalen College. Dan Tyler deserves particular thanks for tracking down the illustrations with such efficient good humor, and I have been especially fortunate to have had Maria Ascher as my copyeditor: nobody's eye could have been sharper; nobody's touch lighter. I would also like to thank Kathryn Blatt for proofreading the final manuscript, and Tom Broughton-Willett for compiling the index.

Among the many libraries and other organizations that assisted with research inquiries, I am grateful to the Alfred Dunhill Museum and Archive; the Bodleian Library; the British Library; the British Museum; Cambridge University Library; Corpus Christi College, Oxford; the Dickens House Museum; the English Faculty Library, Oxford; the Free Library of Pennsylvania; Getty Images; the London Metropolitan Archive; Magdalen College, Oxford; the Museum of London; the National Portrait Gallery; the New York Public Library; Pollock's Toy Museum; the Senate

House Library, London; the Shakespeare Birthplace Trust; the *Times* Archives; and the Victoria and Albert Museum.

Specific debts to earlier biographies and critical works are recorded in the Notes.

Although every effort has been made to trace the holders of copyrighted material, the author and publishers would be grateful to know of any errors or omissions.

Index